W9-AXV-999

The European Revolutions, 1848–1851

Reaching from the Atlantic to Ukraine, from the Baltic to the Mediterranean, the revolutions of 1848 brought millions of people across the European continent into political life. Nationalist aspirations, social issues, and feminist demands coming to the fore in the mid-century revolutions would reverberate in continental Europe until 1914 and beyond. Yet the new regimes established then proved ephemeral, succumbing to counter-revolution.

In this second edition, Jonathan Sperber has updated and expanded his study of the European Revolutions between 1848 and 1851. Emphasizing the socioeconomic background to the revolutions, and the diversity of political opinions and experiences of participants, the book offers an inclusive narrative of the revolutionary events and a structural analysis of the reasons for the revolutions' ultimate failure. A wide-reaching conclusion and a detailed bibliography make the book ideal both for classroom use and for a general reader wishing to acquire a better knowledge of this major historical event.

Jonathan Sperber is Professor of History at the University of Missouri-Columbia. His previous publications include award-winning books such as *Rhineland Radicals: The Democratic Movement and the Revolutions of 1848–1849* (1991) and *The Kaiser's Voters: Electors and Elections in Imperial Germany* (1997).

NEW APPROACHES TO EUROPEAN HISTORY

Series editors

WILLIAM BEIK, *Emory University*
T. C. W. BLANNING, *Sidney Sussex College, Cambridge*

New Approaches to European History is an important textbook series, which provides concise but authoritative surveys of major themes and problems in European history since the Renaissance. Written at a level and length accessible to advanced school students and undergraduates, each book in the series addresses topics or themes that students of European history encounter daily: the series embraces both some of the more traditional subjects of study, and those cultural and social issues to which increasing numbers of school and college courses are devoted. A particular effort is made to consider the wider international implications of the subject under scrutiny.

To aid the student reader, scholarly apparatus and annotation is light, but each work has full supplementary bibliographies and notes for further reading: where appropriate, chronologies, maps, diagrams, and other illustrative material are also provided.

For a list of titles published in the series, please see end of book.

The European Revolutions, 1848–1851

Second Edition

JONATHAN SPERBER
University of Missouri-Columbia

CAMBRIDGE
UNIVERSITY PRESS

CAMBRIDGE UNIVERSITY PRESS
Cambridge, New York, Melbourne, Madrid, Cape Town, Singapore, São Paulo

Cambridge University Press
The Edinburgh Building, Cambridge CB2 8RU, UK

Published in the United States of America by Cambridge University Press, New York

www.cambridge.org
Information on this title: www.cambridge.org/9780521547796

First published 1994
Reprinted seven times
Second edition 2005
Third printing 2007

Printed in the United Kingdom at the University Press, Cambridge

A catalogue record for this publication is available from the British Library

Library of Congress Cataloguing in Publication data

Sperber, Jonathan, 1952–
 The European revolutions, 1848–1851 / Jonathan Sperber. – 2nd ed.
  p. cm. – (New Approaches to European History ; 29)
 Includes bibliographical references and index.
 ISBN 0 521 83907 6 (cloth) – ISBN 0 521 54779 2 (pbk.)
 1. Europe – History – 1848–1849. 2. Revolutions – Europe – History – 19th
century. I. Title. II. Series.
 D387.S64 2005 940.2′84 – dc22 2004057071

ISBN-13 978-0-521-83907-5 hardback
ISBN-13 978-0-521-54779-6 paperback

Contents

List of illustrations	*page* vi
Preface to the second edition	vii
Chronology of events	viii
Introduction	1
1 Society and social conflict in Europe during the 1840s	5
2 The pre-revolutionary political universe	56
3 The outbreak of revolution	109
4 Varieties of revolutionary experience	157
5 Polarization and confrontation	208
6 The mid-century revolutions in European history	258
Bibliography	284
Short biographies	299
Index	305

Illustrations

MAPS

1.1 Europe in 1848	*page* 6–7
1.2 Dominant agricultural property and production regimes in Europe during the 1840s	14–15
1.3 Predominant religious confessions in Europe during the 1840s	36–37
3.1 Scenes of barricade fighting in January to March 1848	118–119
5.1 Revolutionary regimes in the spring of 1849	248–249

FIGURE

1.1 Real wages in France and Germany, 1820–47	24

Preface to the second edition

The one hundred fiftieth anniversary of the revolution of 1848, that produced a small flood of exhibitions, conferences, lecture series, commemorations, and scholarly publications in the years around 1998, also provided the impetus for a second edition of this work. As part of the relevant revisions, the bibliography has been completely rewritten and brought up to date with the latest literature, much of it appearing in conjunction with the revolutionary sesquicentennial. The account of the 1848 revolutions has been modified as well, to take into consideration the latest scholarly findings. As a result of them, the discussion of the 1848 revolution has been expanded, both topically and geographically, including new material on events in the Low Countries, Scandinavia, and the very interesting developments in the Danubian Principalities of Moldavia and Wallachia. I have added new examples for some of the assertions in the book, introduced new themes, particularly a section on the memory and commemoration of the 1848 revolutions. A number of smaller mistakes present in the first edition have been corrected.

More generally, though, most of these newer scholarly investigations have offered further evidence to support the general approach to and interpretation of the mid-nineteenth-century revolutions put forth in this book. Indeed, the first edition of *The European Revolutions, 1848–1851* found frequent and favorable mention in bibliographies and commemorative essays, to say nothing of Internet web sites, appearing in conjunction with the revolutionary anniversary. It is to be hoped that a revised and updated second edition will continue to improve upon this favorable track record.

Chronology of events

1845

Failure of the potato crop produces famine or near-famine conditions in much of Europe.

1846

The potato harvest improved over the previous year, but the wretched grain harvest worsens the food supply situation.

The Bishop of Imola elected Pope Pius IX; widespread expectations that he will introduce liberal reforms in the church and the Papal States and take the lead towards Italian national unity.

Defeat of the opposition in the elections to the legislature in France.

Polish uprising in the Austrian province of Galicia defeated when serfs turn on the noble insurgents and massacre them.

1847

A good harvest ends the danger of famine (except in Ireland) but business conditions worsen and the industrial and commercial economy in Europe enters into recession.

Civil war in Switzerland; the predominantly Protestant and left-wing cantons defeat the predominantly Catholic and right-wing ones.

Friedrich Wilhelm IV of Prussia calls a United Diet to approve new loans. A majority of deputies demand a constitution and liberal reforms, which the king refuses to grant.

Constitutional-monarchist and radical parliamentary deputies from the smaller states of central and southwestern Germany hold separate meetings to discuss plans for national unification, and social and political reform.

The French opposition mounts a banquet campaign to demand a more democratic franchise.

Victory of the opposition in elections to the Hungarian Diet.

Pius IX calls a Consultative Assembly to discuss reforms in the Papal States; liberal deputies to it demand greater concessions than he is willing to make.

1848

January

Italy: Insurrection in Palermo, Sicily, spreads to the mainland and the King of the Two Sicilies is forced to grant a constitution.

France: Intensification of the banquet campaign in Paris.

February

Italy: King of Piedmont-Savoy and the Grand Duke of Tuscany grant constitutions.

France: Parisian banquets end in street demonstrations; crowds clash with soldiers and police; barricades are built. The army refuses to fight, the National Guard goes over to the insurgents, King Louis-Philippe flees and the republic is proclaimed. Provisional Government is an uneasy coalition of radicals, socialists, and moderate "pure republicans."

March

The revolutionary events of this month lead to riots and demonstrations of the urban and rural lower classes throughout the continent, including strikes, land occupations, boycotts of feudal and seigneurial obligations, and assaults on employers, creditors, nobles, and government officials. These continue into the summer.

Italy: Risings in the Habsburg provinces of Lombardy and Venetia, particularly in their respective capitals, Venice and Milan; revolutionary provisional governments created. Austrian General Radetzky retreats with his defeated forces to the fortresses of the Quadrilateral. Carlo Alberto of Piedmont-Savoy declares war on Austria and sends his army to occupy Lombardy and Venetia. Pius IX grants a constitution for the Papal States.

France: Creation of Luxembourg Commission in Paris to investigate and reform conditions of the working class. National Workshops set up to offer jobs to the unemployed. Formation of numerous political clubs and workers' trade associations in the capital.

Germany: Street fighting in Berlin. Insurgents are victorious: the army withdraws from the city; the king of Prussia promises a constitution, appoints liberal ministers, and announces his support for German national unification. Liberal government ministers appointed in most of the smaller German states, sometimes after menacing street demonstrations. German nationalist uprising in Schleswig-Holstein against Danish rule. "Pre-Parliament" meets in Frankfurt and issues call for elections to a German National Assembly.

Austrian Empire: Street fighting in Vienna; Metternich flees the country. A new government ministry is appointed, containing both conservatives and liberals. It names Colonel Jelačić Ban of Croatia and commander of the border troops. National mass meeting of Croatians in Zagreb. Demonstrations in Prague and formation of a National Committee. Riots in Cracow and formation of Polish National Committee. Mass demonstrations in Budapest; the Hungarian Diet moves there from Pressburg and names members of a Hungarian government ministry.

Low Countries: Mass meetings in the Netherlands, particularly in Amsterdam and The Hague; large street demonstrations in Amsterdam on 27 March. The king appoints a commission, chaired by liberal opposition leader Johan Thorbecke, to draft a new constitution. Formation of a "Belgian Legion" in Paris, primarily from unemployed Belgian workers there. Moving to the north of France, it sets up an armed camp and crosses the Belgian border on 25 and 29 March, hoping for promised support from Belgian radicals. These invasions are defeated by Belgian troops. Belgian government introduces a reform packet, including a considerable expansion of the franchise.

Scandinavia: Mass meetings and street demonstrations in Copenhagen lead King Friedrich VII to appoint liberal government ministers who announce elections for a constituent assembly, but also plans for the incorporation of the Duchy of Schleswig with the Danish kingdom, leading to war with the German states. Mass meetings in Stockholm; street demonstrations on 15 March are suppressed by the army, leaving thirty demonstrators dead.

April

England: Great Chartist reform demonstration in London overawed by the police.

France: Radical demonstrations in Paris demanding a postponement of elections to a Constituent Assembly suppressed by the National Guard. The elections, held under universal manhood suffrage, produce a monarchist majority.

Italy: Elections in the Papal States. Pius IX refuses to join the war against Austria. Elections for a parliament held on the mainland of the Kingdom of the Two Sicilies. Sicilian provisional government declares secession from the Neapolitan kingdom; Neapolitan army withdraws from almost the entire island.

Germany: Republican uprising in the Grand Duchy of Baden, which is easily suppressed. Clashes between Polish and German nationalists in the Prussian province of Posen (Polish: Poznań). Prussian soldiers sent to support insurgents in Schleswig-Holstein; war between Prussia and Denmark.

Austrian Empire: The Emperor recognizes the Hungarian government, but also sanctions the call for elections to a Croatian National Assembly. Hungarian Diet introduces reforms, including the abolition of serfdom. Count Stadion, Provincial Governor of Galicia, declares serfdom abolished; Austrian troops bombard the city of Cracow. Czech nationalists announce that they will boycott elections called in the province of Bohemia to the German National Assembly; instead they call for a Slavic Congress to meet in Prague. Growing nationalist hostilities between Germans and Czechs in Bohemia, especially in the capital city, Prague.

Low Countries: Draft of a new, more liberal constitution for the Netherlands completed. Belgian government abolishes the stamp tax.

Principalities of Moldavia and Wallachia: Romanian students and other intellectuals arrive in their homelands, after having taken part in the Parisian February revolution of 1848. They immediately launch political agitation, in conjunction with both liberals and radicals in their home countries. The Prince of Moldavia has a private army of Albanians arrest the revolutionary leaders in the capital city of Iaşi. A few escape and create a "Moldavian Revolutionary Committee" in Austrian Czernowitz, that attempts to coordinate the Romanian nationalist movement throughout eastern Europe.

May

France: Radical demonstrators attempt to storm and overthrow the Constituent National Assembly but are turned back by the National Guard. Leftist and labor leaders arrested; Luxembourg Commission is dissolved. Government is reshuffled in a more conservative direction; General Cavaignac becomes Minister of War.

Italy: Clash between King of the Two Sicilies and parliament in Naples; barricades built, but royal forces are quickly victorious. Disturbances and demonstrations in the provinces; insurrection and revolutionary government in Calabria. The kingdom withdraws from the war with Austria. Plebiscite in Lombardy and Venetia produces large majority for the constitutional monarchist program of union with Piedmont-Savoy.

Germany: Elections to the Frankfurt National Assembly won by conservatives and constitutional monarchists; elections held at the same time for a Prussian Constituent Assembly fall out similarly, if a bit more to the left. Both assemblies begin their work. Polish nationalist forces in the Prussian province of Posen defeated.

Austrian Empire: Elections called for an Austrian Constituent Assembly under a restricted property franchise. Mass demonstrations against this decision organized by Viennese democrats. Conservative ministers resign and are replaced with more liberal ones; the court flees to Innsbruck; a Committee of Public Safety rules the capital. Formation of a "Supreme Ukrainian Council" in Lemberg (Ukrainian: Lviv), with support of Habsburg authorities in the province of Galicia. National mass meetings of the Slovaks, the Serbs, and the Romanians; conservative Habsburg officials and soldiers, seeking to counter the Hungarian government, support them.

Low Countries: Belgian government completes its reform measures by passing a law prohibiting government officials from serving as parliamentary representatives.

Moldavia and Wallachia: Growing political agitation by radicals, especially in the countryside, in Wallachia. Russian consul general in Bucharest presses prince for political repression; his British counterpart, supported by a special French emissary, calls on him to create a liberal regime.

June

England: In this month and throughout the summer, demonstrations and conspiratorial meetings of Chartists and Irish nationalists in industrial cities of northern England, none of which pose any major threat to public order.

France: Government abolishes the National Workshops. Hostile demonstrations follow; barricades are built and three days of fierce street fighting ensue. Forces of order are victorious; their commander,

General Cavaignac, is named prime minister. The last radical government ministers are forced to resign. Many political clubs and trade associations closed.

Italy: Insurrection in Calabria suppressed. Negotiations between Austrian and Piedmontese government over future of Lombardy and Venetia produce no results. Austrian forces recapture much of Venetia. Elections in the Grand Duchy of Tuscany.

Germany: The Frankfurt National Assembly creates a provisional central German government and elects Archduke Johann of Austria imperial regent. First congress of German democratic clubs.

Austrian Empire: Elections held for an Austrian Constituent Assembly, a Croatian National Assembly and a Hungarian National Assembly. Croatian National Assembly meets briefly and hands over all power to Ban Jelačić. The emperor deposes Jelačić from his position as Ban, but he refuses to go and members of the imperial court and the Viennese government secretly support him. Prague Slav Congress meets and debates reorganization of the Austrian Empire. Clashes between the people and General Windischgrätz's soldiers in Prague lead to barricade building and street fighting. The army is victorious and Windischgrätz, to the applause of German nationalists, dissolves the Slav Congress and arrests radical Czech nationalists.

Low Countries: Liberals victorious in parliamentary elections held in Belgium under the new franchise.

Moldavia and Wallachia: Mass meeting in the Danube River town of Islaz proclaims a provisional revolutionary government for Wallachia. The prince flees and a revolutionary regime is created in Bucharest, that institutes political and socioeconomic reforms, calling for an end to serfdom and for elections to a constituent national assembly.

July

Italy: Piedmontese and other Italian troops routed by the Austrians at Custozza. French government considers and rejects military intervention.

Germany: First congress of constitutional monarchist political clubs. Artisans' congress meets in Frankfurt. Masters refuse to let journeymen participate so they call their own workers' congress.

Austrian Empire: Hungarian National Assembly and Austrian National Assembly both convene. Clashes between Hungarian and Serbian forces (each including regular Austrian army units) in the Banat.

Moldavia and Wallachia: Attempted counter-revolution in Bucharest foiled by the people of the capital city. Russian troops enter Moldavia and are stationed, menacingly, on the Wallachian border. Following heavy Russian diplomatic pressure, a Turkish army of intervention enters Wallachia at the very end of the month.

August

Italy: Armistice between Piedmont-Savoy and Austria. General Radetzky's troops reoccupy the rest of Lombardy and Venetia, with the exception of the island city of Venice. Pro-war demonstrations in the Grand Duchy of Tuscany; insurgents briefly seize control of the port city of Livorno.

Germany: Under pressure from England and Russia, Prussia signs the Malmö armistice with Denmark, dropping its support for the German nationalist insurgents in Schleswig-Holstein and not consulting the provisional German central government.

Austrian Empire: Imperial family returns in triumph to Vienna. Negotiations between Hungarian government and Ban Jelačić produce no result. Hungarian government orders the arrest of Romanian nationalist leaders in Transylvania.

Moldavia and Wallachia: As a result of Turkish intervention, the Wallachian government is reorganized, taking on more liberal members; a second attempt at counter-revolution is defeated by the people of Bucharest.

September

France: Government prepares military intervention in northern Italy, and then calls off the expedition at the last minute. Reorganization of the left. Radicals and socialists unite around former Interior Minister Ledru-Rollin; parliamentary caucus calls itself the "Mountain" after radical parliamentarians of 1793.

Italy: Army of the Kingdom of the Two Sicilies invades the island of Sicily.

Germany: National Assembly votes to condemn the Malmö armistice and then reverses itself. Mass meetings in Frankfurt and vicinity; insurgents try to overthrow the assembly but are defeated by Prussian soldiers after barricade fighting. Second republican uprising in the Grand Duchy of Baden is quickly defeated. Founding congress of Workers' Fraternization in Berlin. Second rival congress of constitutional monarchist political clubs.

Austrian Empire: Austrian National Assembly votes to abolish serfdom but offer compensation to noble landlords. Jelačić officially reinstated by emperor as Ban of Croatia; he leads his troops across the river Drava into interior Hungary. Mass meetings and demonstrations in Budapest; the Hungarian National Assembly votes to offer armed resistance. Field Marshal Lamberg, sent from Vienna to command all armed forces in Hungary is lynched by an angry mob. War between the imperial and Hungarian governments. Lajos Kossuth, head of the Hungarian National Defense Committee begins his great agitation tour to gain support among the peasantry. Meeting of Romanian nationalists in Transylvania with the support of Austrian general Puchner prepares for armed resistance to Hungarian authority.

Moldavia and Wallachia: Largely non-violent confrontations between Turkish army of intervention and the people of Wallachia, mobilized by the revolutionary government. At the end of the month, the Russian army of intervention, previously stationed in Moldavia, crosses into Wallachia and overthrows the revolutionary regime.

October

Italy: Mass demonstrations in Florence; the Grand Duke names a moderate democrat as prime minister. National congress of the constitutional monarchists, the "Society for an Italian Confederation." Truce between Sicilian separatists and regular army of the southern Italian kingdom.

Germany: Second national congress of democratic clubs. First national congress of Roman Catholic political and religious associations.

Austrian Empire: Civil war between Hungarian and Romanian nationalists in Transylvania. Hungarians defeat Jelačić's troops and drive them back towards Vienna. Troops ordered from the Viennese garrison to reinforce Jelačić mutiny. Street fighting breaks out; the minister of war is lynched; imperial court, most government ministers, and members of the constituent assembly flee to Olmouc in Moravia. The imperial capital is in the hands of the radicals, who try, mostly unsuccessfully, to gain support in the provinces and countryside. Attempts at mediation by the German National Assembly are rebuffed by the imperial court.

Low Countries: Dutch parliament approves the new, liberal constitution.

November

France: Constituent national assembly finishes writing a constitution for the French Republic; it calls presidential elections for the following month. Formation of Republican Solidarity, national federation of left-wing political clubs.

Italy: The constitutional-monarchist prime minister of the Papal States is assassinated and the Papal government overthrown, in an insurrection led by the city's democratic clubs. The Pope flees to the Kingdom of the Two Sicilies. Vincenzo Gioberti named prime minister of the Kingdom of Piedmont-Savoy; government policy moves towards reopening the war with Austria and vigorous pursuit of national unity. Democrats meet in Florence and call for a national constituent assembly.

Germany: The King of Prussia appoints the conservative Count Brandenburg as prime minister, who brings the army back to Berlin and declares it in a state of seige. The Prussian Constituent Assembly calls for a tax boycott in response. While the capital is quiet, there are riots, demonstrations and uprisings in the provinces, all ultimately suppressed by the army. Elections in Bavaria produce a majority for the left.

Austrian Empire: Soldiers of Generals Jelačić and Windischgrätz assault Vienna (beginning on 31 October) and defeat the insurgents in several days of barricade fighting. Commissioner of the German National Assembly, Robert Blum, is captured, brought before a court-martial, and shot. Imperial soldiers and Romanian nationalists drive most Hungarian troops from Transylvania. Habsburg troops bombard Lemberg and march into the city, dissolving the national guard and Polish nationalist organizations, and placing Lemberg in a state of siege. The Austrian Constituent Assembly reconvenes in Kremsier; Prince Schwarzenberg named Austrian prime minister with the program of the vigorous reassertion of central imperial authority.

December

France: Presidential elections lead to the unexpected victory of Louis-Napoleon Bonaparte.

Italy: Congresses of democratic clubs in Tuscany and the Papal States; formation of a central committee of Italian democratic clubs in Rome. The revolutionary government in Rome repudiates Papal authority and calls for a constituent national assembly.

Germany: Prussian government dissolves the Constituent Assembly and decrees a constitution that guarantees supremacy of the monarch and the executive.

Austrian Empire: Mentally retarded emperor Ferdinand is forced to abdicate by the court and his ministers in favor of his nephew Franz

Joseph. Imperial troops under General Windischgrätz begin a new offensive against Hungary, reaching Budapest at the end of the month and forcing the Hungarian government to flee to Debrecen. A new Hungarian army, under the command of Polish revolutionary József Bem, marches into Transylvania.

1849

January

France: Louis-Napoleon appoints conservative government ministers who prohibit Republican Solidarity.

Italy: Elections in Piedmont-Savoy produce a victory for the democrats. Elections held in the Papal States for a constituent assembly are boycotted by conservatives and most constitutional monarchists, thus producing mainly left-wing deputies. Mass demonstrations organized by Tuscan radicals in favor of a more left-wing government.

Germany: The Frankfurt National Assembly proclaims a Declaration of Basic Rights. New elections in Prussia show strong polarization between conservatives and democrats. Left and extreme left victorious in elections in the Kingdom of Saxony.

Austrian Empire: Beginning of winter campaign in northeastern Hungary by Magyar general Arthur Görgey. Czech and German radicals plot a revolutionary conspiracy.

February

Italy: Roman Constituent Assembly meets and proclaims a republic. Grand Duke and his ministers flee Florence; a revolutionary provisional government takes power in Tuscany.

March

Italy: Piedmont-Savoy resumes the war against Austria and is defeated at Novara. King Carlo Alberto abdicates. On news of these defeats, riots and demonstrations in Tuscany against the revolutionary government. Mazzini becomes member of a three-man executive committee of the Roman Republic with emergency powers. Parliament of Kingdom of the Two Sicilies dissolved by the king.

Germany: The Frankfurt National Assembly finishes writing a constitution for a united German state, without the Germans of Austria. It votes to offer the imperial crown to King Friedrich Wilhelm IV of Prussia.

Austria: The Austrian Constituent Assembly is dissolved; the government decrees a constitution that is immediately suspended. It demands the dissolution of the German National Assembly and the restoration of the pre-1848 German Confederation. Conscription riots in various provinces of the empire. General Bem's forces conquer almost all of Transylvania.

April

France: Louis-Napoleon sends an expeditionary force to Rome; it marches on the city and is driven back by the Roman Republic's forces, commanded by Giuseppe Garibaldi. Inconclusive negotiations follow.

Italy: Revolutionary government in Tuscany collapses and authority of the Grand Duke is restored. Revolutionaries remain in control of port city of Livorno. At end of the month, Austrian troops enter the Grand Duchy. Beginning of Austrian siege and blockade of Venice. Fighting resumes on the island of Sicily.

Germany: Twenty-eight of the smaller states accept the constitution written by the Frankfurt National Assembly but Friedrich Wilhelm IV of Prussia rejects it and threatens to use armed force against its supporters.

Austria: General Görgey's soldiers rendezvous with other Hungarian forces, and defeat the Habsburg armies, recapturing Budapest and marching along the Danube towards Vienna. Hungarian National Assembly declares independence from Austria, names Kossuth interim president. Negotiations between Hungarian government and remaining Romanian insurgents in Transylvania reach no result. Austrian government asks tsar to intervene in Hungary.

May

France: Elections to the legislative assembly. The "Mountain" is the caucus with the most deputies, but the three monarchist factions together have a majority. Louis-Napoleon orders expeditionary force in Italy to break off negotiations, attack Rome, and restore Papal authority.

Italy: Austrian soldiers conquer Livorno and bombard Venice. Troops of the Neapolitan kingdom defeat secessionists and reconquer Sicily.

Germany: Mass meetings, and demonstrations in support of the Frankfurt National Assembly, typically organized by democrats. In a number of cases these go over to armed insurrection and barricade fighting. A revolutionary government proclaimed in Dresden; the King of Saxony flees, but is quickly restored by Prussian troops. Insurgent

regimes seize power in the southwestern Palatinate and the Grand
Duchy of Baden.

Austria: Agreement reached on Russian intervention against the
Hungarian government.

Norway: Founding of the "Workers' Union" by the Christian and socialist schoolteacher Marcus Thrane.

June

France: Left in National Assembly demands impeachment of Louis-
Napoleon for his intervention against the Roman Republic. Street
demonstrations in Paris easily suppressed by the army and parliamentary leaders of the left are arrested or flee the country. Similar demonstrations in Lyon lead to the building of barricades and street fighting,
in which the insurgents are defeated by the army.

Italy: Conflict between French troops and forces of the Roman Republic.

Germany: Prussian troops overthrow the revolutionary regime in the
Palatinate. Frankfurt National Assembly flees to Stuttgart, where it is
dissolved by soldiers of the Kingdom of Württemberg.

Austria: Russian troops enter Hungary; Habsburg forces launch a new
offensive against the Hungarians.

July

Germany: Prussian troops overthrow the revolutionary regime in the
Grand Duchy of Baden, defeating last insurgent forces in Germany.

Austria: Further, inconclusive, negotiations between the Hungarian government and the Romanian insurgents in Transylvania.

August

Italy: French troops conquer Roman Republic, restoring Papal authority.
Besieged Venice capitulates to the Austrians.

Austria: Russian and Habsburg forces conquer all of Hungary; Kossuth
and government must flee the country.

Fall 1849–December 1851

The combats of the summer of 1849 marked the end of open revolutionary engagements. In all of Europe, over the following two years
radical forces are increasingly persecuted, their leaders imprisoned or
forced into exile. Giuseppe Mazzini founds the "European Democratic

Committee for the Solidarity of Parties, without Distinction of Nationality," known for short as the European Democratic Central Committee in London, gathering major exiled democratic leaders in most of Europe. Any activity requires underground conspiracy. Constitutional monarchists attempt to maintain their positions but are increasingly pushed back by conservatives. A few major developments:

France: Growth of radical secret societies, particularly in small towns and countryside of central and southeastern portions of the country. Louis-Napoleon attempts to expand his authority, but his plans to change the constitution so he could be re-elected president defeated by monarchists in the legislature. He launches a coup on 2 December 1851. Paris is quiet, but secret societies rise in the provinces and must be suppressed by the army.

Germany: Constitutional conflict pitting Prince and government ministers in Hessen-Kassel against the principality's legislature, its civil servants, and even its army officers. The Prussian government attempts to create a "little German" national state by diplomatic negotiation (the Erfurt Union). Linkage of the question of German reunification and the conflict in Hessen-Kassel, with Austria supporting the prince and Prussia the constitution. Prussia and Austria are on the brink of war by November 1850, but Prussia accedes to Austria, which has the support of the tsar (the "humiliation of Olmütz"). Restoration of the pre-1848 German Confederation under Austrian leadership.

Austria: December 1851, abolition of the constitution decreed in March 1849 that had never actually been in effect. Attempted creation of a centralized, absolutist regime.

Norway: The "Workers' Union" reaches its high point in 1851, with over 30,000 members. The government arrests its leaders in June of that year and the group quickly vanishes.

Introduction

The European revolutions of 1848 have not always received the kindest of treatment at the hands of historians. Gentle mockery, open sarcasm and hostile contempt have frequently set the tone for narrative and evaluation. More favorable treatments of the period have not been much of an improvement, since their poetic interpretations have subtly downgraded the revolutions as serious political movements, not to be compared to the real business of 1789 and 1917. We might point to three major interpretative traditions.

One is characterized by its description of 1848 as the "romantic revolution." Historians writing along these lines apostrophize the barricade fighting born from a combination of youthful enthusiasm and romantic poetry; they evoke a revolution reaching its climax in the brief euphoria of liberation in March 1848, the "springtime of the peoples" as the contemporary German phrase described it. In this version, attention is often focused on the romantically heroic deeds of individual great figures: Lajou:Kossuth travelling from village to village in the Hungarian plain, to rally the peasants against the invading Habsburg armies; Giuseppe Garibaldi leading the improvised armies of the Roman Republic against the French expeditionary force; Daniele Manin single-handedly rallying the Venetians to fight the Austrians against terrible odds. It was all great and glorious, but primarily in gesture and pathos – whether it really accomplished anything, is quite another matter.

Rather darker is another version of the 1848 revolutions, that views them primarily as farce, a revolution made by revolutionaries who were at best incompetent dilettantes, at worst cowards and blowhards who stole away from the scene when the going got rough. This version features the story of the Parisian revolutionary (most versions have him being Alphonse de Lamartine, the poet who was Minister of Foreign Affairs in the provisional government of the French Republic) observing from his window a demonstrating crowd go by, springing up from his chair, and rushing out, proclaiming, "I am their leader; I must follow them." Another typical victim of retrospective contempt is the Frankfurt National

1

Assembly, the all-German parliament. Historians have had their fun with the "professors' parliament," mocking its lengthy debates about whether Germany should be a *Bundesstaat* or a *Staatenbund*, noting how, after a year of deliberation, the deputies voted to name the King of Prussia emperor, only to discover that he had no interest in the post.

The third, and probably most substantial of the historians' versions of 1848 directs attention to the failure of the revolutions of that year to establish new regimes, pointing out that after a shorter or longer – and usually shorter – interval, the authorities overthrown at the onset of the revolution returned to power. Historians working in this tradition contrast the failed revolutions of the mid-nineteenth century with the more successful ones in 1789 and 1917, and offer a variety of explanations for the differences. Some follow a Marxist analysis – one first devised by Karl Marx and Friedrich Engels, personally, since they were themselves participants in the revolutionary events – that emphasizes differences in class formation and class struggle. Others look to sociological modernization theory to explain the failure of the revolution; still others point to differing diplomatic configurations and the military initiatives of energetic and insightful generals.

None of these ways of understanding the 1848 revolution is totally false. All can testify to a long lineage, going back, ultimately, to interpretations offered by participants in the revolution themselves. Yet, ultimately, none of them seem adequate to the event. Even if the leaders of the mid-nineteenth century revolutions were blowhards and dilettantes, even if the revolutions were ultimately failures, they were still the largest, the most widespread, and the most violent political movement of nineteenth-century Europe. For that reason alone, they deserve to be taken more seriously.

Over the past several decades a different, more appropriate interpretation of the mid-century revolution has gradually emerged. In some ways encouraged by the east-central European revolutions of 1989, that have caused some rethinking of the nature of revolution and some redefinition of the criteria of success and failure of revolutions, this new interpretation has come into its own in many of the commemorative works published in conjunction with the one hundred fiftieth anniversary of the 1848 revolutions in 1998. One aspect of this new approach has been a change in focus. Following the broader trends of social history, newer studies of the 1848 revolution have moved away from the revolutionary parliaments and the capital cities to the towns and villages of the provinces, from the well-known barricade struggles of 1848, to the less emphasized uprisings and civil wars of 1849 and 1851, from the romantic national leaders to the obscure local activists and the craftsmen, laborers, and peasants, who made up a majority of the European population and of the participants in the revolutionary events.

This new interpretation is, admittedly, less romantic and more prosaic, featuring inquiries into the nature of political organization and agitation during the revolution, as well as discussions of the forms and symbols of political activity, both of a peaceful and violent nature. Also characteristic of this interpretation is an attempt to connect the outbreak and course of the revolution with the social, economic, and cultural changes of the preceding decades. All this can – and all too often does – make for less interesting and exciting reading than the drama or contempt of other versions, yet there is nothing inherent in this new interpretation to make it so. The meetings of a political club of a small provincial town can be no less fascinating than the impassioned debates of national parliamentarians; the aspirations and struggles of impoverished and illiterate peasants no less moving than those of romantic poets. The best authors writing in this vein have vividly conveyed the drama and passions of the revolutionary experience of the mid-nineteenth century; whether anything of that sort is accomplished in this book is something its readers will have to decide.

Depending on where one looks, this new interpretation of the 1848 revolution exists to very different extents. Pioneered by French historians, it is most detailed and complete for France, somewhat less so for Germany, and noticeably more sketchy concerning 1848 in Italy and the Habsburg monarchy. Added to these differences in the depth of the scholarly literature, is its polyglot nature, to be expected in studies of a political movement that extended from the Atlantic coast to the Carpathians, from the Mediterranean to the Baltic. I make no pretense to being able to read all or even most of the dozen languages in which works on the 1848 revolution have been written. Still, enough has been written, and is physically or linguistically accessible, that it seems worthwhile to include the mid-nineteenth century revolutions as a topic in the series "New Approaches in European History," and make available to students and interested general readers a synthesis of the latest historical interpretation of 1848, working into it the still useful elements of older views.

One major aspect of these new approaches to the study of the 1848 revolutions has been placing them in their proper historical context. Therefore, the reader should not expect to jump right onto the barricades. Rather, the book begins with a consideration of the background to and causes of the revolution. The first chapter studies social, economic, cultural, and governmental institutions of and developments in Europe towards the middle of the nineteenth century, with an eye to their relevance for the forthcoming revolutionary events. In particular, it pays careful attention to the forms of social and economic conflict that existed even before the outbreak of revolution. The second chapter then outlines the nature of political life in the 1840s, briefly explaining the major ideologies, the forms of political organization, and the political struggles existing before the revolution greatly deepened and broadened them.

Only in chapter three does the revolution begin and do barricades get built. This chapter will concentrate on the early months of the revolution, showing the rapid collapse of most governments in the first months of 1848. It will move rapidly, though, from the barricades in the capital cities out into the provinces, and explain the course of the revolution there and, in particular, how the news of the fighting on the barricades led to an outpouring of social conflicts. The chapter will end with a consideration of where the revolutionary movement stood at the end of the spring of 1848.

The fourth chapter deals with the subsequent year of revolution, in analytic fashion. Its main theme is the explosion of political participation and organization during the revolution. Political clubs and other kinds of organization, elections, petitions, demonstrations, public meetings, and other forms of activities are important topics. An analysis of the participants in the revolution and of the bases of their loyalties to different political doctrines is included, as is a section on a topic of recent considerable interest – the activities of women during the revolution. The chapter ends with a discussion of trends and developments across the year running from May 1848 to May 1849.

The fifth chapter returns to this same period, but in a narrative rather than an analytical mode. It discusses the major events and struggles between the spring of 1848 and the summer of 1849, concentrating on the decline of the initial consensus, the increasing polarization of politics, the defeats of revolutionary forces in the summer and fall of 1848, their rallying and reorganization in the fall of that year and the winter of 1849, and the second round of revolutionary struggles in the spring and summer of 1849. A last section discusses further events until the final struggles of the mid-century revolutions in December 1851. The sixth and final chapter uses the new approaches to the mid-century revolutions developed in the book in order to place them in European history, in the context of the nineteenth century and in comparison to the revolutions of 1789, 1917, and 1989, and in the forms of historical memory and commemoration by which their course and outcome were transmitted to subsequent generations.

1 Society and social conflict in Europe during the 1840s

The countryside

Towards the middle of the nineteenth century, Europe was a continent of peasants. Even in areas that were, by the standards of the day, heavily urbanized and industrialized, such as the Düsseldorf District of the Prussian Rhine Province, or the Austrian province of Bohemia, farmers made up 40 and 55 percent of the regions' respective labor forces. The French census of 1851 counted some 64 percent of the gainfully employed as active in agriculture. Moving east and south, towards the poorer, economically less developed parts of the continent, the presence of the peasantry increased: 85 percent of the labor force in the Austrian province of Galicia, on the Habsburg monarchy's border with Russia; 89 percent of the inhabitants of the province of Basilicata in the Kingdom of the Two Sicilies at the far southern end of the Italian peninsula. "The people" of 1840s Europe were the peasants – a point that would surprise not a few contemporaries in 1848, when "the people" went from being the objects of political rhetoric to the subjects of political action.

Peasant life varied enormously across Europe, and it would take several books to describe the differences in peasants' standards of living, agricultural tenures, farm products, customs, religion or folklore. For our purposes, we can note two broad groups of differences: in the kind of agriculture practiced and in the relations of production. Although European farmers generally did not specialize as they would in the twentieth century, or even in the second half of the nineteenth, it is still possible to delineate three basic forms of agriculture.

One was centered around grain production: in northern and eastern Europe, rye; in the south and west, wheat. All things considered, this was a prosperous and promising field of economic activity. To be sure, the high grain prices of the late eighteenth century and early nineteenth century, the era of the Napoleonic wars, had dropped sharply in the early 1820s, to the particular dismay of noble large landowners, whose complaints have all too often found the ear of historians. From the mid-1820s

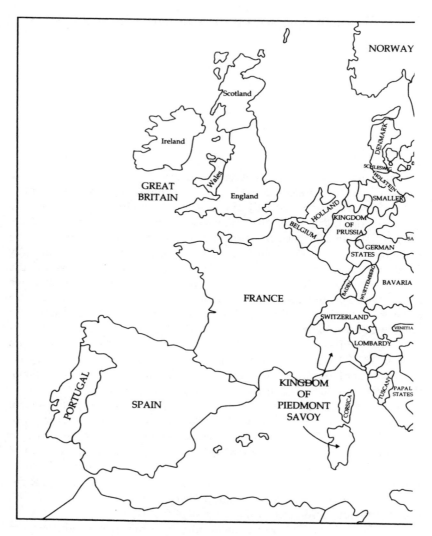

Map 1.1 Europe in 1848

onward, though, grain prices throughout most of Europe began gradually to rise again, on the average perhaps 20 percent in the next two decades. When this price rise was combined with increases in productivity, as the techniques of the eighteenth-century "agricultural revolution" – division and cultivation of the village common lands, cultivation of crops providing a lot of nutritional value in a small area, such as potatoes and corn (maize), elimination of fallow, introduction of soil enhancing, nitrogen fixing crops, like vetch and alfalfa, growth of new, commercial crops, like sugar beets – spread from England to the European continent, the upshot was a favorable outlook, at least for those who had grain to bring to the market.

The new agriculture was most aggressively and successfully practiced on the great northern European plain that extends from the English Channel through northern France and the Low Countries, and across northern Germany to what was then the far eastern end of the Kingdom of Prussia. Here, fertile soil and easy access to water transportation encouraged a productive, modern, market-oriented agriculture. Conversely, that minority of grain growing regions where such agricultural progress did not take place were areas with problems of market access. One such was southern Italy, especially the island of Sicily, one of the great granaries of the ancient Roman Empire, where agricultural techniques had changed little in the intervening millennia. Farmers there had few incentives to innovate, since it was government policy in the Kingdom of the Two Sicilies to tax grain exports and encourage imports, so as to keep bread prices low and thus to pacify the teeming masses of the kingdom's capital, Naples, Europe's third largest city. Another unhappy region was the Austrian province of Galicia, one of the poorest regions of Europe, where grain prices remained persistently low, as much as 40 percent below other parts of the monarchy, since the main waterways leading out of the region, the Vistula and Dniester rivers, passed through other countries, whose trade and tariff policies hindered exports. However, such exceptions should not take our view from the rule that for most European agricultural regions, tending to specialize in grain production, the quarter century before 1850 was a period of gradually increasing prosperity.

Most of Europe, particularly its southern half, is climatically and topographically poorly suited to grain growing, and farmers looked to alternative crops. There were many possibilities, ranging from natural dyestuffs to asparagus, to rapeseed, but the three most important at the time were wine, olives, and silk. These were all highly marketable crops, whose sale could bring in substantial returns. It was the prevalence of these non-subsistence crops that made the difference in the first half of the nineteenth century between a more affluent northern and central Italy and a poorer south. Yields on grain were better in the south, but elsewhere the cultivation of market-oriented crops more than compensated for a less favorable natural environment.

The greatest strength of these crops, their marketability, was also their main weakness. While grain growers could feed their families from their own harvest, non-subsistence crops had to be first turned into cash and then back into food. Although price figures for such crops are more uncertain and variable than those for grain, the available ones often suggest a less favorable development, meaning that ever more grapes or raw silk needed to be sold to obtain the same amount of bread, potatoes, or corn (maize). More important than price trends, though, were the uncertainty and difficulties of the market. Some of these crops were quickly perishable and hard to get from the grower to the seller promptly, particularly before the creation of a railroad network. There were potential expedients available to the ingenious, like the peasants of southern France who distilled their low-quality, quickly souring wines into brandy, that kept much better and thus could be sold before it spoiled. More typically, such farmers preferred to avoid specialization, devoting some of their land to growing their own grain, even on and in climates poorly suited to it, rather than placing all their eggs – or olives – in one market basket.

The last version of agriculture we can mention was practiced by those peasants who lived in the hilly and mountainous parts of Europe. The steep terrain and harsh weather of these regions were poorly suited to either of the two forms of agriculture discussed above. Peasants of the uplands turned to pasturage, the most successful and prosperous example being the dairy farming of the Alpine lands. Most hill and mountain peasants were not so fortunate, lacking the land needed to pasture enough cows, sheep, or pigs, to provide for their needs. Life in the rural up-country thus became a miscellany of expedients: selling the meager crops raised and living on chestnuts, cutting (or stealing) wood in the forest areas frequently covering the high country, and, when possible, engaging in large-scale seasonal migration. During the construction season, Paris's masons could be heard talking the dialect of the Limousin, a mountainous, impoverished area of central France; at least twenty thousand mountain peasants came yearly from the northern Italian Kingdom of Piedmont-Savoy to work in southern France. Everywhere in Europe, peasants came down out of the hills and mountains to the more prosperous lowlands each year at harvest time. As all these examples suggest, living standards in the uplands were low, and all the evidence historians have at their disposal, from travellers' accounts, to reports of government officials, to land-tax records, describe the mountain peasants as the poorest people on the continent, at times living on the very edge of starvation.

To complete this discussion of the divisions of mid-century European agriculture, we need to make a distinction between agriculture and agriculturalists, since the prosperity of the former did not necessarily imply the wealth of the latter. This was a result of the division of agricultural property: it was most uneven in the most prosperous grain growing areas, which were rich in large landed estates, and/or substantial peasant farmers, whether actual property owners or large tenants. These held most of the land; most of the people who lived on it were landless laborers or small proprietors whose holdings did not suffice to support their families. While far from egalitarian, landed property in areas of non-subsistence production, or in the mountains, was more likely to be more widely distributed. To give just one simple example from the province of Bologna, at the northeastern end of Italy's Papal States, during the 1840s in the fertile, rice growing plain of the Bolognese, tenants, sharecroppers, and day laborers made up some 95 percent of the agricultural population. They worked for or rented from large, often noble landowners or urban absentee landlords. In the far poorer mountainous regions of the province, on the other hand, landowners, mostly small proprietors, made up 45 percent of the agricultural labor force with about 22 percent tenants and sharecroppers, while laborers were just above one fifth.[1] To be sure, a landless rural laborer in a wealthy farming area might well be better off than a property-owning peasant on a barren patch of land in the hills, but would be living in a far more inegalitarian social environment.

Ownership of the land had a quite different meaning across the continent and this brings up the second major division of rural society in Europe during the 1840s, the freedom or unfreedom of the land and those who worked it. We can point to a tripartite distinction reflecting the influence of the French Revolution of 1789 on feudal and seigneurial conditions in the countryside. One version was prevalent in the western part of the continent: France, Spain, the states of the Italian peninsula, the Low Countries, Switzerland, and western Germany, as well as to the north in Scandinavia. There, feudal and seigneurial relations had been abolished and the rules of the free capitalist market prevailed in agriculture. Anyone could own, rent, mortgage, sell or otherwise freely dispose of land. This right to own land did not necessarily mean that all or even most of the peasants in those areas actually owned it, as the many

---

[1] Figures from Luigi del Pane, *Economia e società a Bologna nell'età del Risorgimento introduzione alla ricerca* (Bologna, 1969), 403.

agricultural laborers of Italy's Po Valley, the numerous sharecroppers of southern France and central Italy, or the Norwegian cotters testified. However, if people in those regions worked on the land, they did so as free laborers, toiling for compensation (not necessarily in cash, of course; much agricultural labor was paid in kind), and at least legally able to leave and seek better employment.

At the other end of the continent, in parts of eastern Germany, the eastern reaches of the Habsburg monarchy, including its Hungarian provinces, the tsar's empire and the Danubian Principalities of Moldavia and Wallachia, then under Turkish overlordship, the effects of the French Revolution had been unavailing or transitory. As late as the 1840s, these areas remained the realm of feudalism. Most peasants were serfs who were required to work, uncompensated, for their noble landlords; they could not dispose freely of the land they farmed on their own account; and many of them could not even leave this land without their lord's permission. These were economic relations based on compulsion, not on market exchange, and particularly in the poorest and most backward of these areas of feudalism, say the Habsburg provinces of Transylvania or Galicia, such compulsion was physical and literal, characterized by the liberal use of the whip and the stick.

Finally, a third region of Europe was located both geographically and socially between these two, encompassing most of central Germany, including the western and German-speaking provinces of the Austrian empire. Peasants living in this region were free to move about, and usually to dispose of the land they farmed; they were legally required, however, to pay dues and fees of various sorts to their noble landlords, who maintained certain rights over the land their subject peasants farmed. Typically by the 1840s, peasants of those areas had the possibility of ending such seigneurial relations by making a large, one-time cash payment to their lords as compensation. It was a rarity, though, for peasants to take advantage of this possibility, since the money was usually not available, or only to be had on very unfavorable credit terms.

Even before the French Revolution had put a dramatic end to seigneurial and feudal relations in the agriculture of western Europe, the question of its abolition had arisen in the eastern part of the continent. The great eighteenth-century reforming Austrian Emperor Joseph II had attempted to codify and limit the services peasants owed their lords; even in the mid-nineteenth century, memories of this "good emperor," the "peasants' emperor," remained alive among restive serfs. However, by this time, the advance of modern, market-oriented agriculture had led even feudal lords themselves to wonder if forced labor, performed sullenly and reluctantly, accompanied by the occasional peasant uprising, was the most efficient and profitable way to run their estates. If serfdom was seeming less efficient, emancipation would pose its own problems. Why would peasants work on their lords' estate if they were no longer compelled to do so? If the peasants did not work for their lords, then how would the nobles exploit their lands?

A potential answer to this question had been found in the Kingdom of Prussia, one of the two largest states in Germany, in the first decades of the nineteenth century. The kingdom's reform-minded government officials had devised a program by which peasants were freed of their obligation to perform feudal labor services for their lords, in return for which they provided the lords with compensation – not in cash, but in land. While for some ex-serfs this meant that they would become substantial peasant farmers, most were left with small plots of land, insufficient to support their families. To do so, they found it necessary to work as free laborers on their former landlords' large estates. This elegant solution, combining capitalist social relations, modern agricultural techniques, and a powerful and prosperous position for the landowning nobility, had been largely implemented by the 1830s in most provinces of the Prussian kingdom, with the peculiar exception of Silesia, whose nobility stubbornly refused to accept such arrangements. It was an interesting and influential model for a potential end to feudalism in Europe, but debates about the abolition of feudal and seigneurial relations where they existed remained largely just that – debates. Serfdom and feudal dues continued to bedevil the lives of peasants in large portions of central and eastern Europe down through the 1840s, and the existence of these circumstances would have a decisive impact on the mid-century revolution.

Crafts, manufacturing, and their social order

Visitors to the 1851 International Exhibition in London, dazzled by the array of British manufactured goods displayed there, came away referring to the United Kingdom as the "workshop of the world." There was an implicit negative reference contained in this sobriquet: namely, that the countries of continental Europe were not workshops, or, to put it differently, that the process of industrialization on a broad scale which had so transformed the society and economy of the United Kingdom in the first half of the nineteenth century, had largely not occurred elsewhere in Europe. Steam engines, textile mills, blast furnaces, and railways were not unknown on the continent before 1850, and their presence was clearly on the increase during most of the decade of the 1840s. However, industrial production in continental Europe during the first half of the nineteenth century was economically much less significant than agriculture in terms of employment, and as a proportion of both net investment and the gross domestic product. The use of steam power in production was limited to a few industries and within them to a few regions. Most non-agricultural production continued to be done by hand, and most people employed in this production worked in artisanal trades.

Widespread use of steam power before 1850 was confined to three geographically contiguous regions, each of which was sprawled across state boundaries. Perhaps the largest and most significant of them ran from northern and northeastern France through Walloonia (French-speaking Belgium) into the Prussian provinces of the Rhineland and Westphalia in northwestern Germany.[2] A second, further south and east, included portions of the Kingdom of Saxony and of the neighboring Austrian province of Bohemia. The third, and smallest, encompassed areas of Alsace, in eastern France, as well as neighboring portions of southwestern Germany and northwestern Switzerland. Outside of these areas, steam power and large, mechanized workshops were present only in scattered locations. The three major capital cities, Paris, Berlin, and Vienna, all had a fair number, as did an occasional urban center, like the French manufacturing town of St. Etienne, north of Lyon, but in large stretches of the wealthiest countries of western Europe – to say nothing of the poorer states to the south and east – steam engines and factory industry were not to be found.

Far and away the most important industrial sector was textile spinning, typically cotton or woolens. There were some steam-powered weaving mills as well, and, to a lesser extent, industrialized metallurgical production, more often than not in connection with the railroads, whose construction had begun in scattered fashion in the mid-1830s, and had experienced something of a boom ten years later. These two branches, textiles and metal working, largely exhausted the list of industrialized economic sectors in continental Europe before 1850.

The most common form of large-scale manufacturing had little to do with either factories or steam power. This was the system of outworking, by which dozens, hundreds or even thousands of craftsmen worked at home or in a small workshop for a merchant capitalist, who provided them with the raw materials, and sometimes the tools of their trade as well (both usually on credit), bought their finished product, and then sold these wares in a broader, continental, or even world-wide market. Just how

---

[2] Belgium is sometimes described as a European country which had achieved a major degree of industrialization before 1850, but it might be more accurate to say that it was not so much industrialized as small: its share of the northwest European industrial region took up most of it.

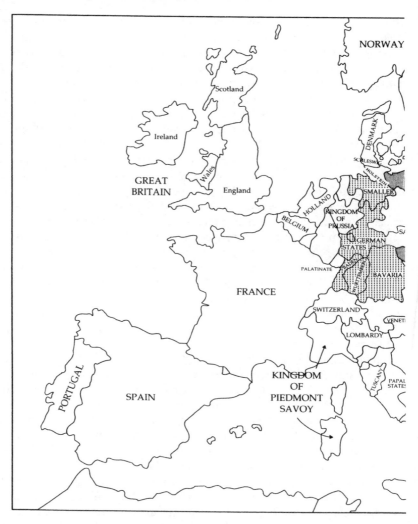

Map 1.2 Dominant agricultural property and production regimes in Europe during the 1840s.

SWEDEN

Free Capitalist

Seigneurial

Serfdom

KINGDOM
OF
PRUSSIA

SAXONY

RUSSIAN
EMPIRE

Galicia

AUSTRIAN EMPIRE

Hungarian
Provinces

MOLDAVIA

Transylvania

CROATIA

BOSNIA

SERBIA

WALLACHIA

OTTOMAN

EMPIRE

KINGDOM
OF TWO
SICILIES

GREECE

outworking was organized can be seen from this description, written in 1842, of silk manufacturing in the Wupper Valley in western Germany:

[weavers] work on the material given them by the manufacturers in their apartments and on their looms at a wage determined in advance...almost all the master dyers, both in the city of Elberfeld [the major city of the Wupper Valley] and elsewhere in the county, dye for wages [but] independently, the cloth given to them by a manufacturing establishment...Spinners spin the silk given them on their own spinning wheels for a predetermined wage...[Virtually all] finishers, pressers, fabric gluers, ribbon weavers, cloth printing form makers, and cloth printers...practice their trade in their own dwellings; that is, they prepare for a wage the material given them by one or even many manufacturers.[3]

Outworking was particularly common in textile manufacturing, but was also used to produce knives, scissors, razors, leather goods, straw hats, toys, musical instruments, playing cards, and even such exotica as religious pictures painted on the reverse side of a piece of glass.

This version of large-scale enterprise was not new; forms of it had existed in Europe since the Middle Ages. Many of these older craft manufactures were in decline during the first half of the nineteenth century. The woolens manufacture of Florence and Bologna, pride of these two cities during the Renaissance, had largely gone out of existence; outworking woolens manufacture in southwestern France, vigorous as late as the 1770s, was in its final agonies. Particularly hard hit was the manufacture of linen cloth, a product that had a very hard time competing with more popular and better quality cotton textiles. The decline of the large-scale outworking production of linen cloth in Silesia, in the southeastern corner of the Prussian monarchy, or in Westphalia, at the opposite end of that kingdom, had reached crisis proportions by the 1840s.

These sorts of examples have often led historians to speak of a decline of or even a catastrophe for outworking because of mechanized competition, modeled perhaps on the sad story of the English handloom weavers, for whom the first half of the nineteenth century was an unmitigated disaster. What this gloomy view overlooks is the expansion of many branches of textile outworking between 1800 and 1850. Silk production, unmechanized in continental Europe until the last quarter of the nineteenth century, was a prime example. Silkworms were raised and raw silk processed throughout northern and central Italy. Silk was woven there and in and around Lyon and St. Etienne in central France, around Krefeld and Elberfeld in northwestern Germany, and in and around the Austrian capital of Vienna. These latter areas were also centers of silk

---

[3] Cited in Jonathan Sperber, *Rhineland Radicals: The Democratic Movement and the Revolution of 1848–1849* (Princeton, 1991), 24.

ribbon and stocking weaving and of the finishing and dyeing trade, all largely conducted on an outworking basis.

Early industrial development in continental Europe was, if anything, actually favorable to the growth of artisanal outworking. Cotton and woolen spinning was mechanized on the continent decades before weaving was. Consequently the building of mechanized spinning mills increased the output of thread and demand for artisanal handloom weavers. In the Düsseldorf District of the Prussian Rhine Province, an important part of the northwest European center of early industrialization, the building of steam-powered cotton-spinning mills led to a doubling in the number of handloom weavers between the 1820s and the middle of the century.

Overall, outworking was thriving and expanding in Europe during the first half of the nineteenth century. Outworkers and outworking establishments greatly outnumbered mechanized factories and those who worked in them. Even language use testified to this. The words "fabrique," "Fabrik" or "fabbrica," in today's French, German, and Italian meaning "factory" in the sense of a large, mechanized industrial establishment, then referred to a large-scale manufacturing enterprise, more likely an outworking establishment than a steam-powered workshop.

Such large-scale outworking establishments were far from being identical with the crafts. At least as many, and in most places more artisans worked for small-scale and local markets, providing for basic needs of food, clothing, and shelter. Besides the nursery rhyme butcher, baker, and candlestick maker, we could mention tailors, shoemakers, cabinetmakers, masons, and construction carpenters as the most common of these crafts. There were three features tending to distinguish these small-scale craftsmen from outworkers. They were more likely to reside in cities and towns than outworkers, the latter an often – and in the middle decades of the nineteenth century increasingly – rural group. Small-scale craftsmen were also usually in heavily male trades, while the ranks of outworkers included larger numbers of women. Finally, such craftsmen had, at least in theory, a formal occupational structure, a lifetime career path. It led from apprentice, a teenager learning the trade, through journeyman, an itinerant worker in the field, to master, an older, settled man, with his own workshop, employing his own journeymen and training his own apprentices.

Prior to the French Revolution, these occupational structures had been shaped and regulated by the guilds, groups of master artisans legally empowered to set prices, wages, and output in their respective crafts, determine who might practice the craft and, more generally, keep an eye on the morals and private lives of all those in it. Such a hindrance to the free market economy was anathema to the revolutionaries, and their legislation of 1791 abolishing the guilds retained its effect, not just in France, but in a large portion of western and southern Europe, closely (if not always exactly) following the areas in which the feudal system in agriculture had been swept away. In Scandinavia, the Habsburg Empire, the Principalities of Moldavia and Wallachia, and many of the German states, on the other hand, guilds had survived into the mid-nineteenth century with at least some of their powers intact, if by the 1840s increasingly supervised by a not always friendly state bureaucracy.

Yet even where guilds had no legal standing, or had been suppressed by the law, they had not vanished from the thoughts and actions of craftsmen. Compulsory guilds might be gone, yet in many cities the masters of a trade were somehow all members of the same mutual benefit society (friendly society) or religious brotherhood. The French "compagnonnages," brotherhoods of journeymen artisans, who had alternately fought against and tacitly cooperated with the master craftsmen's guilds under the old regime, and had been outlawed with the guilds in 1791, continued through the 1840s to guide journeymen in taking the "tour de France," as they moved around the country practicing their trades and seeking work. The attractions of the ordering and organizing principles of the guilds were not lost on artisans, no matter what the laws or pro-free-market economists said about them, a point which would emerge in a striking way in 1848.

Craftsmen clung to such ideas at least in part because the world of small-scale craft production of the 1830s and 40s was moving ever further away from the ideas of the old guild system. Some of the same forms of production seen in outworking were beginning to make their appearance. Nominally independent master artisans found themselves increasingly working for and in debt to merchant capitalists, who organized the trade – "usurious middlemen, who have pushed themselves in between the public and the producers," as the cabinet-makers of Berlin described them in quite unfriendly language.[4] The line between master and journeyman, between being economically dependent and having one's own business, had become blurred.

Guilds had been designed to prevent the blurring of such lines, but even where they still existed they were unable to halt these developments, since ingenious capitalists were able to hide their position by working through straw men. Perhaps the high point of such practices was in the tailoring trade of Paris, continental Europe's largest city. Merchant capitalists had created a complex system of sub-contracting and sub-sub-contracting that included a substantial amount of female labor – a

---

[4] Cited in Rüdiger Hachtmann, *Berlin 1848. Eine Politik- und Gesellschaftsgeschichte der Revolution* (Bonn, 1997), 74.

disgrace to any self-respecting male artisan's honor, and a threat to his economic position, since women were paid noticeably less than men and threatened to bring down wages throughout the trade.

These forms of outworking had become ever more prevalent among the craft trades of major metropolitan centers such as Paris and Berlin, but were also in common use in smaller, more provincial cities such as Turin or Düsseldorf. They seem to have had an especially strong hold in the three large and relatively less skilled crafts of tailoring, shoemaking, and cabinet-making. The food trades, on the other hand, were less affected; bakers and butchers continued to follow the traditional patterns of their crafts, including, among the latter, a tendency toward strong religious devotion and disregard of sanitation.

There were two more groups among the urban – more precisely, the non-agricultural – lower classes worth noting here. One was the unskilled laborers, working by the day as longshoremen (dockers), porters, tow-men, construction helpers, and the like. All pre-industrial cities were rich in opportunities for men (and it was mostly men who did such things) to haul, push, carry, or lift. Many of these men were temporary residents, seasonal migrants from rural areas, who might live among themselves in their own neighborhoods and have strikingly little contact with the urban world in which they worked. Craftsmen wanted little to do with them – a feeling that was often reciprocated – and regarded it as a great disaster to be forced to work outside their trade as unskilled labor.

Surprisingly, in view of the many temporary migrants working these jobs, the casual nature of employment in them, and the lack of skill required for them, those who worked in them were sometimes able to create organizations to regulate their labor market. The most remarkable example was the longshoremen of the port of Marseilles, who had succeeded in preserving their old regime guild (it is in and of itself interesting that unskilled laborers, in no way master craftsmen, had their own guild) even after it had been officially outlawed, and in fact dominated the docks with it until the 1860s. Other examples would include the guilds of porters in many Italian cities, who continued to influence the labor market in the 1840s, well after artisans' guilds had been abolished or had faded into insignificance, or the organization of tow-men, who claimed the exclusive right to tow any boats passing upstream through the Rhine river ports of Cologne and Mainz.

There was a female pendant to this world of male unskilled labor: domestic service. Often amounting to as much as 10–15 percent of a city's inhabitants, household servants were disproportionately from rural backgrounds, and, by the middle of the nineteenth century, very largely women. The retinues of male lackeys, with which old regime aristocrats had surrounded themselves in their public appearances, were increasingly *passé* by the 1840s, giving way to a more bourgeois conception of the servant as devoted to the female realm of hearth and home.

Social structure and elites

Given the dominant position of agriculture in continental Europe during the first half of the nineteenth century, it is hardly surprising that the sources of wealth and power were to be found on the land. France was an industrially advanced and urbanized country by the standards of the day, and also one of the best administered, thus possessing some of the highest-quality statistics. Exploiting these references, the historian André-Jean Tudesq has studied the "great notables," of the early 1840s, the 160,000 most highly taxed individuals, from whose ranks came the top government officials, legislators, and dominant figures in the economy. He found that 65 percent of these were large landowners, outnumbering merchants and manufacturers by over four to one. The latter groups were more numerous among the wealthy and powerful of Alsace, an early center of industrialization, or in the port cities of Marseilles and Bordeaux, but such areas, and this is the whole point, were still isolated in an agricultural landscape.[5] What was true of France was even more the case in less urban, less industrial, less economically developed regions to its east and south. The upper class of mid-nineteenth-century Europe was above all a class of landowners, followed at some distance by affluent merchants and bankers – many of whom dealt in agricultural products, or financed the trade in them – and, finally, at even greater distance, by a small group of manufacturers, including both factory owners and rather more merchants with their outworking establishments.

If landowning formed the basis for a continental European elite, the composition of this elite, and with it the nature of the social structure, differed sharply in different parts of the continent. To the west and south, basically in the same area which had seen the abolition of seigneurialism during the era of the French Revolution, membership in the elite was open to anyone with the money for it. Aristocratic families who proudly traced their lineages back to medieval times were a part, along with more recently ennobled families, whose blood was not quite so blue, and quite ordinary commoners, who had no distinction beyond their wealth. The relative proportions of these groups varied in different regions: the

---

[5] André-Jean Tudesq, *Les grands notables en France (1840–1849)*, 2 vols. (Paris, 1964), 1: 96–97.

Romagna, in central Italy, for instance, was dominated by great aristocratic families, while in the Palatinate, in the extreme southwestern corner of Germany, it was a "bourgeois aristocracy" of vineyard owners who possessed a large share of the land. Large landowners might live in the country on their estates or in cities as absentee landlords; nobles and commoners among them might have different attitudes toward politics or religion, and different memories of the era of the French Revolution, but together they formed a legally and economically homogeneous elite.

To travel east into Europe, through Scandinavia and central Germany into eastern Germany and the eastern provinces of the Habsburg monarchy, was to move steadily away from this social arrangement and toward one in which wealth and power were concentrated in the hands of an hereditary aristocracy. In part, this is just another way of saying that the impetus from the French Revolution to alter or abolish feudal and seigneurial relations in agriculture weakened as one moved eastward in Europe. However, this state of affairs also reflected the peculiar relationship between city and country in east-central and eastern Europe. Not only were cities and urban sources of wealth scarce there, but the urban capitalists, and to a certain extent all town dwellers, were alien bodies within rural society.

A modest version of this difference might be seen in the Prussian capital of Berlin, where one study of industrial entrepreneurs in the first half of the nineteenth century has found that half were Jews, a religious minority group lacking equal rights with the Christian population and culturally distinct from them. This contrast was even sharper in the further eastern reaches of the Habsburg Empire, where the majority of townspeople spoke a different language and often practiced a different religion from the rural inhabitants of the vicinity: the Yiddish-speaking Jews who were a majority in many towns of the Habsburg province of Galicia, whose rural inhabitants were Roman Catholic, Uniate (Greek Catholic) or Orthodox Christians, speaking Polish or Ukrainian; or the Germans who dominated the city of Pressburg, which is today the Slovak capital Bratislava, and was in the 1840s seat of the Diet, the Hungarian feudal legislature.

Not only did the position of the nobility among the elite or the relationship between town and country in eastern Europe differ from those existing in the west, but the very nature of the nobility did as well. In France, Italy or Germany of the eighteenth or early nineteenth centuries, nobles were a small group, rarely exceeding 1/2 to 1 percent of the population. In the 1840s, 6 percent of Hungary's inhabitants were nobles. If we just count Magyar (Hungarian) speakers, and not those whose native language was Romanian, Slovak, Ukrainian or Serbo-Croatian, then about 12–13 percent of those Magyar-speakers belonged to the nobility. Similar proportions of nobles could be found in the Polish-speaking areas of eastern Europe. The nobility in that region was a mass nobility: great magnate families, like the Radziwills and Esterházys, who owned tens of thousands of acres and almost as many serfs; modest gentry families, with just a few hundred acres at most; and large numbers of the "peasant nobility," simple farmers who were nobles because they were not serfs.

This arrangement had consequences throughout the entire social structure. The middle class in western Europe consisted in part of more modestly affluent individuals: lesser landowners, smaller merchants, and manufacturers. In the eastern part of the continent, on the other hand, the urban version of such a middle class was either lacking or was made up of alien outsiders; the mass nobility ensured that the "middle class" of the Polish or Hungarian regions of Europe were nobles too.

Property owners and businessmen were only a part of the middle class in mid-nineteenth-century Europe. Another major segment consisted of members of the professions: clergy, lawyers, notaries, physicians, apothecaries, secondary school and university teachers. Although individuals within this professional middle class might themselves be property owners or entrepreneurs, the source of their social position came from the education they had received and the services they offered, both of which were provided, guaranteed or regulated by the state. In central and eastern Europe, such professionals were likely to be employed by the state, thus making civil servants a substantial part of the middle class there. Even attorneys in private practice, themselves substantially outnumbered by jurists working directly for the government as judges, state's attorneys or state administrators, were on the state payroll or appointed to practice at a particular court by the government. By contrast, in the western part of the continent a combination of greater opportunities and lesser governmental regulations allowed more professionals to work on their own account.

Together, the upper and middle classes made up at most 20 percent of the continent's inhabitants. The large, less fortunate majority could be divided into two groups, membership of which would be determined by whether the main provider brought in enough to secure the basic physical needs of a family. If not, then the unpleasant alternatives would be celibacy, avoiding founding a family; a family in which both spouses worked at separate, poorly paid occupations, an option difficult to maintain once there were children; or a life on the ragged margins of subsistence.

In the first, more favored group would be all those peasants whose landholdings, crops, and servile obligations – or lack of them – were combined in a favorable manner (note that in eastern Europe, this group would include members of the nobility!), some clerks, shopkeepers, and master craftsmen, as well as the occasional highly skilled factory worker and manufacturing outworker. The second group encompassed the less fortunate peasant farmers and all landless rural laborers, those master craftsmen in the less prosperous trades (which were also the most common ones), virtually all lower-class, female-headed households, as well as most outworkers, journeymen artisans, factory workers, day laborers, and servants. The size of the two groups varied from region to region and with the harvest and the business cycle, so it is impossible to give an exact idea of their proportions. A fair guess might be that in the most prosperous parts of the continent, they were close to equal; in the poorest areas, the least fortunate might outnumber those holding their own by four or five to one.

Throughout Europe there existed a society in which wealth was closely associated with ownership of land and where a substantial portion of the middle class was sponsored by and involved with the state. The large majority of the population was divided into two groups, not by the ownership of property or a business as such, since many landowning peasants and at least nominally independent master craftsmen were themselves very poor, but by the ability, whether through one's own business or property, or (less likely) by one's own labor, to support a family. If these features of social structure were common to the whole continent, strong differences existed between its western and eastern parts. The large presence of the nobility, the strong contrast in the countryside between free and noble inhabitants on the one hand, and serfs on the other, and the extreme degree of alienation between rural and urban society, set eastern Europe off greatly from the west. As political ideas and movements went from their origins in western Europe, especially France, toward the east, they would develop a different meaning in this different society, a point which would become particularly apparent in 1848 and shape much of the course of the mid-century revolution.

Social and economic trends

One way to understand trends in the economic development of continental Europe during the first half of the nineteenth century is to place them in the context of a population that had been steadily growing since the 1750s, and whose growth had accelerated to an annual rate of 0.5–1.0 percent since the early years of the nineteenth century. The 17 million inhabitants of the Italian states in 1800 had become 24 million by mid-century; the 22 million Germans (excluding the Germans living in the Austrian Empire) of 1816 were the 33 million of 1850; even the French, those precocious practitioners of birth control, saw their numbers rise

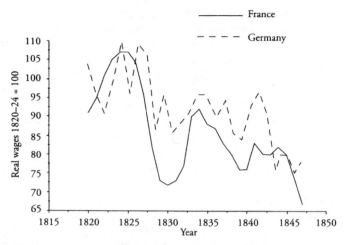

Fig 1.1 Real wages in France and Germany, 1820–47

from 26 to almost 36 million in the first half of the century. While these increases may seem modest when compared with the population growth rates of many African or Asian countries in the last half of the twentieth century and at the beginning of the twenty-first, they were unsettling to a society lacking experience in a rapid rise of numbers. How would these extra mouths be fed, these extra backs be clothed, these extra hands be given work to do?

The model answer to these questions came from Great Britain: introduction of modern agricultural techniques, so that fewer farmers could feed more people; industrialization, to expand greatly the output of consumer goods, provide work for additional people, and generate wealth to employ more in services and the crafts. It was a solution, which, in the long run, worked reasonably well – except for the Irish, as the terrible potato famine would show – but it was only partially emulated on the European continent. There, agriculture was modernized more slowly – rapidly enough to keep up with the growing population, but outstripping it only with difficulty. The industrial revolution, on the other hand, did not take place before 1850, and the increase in the non-agricultural labor force occurred mostly in outworking or from crowding into the traditional crafts. While these did produce additional wealth, it was not on the same scale as could be achieved by the productivity increase of industrialization.

Under these circumstances, one might expect that the supply in the market for labor and craft products would exceed demand, while just the opposite would entail in the market for basic foodstuffs. This seems to have been exactly the case in the two decades between 1825 and the onset of the economic crisis of the mid-1840s, immediately preceding the 1848 revolution. As we have seen at the beginning of this chapter, substantial farmers and landowners of the north European plain, who could easily bring grain, potatoes or meat to market, did well in this period. Wage earners, on the other hand, whether day laborers, factory workers, journeymen artisans or outworkers, saw their wages either decline or at least not keep pace with the rise in food prices. Both (admittedly not very reliable) national real wage series which exist for France and Germany, as well as scattered information on wages and prices in various localities and for different trades throughout the continent, suggest a decline of some 20 percent between the mid-1820s and mid-1840s. Many master craftsmen, themselves sometimes wage earners or outworkers, also probably suffered a similar fall in income. Statistics on urban meat consumption, available for cities in Belgium, France, Germany, and the Habsburg monarchy, support this assumption: they all show a decline or at best a long-run stagnation beginning in the 1830s and not turning around for twenty-five to thirty years.

In these circumstances, entrepreneurial initiatives to expand production were risky ventures, involving producing for a market whose physical accessibility was unclear and whose mass purchasing power was in decline. It was easier for businessmen to avoid such initiatives and look for secure forms of investment, such as floating government loans – the main activity of large bankers, such as the famous Rothschild brothers, and chief issues traded on the major stock exchanges – buying and reselling real estate, or trading agricultural products.

A good, if exaggerated, example of the main forms of capitalism practiced in Europe before 1850 comes from the mercantile and financial oligarchy of the city of Naples. The city's large capitalists did a brisk business advancing money to the government of the Kingdom of the Two Sicilies against its tax receipts, even offering their services in collecting the taxes for the money owed to them. Their other main sphere of activity was monopolizing the grain trade. Grain was grown mostly in the kingdom's eastern provinces, on the coast of the Adriatic Sea, and consumed in Naples to the west. These areas were separated by the high Apennine mountains. By controlling the grain warehouses on the Adriatic coast and the coastal fleet connecting the two regions by sea, the Naples merchants and bankers could impose a differential between prices paid to producers and demanded of consumers, netting them a tidy profit. Investment in modernizing and improving production would hurt, not help their business, so they were unwilling to do it – unless, as happened in woolens manufacture, the government was willing to grant them a monopoly and a guarantee against outside competition.

There was a way out of this situation, by expanding the potential market for more productive investments. No force could expand markets in the mid-nineteenth century like the railway: it could widen commercial networks beyond rivers and seaports; bring perishable, non-subsistence crops to market; and bring coal to iron ore (or vice versa) so that iron and steel could be forged in coke-fired blast furnaces, instead of inefficient charcoal-fired forges. Building a rail network in itself would stimulate enormously the demand for labor and for iron and machinery. Contemporaries were intensely aware of this revolutionary economic potential of the railway and followed closely and with substantial expectations the building of a railway network. Beginning in western and central Europe around 1840, the network had reached some 10,000 kilometers – a substantial amount, but still very incomplete – by the end of the decade.

Building railways in continental Europe invariably brought the government into the investment process. Some states built the railways themselves; others, while leaving construction to private corporations, guaranteed rates of return for railway stock shares or simply offered subsidies for construction and operation. Everywhere, governments planned railway lines – a matter of economic life and death for cities and whole regions, which would either have access to the railway, and the economic benefits it would bring, or be shut off from them and from the possibility of future prosperity. Railway building was inevitably politicized.

The general characteristics of social and economic development in the quarter century before 1850 could be summed up by saying that social wealth was visibly increasing, and yet poverty was increasing as well, and the living standards of the majority of the population seemed to be in decline. In many ways, it was an era in which the capitalist market economy showed its least attractive features. The market's disruptive force, dissolving previously existing social and economic arrangements and exacerbating inequality, outweighed its ability to create new wealth. At the same time, such non-market economic institutions as the guild system and feudal or seigneurial agricultural tenures, existing primarily in central and eastern Europe, did not so much counteract these market trends as amplify them. The beginnings of a way out of these difficult circumstances – the construction of a rail network, industrial enterprises, a more specialized and efficient agriculture – were becoming apparent in the 1840s, but their economic effect had not yet become dominant when the economic disasters of the middle of that decade, the harvest failures of 1845 and 1846 followed by the severe recession of 1847–48, created a crisis situation and helped bring about the outbreak of revolution.

The state

Since government in the twentieth century does so much, employs so many people, and takes up so much of the gross domestic product, it might be helpful in talking about the state in mid-nineteenth-century Europe to begin by emphasizing what it did not do. All its modern, social welfare functions – unemployment, illness and old-age insurance, support for the impoverished or for mothers and children – did not exist. People needing assistance had to turn to their families, to voluntary associations such as mutual benefit societies, or to charity, usually administered by the church. The elaborate educational and cultural activities of contemporary governments were present only in the most rudimentary form: some support for a theater, opera or orchestra in the capital city, and the maintenance of a skeletal and sparsely used system of secondary and higher education. Financing of elementary education was left largely up to the good will of cities and villages, the central government providing at most some guidelines and occasionally a little financial help.

Within the sphere of culture, broadly defined, the main arena of government policy was religion. Separation of church and state was unknown. Senior clergy, Roman Catholic or Eastern Orthodox bishops and their Protestant counterparts, were appointed by the government; in many states, all clergy were. Part of church funds came from the public treasury. Education of the clergy stood under government supervision and the authorities did not hesitate to intervene, openly or covertly in even seemingly esoteric theological or doctrinal disputes, when they felt such disputes might have a political relevance.

While governments of the mid-nineteenth century did try to encourage and direct economic activity, they did so with a meager arsenal of resources, largely confined to taxes, tariffs, and scattered subsidies or interest rate guarantees. The possibilities open today to a government which spends 30–50 percent of a country's GDP were not available when the proportion of government spending in total output was one tenth or one twentieth as great. Actions taken to influence interest and exchange rates or the money supply were either technically or conceptually impossible in an age of fixed exchange rates, gold and silver backing for the currency, and a belief that tampering with either of these elements was the moral equivalent of embezzlement or bank fraud. Of all the Great Powers, the only one lacking a currency backed by precious metals was the Austrian Empire, and its rulers treated this fact as a shameful state secret to be hidden at all costs both from the general public and the financial world. The major contribution that governments of the mid-nineteenth century could make to economic development was to facilitate transport and communication, by building roads, digging canals, making rivers navigable and, above all, by building or helping to build railways.

Most of what governments did do can be summed up in a few phrases: administer justice, preserve public order, raise a standing army, and collect taxes to pay for these activities. Yet many of these efforts were hampered by the small numbers of officials who actually staffed the government. In France, the most heavily policed and extensively administered state in Europe, there was just one gendarme (paramilitary policeman) for every two thousand inhabitants during the 1840s, while in the Kingdom of Prussia, usually regarded as a state with a numerous and powerful police, the figure was a mere one in seven thousand. Even this very modest police presence was substantial when compared with other parts of the continent. In the Hungarian provinces of the Habsburg monarchy, for instance, there were only 4,300 government employees of any and all kinds – including the workers in the state-owned salt mines and postal clerks – for 10.2 million inhabitants.

To carry out even the most minimal and basic functions, European states of the time had to resort to a number of expedients. The king's servants in the Hungarian provinces of the Habsburg monarchy were outnumbered four to three by the employees of the county governments, which were elected and controlled by the nobility. These counties were both the agents of the royal power and the courts of first instance, giving them the right to rule on the legality of their own decrees, a situation that, to put it mildly, contained within it substantial conflicts of interest. In the eastern provinces of the Kingdom of Prussia, even where feudalism had been abolished, the owners of former feudal estates continued to be the agents of royal authority for their former serfs: policemen, administrators, and tax collectors, in the name of the king. In western Europe, where feudalism was gone and state administration more extensive, basic governmental functions were carried out with additional assistance, by urban policemen, for instance, appointed by municipal governments, or forest and field watchmen chosen by villagers.

What all this suggests is that the state of internal order in most European countries of this period was a precarious one, since governments lacked the necessary resources to impose it. It may come as no surprise to learn that organized banditry was rife in the mountains of southern Italy, and the authorities of the Kingdom of the Two Sicilies were helpless against it, or that cattle rustling was one of the main occupations on the island of Sicily. Such conditions lasted throughout the nineteenth century and well into the twentieth. However, it does go against the usual picture of Prussian discipline and German devotion to law and order to note that smuggling was ubiquitous in the border districts of the Kingdom of Prussia, and the authorities could not stamp it out. Contraventions of the forest laws were equally a problem in the Prussian kingdom; poachers and government foresters engaged in running gun battles.

In these circumstances, smooth functioning of the machinery of state, in particular the collection of taxes, without which nothing could be done, required the tacit acceptance by the mass of the population of the legitimacy of the government. This state of affairs explains the keen interest the authorities displayed in the church, which was seen, correctly, as an important agent of political legitimization. Even a moderate degree of popular resistance to the government outdid the coercive power of the civilian state authorities. They were then dependent on local agents, whether Hungarian county officials or French village field and forest watchmen, themselves neither numerous nor imposing and, in addition, chosen by people whose interests might not coincide with those of the central government.

One area where government did show a certain efficiency of function was in the maintenance of armed forces. Great Britain's all volunteer military was a great exception in the first half of the nineteenth century; all the continental European powers raised their armies by means of conscription. Only the Kingdom of Prussia, in terms of population the smallest of the Great Powers, and so needing to draft the largest proportion of young men to have a respectable army, attempted to hold to the ideal of universal military service. In theory, all physically fit young men served on active duty for two years, followed by a more lengthy period in the reserves. (In practice, budgetary constraints limited the proportion of eligibles actually drafted.) The other Great Powers and the smaller states used the French system of conscription, in which a draft lottery was held, and the smaller proportion of eligible young men drawing an unlucky number would be conscripted for a lengthy period of time. In France, service lasted for six years; for the unfortunate draftees of the Hungarian provinces of the Habsburg monarchy, for life – until army reforms of the 1840s reduced the term first to ten years and then to eight. These lengthy terms of service might seem frightening today – and, as will be seen below, young men often tried to evade them. However, soldiers in this system were furloughed for the better part of the year, and just on active duty for a few months at a time.

This system worked surprisingly well, perhaps because there was so little warfare. In the almost four decades between the Battle of Waterloo in 1815 and the outbreak of the Crimean War in 1854, the Great Powers of Europe – England, France, Austria, Prussia, and Russia – were at peace with each other. The few campaigns in which they actually engaged – the

French intervention in Spain of 1823, and the conquest of Algeria in 1830, or several Russian clashes with the Turks – were more in the nature of skirmishes than any serious armed conflict.

While lacking opportunity to win glory on the field of honor, soldiers were not totally unemployed. If the available civilian means for preserving public order failed, as would happen during a riot, or even a widespread crime wave, then government officials would either have to acquiesce in the flouting of their authority or call in the armed forces to enforce it. Being the policeman of last resort was the army's main task in this period, its chief opportunity to fire a shot or wield its bayonets in anger. Use of the army for crowd control or crime fighting was a provocative act that could easily anger the crowd being controlled and sharply escalate the level of violence. Under the right circumstances, as would exist in the first months of 1848, the cycle of violence, armed repression, and more violence could end with barricades being built and the government overthrown.

For all their common features, European states of the mid-nineteenth century differed strongly, their differences existing along the same west–east axis denoting the presence of feudal and seigneurial relations in agriculture. France, to take one model version of governmental organization, was a centralized, unified state, with one code of law, valid across its entire territory and for all of its citizens. The very same taxes, at the very same rates, were collected everywhere, from Lille in the north, to Marseilles in the south, from Nantes in the west, to Strasbourg in the east. One centralized governmental administration covered the entire country, its representatives, the prefects – one in each of the eighty odd departments into which the country was divided – all executing (or attempting to execute) the orders they received from the government ministers in Paris and reporting back to them.

These characteristics of uniformity in administration, equal application of the law, and centralization could also be found in the Low Countries, the Italian states, and, to a lesser extent, in the smaller states of western Germany. Moving further east into the Kingdom of Prussia, we do find a centralized administration, and government ministries in Berlin, issuing laws and decrees valid for the whole kingdom. Different codes of law existed in the kingdom's different provinces, though; tax rates varied among them, and, in different provinces, the nobility retained different legal privileges. A smaller version of this state of affairs existed in the Kingdom of Denmark, where a central administration in Copenhagen ruled a conglomerate state with somewhat different legal institutions in the kingdom proper, the duchies of Schleswig, Holstein, and Lauenburg (today the northern tip of Germany), the north Atlantic possessions, the

Faroe Islands, Greenland and Iceland, and the small colonial holdings in the West Indies.

In the Habsburg monarchy, this entire paradigm of uniformity, central administration, and equality before the law was completely irrelevant. The small central bureaucracy in the imperial capital of Vienna oversaw (governed is probably too strong a word) a realm sprawled across central and eastern Europe, covering all the territory in today's Austrian, Hungarian, Czech, Slovak, and Slovenian republics, as well as parts of Italy, Poland, Croatia, Yugoslavia, Romania, and Ukraine, and consisting of a collection of separate provinces, each with its own rights and privileges, containing different forms of administration, varying kinds of taxation, and widely differing legal systems. The Alpine province of the Tyrol, to take just one example, jealously guarded its "unity of faith," its right to refuse to allow anyone not of the Roman Catholic confession to live there, and its medieval privilege of paying only enough taxes to outfit five thousand men at arms, a very favorable deal by the standards of the nineteenth century.

The nature of the monarchy's administration is best seen in the provinces that made up the "Crown of St. Stephen," or the Kingdom of Hungary, although in the eyes of the monarchy's rulers, at least, this area did not obtain such a status until the compromise of 1867 turned the Habsburgs' realm, the Austrian Empire, into the Austro-Hungarian Empire. Before 1848, there was a separate chancellory in the Viennese central administration for Hungarian affairs; its representative in Hungary itself was the "Palatine," or Viceroy, traditionally a prince of the imperial family, whose office was in the city of Buda (as yet lacking a permanent bridge to its sister city Pest, on the other side of the Danube). The Hungarian feudal parliament, the Diet, with its lower house elected by the nobility of each county, and its upper house consisting of the great noblemen of the land, whose consent was required for the passage of laws relating to Hungary, did not meet in Buda, with the viceroy, the kingdom's chief executive, but in Pressburg (today's Bratislava), almost a suburb of Vienna.

This setup, complicated as it was, only applied to "interior Hungary," more or less equivalent to today's Hungarian Republic. The six counties of the province of Croatia-Slavonia were part of the Crown of St. Stephen, but they had their own Diet, that met in Zagreb, and their own Provincial Governor, the "Ban," appointed directly by Vienna. These six counties were also represented in the Pressburg Diet; litigants in their courts could appeal to the Hungarian courts; and the Ban was, theoretically, subordinate to the Viceroy in Buda.

Also part of the Crown of St. Stephen was the Province of Transylvania (today in Romania) governed by a separate Transylvanian Chancellory in

Vienna, which gave its orders directly to the royal administration, the "Gubernium," with its seat in Hermannstadt – today the Romanian city of Sibiu. Transylvania also had a Diet, whose members were representatives of the nobility, and of the free German farmers, the so-called Transylvanian Saxons, who had settled there in the Middle Ages. It was not much of a representative body, since a majority of its members were appointed by the government, and the large majority of the inhabitants of Transylvania, Romanian speaking, mostly serfs had no representation of any kind.

There was an additional and still different part of Hungary, the military border district. Most of it lay next to Croatia-Slavonia (there was a separate, smaller part in Transylvania); its inhabitants were to the Austrian Emperor what the Cossacks were to the tsar: peasants freed of servile obligations to noble landlords and given their own lands to cultivate under strict military regulations, in return for their service as light infantry and cavalry of the imperial armies. They had been placed there for their part in the Emperor's wars against the Turks that had been going on since the sixteenth century, although by the 1840s the Habsburg Monarchy had been at peace with the Ottoman Empire for six decades and the exact reason for the existence of such troops was getting hard to understand. Whether actually engaged in war or not, the border districts were a realm of martial law, directly under the control of the War Council in Vienna. Yet they were also integrated into the civilian government of Hungary, since their military commander was, simultaneously, the Ban of Croatia-Slavonia.

This discussion of the government and administration of Hungary – actually somewhat simplified, since nothing was said about the three free districts of the Jazyger-Kumanen, the six Hayduck and sixteen Zisper cities, or the "corpus separatum" of the Fiume coastal district – should give some notion of the variegated, complex, and baroque state system of the Habsburg monarchy. It was an amalgam of medieval traditions and privileges, years of prolonged warfare with the Ottoman Empire, eighteenth-century attempts at administrative reforms, early-nineteenth-century attempts to revoke the eighteenth-century administrative reforms, all of which existed side by side, seemingly in contradiction to each other. It seems archaic today, and by the 1840s it did to many contemporaries as well. Certainly, in comparison to the more uniform and linearly organized French and Prussian administrations, it produced less government at greater expense. Yet it fitted well into the partly feudal society of much of eastern Europe and, when put to the test in 1848, would prove to have some surprising and unexpected strengths.

Education and religion

Some idea of the state of elementary education in mid-nineteenth-century Europe can be obtained from the extent of literacy. It was most common in the German states and Scandinvia, where upwards of three-fourths of the adult population could read and write. Following them came France, the Low Countries, and northern Italy, where literacy rates were in the 40–60 percent range. Moving south and east, knowledge of these elementary skills dropped off fast, declining to as little as 5–10 percent of adults in the eastern provinces of the Habsburg monarchy and in southern Italy. Throughout the continent, men were more likely to be able to read and write than women, townspeople than countryfolk, and Protestants than Catholics.

To some extent, the middle decades of the nineteenth century saw an education boom. In France, for instance, between 1833 and 1847 the number of schools doubled and the number of children in them tripled, reaching some 3.6 million by the latter year. Quality and education of elementary schoolteachers was gradually increasing as well: the half-literate tailors, retired NCOs, and inhabitants of poor mountain villages, seeking to earn additional money, but too weak for heavy physical labor, if not entirely banished from the ranks of the occupation, were giving way to younger instructors, trained in teachers' colleges.

Still, there were substantial limitations to the place of teacher and of schools in the world. School attendance was erratic, especially in the summer when children were needed in the fields and pastures. Textbooks, to say nothing of maps, charts, and other basic school supplies, were few and far between. Too often, the curriculum consisted primarily of learning the catechism, religious songs, and Bible stories, with reading, writing, and arithmetic thrown in as an afterthought.

The social esteem of the schoolteacher's occupation and the pay for exercising it were equally low. Village teachers often earned little more than an unskilled day laborer and were forced to take on additional work to make ends meet: as choirmaster, organist, bell-ringer, and janitor in the church, or as scribe for the village mayor. In most of Europe, supervision of the local schools was in the hands of the parish clergy, who made their opinions about the subordinate condition of teachers crystal clear. France, with its purely secular system of school administration, was already an exception to this rule, but even there lay teachers faced the competition of the religious, who would work for much less.

These circumstances, as difficult as they were, characterized those parts of Europe where elementary education was well established and where there existed a consensus about its necessity and desirability. In the south and east of the continent, this benign attitude was far from present. The Kingdom of the Two Sicilies was a realm of almost complete illiteracy, with just one pupil for every 150 to 170 inhabitants. There, Monseigneur Guiseppe Mazzetti, in his 1838 tract on education reform, called for a system that would "prevent the movement of the masses, restrict the number of the literate, make them good and tranquil, which would exclude the people from any instruction making them useless or harmful." If these were the thoughts of an educational reformer, it is not hard to imagine the opinions of enemies of public education. A revealing moment of openness came at the 1840 meeting of the Provincial Estates of the Austrian province of Galicia. To a proposed expansion of public education in the countryside, noble deputies replied, "Shall we found schools in the country, so that the peasants [i.e., the nobles' serfs] can direct complaints against us to government officials?"[6]

Secondary and higher education were very modest affairs, with at most 1 percent of the relevant age group – exclusively boys and young men – taking advantage of it. Tuition fees were high and, more importantly, most families could not afford to support for years an adolescent scholar whose efforts were bringing in no revenue. Secondary school curricula, centered around the study of classical languages, had a limited appeal, especially to practically minded businessmen, who could otherwise have afforded to give their sons a more advanced education. Yet in spite of these less than propitious circumstances, education was advancing. Secondary school and university enrollments almost doubled between the 1820s and the 1840s. Unfortunately, the supply of jobs in secondary education, universities, the church, public administration, and the professions, for which graduates were trained, was not growing anywhere near so rapidly. Particularly in the German and Italian states and the Habsburg monarchy – less so in France – there seems to have been an increasing incidence of unemployment among the educated classes, and contemporaries began talking darkly about the existence of an "academic proletariat."

If the school as an institution and education as an organized social process had still not emerged from their previous marginal position in mid-nineteenth-century Europe, quite the opposite was the case with religion and the church. Many people may not have known how to read or write, but everyone knew how to pray. The calendar of church services

---

[6] Quoted in Luigi Parente, "Stato e contadini nel mezzogiorno d'Italia tra il 1830 e il 1845," *Cahiers internationaux d'histoire economique et sociale* 13 (1981): 252 and Roman Rosdolsky, *Die Bauernabgeordneten im konstituierenden östererischschen Landtag 1848–1849* (Vienna, 1976), 7, n. 1.

and religious holidays – just about the only kind of public holidays, incidentally – shaped the year. In so far as clubs and voluntary associations existed, they were most likely to be religious ones: religious brotherhoods, Bible study groups or missionary societies. Spectacular religious events, such as Protestant revival meetings or Roman Catholic pilgrimages, attracted enormous crowds, far overshadowing more secular attractions. The great pilgrimage to the Holy Shroud of Trier in 1844, for example, had more than half a million participants – a particularly astonishing figure, considering that since there were no railroad or steamship connections, almost all the pilgrims came on foot. The priest or pastor was a man of power and influence, especially in the countryside, where he might have been the only person with anything beyond an elementary education. In many villages of southern and eastern Europe, he was the only person who could read and write. This position of religion made it a powerful form of broad group identity, challenging nationality or loyalty to a ruling dynasty for primacy in the minds of the less educated lower classes.

Confessions were far from randomly scattered about Europe; each major religion had its own regions where its faithful made up the overwhelming majority of the population. Roman Catholics were found especially in the south and west of the continent. Virtually everyone living in France, Spain, Portugal, and Italy was Catholic, except for a few small enclaves of Protestants in southern and eastern France and Eastern Orthodox in southern Italy. Roman Catholics also made up a smaller, if still predominant proportion of the population of western and southern Germany and of most of the lands of the Habsburg Empire. Scandinavia, by contrast was almost entirely Protestant, and Protestants dominated the population of central and eastern Germany. They were found in lesser proportions in western Germany and in Hungary. The province of Transylvania, in fact, had the unusual distinction of being the only place in the world where Unitarianism was an officially recognized and state supported religion. Most of Europe's Orthodox Christians lived in the realm of the tsar, but substantial numbers of them were present in the eastern provinces of the Habsburg monarchy – Galicia, Transylvania, Croatia-Slavonia, the Banat – and in the neighboring Danubian principalities. Precisely in these border regions there were also hundreds of thousands of Uniates, or Greek Catholics, Christians who practiced their religion according to Eastern Orthodox rites, but recognized the authority of the Pope. Jews lived in small numbers scattered throughout Europe; substantial concentrations of them existed only in the west of the tsar's empire and in the Austrian province of Galicia, where they were a majority of the inhabitants of a number of towns.

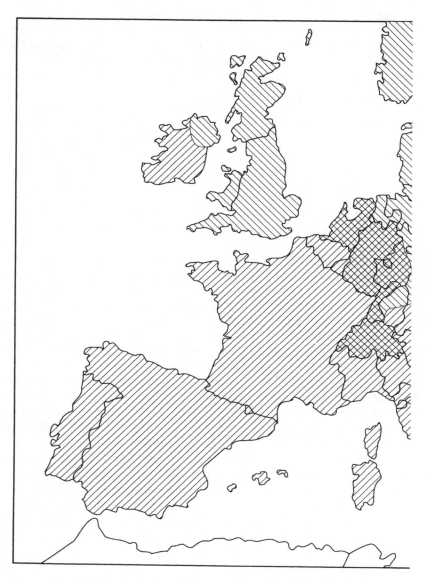

Map 1.3 Predominant religious confessions in Europe during the 1840s

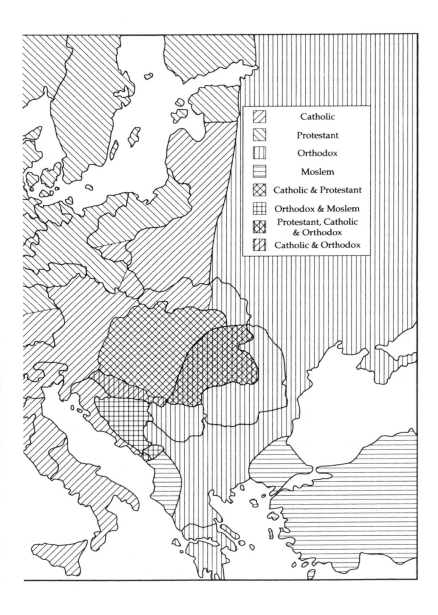

Catholic	
Protestant	
Orthodox	
Moslem	
Catholic & Protestant	
Orthodox & Moslem	
Protestant, Catholic & Orthodox	
Catholic & Orthodox	

To put it differently, the religious map of Europe consisted of three large blocs, a Catholic one to the west and south, a Protestant one in the north and center, and an Orthodox one to the east. Where the blocs met, there were zones of an uneasy mixture of the confessions. One such zone lay along the Rhine, from Holland south through eastern France and Rhenish Germany to Switzerland; Protestants and Catholics were scattered about it. Much of the Kingdom of Hungary formed another such zone, and a particularly complicated one, since it encompassed Catholics, Orthodox, Uniates, and several varieties of Protestants. Finally, the neighboring Habsburg provinces of Galicia and Bukovina were a zone where Catholics, Orthodox, and Uniates were mixed. "Mixed" is perhaps too pronounced a phrase, for except in larger cities the two confessions tended to live separately, villages usually being inhabited exclusively, or almost so, by members of one of the Christian confessions. Even when villages did house two substantial and different religious communities, they kept their distance. In religiously mixed villages of the southern Rhineland, Protestants and Catholics had their own churches and cemeteries (or quarreled constantly over them, when required to share), their own festivities, their own, opposing candidates in elections to the village council. They even drank in separate taverns. Such inter-confessional barriers, between different types of Christians, and, even more so, between Christians and Jews, were another way of expressing the power and influence of religion as a form of group identity.

For all the significance of the church in public and private life, it is also important to note that by the 1840s the place of religion in Europe was not as self evident as it had been a century earlier. Here, as in so many other respects, the French Revolution of 1789 was the relevant event, creating a great challenge to the church. The revolution, and the wars and political upheavals stemming from it, had led to the physical and institutional disruption of the church in many parts of Europe, including the confiscation of church property, the rearrangement of ecclesiastical administration, even the destruction of church buildings and, for a short time, the prohibition of the public exercise of religion. Yet for the physical destruction and disruption caused by the revolution, the intellectual challenge it offered to religion was even more significant. The revolution proposed and attempted, ultimately unsuccessfully, to create a new form of government, one not previously seen in Europe, although in some ways anticipated in the young North American republic: a secular political realm, in which public affairs would not be oriented around religious principles.

By the 1840s, most of the institutional damage done to the church in the era of the French Revolution had been repaired. (As with feudal relations in agriculture, the revolutionary era's challenge to religion had been most intense in western Europe and the disruption of church life fell off as one went further east.) The intellectual challenge, however, had not been forgotten, and the movements of religious renewal and revival, that would characterize both Protestantism and Catholicism in the mid-nineteenth century, focused on finding new ways to engage the mass of the faithful, combat any decline in devotion, in doing so striving to regain or preserve the mass of ordinary believers to the church. One method employed was a revivification of preaching: both Protestant revivalists and Catholic Jesuit *patres* specialized in this with considerable success. Another was the founding of associations and societies for charitable, sociable, and pious purposes: Marianic Sodalities, St. Vincent de Paul charitable conferences, Bible study groups, temperance associations, missionary societies, and the like. Characteristic of all these efforts was the realization that popular loyalty to the church was no longer as totally self-evident as it had been before that great dividing line which was 1789.

Objects of social conflict in pre-1848 Europe

Conflicts in mid-nineteenth-century Europe took on a special form due to the nature of politics. In the two decades between the revolutions of 1830 and 1848 exposure to political life – the franchise, participation in political debates, even reading newspapers – was usually restricted to a very small group of the population, whose size declined from west to east and from north to south in Europe. Consequently, there was frequently a separation between politics, that is the conscious attempt to organize the state, economy, and society, and instances of contention about them. To put it more concretely, peasants trying to murder a tax-collector or out-working weavers screaming curses at the merchant who employed them (to take two common forms of conflict) were implicitly suggesting a different way of running things. They did not clearly articulate just what that way would be, even to themselves.

Historians sometimes refer to these forms of contention, in which at least some of the participants lacked an articulate expression of their goals, as "social conflict," describing "political conflict," on the other hand, as antagonisms whose protagonists were attempting to move economy, society or state in a consciously pre-chosen, expressly articulated direction. These two forms of conflict are not absolutely distinct; with the development of mass political participation in the revolution of 1848 they began to overlap and partially to merge. To understand this development, a crucial feature of the mid-century revolution, we need to look first at the two forms of conflict separately. Political life and political conflict will be the subject of the next chapter; in the remainder of this one we will consider social conflict, working from the previous description of social structure.

Conflict in the countryside

If there was one single kind of social conflict more prevalent than any other in mid-nineteenth-century Europe, it was conflict over the collective use of agricultural land. Such conflict came in many forms, but they were all ultimately due to the incompletely individualized nature of farming. Portions of land were owned in common by villages and used in common by all of the villagers, or at least all of them who had the right to do so. Even "private" property was not completely private, and in many parts of the continent, peasants could pasture animals on the property of others at certain times of the year or cut and gather wood in the forests belonging to others. These "burdens" or "servitudes" on private property, as contemporaries referred to them, were a legacy of feudal relations in agriculture, but unlike serfdom, or seigneurial dues, they were a legacy which the French Revolution had not abolished. They existed everywhere on the continent, even in regions where the otherwise unfettered use of private property was to be found.

The economic circumstances of the first half of the nineteenth century put these customary usages under considerable strain. Population growth was one problem: more people meant more wood for construction and heating, only the supply of wood from forests was hard to increase without environmentally dangerous overcutting. Yet measures to achieve economic growth and to relieve population pressure on natural resources also pressed on traditional usages. Introduction of modern farming techniques meant that fields no longer stood fallow, allowing just anyone's cattle or sheep to graze on them. Agricultural innovators pressed to divide the village common land, or to rent it out in one large block, a measure that would have been disastrous for the rural lower classes who needed the common land to pasture their few farm animals. Equally frustrating to the rural poor was the misuse of common rights, as enterprising affluent peasants or absentee landowners proceeded to pasture several hundred sheep (their wool to be sold to textile manufacturers) on the common land, instead of the two or three per family of subsistence usage. Iron and leather manufacture, two economic growth areas, both involved the substantial use of forest products – oak bark for tanning and charcoal to forge pig iron from ore – as did the expansion of winegrowing, since vintners needed wood for stakes to hold up their grape vines and for barrels to store their product.

In these circumstances, all the options – whether preserving customary collective usages, continuing them in different ways or abolishing them – touched on issues of economic survival and set off angry confrontations. Sometimes they might originate in a legal step directly intervening in the question of usage, like the French forest code of 1827, that subjected to government regulation usage rights in village-owned woodlands, or the Austrian government decree of 1839, calling for the sale of all village forest held in common. Governmental actions in the Kingdom of the Two Sicilies taken in the opposite direction to preserve customary usage rights also set off large-scale confrontations in the southern Italian countryside. Most European states took no such definite action on the issue, one way or the other, but just tried to muddle through. This did not stop conflicts from emerging either, on a broad scale and in a striking variety of forms.

Farmers in southern France and western Germany engaged in decades-long lawsuits over usage rights to forests owned by large landowners, noblemen still possessing some seigneurial rights, or the government. Peasants of southern Italy began a tactic they would continue to use into the twentieth century, the occupation of disputed forest lands. Historians have counted thirty-four land occupations in two districts, Melfi and Potenza, of the province of Basilicata, between 1813 and 1847, or an average of one per year. The peak area of these southern Italian land struggles was in the forested Sila mountain chain of the neighboring province of Calabria, where the division of the common lands and abolition of rights to common usage during the era of Napoleonic rule at the beginning of the nineteenth century had left much of the forests in the hands of large landowners. Over the following three decades, smallholding peasants and rural laborers went to court, submitted petitions to the government of the Kingdom of the Two Sicilies, engaged in collective land occupations, or simply cut the wood necessary for their subsistence.

Indeed, the single most common way that the conflict over usage rights expressed itself was in wood "theft," or peasants' reiteration of their right to use forests that they did not own. By the mid-1840s, in the Bavarian province of the Palatinate in southwestern Germany, one inhabitant in three (including infants and the elderly) was convicted of this crime each year. Some 320 km northeast, in the Prussian province of Westphalia, peasants' insistence on using the forests belonging to the nobility, and the authorities' equally stubborn insistence on preventing them, led to a minor civil war leaving twenty peasants and foresters dead in the quarter century before 1848. Only "fear protects the wood," the Prussian authorities concluded, and their strategy of intimidation included supplementing the badly outnumbered foresters and gendarmes and the blatantly unreliable village watchmen with soldiers on active duty.

Prussian authorities were not alone in noting the significance of wood theft. In an autobiographical note, Karl Marx, whose lawyer father Heinrich had represented the peasants of the mountain village of Thalfang in their ultimately unsuccessful legal challenge to the Prussian government's curtailment of their forest usage rights, recalled that he had begun to think about the "social question" as a young journalist in the early 1840s. The incentive for the future communist revolutionary's first thoughts about private property came from an investigative piece he did on wood theft among the winegrowers of the Moselle Valley, near his native city of Trier. We might agree with both the Prussian government and Karl Marx, one of its most determined enemies, that forest conflict was ubiquitous and a significant sign of the strain on social and economic structures. Forest conflict was the most common form of conflict over collective use rights, a conflict situated at the intersection of customary forms of agricultural usage that were being legally questioned, while they were simultaneously being threatened by population growth and new forms of productive activity associated with the expansion of the market economy.

Struggles over usage rights did not directly translate into a conflict between classes since the nature and protagonists of such struggles varied considerably. Different groups of villagers could be arrayed against each other, inhabitants of one village against those of a neighboring one, peasants against forest landowners, whether wealthy commoners, nobles still possessing seigneurial privileges, or the state. Struggles could pit villagers wishing to use their own common forest property against foresters enforcing government regulations prohibiting such usage. Another version of rural conflict clearly did take on the contours of a direct class struggle, the conflict between lord and serf, between noblemen outfitted with seigneurial privileges and peasants burdened with servile obligations. Everywhere that the measures of the French Revolution had not taken hold, that is throughout most of central and eastern Europe, this conflict raged.

Much of the conflict was conducted at the legal level, with court cases and appeals to the administrative bureaucracy. Romanian peasants in Transylvania flooded the Austrian officials with complaints about how the Magyar nobility had imposed additional burdens of labor services on them and worsened their conditions of servitude. Peasants and nobles in southern Germany went to court over the validity of feudal dues and hunting rights and possible payments to redeem them.

Conflict also occurred at the level of daily confrontation, as serfs refused to perform their labor services, or did so lazily and sloppily; noble landlords responded with the whip and the stick. Noble hunting rights were routinely ignored by the peasants, who illegally shot the rabbits, birds, and deer threatening their crops. On occasion, these petty forms of physical defiance escalated into broader anti-feudal peasant uprisings. The revolution of 1830 saw a wave of attacks on nobility and noble privileges in many parts of central and eastern Europe, most drastically the following year in northern Hungary, today's Slovakia. Serfs were convinced that the cholera epidemic of 1831 was caused by nobles poisoning the wells, and they rose up against them, burning castles and killing a few. The most drastic example of serf hatred of the nobility came in 1846, in the Austrian province of Galicia, where a badly bungled attempt by Polish conspirators to lead a revolution created a situation in which the serfs of the area felt free to murder the nobility and their estate administrators – which they did, dispatching over a thousand of them.

In the countryside of western and southern Europe, the areas of capitalist property and production relationships, there were certainly class tensions – between large landowners and day laborers, between landlords and their tenants and sharecroppers, between large peasant farmers and smaller ones who worked for them – but no such violent, murderous hatreds as existed on the territories of serfdom. A more significant arena of conflict (which also could be found in the servile lands) was the one between debtor and creditor. Peasants were frequently borrowers, whether to get cash until they could sell their crops, to invest in more modern agricultural techniques, to buy out seigneurial obligations, or simply to purchase food in a year of bad harvest. Financial services, however, were poorly and primitively arranged in pre-1850 Europe. Even substantial businessmen had trouble getting credit on favorable terms, and peasants had little choice but to turn to petty moneylenders charging high interest rates and demanding unfavorable repayment conditions. The possibility of forced sales to repay a defaulted loan was a constant presence and rural hostility against moneylenders – in some regions of central and eastern Europe, where Jews dominated the trade, taking the form of angry anti-Semitism – was a constant presence in village life.

Conflicts in manufacturing and crafts

Conflict in non-agricultural production during the middle decades of the nineteenth century was unusually fragmented and complex, reflecting the nature of production itself. Overall, three different varieties of social conflict appeared. There were conflicts between masters and journeymen artisans, survivals from an era when guilds dominated economic life. Another form of conflict, perhaps the single most prevalent one, pitted nominally independent, outworking small producers against the merchant contractors who were their employers and often creditors as well.

Finally, there were also examples of more familiar kinds of labor disputes: conflicts between capitalists and laborers over wages, hours, and working conditions, leading to or accompanied by strikes.

Conflicts between masters and journeymen centered around control of the labor market. An issue of repeated controversy was who would greet newly arrived journeymen come to town looking for work and make arrangements between them and the masters looking for help. In the German city of Nuremberg, a center of craft production carried out in small workshops and with powerful and effective guilds, the masters had, with the help of the municipal government, forcibly seized the power to direct this process in 1806. A list of masters needing help was drawn up and journeymen come to town were given no choice but required to go the workshop at the top of the list. Decades-long efforts by journeymen to break the masters' hold were unavailing. Just the opposite was the case in the hatting trade of France's two largest cities, Paris and Lyon. There, it was the journeymen themselves who made the arrangements for their newly arrived comrades, and only sent them to masters who agreed to the journeymen's conditions for employment. Such journeymen's control over the trade could lead to conflicts among the journeymen themselves, between locals, often married and settled, and usually single outsiders come to look for work.

Another issue of controversy was the traditional customs of the journeymen. Their rites and ceremonies have been studied in loving detail by folklorists and anthropologically minded historians, but nineteenth-century master craftsmen lacked this cultural interest. What they saw about these ceremonies was that they all required the journeymen to work less and drink more while on the job. Masters tried hard to stamp out these customs, often demanding that the government authorities support them in their efforts; journeymen resisted stubbornly such initiatives.

Another version of the conflict over control of the labor market was only possible in those regions of central and eastern Europe where guilds still existed and retained at least some power to regulate economic life. Master craftsmen would use their guild position to refuse to allow journeymen to settle and set up as masters themselves. This was, for the masters, a basic form of economic self-defense, given the rising number of craftsmen and declining popular purchasing power, but it was deeply painful to the journeymen. Their journeying, which had lasted five to ten years in the eighteenth century, was going on for fifteen or twenty by the 1840s. To make the situation still more painful, in some of the smaller states of southern Germany, the right to marry and have a family was dependent on being a master, condemning journeymen to celibacy until they reached middle age, or forcing them to enter into an informal union, which the courts, the church, and educated public opinion condemned as immoral concubinage.

Disputes between merchants and outworkers in weaving, the most common outworking craft, centered on rates of pay for each piece of woven goods turned in. Not surprisingly, merchants would demand lower and weavers higher rates, but such disputes were often carried out in an indirect way. Capitalists would not directly lower their price but would charge fines for low-quality work, and short-weigh or short-measure the cloth they received from the weavers. Lines at the merchant's office, with weavers waiting impatiently to turn in their work while one of their number argued bitterly over a disputed piece of goods, were scenes of social confrontation and carried in them seeds of revolt.

Weavers had their own weapons of indirection in this struggle. They could steal goods, turn them in late, pocket advance payments and not deliver the work. Such tactics were only successful in boom conditions; in more slack times they were worthless. Then the weavers would turn to more direct action, launching large-scale and violent demonstrations aimed at merchant manufacturers who were cutting the weavers' pay. Whole communities of weavers would parade in public demanding fairer terms, perhaps smashing the windows in a merchant's house and office to add additional emphasis.

On three occasions between 1830 and 1848, such demonstrations were held on so large a scale that they seemed to contemporaries to be veritable uprisings, harbingers of a new form of social struggle and perhaps even a new form of society. Two of these uprisings, in 1831 and 1834, were carried out by the silk-weavers of Lyon, France's second city, to the ominous motto, "Live working or die fighting." A similar uprising in 1844 of the linen-weavers of the Prussian province of Silesia was celebrated in a widely read poem of Heinrich Heine, with its refrain, in which the weavers announce "We are weaving old Germany's funeral shroud." Echoes of the Silesian weavers' uprising can be found in the philosophical writings of the young Karl Marx; a half century later, it remained a living theme in the work of dramatist Gerhard Hauptmann and artist Käthe Kollwitz.

There was an additional complication in the relations between out-workers and merchants. The outworking craftsmen were themselves often employers, with their own journeymen and apprentices. Sometimes, as was typical in the silk manufacture of western Germany, they would make common cause with the merchants against the journey-men. In the Parisian tailoring trade, on the other hand, journeymen tailors' strikes in the 1830s and 40s, ostensibly aimed at the masters who employed them, were in reality directed against the merchant contractors and sub-contractors who controlled the master craftsmen and the entire trade.

The reader may have noted how different these disputes are from later nineteenth- and twentieth- or twenty-first century labor conflicts. Wages, hours, and working conditions, the basic issues of later disputes, only appear in these earlier conflicts indirectly, via questions of fines and short-measuring or drinking on the job. Forms of conflict differed as much as the issues involved. Unions, employers' associations, strikes or collective bargaining were nowhere in evidence. These circumstances reflect in part different legal conditions, since both unions and strikes were strictly illegal in continental European countries during the first half of the nineteenth century. They also reflect differences in the relations and organization of production. A master silk-weaver, in charge of his own workshop, but under contract and in debt to a merchant contractor, for instance, could hardly make demands about hours or working conditions, both of which he set himself – albeit under the constraints of his situation.

One might expect the nascent industrial labor force of the time, pioneer of future forms of production and economic organization, to have championed these more modern forms of labor conflict, but this was hardly the case. Strikes did occur in pre-1848 Europe; historians have counted some seventy in France during 1833 alone – admittedly an unusually unruly year. These strikers were not factory workers but craftsmen, often in the construction trades or in printing, where workshops were large and masters employed fairly sizeable (i.e., ten to fifteen men) work forces. Even here, boundaries between more recognizably modern and older forms of labor conflict were fluid. All the masons on an 1830s Parisian construction site might have cursed their employer, quit en masse, and gone to look for new jobs – behavior that would have been thoroughly recognizable in the eighteenth century – but before leaving they might also have explained how higher wages would keep them at work.

Perhaps the one example of a newer labor group engaging in workplace conflict was the railroad construction workers. Laying track and leveling the terrain for it required gathering together gangs of as many as several thousand men, mostly itinerant, unskilled laborers. This was frankly a terrifying sight, both for their employers and for the inhabitants of the area where the work was being done, and the authorities were confronted with constant requests for police or even troops to protect solid citizens from this dangerous mass of unruly proletarians. When such workers did take action, their demands, if brought forth in crude and turbulent fashion, proved to be quite rational and planned out: higher wages when the railroad company was squeezed to meet its construction schedule, or simply a demand that back wages be paid, since companies often tried to maximize their cash flow by not paying construction workers for months at a time. Such demands could be settled easily – provided the military did not intervene and turn the situation into a major riot.

If the railroad laborers' strike behavior seems more recognizable by contemporary standards than that of, say, journeymen shoemakers, the very nature of railroad construction, with its constant fluctuation of personnel and continuous movement of the construction sites themselves, prevented any permanent form of organization from emerging. Labor relations and forms of conflict in non-agricultural employment during the first half of the nineteenth century were quite different from what they would be in the second half of the century and in the subsequent ones. This is a point relevant to the 1848 revolution, which would see particularly dramatic examples of such conflicts, as well as the founding of associations devoted to workers' issues. In considering these associations, it is important not to confuse them with the trade unions or labor parties of the late nineteenth and twentieth centuries; the associations were as different as the social conflicts and relations of property and production from which they emerged.

Conflicts with the state

As we have seen previously, the government's sphere of activity in the first decades of the nineteenth century was relatively limited, thus restricting the range of possible confrontations between the state and its subjects. Yet even the few things that the government did were enough to provoke substantial conflicts. Two sources of trouble were particularly apparent: the armed forces and the collection of taxes.

The very thought of being a soldier was far from popular, in view of the long terms of service awaiting most eligible young men unfortunate enough to be drafted. When the draft commission entered an Austrian village, the eligibles immediately fled into the hills and forests. Others never waited around to be registered. Census figures from the period show a suspiciously high female to male ratio precisely in the ages of eligibility for military service. Pedlars did a brisk business in amulets and prayer booklets, which ensured supernatural intervention for a favorable number in the draft lottery. Somewhat more practically, there was usually the possibility of purchasing a replacement, paying someone to serve in place of the draftee. There was a semi-organized market for such replacements, and the going rate was substantial, so this was an option open primarily to the sons of the well-to-do. Ingenious French entrepreneurs attempted to democratize this practice, selling conscription insurance.

Premiums would go to purchase a substitute, should the policy-holder draw a bad number.

Once dragooned into the ranks, soldiers found their relations with civilians seriously strained. For all the business that a military garrison could bring into a town, its presence was also strongly disruptive. If barracks were insufficient, soldiers could be quartered on civilian households. Off-duty soldiers took on odd jobs and helped drive down already low wage levels. The armed forces' constant desire for female companionship attracted large numbers of prostitutes to garrison towns and also encouraged frequent and nasty brawls between soldiers and civilians over women, such hostilities usually lubricated by the excessive consumption of alcoholic beverages.

All these frictions, repeated from day to day, led to an accumulation of bad blood between soldiers and civilians. In the suburbs of Milan, capital of the Habsburg Empire's northern Italian province of Lombardy, bands of civilians would jump on individual soldiers at night, beat them, strip off their clothes, and leave them tied to trees. Street urchins in Cologne, largest city in the Prussian kingdom's far western Rhine Province, were given to screaming epithets at the soldiers stationed there, such as "Prussian bums in rags," or "filthy Prussians." One could attribute this to juvenile high spirits, only every year at Carnival (Mardi Gras) time, when otherwise unlicensed behavior was sanctioned, crowds of grown-ups joined in the taunts as well. The ill feelings produced regularly led to violence. Historian James Brophy has counted thirty-nine different large-scale street and tavern brawls between Prussian soldiers and civilians in the monarchy's far western Rhine Province between 1830 and 1846.[7] The largest and most bloody occurred when the soldiers were required to act as riot police and would bring to this task their anger and frustration from their everyday experiences. Called out to preserve order during a parish fair in Cologne in 1846, the troops ran wild, clubbing and bayoneting civilians for no good reason. Order was only restored when the garrison's commandant pulled his men back into their barracks and allowed civilian volunteers to patrol the streets and escort the massive funeral procession of a victim of the army's violence.

Paying taxes is an action which has never known much popularity throughout human history, but the burdens of taxation were particularly apparent in the two decades before 1848, a time when standards of living seem to have been gradually declining. Direct taxes, the most important of which was a tax on landed property, did sometimes lead to complaints

---

[7] James M. Brophy, "Violence Between Civilians and State Authorities in the Prussian Rhineland, 1830–1846," *German History* 22 (2004): 1–35.

about unfair assessment or unequal distribution of the tax burden, but for all the grumbling about them, these taxes were usually paid. Indirect taxes, particularly those levied on the consumption of food and drink, were another story; they were strongly resisted.

Smuggling was a form of tax resistance that offered substantial economic benefits to both smugglers and their customers. For the inhabitants of coastal and border regions, smuggling was a way to earn a living, supplementing fishing or farming, or even being the main source of income. Frustrated officials of the Kingdom of the Two Sicilies noted that the inhabitants of the coastal village of Rodi had twenty-six small boats constantly out on the water, bringing in contraband. Prussian customs agents were no less annoyed with the townspeople of Breyell on the kingdom's border with Holland, especially as the authorities' efforts to enlist the solid citizens in a campaign to snuff out the crime was unavailing because the smuggling business was the basis of those very same citizens' fortunes. Both groups of smugglers brought in coffee and sugar and this points to the other economic basis of smuggling: its providing cheap food (or drugs, since the coffee was used by handloom weavers to stay awake and alert at their looms for twelve to fourteen hours a day) for a population needing every break it could get in food prices.

Food and drink prices marked the other main area of popular hostility toward taxation. The octroi, a tax on food brought into the city limits, or related duties on slaughtering and flour milling, were particularly hated forms of taxation. Popular hatred peaked when food prices rose, for then the taxes could be the final blow in making basic necessities unaffordable. A run of poor harvests between 1828 and 1832 provoked such a situation in Europe, and in those countries which underwent a revolution in 1830, as well as a number which did not, there were riots and tumultuous gatherings whose participants demanded an end to the octroi, refused to pay it, and assaulted officials trying to collect it. The authorities of the Kingdom of the Two Sicilies hastily abolished the *macinato*, the tax on grain milling, in 1831, in the – correct – expectation that such a move would ease social tensions. The decade after 1832 generally saw better harvests and only a gradual increase in food prices, so that disturbances about these food taxes calmed down, but police reports on public opinion continued to mention them as a source of disturbance, one that would re-emerge with any sharp rise in food prices.

Although purists may assert that alcohol is no basic necessity, Europeans resisted taxes on it as much as on bread. Attempts during the 1830s and 1840s to levy an alcohol tax on informal drinking clubs in southeastern France, or the rural wool-weaving districts of the Biellese valleys of northern Italy, were met with steadfast refusal to obey the law and even violent mob resistance to authorities when they tried to close down the clubs boycotting taxes. Throughout these decades, the vintners of the Rhineland constantly murmured about the Prussian tax on must, that is fermented grapes, still levied at levels of the 1820s, even though wine prices had fallen by 50–60 percent since then. What was true in that case, as well as in all the other examples of conflicts over taxation, is the way that these conflicts brought together economic and political issues. In 1848, when such conflicts were politicized, questions of taxation would prove to be an extraordinarily powerful force for political mass mobilization.

Conflicts over religion

Conflicts centered on religious issues were as pervasive in pre-1848 Europe as religion itself was within European society of the time. Conflict often raged between members of different religious confessions, but membership in the same confession was no guarantee against religious conflict. Both intra- and inter-confessional conflicts could easily be mixed with social antagonisms or conflict with the state.

Considering the distance members of different Christian confessions maintained toward each other, even when they lived in close proximity, it is not surprising that suspicious distance gave way to open conflict. One example of this transition from suspicion to violent antagonism occurred in the German city of Essen, later famous as the home of the Krupp steel works, but in the 1840s still a modest market town with a population about evenly divided between Protestants and Catholics. During the 1845 Corpus Christi procession, the rumor spread that the Protestants had stolen one of the sacred flags used in the ceremony, and the religious holiday ended with the processioners trying to storm city hall. On later investigation, it turned out that the flag had not been stolen at all, but that the teenage girl carrying it had found it too heavy and an aspiring male admirer had chivalrously volunteered to take it off her hands.

Of course, the real point was the feelings of suspicion and hostility between the confessions, which made out of this incident incipient religious warfare. While the level of violence provoked was unusual, the feelings of suspicion and hostility were not. Throughout the confessionally mixed zone along the Rhine, Protestants were refusing to take off their hats when Catholics held religious processions, Catholic priests would not sanction religiously mixed marriages, unless the couple agreed to bring up their children in the Catholic confession, and mutual accusations of proselytizing and disturbing the peace of the region by subverting confessional coexistence were constantly being leveled. An example of this attitude, and particularly the badly overheated language in which it was expressed, comes from the assertion of the Catholic parish priest in the village of Lampertloch in Alsace, who stated in 1846 that "the Canton of Woerth is just like the crater of a volcano in full eruption, constantly spitting out as lava the spirit of that rotten sect, Lutheranism."[8]

Conflicts were just as prevalent and every bit as pronounced within the individual confessions. One version that ran through Roman Catholicism, most strongly in the Mediterranean world, but elsewhere in Europe as well, was the clash between clericalism and anti-clericalism. At least some men from the middle and upper classes, although baptized Catholic, rejected their religion. They would mock priests, publicly sneer at processions (and even throw things at them), or make fun of church services by bringing a picnic lunch to them. Such free thinkers gathered together in Masonic Lodges, strongholds of anti-clericalism. They might cap off a lifetime of impiety by ceremoniously refusing the sacraments on their deathbeds. The clergy fumed and fulminated in the pulpit against such sinners in the ranks of the faithful.

These ranks, the peasants, craftsmen, laborers, and small businessmen of Catholic Europe, were little affected by an intellectualized hostility toward religion. However, conflicts between laity and clergy arose within the framework of religious devotion. As part of their effort to revive and shore up popular loyalty to the church, Catholic priests began to attack many of its traditional institutions and practices. The clergy felt that religious brotherhoods, saints' days, processions or pilgrimages increasingly provided occasion for thoroughly secular dancing, drinking or illicit sexual contacts, and that they contained many scarcely hidden pagan elements, unworthy of Christian religion. Their attempts at pious reform were often poorly received by the devout masses who were strongly attached to their religious practices.

A celebrated, if possibly apocryphal, story describes such a confrontation in Provence, in southeastern France, a region of particularly strong conflicts between popular culture and the clergy's Catholicism. The feast of St. Ely was the occasion for the parish priest to bless the assembled farm animals. He hesitated to do so, strongly suspecting the pagan superstitious element in the occasion. A peasant came to him and said, "Come, Monsieur le Curé. All the horses, mules and donkeys are there; you're the only one missing!" The priest refused to perform the ceremony; his parishioners promptly rioted against him and the authorities had substantial difficulty in restoring order.[9]

---

[8] Cited in Tobias Dietrich, "Confessionelle Gegnerschaft im Dorf im 19. Jahrhundert," in Olaf Blaschke (ed.), *Konfessionen im Konflikt* (Göttingen, 2002), 203.

[9] Maurice Agulhon, *The Republic in the Village: The People of the Var from the French Revolution to the Second Republic*, trans. Janet Lloyd (Cambridge, 1982), 104–5, 325 n. 64.

There were similar tensions within Protestantism, although they played themselves out in somewhat different fashion. Loyalty to the church was noticeably weaker among the Protestant lower classes than their Catholic counterparts. While peasants and inhabitants of small towns generally retained the practices of their faith, the working class of such large urban centers as Berlin or Hamburg had increasingly abandoned church attendance. On the other hand, popular and intellectual opposition to the dominant forms of religion tended to be more coordinated among Protestants than Catholics. Religious rationalism and even Unitarianism attracted a strong following among both educated and lower-class German Protestants during the 1830s and 40s, within the established state churches and outside them, in the form of "free congregations."

One circumstance helping to exacerbate religious tensions was the way they overlapped with other social conflicts. In a number of manufacturing centers – Krefeld and Mönchengladbach on the lower Rhine, Montauban and Nîmes in southern France – the merchant contractors were a heavily Protestant group, while the outworkers they employed were disproportionately Roman Catholic. Tensions stemming from confessional differences and from workplace conflicts overlapped and reinforced each other. A similar multiplication of conflicts occurred in rural areas of eastern France and southwestern Germany between Christian peasants and Jewish villagers. The peasants were determined to keep the Jews from asserting any usage rights to the village common lands; they harbored additional resentments against the religious aliens in their midst, most of whom earned their living by lending money and by dealing in farm products and livestock.

Religious conflicts and conflicts with the state also overlapped and fed on each other, given that church and state were not separated and European states of the first half of the nineteenth century were rarely confessionally neutral. A complex example of the overlapping of conflicts can be seen in the grievances of the Romanians of the Habsburg province of Transylvania. Most were serfs and exploited by their feudal overlords. Unlike the Magyar nobles and the free German peasants, they were not represented in the provincial Diet. Additionally, most Romanian speakers were of the Eastern Orthodox faith, which, unlike Catholicism or Protestantism in the province, was not a recognized religion and so received no financial support from the government.

A simpler example comes from the kingdom of Bavaria, whose ruling dynasty and majority of inhabitants were Roman Catholics, vociferously so. In Bavaria, the army and militia accompanied the Corpus Christi procession and knelt at the sight of the consecrated sacrament. All soldiers and militiamen had to do so – including the Protestants from northern Bavaria, who were, to say the least, angry about being forced to take part in a Catholic religious ceremony, one which had been promoted since the Counter-Reformation as a sign of opposition to Protestantism.

Much the same sort of conflict, only with the confessional signs reversed, occurred in the kingdom of Prussia, whose Protestant monarch ordered all army conscripts to attend Protestant church services on Sundays, giving no thought to the offense this caused Catholics in his army. During the 1830s, when Catholic priests in Prussia began refusing to perform religiously mixed marriages without receiving a promise of Catholic upbringing for the offspring, the Prussian government responded by arrested two archbishops and ordering them to be deposed from their sees. Roman Catholic Prussian subjects saw this – not entirely incorrectly – as proof of their oppression by Protestants. There were demonstrations and riots directed against the government and against Protestants in predominantly Roman Catholic regions of the Prussian monarchy for a number of years, until the authorities negotiated a solution to the controversy with the Vatican.

Given the salience of religion for group identity and the close involvement of the government in religious affairs, it is easy to see how conflicts relating to religion could become explicitly political, that is the subject of conscious plans to change the government. In 1848, religious controversy would be strongly politicized and intra- or inter-confessional conflict would become an important factor in shaping the path of the revolution, albeit one not often considered in most historians' accounts.

European society and its conflicts in the 1840s

The German historian Hans Medick has described a "long eighteenth century," a period of fairly continuous social and economic development, running from 1648 to 1848.[10] Although coined specifically for central Europe, and most applicable to conditions there, it is arguably the best way to understand social structure and social conflict throughout the entire continent in the first half of the nineteenth century. True, there were new elements of social and economic development, particularly in the 1840s: the beginnings of a rail network, the first textile mills and coke-fired blast furnaces, the increasing sales of specialized farm products. Yet even in northern and western Europe, where most of these new departures were to be found, they were less significant than other trends that

---

[10] See the discussion of this concept in David Sabean, *Property, Production, and Family in Neckarhausen, 1700–1870* (Cambridge and New York, 1990), 47–51.

had been continuing since at least the mid-eighteenth century: the pressure of a growing population on natural resources, the introduction of innovations raising agricultural productivity, the growth of outworking and its spread throughout the field of craft production. In eastern and southern Europe, even the modest new departures of the more advanced parts of the continent were hard to find.

conflict sources?

The same story could be told about social conflict. Antagonism between lord and serf, conflicts over forest use, resistance to taxation, clashes between master and journeymen artisans, hostility between Catholics and Protestants or between Christians and Jews: all these versions of social conflict in the 1840s would have been quite familiar to contemporaries a century earlier. Although we can point to an occasional new departure in this arena, usually in the more advanced countries of western Europe – for instance, the gradual development of strike activity over wages, hours, and working conditions in France –,once again, continuity outweighed change.

1789

All this is not to say that Europe in the 1840s was essentially the same place as it had been in the 1740s. For there had been a fundamental change in the intervening century, brought on by, in the wake of, and in opposition to the French Revolution of 1789. Following ideas first proposed by thinkers of the Enlightenment and tentatively tried out by eighteenth-century reforming monarchs, such as the Austrian Emperor Joseph II, the revolution had produced a complete model of a new form of governmental organization and political participation, new versions of production and property relations in agriculture and the crafts, a new and subordinate place for religion within society and public life. We could describe, at the most general and abstract level, these changes as involving a replacement of an old regime society of orders with a post-revolutionary civil society of property owners.

In the society of orders, different social groups, membership of which was usually set at birth, and typically was connected to membership of an established church, had different legal rights and privileges that both set the pattern for their ways of making a living and also determined their possible participation in public life. By contrast, in the post-revolutionary public order all citizens (male citizens, anyway; women had a subordinate position in both forms of society), regardless of their status at birth or their religion, were equal under the law, and equally entitled to pursue the acquisition of property. Participation in public life was generally connected to the possession of property and not to status at birth or religious confession.

These changes proposed by the revolutionaries had been partially implemented in the quarter century following 1789, most in the countries of western Europe, less in the center of the continent, and virtually not at all in the east. Yet even where the actual changes wrought by the revolution had been at their least, in the eastern provinces of the Habsburg monarchy, the model created by the French Revolution existed as an agenda, a program for potential change.

Another way of putting this is to say that the revolution introduced a new group of political ideas; it had created a new political universe in Europe. Much of the tension leading up to the 1848 revolution can be understood as involving the interaction of these new political ideas, ultimately stemming from the French Revolution, with a social structure and a structure of social conflict, which, for all the new departures in them, were still those of the eighteenth century. We have looked at social structure and social conflict of 1830s and 1840s Europe in this chapter; we will now go on to consider political practice and political ideas at that time.

creating new way of political life

The framework of political life

The typical characteristic of political life throughout Europe at the beginning of the 1840s was a negative one: the lack of republicanism and democracy. In an audacious outburst of experiment, late eighteenth-century revolutionaries had suggested that large, complex states could be ruled without a king and the years around 1800 had seen republican government at its greatest extent since classical antiquity. While a half-century later, this experiment continued in the Americas, in Europe it seemed to have been given up. The only republican governments were those covering small areas: the Swiss cantons, county-sized political entities bound together in a loose confederation, and the German city-states of Frankfurt, Hamburg, Bremen, and Lübeck, themselves only semi-autonomous parts of the larger German Confederation. Elsewhere, there were monarchs, who both reigned and ruled.

They ruled without counting on the consent of the governed. Even in those monarchies that possessed legislative bodies and a constitution or charter of privileges to empower them, the men who sat in them were scarcely the people's representatives. The franchise was restricted or exercised very inequitably. Nowhere was universal manhood suffrage a reality, to say nothing of women having the vote. The stringency of these limitations might be seen from conditions in France, where those possessing enough property to be eligible to vote in elections to the Chamber of Deputies, the lower house of the bicameral legislature, made up just 5 percent of all the adult males in the country.

Within this common framework of monarchism and restricted suffrage, we can distinguish between two very different forms of governmental structures in 1840s Europe. One version, found in France and also in the Netherlands, Belgium, Norway, and most of the smaller states of western and southern Germany – Bavaria, Baden, and Saxony, for instance – was the constitutional monarchy. As the name indicates, such regimes possessed a constitution, a fundamental law regulating the exercise of political power. It guaranteed citizens basic rights and delineated the nature and competence of the executive, legislative, and judicial branches of government.

Typically, such constitutions created a bicameral legislature with a lower house elected indirectly by some sort of property franchise and an upper house composed of the hereditary nobility and other special dignitaries. The legislature's consent was required for the making of law, the imposition of taxes, and the expenditure of government funds. The monarch was, under these constitutions, the head of state, but his (in continental Europe, reigning monarchs were all men) governmental role was far from exclusively symbolic. He was also commander-in-chief of the armed forces, and director of the executive branch of government, carrying out the business of the regime through a council of ministers. In France and Belgium, the ministers were chosen from the leading parliamentary deputies, in the Netherlands and the German states from the upper ranks of the civil service. The right of the legislature to approve these ministers, or to vote them out of office, already well established in Great Britain, was in no way secure in the constitutional regimes of continental Europe. Constitutional arrangements usually also included an independent judiciary and some guarantees of freedom of speech, the press, association, exercise of religion, and disposition of property – although these freedoms were far from absolute, and many of the constitutions did not so much grant them as set the framework for legislation restricting them.

Yet these meager accomplishments of west European constitutionalism loom large – and loomed large to politically interested contemporaries – when set against conditions in the rest of the continent. In the states of the Italian peninsula, in the kingdom of Prussia, and in the Austrian Empire, there were no constitutions at all, that is, no universally valid checks on monarchical power, no guarantees of any sort of civil rights. If anything, certain rights, freedom of the press, speech, and association in particular, were certain not to be granted. These parts of Europe were the realm of political absolutism.

Even absolute monarchs did not rule absolutely. In practice, there were two institutional barriers to monarchical power. Like their west European counterparts, absolute monarchs ruled through a council of ministers, and a professional civil service. If the actions of the latter were not subject to parliamentary control, they sometimes demonstrated a will of their own, not always in conformity with the commands of their royal masters. The bureaucracy of the kingdom of Prussia was particularly noted for its strong *esprit de corps* and sense that it was the actual ruler of the country, all the while professing to be the king's most obedient servant.

A second limitation of royal power lay in the feudal legislatures, the estates, or as they are often translated into English, the diets. They were unknown in most of Italy, but virtually every province of the Habsburg monarchy and the Prussian and Danish kingdoms had its own. The powers of these diets were limited, sometimes to just advisory functions, in every case to the provinces for which they were elected. Estates general, diets for the entire realm, existed in smaller states, such as the principalities of Moldavia and Wallachia, and the kingdom of Sweden, but not in any of the Great Powers. In view of what had happened to the king of France when he convened such a body in 1789, the absolute rulers of these powers were in no hurry to repeat the experiment fifty years later.

The franchise for such legislatures ran along the lines of the old regime society of orders, being determined by social category set at birth. The nobility elected its own deputies (sometimes there were deputies elected separately by the higher and the lesser nobility), townspeople chose theirs, the clergy might have its own representatives, and, occasionally, the peasantry as well. Representation was never proportional to the population being represented; indeed, the whole point of the diets was to avoid this. The nobility, at best a modestly sized group, always had the largest number of deputies, frequently an absolute majority.

In comparison to the legislative bodies of the constitutional monarchies of western Europe, the diets of the Great Powers of central and eastern Europe lacked power and influence. (The estates of the kingdom of Sweden, by contrast, had many of the powers of the legislatures of western European constitutional monarchies.) Their power to make law or to consent to taxation, when existent, was confined to individual provinces; their connection with the inhabitants they were supposed to represent not much in apparance, except for the badly over-represented nobility. Unlike constitutional legislatures, they were poor sounding boards for public opinion. The provincial diets of the kingdom of Prussia and some of those in the Austrian Empire, for instance, were prohibited from publishing their proceedings, so that the voters literally did not know what the representatives they elected had done.

If there was an exception to this picture of powerlessness and irrelevance, it was the Hungarian diet. To be sure, the nobility was grossly over-represented there too, but since the nobles formed such a large proportion of the population, the effective electorate was greater and had a much broader scattering of wealth than was the case in France at the time. Like the other diets of the Habsburg Empire, the Hungarian one was regionally limited in its representation, only the politically active individuals in the region it represented claimed that Hungary was not just another province but a sovereign kingdom within the empire. Even here, the public influence of the diet was restricted by the tradition of carrying on its debates in Latin.

We might sum all this up by saying that representative political institutions were weak throughout Europe, and that the circle of those represented in them was extremely narrow. Such basic civil rights as freedom of speech, press, and association, fundamental pre-conditions of political participation, were at best only partly guaranteed. The possibilities for representative politics were greatest in the constitutional monarchies of western Europe and weakest in the absolutist regimes of the south and east of the continent. Everywhere, however, politics remained a matter for relatively small groups, a state of affairs that would have surprising and dramatic consequences when mass political participation suddenly became a reality in the spring of 1848.

Forms of political participation and organization

Political life was severely limited before 1848, but was not totally impossible, and it is helpful in understanding the explosion of political participation at the outbreak of the revolution to see what had gone on before. We can divide a discussion of political life in 1840s Europe into two parts, a consideration of the possibilities of political participation, and an account of the chances for political organization.

Before being involved in politics, one has to be informed about public life, something accomplished in the middle of the nineteenth century primarily by reading newspapers. The technological and economic limitations on the press were then considerable. Type had to be set by hand, creating a publishing bottleneck that even the introduction of the steam-powered printing press could not abolish. Newspapers were rarely more than six to eight pages long. Daily papers were uncommon; a publishing schedule of once or twice a week was the rule. Press runs were modest. The Parisian daily *Le Siècle*, with a press run of 30,000, was the newspaper with the largest circulation in France and all of continental Europe. This was far above most other major national or regional newspapers, which were lucky to appear in the 3–5,000 copy range. These in turn were more significant than the typical paper: a small city or town weekly appearing in a press run of a few hundred.

Readership was larger than these modest figures suggest, since individual copies were purchased by proprietors of taverns and cafés for their customers to read, or were subscribed to by social clubs, so that all members might have access. Even so, only a small proportion of the adult male population – and an even smaller proportion of the female one – can have had regular access to the press. Of course, in those areas of eastern and southern Europe where literacy was uncommon, even access to the press would not have done much good.

These material and marketing difficulties were just the beginning of problems for reporting the news. Outside the constitutional monarchies of western Europe, publishing a newspaper required a government concession, one which was generally not forthcoming. Furthermore, newspapers, like all other forms of publishing, were subject to prior censorship. Anything the censor disliked or felt the public ought not to know could not appear. The system of censorship reached its extreme in the Habsburg monarchy, where even literary classics, like the works of Friedrich Schiller, were deemed subversive, but it was exercised throughout central and eastern Europe. Newspapers might challenge the censor, openly defying his commands, printing blank spaces where articles were cut out, or using allegory and allusions to make a political forbidden point. Karl Marx employed these tactics in his first venture into politics, as the editor of the oppositional *Rheinische Zeitung* in the city of Cologne during 1842–43. The fate of the newspaper also suggests what happened to those who defied the censor: the authorities revoked its license to publish.

Even in constitutional regimes with a guaranteed freedom of the press, inventive authorities could place limitations on unwelcome journalism. The classic example of such restriction was the French press law of 1835. It required newspaper publishers to deposit a large sum as caution money, to guarantee that they could pay any potential libel verdicts. Publishers were also required to designate one individual as legally responsible, so that he might go to jail, should the newspaper be convicted of attacking the royal family or advocating the introduction of a different form of government. Such legislation's use – or misuse, not easy to distinguish from its use – while not as effective as open censorship in putting a barrier between journalists and their public, nonetheless helped keep an independent and oppositional press under control.

A more effective means of reaching a wider public for political purposes was the use of festival and celebration. The most celebrated example was the great banquet campaign, launched by the political opposition in Paris at the end of 1847, and leading directly up to the revolution of the following year. Since actual political meetings required police consent, which the authorities were not about to grant, oppositional leaders sponsored a series of banquets, ostensibly just public meals. The entry fees were low, however, attracting thousands of potential celebrants, and not much food or drink was in appearance, while angry speeches denouncing the government were. By this time, though, the banquet tradition of politics was a good two decades old, widely practiced throughout

France and Germany, and as far off as Sweden, as a means of expressing political opposition. Such forms of politics had in the past tended to be more elite oriented, with more serious emphasis on the eating and drinking, a more limited circle of invitees, and correspondingly higher fees for admission. The 1847 Paris banquets were a new departure only in so far as they aimed at achieving a substantial popular political participation.

Banquets were just one form of festivity utilized for political purposes. Carnival, the pre-lenten festival of Catholic Europe, offered another major opportunity, especially given the traditional theme of the celebrations, the one time in the year when the world was turned upside down. Authority could be – and was – attacked with impunity, while its attackers hid behind the claim that their mockery of the king of Prussia or of the tsar was all in the humorous spirit of this exceptional season. There was a wide variety of other opportunities: the festivals of gymnastic, sharp-shooting, and choral societies, for instance, particularly common in central Europe, or feasts of saints, which the conservative Legitimists in France frequently tried to turn into demonstrations against the liberal Orléanist regime, come to power in the revolution of 1830.

The politics of public festivity marked a transition toward the future mass politics of the 1848 revolution. Heinrich von Gagern, a prominent liberal figure in southwestern Germany, and president of the German National Assembly during the 1848 revolution, described his speech at the 1846 fair of the provincial agricultural improvement society as being on the "hustings," using the English word in his account, thus showing his own understanding of the political implications of his actions.

Even elections could be turned into political festivals. The 1847 campaign of Lajos Kossuth, then leader of the opposition to absolutist Habsburg rule in Hungary, two years later president of an insurgent, independent Hungarian government, for a seat in the Hungarian diet from the county of Pest, was a long series of banquets, public speeches, and parades, culminating on election day in processions of voters to the polling places, wearing feathers in their caps with the red, white, and green national colors. It would not be unfair to say that the political significance of his election was above all in its festive aspects, which reached a much wider circle of the public than the far more circumscribed group of eligible voters.

All these examples suggest that political mobilization and mass political participation were possible before 1848, in spite of the very limited franchise and restrictions on or lack of basic civil liberties. Before 1848, these forms of a nascent mass politics might be seen in capital cities such as Pest or Paris, or in regional metropolises like Toulouse or Cologne. Heinrich von Gagern's mounting the hustings at an agricultural fair, though, was very much an exceptional act. Smaller towns and especially the countryside, where most Europeans lived, were rarely scenes of mass political participation. When politics was practiced there at all, it was only among an extremely limited group of the affluent and educated. Social conflicts of the sort described in the previous chapter were a common occurrence, but between the peasants stealing wood or threatening the tax-collector and the notables at their banquet table there was little or no connection.

If political participation was limited, political organization was even more so. Political parties in the modern sense, with a national organization, central leadership, a program, and dues-paying members, were legally impossible. In the absolutist states, the very existence of such an association was illegal, since it implied that politics was not just a matter for the ruler, his officials, and perhaps the feudally organized estates. In the constitutional monarchies, the formation of associations required the explicit permission of the authorities, which was not forthcoming for such groups of potential trouble-makers. Even if political parties had been permitted, they would have faced severe obstacles given the poor quality of communication and transportation, the modest circulation of the press, and the low level of popular interest in politics.

If political parties were legally and logistically impossible, there were several alternative forms of political organization practiced before 1848. One was an organization centered on the editorial staff of a newspaper. The journalists employed on the Parisian dailies *Le National* and *La Réforme* were known as the leaders of the militant, leftist opposition to the liberal Orléanist monarchy. When a provisional republican government was formed after the revolution of February 1848 overthrew the monarchy, its key members came from the two newspapers' staffs. In 1847, to give another example, a group of pro-Prussian German liberals founded a newspaper, the appropriately named *Deutsche Zeitung* (the German News) in the university town of Heidelberg, to represent their political program throughout the German states.

Heidelberg was not in Prussia but in the Grand Duchy of Baden, one of the smaller German states possessing a constitution and a relatively lax press censorship. The pro-Prussian liberals could not locate their newspaper in Prussia, since the authorities of that absolutist monarchy would not permit it. This decision points to the chief weakness of using a newspaper as a form of political organization: in so far as it worked, it only worked where the press was not licensed or censored. This left out most of the south, center, and east of the continent.

If legal political organization was difficult or impossible, the obvious alternative was to work illegally, thus bringing us to another major form of pre-1848 political organization, the secret society. Such groups were most common in Italy, where they had a long tradition, going back to the first decade of the nineteenth century. Working from exile in Marseilles, the indefatigable revolutionary Giuseppe Mazzini organized the largest secret society in the early 1830s, "Young Italy," that counted perhaps as many as 50,000 members throughout the entire peninsula, most concentrated in the center, in Tuscany and the Papal States.

The Italians were scarcely alone in their use of secret societies. Driven into exile after their unsuccessful rising against Russian rule in 1830, Polish revolutionaries spun a net of conspiracy throughout the Polish-speaking lands divided among the Prussian kingdom and the Austrian and tsarist empires. Looking for allies, they organized similar groups in southeastern Europe, among the inhabitants of Serbia, Moldavia, and Wallachia. German students and journeymen artisans, two of the more mobile and more unruly groups of central Europe, organized secret societies, both at home in Frankfurt or Mainz, and abroad, in Zürich, Belgium, London, and Paris. As the premier city in continental Europe and in many ways its political center, Paris was also the center of secret conspiracy. This was certainly true for exiles, and secret groups of Poles, Germans, and Romanians existed in the French capital during the late 1830s and early 1840s. It was also true for indigenous French radical and extreme radical secret societies, which abounded in Paris and, to a lesser extent, in Lyon, Toulouse, and other larger cities in France. Louis-Auguste Blanqui, the prime promoter of such groups, spent a lifetime at it. Between 1830 and 1880, he was either organizing a secret society or in jail for the consequences of his actions.

Blanqui's fate indicates the problem with secret societies. If they were to be effective, they would have to have a large membership, but if they had a large membership, they would no longer be secret, and they would then be broken up by the authorities. Ultimately, this is what happened to all of them. Attempts to mount an insurrection, the basic purpose of such groups, would only accelerate the process. Secret societies frequently tried to mount an uprising before 1848. Some of the larger and the more serious of these efforts include one carried out by German student conspirators in Frankfurt am Main in 1833; a major attempt by Mazzini's Young Italy the following year; one in Paris under Blanqui's leadership in 1839; one in the Austrian province of Galicia by Polish activists in 1846; and one in southern Italy that year. All were dismal failures.

If neither open use of the press nor secret association proved entirely successful, what forms of political organization remained? The answer, and the most common form of political organization in pre-1848 Europe, was the informal one. Like-minded individuals would gather, either in an organized but ostensibly non-political setting, or would just come together in a public place for casual conversation. Here, once again, the variety of possibilities was extraordinarily wide. The Juridical-Political Reading [and social] Club was the one place where independent political discussion could be found under the authoritarian rule of the Habsburgs' chancellor Prince Metternich. Throughout southern Europe, Masonic Lodges were another focus of political conversation. From the opposite religious viewpoint, strongly anti-Prussian, devout Catholics of Koblenz, on the Rhine, talked politics in the city's Rosary Brotherhood. Radicals in Pest gathered at the fashionable Café Pilfax, in Cologne at Romberg's coffeehouse, and in Rome at the aptly named "Café of the Union of the People."

This list could be extended indefinitely. By the 1840s, cities and towns throughout Europe were honeycombed with such informal meetings; they were the main forum of political discussion. In a constitutional monarchy, the combination of these informal groups with parliamentary debates and their reporting in the press – subscribed to in the taverns or social clubs where these groups met – created loose political networks in the entire country. Like-minded parliamentary deputies belonged to a common caucus in the legislature; their speeches reached the provinces via the press; those who agreed with the viewpoints expressed in these speeches gathered in informal settings to read and discuss them and, when election time came, tried to elect as their own deputy someone espousing these ideas.

In the absolutist regimes, on the other hand, these links between different levels of political life did not and could not exist. Lacking a free press and a parliament to articulate specific positions, political opinions remained diffuse. Discussion circles included a wide variety of overlapping and sometimes mutually contradictory opinions. Recalling such a group meeting in Bologna during the 1840s, one participant described how "nationalists and neo-Catholics, partisans of free competition and of the organization of labor [i.e., an early version of socialism]" all met together on the common ground of the "redemption of Italy."[1] It would only be with the freer political environment of the 1848 revolution, when they could actually take action to redeem Italy, that the strong differences in their political viewpoints would become clear.

For all the prevalence of informal discussion groups, their membership was small and their social composition restricted. In both constitutional and absolutist regimes, even these very modest forms of political

---

[1] Quoted in F. Catalono, "Socialismo e comunismo in Italia dal 1846 al 1849," *Rassegna Storica del Risorgimento* 38 (1951): 306–16.

organization were limited to the middle and upper classes. Peasants had no connection with them; laborers and craftsmen only occasionally, in some of the larger cities of western Europe. As one government official in the Department of the Vaucluse in southeastern France noted in regard to political life before 1848, "those eligible to vote [i.e., the wealthiest 5 percent of adult males] were everything; the rest of the population nothing."[2]

Political doctrines and political movements in mid-nineteenth-century Europe

The single most important, if not the only factor shaping political doctrine in mid-nineteenth-century Europe was the heritage of the French Revolution of 1789. The revolution had created the now familiar idea of a political spectrum, that is, the placing of political positions on a left to right scale. Moreover, the specific political doctrines of the 1840s were based on questions posed by the revolution: sometimes the answers proposed were themselves based on the ones first offered in the decade after 1789; sometimes, they arose from a desire to go beyond the solutions tried then. In either case, they testified to the enormous shaping power of the revolution for nineteenth-century developments.

Liberalism

The best place to start a discussion of the political spectrum is in the middle, with the doctrines of liberalism. Certainly the single most important political idea and political movement of the nineteenth century, liberalism was also in practice amorphous and malleable, having widely differing meanings in different parts of the continent. Liberalism as a political doctrine has also undergone a long process of evolution, that has left it in the early twenty-first century, very different from what it was 160 years previously. To denote this difference and avoid evoking connotations from today's politics, it is helpful to use the term favored by contemporaries in the 1840s, who spoke less of liberalism and more of constitutional monarchism.

First articulated by the French politician and man of letters Benjamin Constant in the early decades of the nineteenth century, and common to liberals in Italy, the Low Countries, the German states, and the Habsburg monarchy by the 1840s, constitutional monarchism might be seen as a

---

[2] Quoted in Philippe Vigier, *La seconde république dans la région alpine*, 2 vols. (Paris, 1963), 1: 181.

doctrine offering a cautious and limited consent to the ideals of the French Revolution, often colored by a look across the channel towards conditions in Great Britain. A constitution would guarantee basic freedoms. As Constant put it in 1819, such freedoms meant:

for everyone to be under the dominion of nothing but the law, not to be assisted, detained or put to death, nor maltreated in any way, as a consequence of the arbitrary will of one or more individuals. It is for every one to have the right to express his opinion, to choose and exercise his occupation, to dispose of his property and even to abuse it, to go and come without having to obtain permission and without having to give an accounting of his motives or actions. It is the right of each person to associate with other individuals, either to discuss their interests or to practice the form of worship they prefer or simply to fill the days and hours in a way which best suits their inclinations and fancies.[3]

In other words, a liberal constitution would guarantee equal treatment under the law, enshrine such basic civic rights as freedom of speech, press, association, and religion, and ensure the freedom to dispose of private property – a freedom particularly cherished by nineteenth-century liberals. The question they faced was what kind of government would best secure such freedoms. Historical experience suggested that an absolute monarchy on the one hand, and a radical republican regime, as had been tried in France under the Jacobins in the 1790s, would be more likely to suppress these basic freedoms than to guarantee them. This, as Constant observed, was because such regimes had just one pole of political power – a monarch or a revolutionary legislature. By contrast, a constitutional monarchy, that is a regime in which a legislative and executive branch of government existed independently of each other, and whose actions would be mutually restrictive (an idea very similar to the Anglo-American doctrine of constitutional "checks and balances") would be the form of government most likely to safeguard these freedoms. For most mid-nineteenth-century liberals, this independent executive power would be most effective if its leadership, the government ministers, was appointed by a hereditary monarch who would provide continuity and stability as head of state, and who could mediate between the ministers he appointed and the elected legislators. This endorsement of a monarch as head of state made most liberals of the 1840s constitutional monarchists. Only in France were there liberals – in 1848, they would be called "pure republicans"–who could imagine following the North American practice and investing executive power in an elected president.

[3] Cited in Guy Howard Dodge, *Benjamin Constant's Philosophy of Liberalism: A Study in Politics and Religion* (Chapel Hill, 1980), 38–39.

Liberal social doctrine was intrinsically related to the constitutional monarchist conception of government. Society, for mid-nineteenth-century liberals, consisted of (usually male) property owners and it was naturally self-regulating, working best when "artificial" interference with it was kept to a minimum. A constitutional monarchist regime, liberals felt, would be most likely to restrict governmental activity to protecting the natural workings of society and least likely to interfere with these workings. This followed from the existence of a constitution regulating governmental activity and securing civil rights, the mutual checks imposed on each other by legislature and executive, and by a third basic element of liberal doctrine, the property franchise. Only people possessing the ability to form an independent judgment, liberals felt, should be eligible to vote. It helps to understand this idea if we remember that the secret ballot was uncommon, and voting was generally public and oral, so that employers, creditors, government officials, and other interested parties could observe anyone casting a ballot. Women, naturally dependent on men, as most people of the first half of the nineteenth century thought, should not have the franchise, in the opinion of constitutional monarchists, but neither should workers, who were dependent for their livelihood on their employers. Liberals were uncertain and divided about the exact amount of property needed to secure one's independence and so exercise the franchise: some supported allowing most male property owners to vote; others wanted to see the ballot limited to a small minority of the well-to-do.

Liberals asserted – and asserted forcefully – that they represented the people, only they made a distinction between "the people" and "the mob" or "the rabble." As the Aachen wool merchant David Hansemann, a prominent German liberal of the 1840s, explained, what counted was the "true majority," as distinguished from "the majority by head count." This "true majority," had a "broader education [which] afforded it greater insight and its wealth [which] gave it a greater interest in the existence of a solid, strong and good state government."[4]

The liberal attitude towards suffrage was expressed in classic terms by François Guizot, a leading political figure of the post-1830 liberal French monarchy. Responding to a complaint about high property qualification for voting, he responded, "Enrichissez-vous," "Get rich." A liberal society would be one in which enterprising men might have the opportunity to accumulate property or gain a significant position in the government or professions, as expressed in the liberal slogan, "careers open to

---

[4] Cited in Dieter Langewiesche, *Liberalism in Germany*, trans. Christiane Bannerji (Princeton, 2000), 12.

the talents." In that way, any man would have the prospect of being able to gain a voice in public affairs. Mid-nineteenth-century European liberals looked at existing social institutions primarily from this point of view and judged governmental activity, or inactivity, by its efficacy in leading society in this direction. This interaction between constitutional monarchy and a society of male property owners, equal before the law, was both prescriptive and descriptive for liberals.

Feudal and seigneurial tenures in agriculture, and a society of orders based on distinction at birth, from which they sprung, were illegitimate to liberals, violations of equality before the law, not allowing all men chances at a career, and restricting the free disposition of property. In central and eastern Europe, where such agricultural tenures existed, liberals were unanimous in demanding their abolition. Liberals were equally unanimous in agreeing that labor organization, in the form of strikes or trade unions, was an illegitimate interference in the natural workings of the labor market, so that liberals advocated the suppression of these groups and activities. This did not imply that liberals felt nothing but contempt for working people's attempts to improve their lot; rather, they supported and even took the lead in founding institutions that would allow workers to acquire their own property: savings banks, mutual benefit societies, and institutes of technical and vocational education.

We might be tempted to generalize these positions, as textbook accounts often do, to the statement that liberalism was a doctrine advocating free trade, economic growth, and the industrial revolution. This was certainly the case in mid-nineteenth-century England, the period of the great liberal agitation in favor of the repeal of the Corn Laws. To some extent, this was also true on the continent. The German customs union of 1834, the *Zollverein*, found liberal favor and Italian liberals talked increasingly of a similar arrangement among the states of the peninsula. Some continental liberals were uncompromising free traders although it is characteristic that the leading German publicist for such a point of view was the expatriate Englishman John Prince Smith. Others were more skeptical of unlimited *laissez-faire* and industrialization precisely from allegiance to the liberal social principles implicit in constitutional monarchism.

In central Italy and southern Germany, liberals were openly hostile to the British model of industrialization, which, they asserted, had reduced the possibility for adult males to become property owners, creating, instead, an ever greater number of propertyless proletarians. To put it in Guizot's language, they feared that the advance of industry would mean that most men would never have the chance to get rich, or even to be modestly comfortable. South German liberals went so far as to support the continued existence of the guilds, viewing their existence as part of the natural workings of society, seeing their role in preserving the position of master craftsmen as helping support independent property owners with a stake in society. For these liberals, guilds represented the natural working of society, and efforts to abolish them and allow freedom of occupation were an example of government interference in these natural workings!

Some liberals, on the other hand, opposed free trade, because they supported industrialization. The most articulate theorist of this point of view was Friedrich List, the German journalist and economist, who pointed out that free trade between countries with a high level of industrial development – say, England, France or Belgium – and those with a lower level – the German states, for instance – would prevent the latter from ever acquiring modern industry. List advocated the introduction of protective tariffs until such time as industry had developed sufficiently to compete on equal terms with the more advanced countries. Liberals in centers of factory industry – the Rhineland or Alsace, for instance – were attracted to this assertion. In economically less developed parts of Europe, Hungary being a particularly good example, liberalism was associated with an effort to catch up with the wealthier parts of the continent. In part using List's ideas as justification, Hungarian liberals advocated, and even supported with their own money (most of which they lost), the creation of industry, the building of railroads, and the founding of a Hungarian seaport on the Adriatic coast for their nation's economic development.

Mid-nineteenth-century liberals also saw another sphere of government activity, designed, ultimately, to help create a society of male property owners with a voice in public affairs. This was public education, which liberals, as a group, strongly supported. François Guizot's law of 1833, requiring every city, town, and village in France to have a public elementary [primary] school for boys (although not opposed to education for girls, he did not accord it quite the same priority) might stand as something of a model of liberal aspirations and accomplishments. At least potentially, such a stance had the effect of leading liberals into confrontation with organized religion, which also had strong claims on the administration and goals of public education.

In fact, anti-clericalism was a major component of liberalism, reflecting the extent to which most churches had strong ties to the absolutist government and society of estates that liberals opposed. This connection between liberalism and anti-clericalism dated from the French Revolution and even before it, from the eighteenth-century Enlightenment. It continued unabated in the middle decades of the nineteenth century. The same Masonic Lodges or social clubs in southern Europe that were centers of free thought were often centers of liberal ideas as well. The liberal revolution of 1830 in France had gone along with the storming of churches, and the tearing down of crosses and religious statuary.

In areas of religiously mixed population, Protestants were noticeably more likely than Catholics to be supporters of liberalism, less a reflection of a special connection between Protestant religion and liberalism than of the extent to which free-thinking was more prevalent among Protestants than Catholics. A number of attempts were made, in France, Germany, during the 1830s and 40s, to reconcile Catholicism and liberalism. Although for a time showing some success, in the end all proved unavailing, as the events of 1848 would demonstrate once and for all. The Catholic Church and the liberal political movement remained unreconciled for the rest of the nineteenth century.

This last paragraph broaches a significant question, namely that of the supporters of liberalism. Given its views on state and society, liberalism tended to be a political movement of the notables, that is of the locally most influential and affluent men. Liberals could be found in private clubs or the more exclusive taverns, their ranks including merchants, manufacturers, landowners, professionals, and civil servants – a surprising number of whom had liberal sympathies, even when serving absolutist governments strongly hostile to liberal ideas. In smaller towns, where circumstances were more modest, so were the notables and the liberal adherents: small rentiers, tavernkeepers or shopkeepers, for instance. In Hungary, where the nobility was so large a proportion of the population, most liberal leaders and activists were from the nobility.

Indeed, we might turn the question around and ask who among the wealthy and powerful were not liberals. The answer is twofold. First, those who profited from the absolutist government and the old regime society of orders liberals opposed: noble landowners of eastern and central Europe who clung to their serfs or their seigneurial privileges; royal courtiers and the upper levels of government service and the armed forces in absolutist regimes; businessmen who earned their often considerable fortunes as government contractors or financiers for these regimes. As Antonio Scialoja, a southern Italian liberal noted of the members of the Naples merchant oligarchy, who had precisely these functions in the Kingdom of the Two Sicilies, "to tell the truth [they are] the most indifferent to political liberty."[5]

The second group, which overlapped considerably although not completely with the first, were the religiously devout. The pious Catholic

[5] Quoted in John Davis, "Oligarchia capitalistica e immobilismo economia a Napoli (1815–1860), *Studi Storici* 16 (1975): 378–426.

nobility of Brittany, horrified by the liberal and anti-clerical revolution of 1830, retired to their estates in western France, muttering anathemas at the new Orléans dynasty, which had come to the throne. When the Orléans king Louis Philippe was overthrown in turn in 1848, these nobles saw the revolution as a judgment of God on his impious and insubordinate enterprise of eighteen years previously. Protestant revivalist manufacturers of the Wupper Valley in the Prussian kingdom's Rhine Province were at best deeply skeptical of liberalism, and convinced supporters of the absolutist rule of their king, unlike a large majority of the more constitutionally minded bourgeoisie of their region. Most clergy, except for those professing rationalist and Enlightened forms of religion, could be counted upon to reject liberalism.

We can come at the question of support from another angle and ask whether liberals had lower-class supporters, or whether they wanted them. Liberals themselves were more than a little ambiguous about popular support. They did affirm the ideal of equality under the law and the related principle of the "career open to the talents"; hereditary social distinctions were not for them. Any adult male was a potential property-owning citizen. At the same time, liberals were aware that most adult males did not own any substantial amount of property; if they looked social change squarely in the face, they would have to admit that the number of property owners seemed to be declining in the decades before 1848. The experience of the French Revolution, when Europe's original constitutional monarchists had enlisted popular support in their struggle with absolutism and a society of orders, but soon found themselves involved in a radical republic, complete with a reign of terror and European-wide war, weighed heavily on nineteenth-century liberals.

All things considered, by the 1840s most liberals in Europe preferred an affluent following and a politics of reform and gradual, moderate steps, to one of mass support and political confrontation. On the eve of the 1848 revolution, Marco Minghetti, moderate liberal of the city of Bologna, in the Papal States, praised English politics and the great liberal campaign to repeal the Corn Laws. Whether his observations of England were accurate or not, is certainly a debatable matter, but they do suggest what he and many other European liberals regarded as a desirable form of politics:

[T]here [in England], the progress of public opinion does not occur via machinations or via attempts at revolution but with a balanced and temperate movement so that the evils and needs of the day come out into the open and their remedies may be conveniently sought. Thus it is that the lower classes never act outside the forms that the law commands, and the classes which have in their hands the governing of public affairs not only do not oppose certain irresistible tendencies of the century, but search, in moderating fashion, to lead them to a good end.[6]

However, the preference for certain forms of political action depended on the political circumstances in which liberals found themselves. In the constitutional monarchies of western Europe, above all in France, under the Orléans dynasty, come to power following the revolution of 1830, liberalism became governmental. Public policy, from seeking to limit the independence and influence of the Catholic Church, to promoting public education, from using tariffs, tax policy, and government loans to encourage railroad construction and industrialization, while suppressing a nascent labor movement, from granting freedom of the press to devising laws which harassed oppositional journalists who tried to make use of it, followed along liberal lines. Government influence on a university graduate who wanted to have a career in public administration, or a businessman, interested in having a railroad line pass through his city, could be exerted for liberal political ends. It is not entirely surprising that in these circumstances most of those elected to the Chamber of Deputies, the lower house of the French parliament, supported the government's – that is liberal – political positions. French liberalism was increasingly a party of the status quo, one that could live comfortably within the existing political system, in which just 5 percent of the adult males had the vote. Aspirations towards mass politics existed primarily on the left and the right, among the republican and legitimist (conservative adherents of the Bourbon dynasty overthrown in 1830) enemies of the regime.

In the rest of Europe, liberalism continued to be an oppositional political movement. Official policy in the absolutist regimes of Prussia, Austria, and the Italian states was dead set against liberal demands for a constitutional monarchy. The authorities were equally determined to maintain existing noble privileges in central and eastern Europe against liberal belief in equality under the law. Although they usually could make distinctions between liberals and more radical and extreme opponents of their rule, in moments of irritation, they were likely to throw them all together into one group of enemies of the state, equally liable to prohibition and persecution. Although liberal notables in these countries might have liked to work with the government, and frequently offered their cooperation, they were consistently spurned by the authorities, forcing the liberals to adopt a sharper and more popular stance, often enough against the better judgment of the liberals themselves.

[6] Cited in dal Pane, *Economia e società a Bologna*, 518.

Circumstances were similar in the smaller German states, many of which were constitutional monarchies, but, unlike France, not liberal ones. State policy partly determined by the monarch and his ministers, chosen from the nobility and the upper ranks of the civil service, and partly by pressure from the powerful absolutist regimes Prussia and Austria, usually moved in the direction of vitiating constitutional guarantees of civil liberties, weakening the position of the parliaments, and preserving remaining noble privileges. Unlike the absolutist regimes, however, liberals in Baden or Saxony could use the possibilities open to them by the existence of parliament to mount an opposition to the government. Through their participation in political or politicized festivals, and via the distribution of fliers or of autographed lithographs, these liberal parliamentarians could become, "men of the people," "heroes of the chamber [of deputies]," and in this way leaders of a more popular political movement than most liberals might have expected. Something similar could be said about the liberal opposition in the Hungarian Diet, an unusually populist body for a feudal legislature, in view of the large proportion of Hungarians belonging to the nobility.

If we were to sum up the position of liberalism as a political doctrine and a political movement in Europe during the 1840s, it might be in a series of firm statements, each followed by a qualifier. Liberals were for equal treatment under the law, but their espousal of equality ended when it came to the franchise. Sharing the Enlightenment's criticism of absolutism and a society of orders, liberals supported the ideals of the French Revolution, but not to the point of endorsing democracy or republicanism. A movement self-consciously opposing privilege and representing the people, liberals confined their definition of the people to substantial, educated property owners, at a time when most Europeans were not educated and even more had little or no property. Liberalism was itself a movement of notables, of the influential and affluent. Certainly by the 1840s, most liberals shunned political violence or even taking drastic, peaceful measures. They were reluctant to stir up popular support, preferring a policy of moderation, reform, and cooperation with the existing authorities – only in most of Europe, excepting (naturally, a very important exception at that) France, they had little prospect of obtaining power except by drastic means. It would, in fact, take the drastic, unexpected and often unwanted step of violent revolution in 1848 to bring liberals, however briefly, to power.

Conservatism

Conservatism as a political movement began as a reaction against the challenges posed by the free-thinking ideas of the Enlightenment and the efforts of reforming eighteenth-century monarchs, inspired by Enlightenment ideals. The French Revolution of 1789 greatly magnified these challenges and reshaped conservative opposition to them. Absolutist monarchs and their servants, noble leaders of the estates, along with clergy and their devout lay followers, groups often strongly opposed to each other for centuries before 1789 (and by no means united in rejecting Enlightened reforms), were forced to band together in order to confront the revolutionary movement that threatened the position in state and society of all of them. Although in the end, after a quarter century of warfare, the military threat emerging from revolutionary and Napoleonic France was defeated in 1815, the social and political changes wrought by the revolution could not be completely undone. The possibility of a renewed or even expanded outburst of revolution remained present, as the events of 1820 and again 1830 confirmed. Consequently, conservatives were continuously pressed to maintain their counter-revolutionary stance.

Part of this stance was the development of a positive political doctrine, a justification of conservative positions beyond opposing revolution. The years between 1815 and the revolutions of 1830, the era of the Restoration, were the period of the formation of conservative political thought. Three main themes dominated it, historical tradition, patriarchalism, and divine justification. All three of these contained strong opposition to the principles of the French Revolution.

Conservatives often asserted that governmental institutions should be perceived as living organisms, products of a long historical development, in the course of which particular traditions had been created and become part of the existing state of affairs. A newly written constitution, a declaration of fundamental civic rights, or an entirely new code of law, such as the one promulgated under Napoleon, were impossible in this point of view. These revolutionary actions, conservatives would assert, involved an abstract and universalist view of human beings, while there were only particular governments with their own, historically developed traditions. The imposition of such rationalist documents, conservatives would add, distorted the natural, organic course of historical development. The main proponents of this argument were members of the Historical School of Law, that developed at this time and dominated jurisprudence in Germany for decades to come, but it was a point of view common to conservatives throughout the continent.

The second main theme of conservative thought, patriarchalism, looked on state and society as an expanded version of a family. Adam Müller, a conservative political thinker of the early nineteenth century, and later advisor of Austria's conservative Chancellor Prince Metternich, asserted that a prince was "to his people as a paternal head of household is to his family." Müller described the servile peasantry as "nothing else than the wider family of the noblemen."[7] A king ruled his subject and a lord ruled his serfs with the love and sense of duty appropriate to the paternal role, but could also, in paternal fashion (at least as contemporaries saw child-raising) chastise them if they were disobedient. While this line of argument may seem extremely naive today, it had a number of useful political points. First, it could be used as a criticism of government bureaucracy – often suspected of possessing liberal sympathies. What father, after all, runs his house with the assistance of a tenured civil service? Secondly, it provided a gender-based club with which to beat conservatives' opponents. Conservatives pointed out that if patriarchy was not an appropriate political organizing principle, if all men were equal under the law, as liberals asserted, or should participate actively in politics by possessing the franchise, as the radical left maintained, then why should legal equality or the vote be denied to women? There were no liberals, and, as we shall see, precious few radicals, willing to take on this argument and concede that their own point of view led logically to women's equality of rights with men.

Both tradition and patriarchal power were divinely blessed in conservative thought. Ernst-Ludwig von Gerlach, one of the leading Prussian conservatives, asserted "kings, the institution of monarchy and kingdoms are God's first creation, and in their very essence sacred."[8] This is rather different from the liberal conception of a monarch deriving his powers from a distinctly human, written constitution. Conservatives wished to see an organized and established church in charge of public education and public morality. Their ideal government was a "Christian state," whose fundamental precepts would be taken from the teachings of revealed religion, and not from a rationalist Rights of Man, as Enlightened thinkers, the French revolutionaries of 1789, and their nineteenth-century followers wished. Indeed, religiously based conservative opposition to the principles of the French Revolution had something of the apocalyptic to it. Friedrich Wilhelm IV, the conservative and devout King of Prussia, was given to describing the French Revolution as the Beast of the Book of Revelation (the one whose number is 666), and this feeling of being engaged in a struggle between divinely blessed good and satanic evil was not unusual for European conservatives in the

---

[7] Quotes from Robert M. Berdahl, *The Politics of the Prussian Nobility: The Development of a Conservative Ideology, 1770–1848* (Princeton, 1988), 173, 175.

[8] Quoted in Hans-Christof Kraus, *Ernst Ludwig von Gerlach. Politisches Denken und Handeln eines preussischen Altkonservativen*, 2 vols. (Göttingen, 1994) 1: 219.

first half of the nineteenth century. We can see this crusading spirit in the response of Friedrich Wilhelm IV in 1847 to liberal demands that he grant a constitution. The monarch proclaimed that "no power on earth will succeed in moving Me to transform that natural relationship between ruler and people . . . into a legalistic or constitutional one and I will never allow a written piece of paper to come between Our Lord God in heaven and this country."[9]

If conservatives supported organized religion, the churches usually returned the favor. Connections between conservative politics and adherents of religious renewal in the first half of the nineteenth century were particularly close. The Jesuits and Redemptorists, whose "popular missions" began in France after 1815 to combat the ravages done to the church during the revolutionary era, consistently informed the faithful that besides attending mass regularly, taking communion, venerating the Virgin Mary, and avoiding drinking, dancing, and fornication, they should also obey the orders of the restored Bourbon dynasty. The revolution of 1830, that overthrew the Bourbons' conservative regime, included a wave of attacks on its clerical supporters.

Much the same was the case among Protestant revivalists. The brothers Ernst Ludwig (whose opinions about a divinely endowed monarchy were cited above) and Leopold von Gerlach, the organizers of an assertively and self-consciously conservative group among the Prussian nobility and higher bureaucracy in the 1830s, were both prominent lay supporters of revivalism and found many of their supporters in revivalist circles. One of their main finds was an obstreperous young nobleman named Otto von Bismarck, who came to their cause after marrying a young woman from the pious Puttkamer family and being converted to her way of thinking about religion. Although Bismarck's glory days would come later, in the 1860s, he began his political career in 1848 as a spokesman for the extreme right in Prussian politics.

This alliance of "throne and altar," as contemporaries described it, generally worked well for subjects of the same confession as their royal family. But what happened when king and subject belonged to different religions? Did a devout and otherwise conservative Roman Catholic owe allegiance to a Protestant King of Prussia, a Protestant to a Catholic King of Bavaria, an Eastern Orthodox Serb to a Catholic Habsburg Emperor? Answers both clergy and laity gave to these questions varied and weakened the conservative political potential in religious devotion present when monarch and his subjects were of the same confession.

---

[9] Quoted in David Barclay, *Frederick William IV and the Prussian Monarchy 1840–1861* (Oxford, 1995), 128.

Yet conflicts arising out of confessional differences could also help promote conservatism as a political movement. The Roman Catholic noblemen of the Prussian province of Westphalia put themselves forward, quite ostentatiously, as supporters of the Catholic Church in its struggles against the Protestant government. In doing so, they hoped to gain popular support and divert the peasants' attention away from the nobility's stubborn insistence on preserving its seigneurial rights, object of scathing criticism by the province's liberals. Much the same attitude was taken by the nobility of Croatia, who strongly disliked the program of Hungarian liberals, because it demanded both the introduction of the Magyar language and the abolition of serfdom. The nobles positioned themselves as defenders of the Catholic faith against the Hungarian liberals, many of whom were from Calvinist families.

Conservative views on society and economy were often heavily colored by political and religious positions. Traditionalism and paternalism were frequent leitmotifs, conservatives calling for the predominance of agriculture in the economy, the preservation of feudal and seigneurial privileges, and the continued existence or reintroduction of the guilds. Prussian conservative Ernst-Ludwig von Gerlach explained that these forms of social and economic organization were of divine origin. "It is a truth," he wrote, "that God Himself has ordained the orders of society and their ranking from the highest to the least."[10] Such divinely inspired institutions were the conservative answer to the social problems of the first half of the nineteenth century. Employers, whether large landowners, substantial farmers, master craftsmen or manufacturers, should treat their hired help as a father treats his children. Charitable assistance to the poor on the part of those more fortunate was another conservative and Biblically mandated response to difficult economic circumstances.

Laissez-faire, industrialization, and economic individualism, all of which went against conservatives' notions of a divinely inspired hierarchical social order, often drew conservative fire. Prominent right-wing politicians, from Austrian Chancellor Metternich to the Prussian king Friedrich Wilhelm III, were skeptical about the usefulness of railroads and even openly fearful of their revolutionary effect on society. The thundering denunciation of industrial capitalism by the south German, Catholic-conservative social theorist Franz von Baader, with his merciless dissection of the alienation of the factory labor force, is strikingly reminiscent of socialist polemics. Perhaps best summing up this point of view, Count Villeneuve-Bargemont, a prominent French Legitimist, wrote a

---

[10] Cited in Kraus, *Ernst-Ludwig von Gerlach*, 1: 201.

Christian Political Economy, praising the social values of charity and paternalism, and denouncing the godless individualism of Adam Smith.

Yet just as it is exaggerated to see liberals as solidly in favor of *laissez-faire* and industrialization, it is equally questionable to understand conservatives as resolute defenders of economic traditionalism against the forces of industrial and free-trading modernity. The large landholding nobility of the eastern provinces of the kingdom of Prussia, as a group pronouncedly right wing, hostile to constitutionalism, supportive of the semi-feudal provincial estates and strongly loyal to its monarch, had made itself quite at home in the world of agricultural capitalism following the agrarian reforms of the early decades of the century. These same landowners were among the staunchest partisans of free trade in Germany, given their strong interest in grain, timber, and wool exports, and in the duty-free import of manufactured goods. Religiously devout industrialists – the pious Catholics of northern France or the Protestant revivalists of the Wuppertal in western Germany – effortlessly combined hard-headed business sense with right-wing politics.

This last paragraph suggests something of the social basis of conservatism as political movement. It was, in many ways a mirror-image of the supporters of liberalism. Those elite groups that benefited from the absolutist state and the privileges of the estates – nobility, leading government officials, senior officers of the armed forces – were both leaders and much of the rank and file of the conservative cause. Conservatism also possessed an appeal to the devout from all social classes, and this appeal would prove a true strength for conservatives in the period of mass politics opened up by the revolution of 1848.

This political potential of religious devotion was not entirely apparent before the outbreak of the revolution and for much of the 1840s conservatives in Europe found themselves on the defensive. Ensconced in the structures of power and privilege throughout most of the continent, conservatives saw with apprehension the growth of oppositional movements, the increasing liberal demand for a constitution, and the development of even more threatening forms of radical and socialist forms of political opposition. Their own future seemed increasingly problematic. Austrian Chancellor Prince Metternich, the great architect of conservative politics in Europe since 1815, soldiered on in existential despair, knowing that the political order he worked to uphold could not stand indefinitely, yet striving to preserve it as long as he could.

In France, as was so often the case, circumstances were somewhat different. A liberal regime had been in power there since the revolution of 1830, and conservatives had to face the problem of political activity in opposition, lacking the possibilities open to those in the government, holding the reins of power. There were four possible options practiced by conservatives under these circumstances. One was boycotting politics, refusing to take the oath of loyalty to the Orléans monarch Louis-Philippe, come to power via a liberal revolution that had overthrown the traditional ruling Bourbon dynasty. Much of the nobility of western France took this option, as did many of the bishops of the Catholic Church, who conspicuously refused to pray for the welfare of the king on St. Philip's day.

Another, quite different possibility was to join the political game under the liberal regime, campaign for office, compete in elections, and strive for political power. A prime advocate of this point of view was the Marseilles attorney Pierre-Antoine Berryer, one of the great courtroom orators of his day. He and his followers attempted to exploit the economic grievances of merchants and landowners of southern France, who had an interest in free trade for the export of agricultural products and were skeptical of the government's protectionist policy of encouraging industrial development, largely in the north of the country. Pursuing an oppositional role, these conservatives even forged electoral alliances with the left-wing republican opposition, achieving a certain success, albeit at the cost of renouncing what many on the right, including the Legitimist pretender to the throne, regarded as basic political principles.

Yet another alternative, increasingly popular in the 1840s, was for conservatives to rally to the regime. To be sure, it was still a liberal government, born out of revolution and representing religious viewpoints conservatives found less than tasteful. Yet it was also a guarantor of order, a protector of property, and a potential bulwark against radicalism and socialism. In the light of the threats posed by the latter movements, some conservatives felt, the differences between themselves and the liberals were of lesser significance.

Finally, we can point to a different orientation, compatible with any of these specifically political strategies, namely a concentration on religious affairs. Conservatives were involved in founding St. Vincent de Paul societies to provide charitable assistance to the poor; they assisted the Catholic Church in its efforts to rally and regroup the faithful. These varied efforts testified to the popularity of religious issues in conservative politics, often much greater than other tenets of conservative doctrines.

All four of these themes would reappear in 1848. In the politically wide-open situation created by the revolution, conservatives would strive to restore traditional dynasties; they would take part energetically in mass politics and parliamentarism. At crucial moments, moments reoccurring throughout the course of the revolutionary events, conservatives would be found supporting and allied with liberals against the threat of the extreme left. 1848 would also see a strong and often quite successful politicization of the practice of orthodox religion. These developments would prove that political conservatives, in spite of their open contempt for democracy, were quite capable of practicing it.

Radicalism

Even more than the other two main political doctrines, radicalism in mid-nineteenth-century Europe was dominated by the heritage of the French Revolution. The experience of the republican phase of the revolution, the rule of the Jacobins and their successors in France, and their efforts to export their doctrines throughout the continent were both a model for and a challenge to leftists a half-century later. Radicals drew much of their inspiration and symbolism from the great revolution. In the 1840s, leftists all across Europe sang the Marseillaise, officially banned in monarchical France as a republican anthem. They waved tricolor flags, each national group having its own three colors, called for liberty, equality, and fraternity, wore Phrygian caps, planted trees of liberty, denounced their opponents as aristocrats, and even made surreptitious references to the guillotine.

Yet at the same time, radicals were aware that a simple repetition of the events of 1793 was insufficient to the realities of a later time, so they strove to improve upon the original Jacobin model. Giuseppe Mazzini, the dominant figure in Italian left-wing politics from the 1830s through the 1870s, explained that the Jacobin radicalism of the French Revolution expressed the "individualism" of the eighteenth century. "Association" would be the soul of nineteenth-century radicalism, and its center would no longer be in France but in Italy. A similar version of this idea that a nineteenth-century revolution would have a different theme and be centered in a different country than the original one of 1789 can be found in Karl Marx's and Friedrich Engels' *Communist Manifesto*. The manifesto's concluding action program explains that the important nineteenth-century bourgeois revolution is soon to occur in Germany, and it will be different from the previous century's in France, since it will quickly be transformed into another, more radical, "proletarian" form of revolutionary struggle. This whole notion of a new and different revolution was symbolized by the red flag, which during 1848 and 1849 would be flown sometimes in opposition to, sometimes as a supplement to the tricolor of left-wing politics.

If we inquire into the content of the political doctrines expressed by these symbols, we might suggest that the basis of radicalism lay in the idea of popular sovereignty. Ultimate political power came from the people, and was exercised by their democratically elected representatives. Such a democratic political system required for its proper operation the protection of the exercise of basic civic freedoms – assembly, association, speech, the press. In this respect, radical doctrine was similar to liberal ideals and their support for basic civil rights. Both movements also claimed to represent the people, but mid-nineteenth-century radicals, unlike liberals, were democrats. Equality under the law also meant equal rights of political participation; the "people" included all adult males, not just a group of property owners. Radicals were also republicans: they had little interest in a monarchical head of state. Most liberals, it will be recalled, wanted a hereditary ruler as the head of the executive branch of government in order to check, most effectively, the power of the legislature. The republicanism of the left implied a disagreement with this view of the state; unlike liberals, most radicals wanted a strong, active, interventionist government.

Radical activism went beyond proposed future forms of government to encompass current political activity as well. Italian radicals defined themselves as the "party of action," those willing to take the initiative against absolutist and foreign rulers of the peninsula, contrasting themselves to liberals, who might have shared some of these goals, but did nothing but talk about them. Democrats were behind the many abortive uprisings in the almost two decades between the 1830 and 1848 revolutions. Mid-nineteenth-century leftists were a warlike group, their plans for revolution including advocacy of a great European war to destroy their counter-revolutionary opponents.

Anti-clericalism was a sentiment shared by radicals and liberals, only in the former it was carried to extremes. Vehement hostility towards an established church and a disdainful attitude towards revealed religion were characteristic of leftists across Europe in the 1840s. In Protestant areas, this anti-clericalism often took the form of Unitarianism, of the advocacy of a Christianity stripped of its supernatural trappings and transformed into a this-worldly gospel of freedom and democracy. Among Catholics, radical anti-clericalism was sharper, usually going along with a rejection of Christianity in favor of a vague Deism – a favorite idea of Mazzini, and of most Italian radicals – or of open atheism. For most of the two decades prior to the revolution of 1848, the advocacy of anti-clericalism was one of the main forms by which radicalism, in most places a strictly prohibited doctrine, was openly expressed. A government official in the Grand Duchy of Tuscany described the radicals of the town of Montevarchi, a stronghold of the democrats in the mid 1830s, as "[those] troublemakers, and even including the little boys, who have come to dare to speak against the priests and those who praise them. They pour ridicule on Saint Philomena and other sacred things, saying that they are all just the priests' lottery ticket offices and similar remarks."[11]

The reader may have noted that up to now I have said little about the social and economic views of leftists, even though in most of the twentieth century it was precisely these issues that defined left and right. This was noticeably less the case in the 1840s; democrats' views on social and economic issues were both heterogeneous, probably more so than those of other political groupings, and in rapid transition to boot. Reading the social and economic issues of the late nineteenth and twentieth centuries back into the revolution of 1848 is a common but particularly distorting way to understand the events of those years; to do better we must look at left-wing thought of the time without being unduly impressed by its future developments.

There were democrats whose social and economic views were virtually indistinguishable from those of liberals, that is who believed that society was composed of property-owning adult males, and felt that such a society worked best when it was self-regulating, free from governmental interference. While such views were in harmony with the liberal political ideal of constitutional monarchism they seemed out of place for radicals, given their belief in universal manhood suffrage – even for non-property owners – and their advocacy of an activist state. Most radicals did see a virtue in governmental intervention in social and economic issues, although usually in a very different way from the welfare state ideals of the twentieth century. One good way to characterize leftist views on this question might be the two extraordinarily popular slogans coined by the southwest German radical Friedrich Hecker on the eve of and at the outbreak of the 1848 revolution. Hecker asserted that the government should act so as to secure "liberty, affluence and education for all." Exactly what the state should do to secure these ends is in part explained by Hecker's second slogan, which demanded a "rectification of the disproportion between capital and labor." To realize such demands, Hecker and many other radicals called for greatly increased state aid for elementary and technical education, state-subsidized low interest loans to farmers, craftsmen, and small businessmen, perhaps further government credits for the founding of producers' cooperatives, public works for the unemployed, and a redistribution of the burdens of taxation away from the common people to the wealthy via a progressive income tax.

None of these policies involved a repudiation of the idea of a society consisting of adult male property owners, nor were they an attack on the

---

[11] Cited in Franco Della Peruta, *Mazzini e i revolutionari italiani. Il "partito d'azione" 1830–1845* (Milan, 1974), 241.

market economy. Rather, this version of radical social and economic thought – and it was probably the most common – asserted that the workings of society and economy, whether natural or otherwise, were making it difficult for ever more adult males to own property. In view of the actual path of social development in Europe during the first half of the nineteenth century, there was something to these fears. But far from breaking with the ideal of a society of property owners, these radicals proposed to use the power of the state to bring it to fruition. They wished to rectify the disproportion between capital and labor, not abolish it altogether.

It was the socialists who wanted to do that. Socialism had an initial pioneering phase in the 1820s, when the first theorists of socialism or communism, the English industrialist Robert Owen, and the French authors Henri de Saint-Simon and Charles Fourier, condemned capitalist exploitation of labor and the alienation of the industrial worker and proposed the ideas of economic planning, collective control over the workplace, and the abolition of private property. In the two subsequent decades these ideas were taken up by less original thinkers but more effective propagandists and given a wider circulation. Typical socialists of this period included the French trio Louis Blanc, Pierre-Joseph Proudhon, and Etienne Cabet – the last probably the most prominent socialist in Europe before 1848 – the German tailor Wilhelm Weitling and a whole galaxy of German intellectuals who called themselves the "true socialists."

Characteristic of this later group of communists was that they all began their political careers as democratic radicals; in this sense, communism as a political movement emerged from mid-nineteenth-century radicalism. Communists, of course, opposed most democrats' conception of a society of adult male property owners, but they also broke with the democrats on another major issue, namely the significance and nature of political action. Most communists rejected democratic radicals' activities in secret societies, their revolutionary conspiracies, and their aspirations towards a renewed Jacobin republic. These seemed irrelevant beside the socialist plans for social and economic reorganization, to be brought about in peaceful and voluntary fashion. Precisely this reorganization of society would make a political revolution unnecessary.

French followers of Charles Fourier published a newspaper entitled, significantly, *La Démocratie Pacifique*, that is the peaceful, or non-violent democracy. Etienne Cabet produced a work, *The Voyage to Icaria*, in 1838, describing a trip to an imaginary communist utopia. During the 1840s he spread the doctrine among his followers, the "Icarians," through his newspaper, *Le Populaire*, with a circulation of some 5,000 in 1846, by

far the leading exponent of the communist view in Europe. Cabet's effective communist propaganda was always directed to creating Icaria in the
existing society, rather than overthrowing that society to create his ideal
communist regime. Quickly disillusioned with revolutionary politics in
1848, he would call on his followers to actually build his utopia in
Illinois, a dubious project that came to an unhappy end.

In Germany, the communist distrust of radical politics went even
further than in France. The "true socialists" rejected opposition to
absolutism or a society of orders, since it would merely lead to a liberal-
capitalist social and political order, which, as socialists, they wished
to abolish. As the journalist Karl Grün, one of the leading true socialists
put it, the liberal demand for a constitution in the kingdom of Prussia was
just "an egoistical wish of the possessing classes."[12] In making this assertion, Grün rather skipped the question of how the true socialists could
spread their ideas – to say nothing of realizing them – without the guarantees of freedom of speech and of the press to be found in a constitutional
regime. In this respect, one should resist the instinctive tendency, stemming from the experiences of the twentieth century, to see the communists
of the 1840s as being on the extreme left. It might be fairer to say that mid-
nineteenth-century socialists were the first of many groups attempting to
mark out a position beyond the left–right political spectrum.

There was, however, one respect in which socialists were more advanced
than any other political movement of the day, and that was in regard to the
position of women. Conservatives' patriarchal principles led them to deny
legal equality to most adult males, to say nothing of women. The liberal
political universe of property owners was an exclusively male one; women
were represented in it by their husbands or fathers. Even most democrats
went no further than to assert the necessity of companionate marriage,
since a man who was a tyrant to his wife could hardly be a good citizen of a
republic, and to suggest that women should play a political role in bringing
up children to be good republican citizens. Guiseppe Ricciardi, a leading radical in Naples, felt that this female maternal role as "humans' first
educator," made it appropriate for women to have the vote, but Ricciardi's
advocacy of women's suffrage – very unusual among European radicals in
the middle of the nineteenth century – did not mean that he saw women as
equal to men in public life, for he felt that women should not be eligible for
election to most public offices.[13]

---

[12] Cited in Sperber, *Rhineland Radicals*, 123.
[13] On Ricciardi and his ideas about women's suffrage, see Enrica Di Ciommo, *La nazione possible. Mezzogiorno e questione nazionale nel 1848* (Milan, 1993), esp. 178.

Communists, by contrast, were quite enthusiastic proponents of the equality of women with men and of the emancipation of women. Exactly what they meant by that was not entirely clear, indeed hotly disputed among communists, both male and female. It was certainly not today's feminist conception of equal political rights and equal opportunities at work for women. It did seem to include, though, some idea of reform of marriage and divorce laws, a vision of a society in which women would not be subject to male patriarchal authority, an insistence on the equal dignity of men and women, and a commitment to female participation in the communist movement. Such views struck a sympathetic chord among some women and the first proponents of women's political rights in France, who went public with their ideas in 1848 and 1849, had come to politics via communism and socialism.

Democrats reacted with suspicion to the emergence of socialist ideas within their ranks. Many radicals denounced the communist demand for the abolition of private property. Writing on this issue tended to bring out the most turgid in their prose styles; a witty exception came from the pen of the democratic French historian Jules Michelet. Commenting on Pierre-Joseph Proudhon's widely circulated communist slogan, "Property is theft," Michelet remarked that if property was theft, then there were twenty million thieves in France. His *bon mot* had an additional political point, reaffirming the possibility of a society of small property owners that 1840s democrats frequently advocated. Radicals were also worried by the communists' renunciation of political struggle, a particular problem in those parts of Europe, which, unlike France, lacked a constitution and any guarantees of civil liberties.

Nonetheless, there were also signs of a reconciliation of communists and democrats or perhaps a merging of the two only partially separate groups before 1848. Rhetorically, democrats began borrowing phrases from the communist vocabulary, most prominently Louis Blanc's celebrated call for "the organization of labor," a vague demand as easily compatible with a society of property owners as one without property at all. Organizationally, in the world of secret societies, republicanism and communism began to merge. A pioneer in this development was the veteran French conspirator Louis-Auguste Blanqui, who gave an increasingly communist coloring to the secret societies he led. It was Blanqui who invented the expression, "the dictatorship of the proletariat," to describe the regime he imagined would emerge from his planned revolution and the civil war sure to follow.

For posterity, the most famous of these merged communist-democrats were Karl Marx and Friedrich Engels. Having had experiences during the decade of the 1840s with both radical democrats and especially with the "true socialists" in Germany itself and abroad in England and France, Marx and Engels broke with most German socialists on the issue of political action, pointing out that destroying the rule of absolutism in Prussia was a necessary pre-condition for any future socialism. In the *Communist Manifesto* of 1847, written as a political program for the Communist League, a secret society composed of *émigré* German artisans and intellectuals, they went further and asserted that a communist social and economic order could only be realized via a political revolution and a Jacobin republic. This combination of political and social argument would be the wave of the future, but it was still a minority view before 1848.

It is important not to exaggerate the importance of any form of socialist doctrine in this period. Socialism did have a certain influence in France. On the eve of the 1848 revolution tens of thousands, including many craftsmen and laborers in urban areas, had become acquainted with its doctrines. These doctrines were also known in the German states, although mostly among intellectuals; lower-class Germans who had become acquainted with them were likely to have learned them abroad, in Paris, Brussels or London, where many German journeymen artisans had gone looking for work. In the rest of Europe, the specific ideas of socialism were little known. What did exist was the fear they inspired, the "red menace," or, as the *Communist Manifesto* put it, the "specter of communism." Under this rubric, though, were many fears of property owners that had little to do with any specific social doctrine. Serfs rebelling against their feudal lords, peasants seizing wood from the forests, craftsmen demanding a return of the guilds, artisans and laborers going on strike – all these actions were described, and feared, as communism, although most of those inspiring such fears knew nothing of the organization of labor, and either owned property themselves or strongly desired to do so.

As for the communist movement itself, although historical analogies are a notoriously tricky business, it might be helpful to compare the socialists of the 1840s with the "green" environmentalists in Europe during the 1970s and 80s. Both political movements emerged largely from the left of their day, but both asserted that they sought a way to go beyond the standard conflict of left and right, to introduce new issues into politics and a new way of engaging in political action. Ultimately, both movements found themselves back as part of the left from which they had emerged, though not without first causing a good deal of conflict but also getting leftists to think about new questions and confront new political issues.

Moving on from radical political doctrines to radicalism as a political movement, it might be appropriate at this point to consider the supporters and organizations of the political left in Europe during the 1840s. Both had been strongly marked by a change occurring at and shortly after the revolution of 1830. Prior to that date, radicalism as a political movement was still directly tied to the experience of the Jacobin phase of the French Revolution. Leftists tended to be old Jacobins, or their descendants, members of French families, for instance, who had bought church property that had been nationalized during the revolution, or of German and Italian families who had collaborated with the invading French revolutionary and Napoleonic armies.

In terms of social structure, radicals of the 1820s were not all that different from liberals of the time, both groups drawing primarily on free-thinking notables for their supporters. Radicals might have been somewhat more likely to be professionals; liberals, businessmen, and property owners, but the distinctions were not great. This similarity in membership was also found in political position and attitudes towards the government. In the highly conservative atmosphere of Restoration Europe, liberals had been almost as suspicious to the ruling powers as radicals; the two groups had cooperated in opposing conservative regimes.

The 1830 revolution produced a drastic change. First, the new liberal regimes stemming from the revolution in France, Belgium, and the Swiss cantons, opened up new possibilities for political organization and agitation. Political action was increasingly legalized; political distinctions became more apparent. Such possibilities were not limited to the citizens of these countries: *émigrés* from the absolutist regimes in central, eastern, and southern Europe could organize and conspire in Paris, Brussels, Zürich, or Marseilles. Secondly, the policies of the new liberal regimes helped sharpen differences between liberals and radicals, blurred during the Restoration. The 1830 revolution in France, for instance, led not to a republic but a monarchy with a different dynasty on the throne. Those with the right to vote went from being 3 percent to 5 percent of the adult male population, a far cry from the democratic demand for universal manhood suffrage. Over the five years following the 1830 revolution, radicals became increasingly discontent with a regime that most liberals supported.

These events coincided with a generational change in the adherents of radicalism. From being a political movement associated with veterans of past events, leftism became increasingly associated with youth. Giuseppe Mazzini was one of the first to realize this, and for that reason he named his conspiratorial secret society "Young Italy." When Mazzini talked of the "youth" who were to be the vanguard of the liberation of Italy from tyranny and foreign occupation, he meant educated youth, students, and recent graduates; this points to an important social development, which impinged on radical politics. The growth in secondary and higher education in this period, along with the stagnation in the number of jobs available to university graduates, produced a growing number of unemployed or underemployed intellectuals and professionals who increasingly became activists on and leaders of the left.

"Youth" was not restricted to the educated classes. Increasingly, younger artisans, that is, journeymen, were becoming involved with the left, joining secret societies and discussing socialist ideas. The gradually declining standards of living of the urban lower classes, the growth of capitalist forms of production, and the concomitant decline in craftsmen's control over their own labor encouraged them to think about radical social and political demands. Artisans brought their own experiences to political radicalism: they tended to understand socialist doctrines in the light of their own present or past experiences with guilds. Traditional guilds had, after all, carried out the "organization of labor"; socialist or radical democratic ideas along these lines found a ready audience. Gradually, the democratic movement became more democratic, both in terms of the number and the social class of its potential supporters.

Three qualifications about this description of the supporters of democratic politics are in order. First, the idea of radicalism as a youth movement should not be exaggerated. The 1848 revolution, was not, as some over-enthusiastic scholars in the 1960s had it, a generational struggle. If young people were disproportionately over-represented among radicals, there were still many older professionals and master craftsmen on the left. Secondly, the extent of popular support for the left followed a familiar north–south, west–east political pattern. As one moved away from the economically advanced, politically sophisticated regions of western Europe, radicalism became ever more of a matter for the educated upper classes. In Poland and Hungary, where the numerous nobility made up virtually the entire political class, one found the curious circumstance that most democrats were nobles. Finally, and perhaps most importantly, the spread of democratic or especially socialist ideas was confined almost totally to urban areas. Peasants – and once again, remember that most Europeans were peasants – knew nothing of these radical ideas before 1848, and democrats rarely gave much thought to mobilizing the peasantry. The majority of the people were invisible to those who stood for majority rule.

By the mid-1840s, radicalism as a political movement had become strongly differentiated across Europe. In France, there existed a wide variety of left-wing politics, expressed in forms ranging from legal and respectable newspapers to conspiratorial secret societies, with social and economic ideas going from *laissez-faire* to total collectivization, and favoring modes of political struggle stretching from putschism to a parliamentary alliance with the more left wing of the liberals. Such an extraordinary multiplicity was very much the exception, reflecting the legal provisions of constitutionalism, the advanced social and economic conditions, and the history of a modern political life dating back to 1789.

Throughout most of Europe, excepting perhaps some of the more isolated and backward provinces of the Habsburg monarchy, or the Danubian Principalities, there had developed clear distinctions between democratic and liberal opponents of absolutist rule and a society of orders. A good example of this was the yearly meeting of oppositional parliamentary deputies from the smaller constitutional states of southern and southwestern Germany. Occurring yearly since 1839, this gathering of parliamentarians split in 1847 into two groups: a radical one, meeting in Offenburg (it was there that Friedrich Hecker had proposed rectifying the disproportion between capital and labor), and a liberal one in Heppenheim, a few months later. Similar fissures within the leaders of the parliamentary opposition in Hungary were also occurring at about that time. The restrictions of censorship and the prohibition on the formation of political association made it difficult, however, to articulate these differences publicly and bring them to a broader audience. This was even more the case with differences among radicals themselves.

Yet leftists of all political nuances throughout the continent had one thing in common. They were determined opponents of the existing regimes. Even when they considered working within them, as some were willing to do in the constitutional monarchies, they looked forward to a time when these governments would be drastically transformed. Radicals were the party of the revolution. In 1848, they got what they wanted – or what they thought they did, since the advent of democracy in continental Europe would turn out differently from the way its partisans had imagined.

Nationalism

The discussion of political doctrines in the previous section has left out one factor so crucial that it needs to be handled separately, namely nationalism. Both political doctrines and political actions in mid-nineteenth century Europe are not completely comprehensible without taking nationalism into account. Yet for a decisive factor in political affairs, nationalism was an extraordinarily problematic matter. The modern concept of a nation underlying the idea of nationalism was just coming into existence at the time and was far from universally accepted, or even understood; the principles of nationalism, if consequently applied, would have meant the demolition of most political arrangements as they existed in Europe.

In 1846, the Czech journalist Karel Havliček offered a definition of nations and nationalism that captures well the dominant opinion about them on the eve of the 1848 revolution: "A people or nation means, in the purest and most ideal sense, a substantial proportion of the human race who share a common descent, possess their own particular language, form a distinct community (a state), adhere to a particular religion and are clearly differentiated by particular characteristics and customs from other nations."[14] The definition notes the division of human society into distinct, autonomous groups called nations – defined, among other reasons, by common background, history, customs, and, especially, language. Havliček's definition and with it nationalist doctrine went on to assert – and this assertion is what made and still makes the doctrine politically so explosive – that these nations were not just a cultural but a political community. As such, they would be the primary focus of the individuals' loyalty in public life, and therefore every nation should be in control of its own destiny, should have its own nation-state. In other words, nationalists favored national self-determination – a concept that existed by the 1840s, although the actual phrase itself comes from a later part of the century. In theory, this was a simple doctrine, but applying it in practice proved both difficult and violent. Just who constituted a nation and who belonged to one – and which one – was by no means so self-evident as nationalists thought. Even given agreement on the existence of nations, the process by which they would be able to determine themselves, by which they could come to have their own autonomous political entities, was both torturous and conflict-laden.

The problems for nationalism began with the majority of Europeans. They were peasants, frequently uneducated, many illiterate, speaking their own local and regional dialects, very different from the more widely spread educated and written languages of literature, newspapers, and public affairs. The peasants' sense of group identity did not conform to the nationalist model either: they might describe the inhabitants of the neighboring village as "foreigners"; their primary loyalties in public life, in so far as they ever considered them, were likely to be to their village, their religion, and perhaps their ruling royal family, if they had a long

---

[14] Cited in Jiři Kořalka, "Welche Nationalvorstellungen gab es 1848 in Mitteleuropa?" in Rudolf Jaworski and Robert Luft (eds.), *1848/49 Revolutionen in Ostmitteleuropa* (Munich, 1996), 40–41.

experience of rule by the same dynasty. With the partial exception of some of the inhabitants of the French countryside, it was hard for peasants to see themselves as part of the "nation," since they lacked the common language, culture, and sense of destiny required for it. Although nationalists would often claim that the true spirit of their nation resided in the soil and those who lived upon it, the truth was that the nation, and the nationalism that went with it, stemmed from the urban population, especially members of the educated, professional middle class.

The first experiences of nationhood, in a "national theater," or a national literary and cultural society belonged to this social group. Scholarly and learned lectures on the national language or national history were monuments of a developing nationalism. In the early decades of the nineteenth century, secondary school and university students were among the most passionate nationalists; universities and theological seminaries common birthplaces of nationalist movements. The social context of nationalism seems very similar to that of liberal and radical movements of the time, and in the first half of the nineteenth century, nationalism was a movement unquestionably on the left side of the political spectrum. Much of the spirit and the militancy in both movements stemmed from their advocacy of national self-determination and nationalism was integrally connected with their basic political concepts. Both liberals and radicals claimed to represent the people. If you asked them what defined these people as a group, they would answer – and here we can see once more one of the many heritages of 1789 for nineteenth-century political thought and action – that the people were constituted as a nation. National and political self-determination were completely intertwined.

For the same reasons, conservatives strongly opposed nationalism. If one took seriously the idea that the nation was the highest political principle, then dynastic and religious loyalty would have to be subordinated to it, the position of the absolutist monarch and the feudal privileges of the estates judged by it. The conservative idea of tradition and legitimacy as the basis for political rule was strongly opposed to nationalist principles, since existing dynasties, especially the Habsburgs, but others as well, ruled over more than one national group. The many princes of Germany and Italy insisted on their sovereignty, although nationalism would have implied that their realms should be dissolved in favor of a nation state, or incorporated within it.

If, as conservatives generally thought, the existing state of political affairs was the expression of divine will, then nationalism appeared as the enemy of Christianity. Prussian conservatives denounced "nationalist sectarian fanaticism," condemning German nationalists as adherents of "modern heathenism" who had turned the nation into an "idol of worship."[15] Although this vehement denunciation may appear strange today, when both political conservatism and organized religion have come to accept, and, indeed, to embrace, nationalism, it catches an important aspect of nationalism in the first half of the nineteenth century. It was a very powerful alternative source of loyalty and personal meaning for individuals, standing in sharp contrast to those based on dynasty or religion.

Within these general conditions of nations and nationalism, there were many individual variations, related to the level of social and economic development, to the state in which the nation, or potential nation lived, and the historical experiences that could be claimed by each aspiring national group. Not always entirely clear to contemporaries through most of the 1840s, these differences would emerge drastically in the spring of 1848, and play a major role in shaping the events of the mid-century revolution. Let us consider some of these differences in nation and nationalism, moving east across Europe, starting in France.

Nation and nationalism in France

The modern nationalist political program was invented in France in 1789, and by the 1840s it was the nation that seemed closest to fulfilling it. Increasing public education, along with the spread of trade, culture, and communication, were gradually bringing the French language to the countryfolk, helping to create a linguistically unified national area. The French realm, with its celebrated hexagonal shape, and its unitary legal and administrative system, provided a state for the nation. Finally, the events of the great revolution and the era of Napoleon had created a common historical experience that might be judged very differently by people from different social classes and different political positions but which no one could evade.

It was this last point, though, that gave French nationalism of the mid-nineteenth century its distinctive character, for it was strongly identified with one man, the one-time emperor, Napoleon Bonaparte. Particularly to a popular audience, but not exclusively to it, he embodied the sense of nationhood that had emerged from the era of revolution and revolutionary wars. This sentiment was kept alive by the reminiscences of the hundreds of thousands of old soldiers of Napoleon's armies (whose memories of past warfare grew fonder the further they were from its actual experience) and

---

[15] Cited in Alfred von Martin, "Weltanschauliche Motiven im altenkonservativen Denken," in Gerhard Albert Ritter (ed.), *Die deutschen Parteien vor 1918* (Cologne, 1973), 158–59.

by a flood of lithographs, fly-sheets, and cheap pamphlets glorifying the emperor's accomplishments, sold by wandering peddlers all across France and even beyond its borders. During the revolution of 1830 that overthrew the Restoration-era Bourbon dynasty, most of the slogans and cheering, both in Paris and in the provinces, called for the return of a Bonaparte to France, not for a member of the liberal Orléans branch of the royal family to mount the throne, as he did. Once in power, King Louis-Philippe did his best to co-opt Napoleonic nationalism, by completing the construction of the Arc de Triomphe in Paris, begun by Napoleon to celebrate his armies' victories, and by holding a gigantic funeral ceremony in 1840, on the return of the emperor's remains from their long exile in St. Helena.

Napoleon himself was safely dead, and in no position to protest the use and misuse of his name, but, awkwardly, he had left family and heirs behind. His son lived virtually his entire life as a prisoner in Vienna and died very young, but his nephew Louis-Napoleon Bonaparte proclaimed himself the emperor's heir and took to calling himself Napoleon III. Always a political adventurer and active conspirator, Louis-Napoleon, following intrigues in Rome connected with the revolution of 1830 there, set his sights on France. He tried to seize power twice, once in 1836, and again in 1840, both times by making a dramatic appearance in a major garrison town and calling on the soldiers to rally to him, hoping to achieve the same success his uncle had obtained, when he escaped from exile in Elba in 1815 and briefly resumed his rule in France. Neither effort of the nephew was up to the great Napoleon's standards, and the second attempt, when the imperial pretender and his co-conspirators emerged in Boulogne, following a rough crossing of the English Channel, so sea-sick that they could hardly stand, much less carry out a *coup d'état*, had distinct elements of farce. However, both attempts, the widely publicized trial following the second, and Louis-Napoleon's subsequent imprisonment in a fortress (from which he escaped in 1846), established him firmly in the public mind as the heir to Napoleon and the claimant on any future revival of a Napoleonically tinged French nationalism, as the events of 1848 would demonstrate in a most dramatic way.

Nations and nationalism in Italy and Germany

Moving east and south towards Italy and Germany, we find both the sense of the nation and the state to which the nation should belong substantially more problematic than in France. There certainly existed a common literary language in the two countries. Particularly among the educated population, and, to a lesser extent, among townspeople generally, there had developed a sense of the common destiny appropriate to a nationalist movement. The nation, however, could not yet claim a priority on all or even most individuals' loyalty. Dynasty, region, and confession were powerful competitors of the nation, and were arguably more influential, especially in the countryside. If the nation of the nation-state was more uncertain in Germany and Italy than in France, the state was even more so. There was no German or Italian citizenship, no German or Italian armed forces, government administration, no monarch (to say nothing of a republic) ruling over Germany or Italy. Instead, there were the different German and Italian states: Bavaria, Prussia, Austria, Saxony, the Two Sicilies, Tuscany, the Papal States, Piedmont-Savoy, and so on – altogether thirty-nine in Germany, and seven in Italy. The nationalist movement in Germany and Italy thus faced a double task: to spread the sense of nationhood among the population, to turn Bavarians or Sicilians into Germans and Italians, but also to propose some way that this newly perceived nationhood could be expressed in governmental form, that is, to create a unified German or Italian state.

This formulation is a little misleading, because it implies that there existed a nationalist movement, separate and distinct from other political groupings. This was not the case: nationalist goals in Germany and Italy were articulated and furthered by the liberal and radical movements of political opposition. Nationalist demands were a constant presence in the conspiracies of secret societies, the speeches of liberal parliamentary deputies, the meetings of choral and gymnastics societies, and the festivals and banquets of the moderate opposition. One could, I think, go further and say that nationalism was the experience of belonging to one of these groups, of participating in one of these events. Nationalism was the experience of marching behind the tricolor flag, of large-scale collective singing (nationalist songs, naturally), of joining in a large public meeting or a small conspiratorial circle.

When it came to a political program for creating a German or Italian nation-state, nationalists split into two groups, corresponding to their liberal or radical positions on other issues. For the former, national unity was something to be accomplished gradually, without any violent break, "on the basis of the further development of existing institutions," as German liberals put it. Liberals would point to ongoing developments: the meeting of the "Congress of Italian Scientists," that brought together scholars from the entire peninsula, on a yearly basis, starting in 1839, or the similar meetings of the "Congress of German Physicians and Natural Scientists." German liberals could place their hopes in existing institutional frameworks. They praised the *Zollverein*, the 1834 tariff union to which German states belonged, or the German Confederation, a diplomatic league of all thirty-nine German states created by the Congress of

Vienna in 1815. While neither of these were national political institutions as nationalists understood the term, liberals hoped they could become them. The liberal journalist Friedrich von Raumer observed that the *Zollverein* had made Germany into a "great power in the commercial world," even if there was still no German nation-state to be a Great Power in the political world.[16] A common demand was for a "representation of the people," to be added to the German Confederation, some sort of elected parliament to meet besides the existing body of diplomats, thus starting a transformation of the Confederation into a national government. The states of the Italian peninsula had no such common institutions; Italian liberals looked towards the creation of a customs union and a confederation on the German model as potential first steps on the way to national unification. In a variation on this idea, the Neapolitan economist and lawyer Matteo De Augustinis proposed in 1838 the calling of an Italian congress of legal experts, who would meet in Rome to draw up a code of law that would be valid for all the states of the Italian peninsula.

Such a gradualist plan of action would have to find a way to enlist at least some of the existing German and Italian monarchies – themselves most emphatically not national states – into the movement towards a national unification. Many German liberal nationalists placed their hopes in the kingdom of Prussia. It was the largest, most affluent, and militarily most powerful of the German states, hence a logical leader of the process of unification. Prussia's kings and their closest advisors, though, were political conservatives, supporting the principle of political legitimacy, holding fast to the German Confederation as a diplomatic league and not as a future nation-state. They were firmly opposed to liberalism, constitutional government, and a German nation state. Yet this did not discourage the liberals, because they knew that there existed a strong counter current in the Prussian bureaucracy, sympathetic to constitutionalism and national unity, one that had emerged and dominated Prussian policy during the years of the German uprising and wars against Napoleon 1813–15, and had come more briefly to the surface in the diplomatic crises of 1830 and 1840. With the strengthening of the liberal and nationalist movement in the 1840s, liberals hoped that these sympathies would emerge once more.

Such a Prussocentric plan for German unification left open the question of what to do about the Habsburg monarchy. In some ways, Austria clearly belonged to Germany. It was hard to imagine a common German historical experience excluding Austria. The ruling dynasty and much of the higher civil service of the Austrian Empire were culturally German, if

---

[16] Cited in Brian Vick, *Defining Germany: The 1848 Frankfurt Parliamentarians and National Identity* (Cambridge, MA, 2002), 75.

hardly sympathizers with German nationalism, and Germans were the single largest nationality among the subjects of the emperor. Austria was a member of the German Confederation; indeed the presidency of the Confederation's council, which met in Frankfurt am Main, was reserved for the Austrian representative. However, a large majority, some 80 percent, of the Habsburgs' subjects were not Germans and it was difficult to see how the entire empire could be incorporated into a German nation-state without destroying its national character or how the Germans of the Habsburg monarchy could be incorporated into a German nation-state without destroying the Habsburg monarchy.

Liberal nationalists devised various schemes to square this circle. Their exact details are not relevant for our purposes, but two points need to be made about them, since they bedeviled liberal plans for German national unification, before, during, and after the 1848 revolution. First, there was the way that national unity cut across Germans' confessional and regional loyalties. Prussia's ruling house and most of its population were Protestant, distinctly so. A Germany united under Prussia would be a predominantly Protestant state. Most liberals who supported such a plan were themselves Protestants and from the northern part of Germany, where Prussia was situated. Roman Catholics and south Germans were deeply skeptical of Prussia; they insisted on a Catholic, Austrian counterweight. Secondly, a united Germany might conceivably fit the interests of Prussia as one of the European Great Powers, that is be a way to expand its diplomatic and military influence. It was hard to imagine how a German national state could do the same for Austria's interests as a Great Power.

Italian liberals lacked a corresponding state in which to place their hopes. Italy's most populous state, the Kingdom of the Two Sicilies, was also economically the most backward, and ruled by a very conservative Bourbon dynasty strongly opposed to nationalist ideas. The most prosperous, urbanized, best educated, and economically most advanced regions of the peninsula, the northeastern provinces of Lombardy and Venetia, were directly under the rule of the Austrian Empire. Almost all the other Italian states were subject to substantial Austrian influence, and their rulers had no hesitation in calling in Habsburg soldiers to suppress uprisings and conspiracies against their rule. It seems legitimate to use twentieth-century terminology here and call the Italian states Habsburg satellites.

The one exception was the northwestern Kingdom of Piedmont-Savoy. As was the case in Prussia, the Piedmontese royal family had a long history of dynastic rivalry with the Habsburgs. So far so good, only in most other respects, it was less well suited to play the role of national unifier. Unlike Prussia, the Piedmontese kingdom was small, having scarcely more than a third the population of the Kingdom of the Two Sicilies. With its third rate army, Piedmont-Savoy was no Great Power fit to challenge Austria militarily, as Prussia had done and would do in the future. Finally, Piedmont's king, Carlo Alberto, and his closest advisors were strongly conservative, hostile to constitutional government, doubtful of nationalism and sympathetic to the particularly devout wing of Italian Catholicism, which saw the Habsburg Emperor as the primary defender of the faith.

In spite of all these disadvantages, Italian liberal nationalists were stuck with Piedmont for lack of anything better, until, in 1843, the Abbé Vincenzo Gioberti wrote his work *On the Civil and Moral Primacy of the Italians*, in which he proposed the creation of a federal Italian state under the leadership of the Pope. Following the death of the arch-conservative Gregory XVI in 1846, and the election of the liberal (or at least reputed to be so) Bishop of Imola to the Papacy as Pius IX, Gioberti's idea of reconciling liberalism and Catholicism, the supra-national Papacy and Italian nationalism seemed about to be realized. "Viva Pio Nono!" became the battle cry of liberalism and nationalism in the Italian peninsula.

Gioberti's proposal that the Pope become the leader of Italian nationalism is well known; less well known are his writings of two years later, in which he violently denounced the Jesuits, blaming them and those who thought like them for all of Italy's problems and called for religious reforms in the Catholic Church, liberal reforms in the Italian states, and, to accomplish these, a far greater participation of educated laymen, both in the church and in secular public life. Just as the liberal proposal for Prussian leadership in accomplishing German national unification raised the question of inter-confessional hostilities between Protestants and Catholics, so Gioberti's program of Papal leadership for Italian national unification posed questions of clericalism and anti-clericalism, and of the place of the church in Italian society. Thus in both Italy and Germany, the liberal program of national unification, based on the principles liberals espoused of moderation and cooperation with existing governments raised deep-seated issues of popular loyalty which would threaten to make impossible the liberals' own efforts.

Radicals in Germany and Italy were no less nationalist than liberals – if anything, even more so – only they had a very different idea of how to bring about national unity. Leftists asserted that the liberals' belief in gradualism produced much talk but no concrete results. Giuseppe Mazzini had nothing but scorn for adherents of "slow progress, who believe in the regeneration of Italy via such works as infant asylums, scientific congresses, and railroads."[17] His German counterparts were equally skeptical of the

---

[17] Quoted in Della Peruta, *Mazzini e i revolutionari italiani*, 368.

liberals' hopes for the German Confederation, suggesting, with some justice, that the conservative Austrian and Prussian statesmen who dominated the Confederation used it as a vehicle to suppress demands for national unity rather than a means to achieve it.

As part of their attitude towards monarchical government, German and Italian democrats saw them as thwarting the people's – that is the nation's – will. The governments were obstacles to national unity; their overthrow was a precondition for the creation of a unified nation-state. It was, once again, Mazzini who had the clearest plan for accomplishing this. An uprising in one of the Italian states, prepared by members of his secret society and sparked by an incursion from abroad mounted by political exiles, would create an insurgent regime, that would both carry the revolution throughout the peninsula and lead a national war to drive the Austrians out of Lombardy and Venetia. Given the Habsburgs' superiority in conventional military forces, Mazzini saw much of the action occurring in guerilla warfare, which would also have the political advantage of bringing in the rural population, and winning them for the national cause.

The two attempts at this uprising, one led by Mazzini himself, featuring an incursion into Piedmont, in northern Italy in 1834, and a second by the Bandiera brothers in 1846, centered around an incursion into Calabria, in the south, were both dismal failures. Many of the insurgents returning from exile paid with their lives. These failures, part of the broader pattern of unsuccessful insurrections launched by secret societies between the revolutions of 1830 and 1848, left German and Italian radicals by the mid-1840s lacking any concrete means to realize their vision of national unification. Some thought vaguely of receiving French military assistance, following a revolution in France and the coming to power of a radical regime there; others saw nothing better than to support the liberal program of gradual movement towards national unification. The revolutionary events of 1848 would open entirely new prospects for national unification in Germany and Italy, prospects which both liberals and democrats would grapple with. If ultimately unsuccessful, their efforts pointed towards the actual path of the creation of unified nation-states in Germany and Italy in the two decades following 1850.

Nations and nationalism in the Habsburg Empire and eastern Europe

Applying the ideas of nation and nationalism stemming from the French Revolution to the Habsburg Monarchy, with its very different social structure and forms of government, produced strange results. What seemed self-evident in the western part of the continent, and at least reasonable in the center, was dubious and debatable to the east. Sources of consensus in the west became sources of conflict in the east. The nature of the nation, the question of who belonged to the nation, the supporters of nationalism, and the political program of the creation of nation-states all acquired unfamiliar connotations when placed in a new setting.

To start with the nations themselves, the first half of the nineteenth century was the age of the "national reawakening [or rebirth]." As contemporaries understood it, and present-day nationalist historians still assert, it was the period when the smaller, mostly Slavic nationalities of the empire – Czechs, Slovaks, Slovenes, Croats, Serbs, Ukrainians, and the Latin Romanians – remembered their historical traditions, revived their native tongues as literary languages, reappropriated their traditions and folklore, in short reasserted their existence as nations. Much of what happened at the time would seem to fit this self-understanding. In 1834, Simon Bărnuțiu, professor of history and philosophy at the Uniate seminary and lyceum [secondary school] in Blaj, in Transylvania, gave his philosophy lectures in Romanian, to the astonishment of the students, rather than in Latin as had previously been the case. The very same year, the actor and playwright Josef Tyl composed and sung in a musical comedy production in Prague, the Czech language song, "Where is My Homeland?" that would later become the Czech national anthem. Two years after that, a group of students in the Uniate theological seminary in Lemberg published a literary almanac, *The Nymph of the Dniester*, a pioneering work of Ukrainian-language literature. Throughout the eastern reaches of the Habsburg Empire the decades of the 1820s through the 1840s saw the formation of literary societies and cultural foundations, the writing of national histories, grammars and historical philologies, and the publication of books, magazines, and newspapers in languages long thought of as exclusively oral, peasant tongues.

Yet when examined more closely, this national reawakening seems less natural and obvious. The proponents of a literary Romanian, decreed that the Romanian works would be written with Latin letters, since this was the Romanians' historical tradition as descendants of the Roman Empire. Most Romanians' acquaintance with the written word, however, was in the Cyrillic alphabet, the one used in the Eastern Orthodox Church so they could not understand the new Latin writing. The common language, cultural tradition, and common historical experience that nationalist theory takes as defining a nation seem here to be invented, to be at odds with actual common experiences.

A more elaborate but equally revealing example comes from the origins of nationalism among the South Slavs, the Serbs, Croats, and Slovenes. The author and political activist Ljudevit Gaj, leading figure in the

..ndation of both modern literary Croatian and modern Croatian nationalism, asserted that all three ethnic groups were parts of a greater "Illyrian" nation. A nation, he proclaimed in 1835, "has nothing so holy, nothing so precious as its natural language." "All good patriots," he went on, "have the sole wish that all the Slavs living in the old Illyrian states [ultimately, a reference to the Illyrian provinces of the Roman Empire] may be united in their literary language." A rapidly growing number of young Croatian intellectuals followed Gaj's appeal, as for instance the students at the Catholic theological seminary in Zagreb, who, in 1836 founded an "Illyrian National Society." Members swore that they would always make use of the "national language." They, like most Croatian nationalists, including Gaj himself, had to learn their "national language" as a foreign tongue, since Gaj chose as the basis for his literary language the Stokavian dialect, spoken mainly by Serbs, and incomprehensible to most Croats, who used the quite different Kajkavian dialect. In fact, five years before Gaj launched his appeal for Stokavian as the basis for the national language, he had referred to Kajkavian as "our marvelous mother tongue." For Gaj, the idea of a common mother tongue, and a cultural and historical tradition uniting a people together and forming the natural basis for a nation preceded the actual choice of a language designated to fill this role. In other words, peculiar as it may seem, it was nationalism that constructed nations, rather than the other way around. Another sign of the constructed character of this early nationalism was the lack of facility of many of the Slavic nationalist leaders of the 1830s and 1840s in their "own" language. Prominent Czech nationalists spoke and wrote German far better than they did Czech. The leading Czech nationalist, historian František Palacký author of a great multi-volume work exposing the centuries of German oppression of the Czechs, began writing his work in German and continued to use the German language with his family and at home until the 1860s, when he could look back on three decades of nationalist activism. Ukrainian nationalists of the 1840s often spoke Polish far better than they did Ukrainian. During the revolution of 1848, the leading Croatian nationalist newspaper would be the Italian-language *L'Avvenire*, published in the Adriatic port city of Dubrovnik, or as its Italian-speaking inhabitants called it, Ragusa.

This whole development of Slavic nationalism in the Habsburg monarchy is best understood when we remember that nationalists were originally young people of the professional middle class. Nationalism arose in the social context of the growing number of educated young men, who faced a job market with no room for them. It may have been the cynicism of the secret police, when one of Metternich's agents reported from Zagreb in 1844 that "educated young men here have no way of earning a living," and that "the inner disturbances [that is, the Illyrian nationalist agitation] would cease" if they received government jobs, but there was clearly something to the observation. Their invention of literary languages and national customs seems very much in tune with the classical and philological education which such young men had received. It would also help secure a future for them, as teachers and administrators of the nation, the ones capable of speaking and writing the "national" language.

It is important to realize just how restricted a group these nationalists were, given the low levels of literacy and small urban populations of eastern Europe. The Romanian-language *Gazeta de Transilvania*, of Blaj, counted some 250 subscribers in the province of Transylvania. This was a perfectly respectable number for a small-town newspaper, and ones in similarly sized centers of western Europe would not have had a larger press run. However, the *Gazeta* was the only Romanian-language newspaper in the entire province, and its readership made up the entire political universe of Romanian nationalism in the Habsburg monarchy. Even if we accept the editor's contention that he had ten readers for every subscriber, it is clear that the 2,500 nationalists among the two million or so Romanian speakers in Transylvania were a very small group. The political importance of these small groups of nationalists would depend on the extent to which they could approach the vast majority of the population, mostly serfs, who had little interest in nationhood but a strong hostility to their feudal landlords. Much of the story of 1848 in the Habsburg lands would be the interaction of intellectuals' nationalism and peasants' conflicts.

In a different way, the relationship between lord and serf characterized the nationalism of two of the other major national groups of the Habsburg monarchy, the Poles and the Hungarians. Unlike the smaller Slavic nationalities, these could legitimately claim the existence, since medieval times, of a Polish and Hungarian state, literary culture, and nation. However, the states had lost their independent existence, and while the Polish and Hungarian nations still persisted, they were nations in a different sense from those envisaged by the French Revolution. When contemporaries talked of the Polish or Hungarian *natio*, using the Latin word, they meant a nation composed exclusively of the nobility. Serfs or artisans and merchants of the towns were not part of this *natio*, and even though the nobility encompassed an unusually large part of the population, it still meant that the vast majority of people living in Poland or Hungary were excluded from this concept of the nation.

Polish and Hungarian nationalists of the middle decades of the nineteenth century sought to transform their respective *natio* into a modern nation. Latin was the language of the *natio*, of much of law, public life, and literary culture. Nationalists promoted the use of the vernacular, so that everyone, not just the affluent and educated – that is, usually, the wealthier nobles – might participate in the community of the nation. Both as political liberals or radicals and as nationalists, they called for the emancipation of the serfs, so that distinctions of orders might be erased and with it a new, socially encompassing concept of the nation created. The different fates of Hungarian and Polish nationalism during the 1840s indicate some of the difficulties involved in trying to realize the originally western European political program of nationalism in eastern Europe.

The territory of the medieval Polish kingdom had been divided in the late eighteenth century between Austria, Russia, and Prussia. In 1830, Polish nationalists had risen unsuccessfully against the tsar's rule. Thousands of refugees fled to western Europe, dividing themselves in exile into two parties. The more moderate placed their hopes in the liberal Great Powers, France and England, expecting them eventually to go to war with Russia, in the course of which an independent Polish state might emerge. Prince Adam Czartoryski, leader of this group, waited at his headquarters in the Parisian Hotel Lambert for the right moment. He waited over thirty years and the moment never came.

A second, increasingly left-wing group, associating in exile with radicals of other nationalities, decided that a new Polish nation-state would require a democratic revolution that would involve all social groups, including especially the serfs, and set about planning one. They tried their hand at it in 1846, only their conspiracy went wrong from the start when the Prussian police discovered their plan and arrested the group's leaders. Undaunted, the activists in the Austrian province of Galicia went ahead with the uprising, but their movement against the government was a signal to the serfs to move against them. Noble insurgents were captured by serfs and, spurred on by the rumor that the Austrian authorities were offering rewards for insurgents, living or dead (an official had actually offered payment for information about their whereabouts), peasants turned on and murdered over a thousand nobles, priests, and estate managers. One Habsburg official remembered what happened when peasants came to him with the corpse of a Polish noble estate-owner to get their reward.

"We have brought Poles."
"Poles, how could that be," I answered, "what are you?"
"We aren't Poles, we are the emperor's peasants."
"Who are the Poles then?"
"Oh – the Poles! They are the lords, their estate managers, their clerks, the learned men, the well-dressed gentlemen."[18]

[18] Quoted in Brigitte Biwald, *Von Gottes Gnade oder von Volkes Gnaden? Die Revolution von 1848 in der Habsburgermonarchie: Der Bauer als Ziel politischer Agitation* (Frankfurt, 1996), 47.

The peasants thus denounced the revolutionaries and proclaimed their loyalty to the Emperor and even refused to refer to themselves as "Polish." Poles were the feudal landlords. In response to the modern, democratic conception of the nation proposed by the radical insurgents from the nobility, the peasants reasserted the old, medieval concept of the *natio*: the nation was the nobility, their feudal overlords, and they would have nothing to do with them.

Hungarian nationalists were in a more favorable situation than their Polish counterparts, since all the national territory they claimed was grouped together under the Crown of St. Stephen, and they possessed in the Hungarian Diet a political vehicle for their aspirations. Starting in the mid-1820s, and continuing through the next two decades, they strove to gain control of the Diet and turn Hungary from a collection of provinces, each with its own feudal rights and privileges, into a unified nation-state, and the Hungarians from a *natio* of the nobility, into a nation of all social classes. Their program included the introduction of basic civil rights, the institution of free public education, the abolition of serfdom (with compensation to the nobility for its losses), the extension of the authority of the Diet to all the lands of the crown of St. Stephen – that is, the incorporation of Transylvania and Croatia-Slavonia into interior Hungary – and the replacement of Latin as the language of legislation and administration with Magyar. It was the classical liberal political program, as adapted to the conditions of eastern Europe.

Romanian, Slovak, Serb, and Croat nationalists did not see it that way; what they saw was an alien nation trying to suppress their national identity. Nationalism demanded that they oppose the Magyar efforts. After the Hungarian Diet voted to conduct its proceedings in Magyar, the Croatian delegates contentiously continued speaking in Latin; the provincial diet of Croatia-Slavonia voted to conduct its proceedings in Croatian. When officials of the county governments of interior Hungary began conducting their official correspondence in Magyar instead of Latin, the governments of the Croatian counties would refuse to reply, or would answer in their national language. By the 1840s, this had become a steadily escalating conflict, conducted with growing intolerance on both sides.

Hungarian nationalists did not perceive themselves as oppressing other nationalities, imposing the Magyar language, only spoken by a minority of the inhabitants of the lands of the Crown of St. Stephen, but as carrying out a liberal political program, one first envisaged in the French Revolution. As the director of the Košice school district wrote, in opposing the creation of a Slovak cultural society in 1847, "Just as Hungary constitutes one country, so its inhabitants form one nation."[19] His actions were following the precedent of French liberals who, from 1789 onwards, had torn down provincial barriers, built an administratively unified state and imposed the French language on a country of Provençal, Breton, Flemish, Basque, and German speakers. Even in the 1840s, French was not the native language of most of the inhabitants of France.

In the Austrian province of Bohemia, where a similar conflict was building between German and Czech nationalists at the time, Ignaz Kuranda, one of the leading German liberals, actually took a trip to southern France to find out how "France has overcome the linguistic differences of its provinces." "Provence," he noted, "is even richer in literary and national monuments than Bohemia and other Slavic-German provinces."[20] Yet somehow, these linguistic differences had not become a matter of political debate or national antagonism.

What to Hungarian or German liberal nationalists within the Habsburg monarchy was the political irrelevance of linguistic differences was to the nationalists of the smaller nationalities, still struggling to consolidate, or more precisely, to construct a nation, the suppression of their demands for national self-determination. In defense, they invented the doctrine of Austro-Slavism, which asserted that the Habsburg monarchy, with its predominantly Slavic population, should become the nation-state for the different Slavic nationalities. Of course, since the Slavic nationalists were just as much political liberals as the Hungarian or German nationalists, they envisaged a different, liberalized, constitutionalized Habsburg monarchy becoming their Slavic state.

What happened, though, was that the old, unreformed Habsburg monarchy took up their offer. While Prince Metternich was as skeptical of Slavic as he was of any other nationalists, his rival at court, Count Kolowrat, in charge of domestic affairs, looked favorably on the Slavic nationalist movements, seeing them as a counterweight to liberal demands, raised by Hungarian and German nationalists, for constitutional government and the abolition of feudalism. Croatian nationalism enjoyed particular favor. While prohibiting the use of the term "Illyrian," invented by Ljudevit Gaj, the government provided him with a large cash subsidy to continue his activities and bedevil Hungarian liberals. In Hungary, conservative nobles, opposed to the abolition of feudalism, whether their

[19] Cited in Robin Olney, *The Habsburg Monarchy: From Enlightenment to Eclipse* (New York, 2001), 123
[20] Quoted in Francis Loewenheim, "German Liberalism and the Czech Renascence: Ignaz Kuranda, *Die Grenzboten*, and Developments in Bohemia 1845–1849," in *The Czech Renascence of the Nineteenth Century* (Toronto and Buffalo, 1970), 155 n. 25.

native language was Magyar, German or Croatian, and the Catholic clergy, opposed to liberal demands for civic equality for Protestants, ostentatiously supported the Croatian nationalists. Enjoying this support, the nationalists toned down their liberalism and anti-clericalism, to suit their new allies.

The philosopher Hegel once said that tragedy was a conflict of two rights. By this definition, the development of nationalisms in the Habsburg monarchy was the epitome of an historical tragedy. The same population was claimed as part of different nations by different nationalist movements, each applying, validly, the nationalist ideas originating in western Europe to the very different circumstances of the eastern reaches of the continent. Different nationalist movements, all sporting liberal or democratic principles, all opposed, to a greater or lesser extent to absolutist rule and to serfdom and a society of orders, found themselves fighting each other, in circumstances where the only winners would be precisely those supporters of absolutism and feudalism whom the nationalists opposed. The clash of different nationalisms in the Habsburg monarchy would play a major role in defeating the 1848 revolution, not just in the monarchy itself, but throughout Europe.

Party of order; party of movement

Originating in France, and filtering into the general European political vocabulary by the 1840s, these terms referred to the broadest possible distinction between the political forces working for a preservation of the status quo and those attempting to change it. We can conclude this chapter on political life in pre-1848 Europe, by looking at conditions on the continent from the point of view of these two "parties."

The center of aspirations of the party of movement was in France, the home of revolution, and the Great Power most opposed to the settlement of 1815, that ratified France's final defeat in the Napoleonic Wars. To a great extent, France was perceived as Paris writ large. Paris itself had a double significance. It was the capital of a centrally administered state, the key – or so people thought – to controlling it. Paris was also the largest city in continental Europe, with the most politicized inhabitants – and the contrast between them and residents of other large cities, like Naples or Vienna was very strong. It was, one might say, the political capital of the continent.

The street fighting in Paris and the change of regime in France as a consequence of the revolution of 1830 had stirred up the hopes of the party of movement throughout the continent. Coming to power, the Orleanist regime had denounced the treaties of 1815, and the other Great Powers had threatened a military intervention against it. It offered political asylum to revolutionaries from elsewhere on the continent, and even provided financial backing and military training to the refugee Polish insurgents of 1830–31.

All these signs that France was preparing for a repeat of the role it had played in the 1790s as armed patron of revolution in Europe quickly vanished. Disputed questions, most prominently, Belgian independence from Holland were settled peacefully. France took no action to upset the status quo; the other Powers took no action against France and the prospect of a major war that might have brought more upheaval in its wake, dissipated quickly. The most the new French government did was to ensure, in alliance with England, the presence of liberal regimes in Spain and Portugal against the opposition of Russia and Austria, who supported the Iberian liberals' conservative rivals. By the mid-1840s, French diplomats were moving towards securing an alliance with conservative Austria.

Much the same disappointment with developments in France surfaced in domestic affairs. The liberal regime which owed its existence to the 1830 revolution moved steadily to the right, tightening the press laws, harassing the republican opposition, increasingly striving for a reconciliation with the Catholic Church. By the 1840s, growing numbers of conservatives had rallied to the support of Louis-Philippe. If France was to be the center of the hopes of the party of movement, then a new government would have to come to power, probably in revolutionary fashion.

While adherents of the party of movement looked to Paris, those of the party of order had their eyes on Vienna. The Habsburg capital was the home of Prince Metternich, the Austrian Chancellor who had directed the European coalition that had defeated Napoleon, and had invented, at the Congress of Vienna in 1815, the political and diplomatic structures that the party of order was trying to retain. He had preserved these structures through the following three decades, skillfully steering them through the revolutions of 1830 with far fewer losses than anyone might have expected.

It was no accident that the great statesman of the party of order was the Habsburgs' Chancellor, since the Austrian Empire's existence as a Great Power was dependent on the preservation of the status quo. Both absolutism and a society of orders were better preserved in the Habsburg Empire than anywhere outside of Russia; introduction of a constitution and equality before the law, or the abolition of feudalism would have been enormously disruptive. What nationalism would do to an empire containing within it many competing national movements was seemingly too frightening to contemplate.

More than that, the Austrian Empire's position as a Great Power, as a military and diplomatic equal to a more populous Russia or to economically and industrially more advanced France and England, depended on the hegemonic position the monarchy had beyond its borders. Austria presided over the German Confederation, keeping in line its potential rival, the kingdom of Prussia, and guaranteeing its influence over the many smaller German states. Its position in Italy was even stronger, between its possession of the wealthy provinces of Lombardy and Venetia and its powerful influence on the Papacy and on the governments of virtually all the other states of the Italian peninsula. War, revolution, and national unification – contemporaries saw them as all coinciding – could only shatter Austria's position.

If by the mid-1840s developments in France had been increasingly disappointing to the party of movement, Austria's position as stronghold of the party of order was equally questionable, if publicly less obvious. One severe weakness was in the person of the head of state. An absolutist monarchy requires an absolute monarch, only the Emperor Ferdinand, who had succeeded to the throne on the death of his father, Franz I, in 1835, was mentally retarded and unfit to govern. There was no one and no organized way to determine the direction of official policy. Instead, Metternich, Kolowrat, and the Archdukes and Archduchesses of the imperial family all contended for control. The center of government was weak and vacillating, unable to reach quick decisions in a crisis.

A second and greater weakness was the state of public finances, far worse than those of the other Great Powers. The enormous expenses of the wars against Napoleon had forced the empire to declare bankruptcy in 1811; its finances had never really recovered. A continuous and uninterrupted string of deficits since then had forced the authorities to issue a paper currency, which circulated at or close to par, mostly because no one knew (except for a small group of court bankers, who charged dearly for the privilege) how little silver was in the vaults of the state bank to cover the paper. The yearly reports of the state bank were censored to ensure that widespread ignorance remained and prevented a run on the bank and a disastrous decline in the value of the currency.

It would have required a large tax increase to close the budget deficit. Substantial revenues were available if the tax exemptions of the nobility and the privileged provinces were abolished, but of course the privileged groups were precisely those who dominated the government. So there were no reforms, only a greater effort to collect taxes from the most highly taxed: the inhabitants of the capital city and especially those of the Italian provinces. Lombardy and Venetia were the cash cows of the Austrian empire, the only places in the monarchy where paper money did not circulate and the currency was based on silver. Sales of silk from these provinces to France and England brought in silver that was heavily taxed and so brought to the north of the Alps to provide the slim backing for the paper currency used elsewhere in the monarchy and also to provide the cash with which the armed forces were paid.

Austria's finances were extraordinarily precarious, dependent on extremely heavy taxation of some subjects, the steady flow of silver from Italy and the lack of public knowledge of the exact state of government revenues and expenditures. The system existed on the brink of collapse and every extraordinary expenditure raised the specter of a renewed bankruptcy. Just mobilizing the army in the diplomatic crises of 1830 and 1840 had brought the monarchy perilously close to a new financial catastrophe; actually going to war would have been an economic disaster. The lack of a strong hand at the center of power meant that the Austrian government was unable to take decisive action, but even had there been someone really in control in Vienna, determined to employ the army to protect the status quo, he would not have had the money to do so. By the mid-1840s, it was clear that the party of movement could not look to the existing government in France for assistance or encouragement. Yet there was no successor to Paris as the political capital of Europe. The initial impetus for change would have to come from there. Should a signal be given in Paris, though, the prospects for its having a strong effect – a much stronger one, in fact, than was occasioned by the 1830 revolution – were greatly strengthened by the growing weakness of the Habsburg monarchy. There would be no one to check the spread of revolution. It was this prospect, which rendered particularly critical the economic and political crises of the mid-1840s and made them precursors to the most widespread wave of revolution in nineteenth-century Europe.

3   The outbreak of revolution

Preceding the revolution: (1) the economic crisis

It was quite clear to contemporaries that the economic crisis of the years 1845–47 was the precursor to and precondition for the revolution of 1848. Historians have seconded this judgment, but can add to it three important points. What happened in 1845–47 was not an isolated event but part of a broader range of economic difficulties, occurring over a fifteen-year period, running from the early 1840s through the second half of the following decade. Within this broader period, 1845–47 were particularly difficult years, because they saw the interaction of three separate but interrelated crises: a run of very poor harvests; a trade cycle downturn, what would today be called a recession; and a financial and banking panic, reflecting the first two difficulties, but also showing the insufficiency of existing financial institutions. Finally, both the broader crisis and the greater problems of 1845–47 are best understood as a crisis of transition, as part of the movement towards expanded industrial production and a market-oriented agriculture, which would resolve the long-term economic difficulties of the first half of the nineteenth century. This last point is particularly well suited to historians' hindsight, but was no consolation to those who were starving, cold, unemployed, or heavily in debt at the time. Unaware of the prospect of future decades of economic expansion, they were ready to take violent and drastic action to improve their condition.

Problems of food shortages began with mediocre harvests in the early 1840s. Their effects, if at times severe, were localized and limited to the poorer, mountainous regions. Spot shortages of bread in the hilly areas of the southern Rhineland during the spring of 1843 followed the poor harvest of the previous year. Bad harvests in Mediterranean Europe in 1843 led to near famine in mountainous southern Italy the next year. Villagers in parts of the province of Basilicata were reduced to eating the carcasses of donkeys found dead on the side of the road.

1845 saw a broader crop disaster. The outbreak and spread of the potato blight annihilated most of the crop that had become the main food of the poor in northern Europe. Large-scale potato planting was a sign of the development of a productive, modern, market-oriented agriculture, so the famine struck hardest at precisely those areas in the forefront of expanded foodstuff production for the growing population. The harvest of 1846 broadened and deepened the crisis, extending its reach to southern Europe and outside the potato growing areas. The effects of the potato blight were somewhat mitigated that year, but a severely hot and dry summer produced the worst grain crop in almost three decades. By the spring of 1847, both wholesale and retail prices of basic foodstuffs had jumped to an average of twice their levels of the early 1840s; the specter of famine, seemingly banished from Europe, was poised for a reappearance. Throughout the continent, there were bread – or potato – riots as crowds gathered to mob speculators, prevent foodstuffs from leaving the vicinity, or to force their sale at prices well below market levels. In February 1847, two thousand peasants gathered in the town of Varese, in Austrian north-ern Italy, and plundered the wagons of Swiss merchants who had bought up grain. Two months later, crowds in Berlin attacked the market stalls of potato dealers, an event later known as the "potato uprising." Historians have counted over 400 such food riots in France during 1846 and 1847, and 164 in the German states during 1847 alone. Whole troupes of beggars demanded alms in threatening fashion. Nervous governments moved sol-diers to areas threatened with provisioning disaster and drew up plans to hand out weapons to solid property-owning citizens, in order to preserve order when the police could not and the army was unavailable.

In the end, the total famine everyone feared did not occur. A bountiful harvest in 1847 brought down food prices substantially even before the outbreak of the revolution in 1848; continued good harvests over the next several years decreased prices to unusually low levels, before a new series of bad harvests in the mid-1850s raised them to their highpoints of ten years previously. While birth and marriage rates were substantially depressed by the high prices of 1845–47, death rates rose at most slightly, far less than they did in 1849, a year of plentiful food but also of a cholera epidemic.

Probably the single most important reason for avoiding the catastrophe was the vigorous action taken against famine. Municipalities opened soup kitchens and offered subsidized bread, potatoes, or rice for sale. The state authorities prohibited the export of foodstuffs, removed tariffs on food imports, opened army magazines to feed the hard-pressed public, even subsidized the import of grain from Russia and North America. The success of these measures can best be seen by contrast with Ireland, the one place in Europe where the catastrophe did occur. The Irish were unusually dependent on potatoes for subsistence, since the bulk of their arable land went to cash crops to pay their English landlords, making the situation particularly critical for them when the potato crop failed. Much worse, they were ruled by a British government imbued with the doctrines of the free market economy, to the point that it was unwilling to take any of the measures its counterparts on the continent took to combat famine, leaving economists' theories intact and at least one million Irish dead.

If the crisis of subsistence on the continent did not lead to such disastrous results, it does not follow, as some historians have asserted, that it had no serious consequences. Rather, the high grain prices of 1845–47 were the prelude to the next stage of the economic crisis. The more people spent on food, the less they had available for manufactured goods, or for the products and services of artisans. Decreased demand for these products, in conjunction with the normal workings of the business cycle, produced a sharp downturn, beginning in 1847, running through that year and into 1848. Recovery only proceeded sporadically in 1848, the revolutionary events of that year not being encouraging to business, and was not completed until well into 1849. Unemployment was substantial in large cities and manufacturing regions; crowds of the unemployed and columns of workers employed in public relief projects would be a characteristic sight in the 1848 revolution, playing a significant role in the revolution's outbreak and its further development.

Part of the reason for the severity of the slump of 1847–48 was the credit crisis. High grain prices had been accompanied by very substantial borrowing, as food costs outstripped income, and the debt stemming from the years of bad harvest would remain a problem for the lower and middle classes throughout the events of the revolution. Additionally, the subsistence crisis occurred just as the first wave of railroad construction was reaching a peak, straining the capital markets with the enormous sums required for it. The financial system, primitively organized to start with, unable to mobilize savings efficiently or move them around very well to meet demand, and hampered by generally restrictive government monetary policies, collapsed under the strain, producing a wave of bankruptcies. Unable to obtain credit to meet their obligations, businesses suspended payment, bringing down their creditors in a chain reaction of debt.

The 1848 revolution was not a glorified bread riot, a mindless reflex of high food prices; in fact, the revolution began when these prices were falling from moderate levels. However, the wretched harvests of 1845 and 1846 were a major indirect cause of the revolution. They were the culmination of two decades of declining popular purchasing power and were also at least an aggravating factor in the slump of 1847–48, whose debt, unemployment, and sluggish business conditions do go a long way to explaining the marked popular discontent existing at the outbreak of the revolution and continuing throughout it, providing the backdrop for a constantly renewed radicalism and repeated attempts at insurrection.

Preceding the revolution: (2) the political crisis

The years of economic crisis 1845–48 were also the period of a major offensive of the party of movement in European politics. Almost everywhere on the continent political opposition to established regimes intensified, political organization, both legal and illegal, was extended, and new political campaigns were carried out. Sometimes, the opposition used the established institutions. A number of the provincial diets in both the Prussian kingdom and the Austrian empire submitted petitions to the monarch, calling for a constitution and a legislative body with true law-making power for the entire monarchy. As had been the case in the past, it was the Hungarians who made most vigorous use of these institutions. In preparation for elections to the 1847 session of the Hungarian Diet, the opposition even drew up a comprehensive "nation"-wide political platform. Its publication was prohibited by the authorities, who nonetheless could not stop its widespread clandestine distribution. The elections produced a majority for the opposition, although its effectiveness in the early sessions of the diet was hindered by differences between moderates and radicals.

The French opposition, on the other hand, was defeated in the 1846 parliamentary elections. Frustrated by their lack of success among that narrow stratum of the population possessing the franchise, the leaders of the opposition turned in 1847 to a broader audience, launching a nation-wide banquet campaign, calling for political reform. Most banquet speakers were careful to stress their allegiance to the king, and just called for a widening of the property franchise, avoiding both republicanism and democracy. Still, there were occasional toasts offered to the "organization of labor" or to the memory of the glorious days of 1792; the radical politician Alexandre Ledru-Rollin, shortly to lead the left during the 1848 revolution, gave speeches in favor of universal manhood suffrage. Even more important, the campaign itself, by going beyond the usual limits of parliamentary politics, showed the intensification of political life.

The French authorities and the elected legislators made no response to this challenge. Alexis de Tocqueville, the celebrated author and political theorist, elected to the Chamber of Deputies in 1846 as a moderate liberal, had refused to take part in the banquet campaign because of his distrust of the radicals involved. At the end of January 1848, he gave a speech to the chamber, calling on the government to expand the franchise, and, through this reform, avert a potentially revolutionary situation. His appeal, which quickly proved prophetic, was completely ignored.

Elements of both the French and the Hungarian situation appeared in the smaller states of southern Germany. There, the opposition combined intensified election campaigns and parliamentary activity with banquets and festivals, as well as conferences of parliamentary representatives from the different small states to create a common political program.

In many of the Italian states, lacking in parliamentary institutions of any sort, even feudal estates, the opposition's campaign took place more circuitously. When, in 1846, the Grand Duke of Tuscany agreed to allow the formation of a popular militia, a *Guardia Civica*, parades and festivals took place in the Tuscan capital of Florence and in many cities and towns. The marchers praised the Grand Duke and the newly elected Pope Pius IX, but also carried banners calling for the "independence of Italy," the liberation of the northern provinces from Austrian rule. Members of the Agricultural Association of the Kingdom of Piedmont, whose ranks included prominent liberals, pressed the royal government to add to its anti-Austrian diplomatic policies an endorsement of constitutional government. The 1847 Congress of Italian Scientists met in Venice, the first time the scholars had assembled in one of Austria's Italian provinces. Frequent and conspicuous references to "rotten potatoes" in the learned sessions on the recent crop failures produced much subversive amusement, since "potato" was an Italian slang expression for "German." At the beginning of 1848, the campaign against Austrian rule kicked into high gear, when radical nationalists in Milan, capital of the province of Lombardy, called for boycott of the purchase of tobacco, whose sale was a government monopoly. The boycott was widely followed, and when a detachment of Habsburg soldiers marched through the streets of Milan ostentatiously smoking, long-term civilian hatred of the military was politicized in a nationalist direction, leading to nasty riots leaving several dead.

Probably the most interesting and revealing venues of the continent-wide initiative of the party of movement were in the Italian Papal States and in the Kingdom of Prussia. In both places, leaders of a moderate liberalism saw the opportunity to realize their program of national unity and constitutional government in a peaceful, gradual, and legal way, through cooperation with the existing authorities. But the open hand of the opposition was, in both cases, bluntly slapped away by the government. This adamant refusal made it all too clear that it would take revolution to effect even moderate change.

Following his election to the papacy in 1846, Pius IX seemed to fulfill all the hopes placed in his office by Italian liberals, since Gioberti's book three years previously. He began a series of reforms in the Papal states, calling laymen into the government for the first time, and substantially weakening censorship, allowing a much wider and open discussion of political questions. Papal diplomats sponsored the formation of a customs union between the Papal States, the Grand Duchy of Tuscany, and the Duchy of Modena, seemingly a step in the direction of an all-Italian customs union, a long-term liberal demand. The new Pope was dazzlingly popular throughout the peninsula. He could not appear in public in Rome itself without great crowds gathering to demonstrate in his favor; elsewhere, everyone, from the aristocracy to the peasantry, was shouting "Long live Pius IX!"

Capping off his initiatives, Pius called in 1847 for the election of a Consultative Assembly, to advise him on reforms in the Papal government. Here, however, the limits of cooperation between his reforming regime and the liberal movement became clear. His address to the first meeting of the assembly, in which he bluntly asserted that Papal sovereignty came from God, and could not be compromised by a constitution, or any form of power sharing, was an articulation of a distinctly conservative political doctrine and an unmistakable rebuke to the liberals. Unimpressed, the assembly voted an address in response calling for further governmental reforms and insisted on having its proceedings published, a fundamental political innovation in an absolutist regime that had hitherto worked in secrecy.

The clash between absolutist government and liberal movement was even more pronounced in Prussia. Wishing to speed up the construction of railways in the eastern, less prosperous part of the monarchy, and finding that the capitalist profit motive would not induce investment there, the government decided to finance the building of these railways itself. The growing economic and financial difficulties of 1846–47 made it impossible for the state to float a loan, without offering firm guarantees of repayment. Bankers kept pointing to the law of 1820, a last remnant of the era of liberal reform in early nineteenth-century Prussia, which called for new public indebtedness to be guaranteed by an all-Prussian representative assembly. Reluctantly, the monarch and his ministers decided to summon such a legislative body. Rather than call for elections across the entire kingdom, an event that might have given excessive encouragement to constitutionalist ideas, Friedrich Wilhelm IV summoned the members of the different provincial estates, the diets, to meet jointly in Berlin, creating the so called "United Diet" of 1847.

Nonetheless, this legislative body seemed to offer moderate liberals the opportunity they had long been waiting for, of cooperating with the

Prussian government in a program of political reform. They would have the Diet offer to guarantee the necessary loans and even endorse new taxes to repay them, in return for a royal promise to allow the Diet to meet regularly and give it the right of approval for state finances. In following this strategy, liberals were committing themselves to moving slowly, one step at a time, carefully scaling back their demands, not calling right away for a constitution or even protesting the makeup of the Diet itself, with its membership determined by the principles of a society of orders, anathema to the liberals. Like Pius IX, however, Friedrich Wilhelm IV was unwilling to compromise in any way. He showed this attitude when he addressed the Diet and made his celebrated remarks rejecting a constitution as a piece of paper that would come between God and the country, reasserting a conservative political doctrine, also very much like Pius IX. The liberal majority in the Diet, like their counterparts in Rome, would not give in, refusing to guarantee the loans or to approve new taxes. The monarch dissolved the assembly late in 1847, leaving behind a political stalemate.

To a politically interested public, sensitive to the memory of the French Revolution, it was hard to miss the analogy to the events of 1789: the government's financial problems, the attempt to resolve them by calling for what was, in effect, an Estates General, the determination of the majority of the deputies to use state finances as a lever to produce political change. If all these had occurred, could a new storming of the Bastille be far behind? One final event in 1847 made the advent of a new revolution seem increasingly likely, the Swiss Civil War.

Although it sounds extremely peculiar today, order and stability in the Swiss cantons had never been completely restored following the 1830 revolution. Struggles between left and right continued there, at times involving riots, mass demonstrations, and armed incursions from one canton into another. These conflicts peaked in 1847, as radical and predominantly Protestant cantons tried to expel the Jesuits from the Swiss Confederation, and the Catholic and conservative cantons formed a separate, seemingly secessionist league to oppose them. There ensued a brief civil war, in which the left-wing cantons were victorious.

The Swiss Civil War was the first in the series of political confrontations historians generally group together under the heading of the revolution of 1848; it would be the only one in which the forces of change, the party of movement, would be victorious. Although contemporaries could not know this second point, they were acutely conscious of the first: events in the mountains were taken as the precursor to larger and more dramatic changes. As the German radical poet Ferdinand Freiligrath put it, when news of the war's outcome reached him, "In the highlands, there fell the first shot." The feeble response of the party of order only encouraged this mood. Prince Metternich's attempt to create a diplomatic coalition in favor of the secessionist cantons failed, and the Habsburg monarchy's ever more parlous finances made unilateral intervention impossible.

By the end of 1847, all the signs pointed towards revolution. A succession of economic crises had strained the social fabric and left behind a growing popular discontent. Aggressive reform campaigns could not change government policy for the authorities were unwilling to make concessions, an attitude present both in the French constitutional monarchy, and the Prussian or Papal absolutist regimes. Yet these same authorities also lacked the strength to suppress the opposition. Finally, the events in Switzerland had demonstrated that drastic change, even change carried out violently, was possible, and that the defenders of the established order seemed incapable of stopping it. The outbreak of revolution in 1848 and its rapid spread throughout the continent was anything but a surprise.

The verdict of the barricades

The revolutionary events began in January 1848 far off on the periphery of the continent in Sicily, where a group of conspirators planned a rising in the provincial capital of Palermo. There was nothing new about such a rising; they had been occurring in one part of the Italian peninsula or another for some thirty years, and were usually easily suppressed, after securing, at most, limited regional support. In view of the preconditions for and expectations of widespread revolution, 1848 was different. The uprising succeeded and quickly spread to the southern Italian mainland, reaching Naples, the capital city of the Kingdom of the Two Sicilies. After street fighting there, the king yielded to the insurgents, agreeing to implement basic civil rights, grant a constitution, and call for elections to a legislative assembly.

The next and decisive step in the chain of uprisings occurred in Paris, where the banquet campaign begun in mid-1847 was continuing steadily. On 22 February 1848, banquets gave way to street demonstrations; clashes between demonstrators and soldiers followed that day and the next. Barricades were built, over a thousand throughout the city; soldiers showed a marked reluctance to open fire on them. King Louis-Philippe abdicated and fled the country. Crowds invaded and disrupted the session of the parliament, debating the country's future. Converging on city hall, demonstrators demanded the proclamation of the republic, which duly occurred on 24 February 1848. This triumph of the revolution in the capital city of European politics, the center of the hopes of the party of movement, was the signal for similar events almost everywhere.

Mass meetings, followed by street demonstrations demanding a change in regime led to serious clashes between crowds and the authorities, beginning in Munich on 4 March 1848, continuing in Vienna on the thirteenth, Budapest on the fifteenth, Venice and Cracow on the seventeenth, and Milan and Berlin on the eighteenth. Barricades were built and insurgents confronted the armed forces. As in Paris, these confrontations were brief. In Budapest, the authorities gave in without a fight; elsewhere (with one exception), a day or so of skirmishing sufficed. Troops were withdrawn from the capital cities and the insurgents were victorious.

Political changes followed immediately. The kings of Prussia and Bavaria grudgingly dismissed their conservative ministers and appointed liberals in their place. Metternich, the great symbol of the established order, was forced to flee Vienna, one step ahead of the furious crowd, for exile in London. Still more reluctantly, Emperor Ferdinand (actually, the courtiers who guided the retarded ruler's steps) appointed new, liberal ministers in Vienna. However, as a result of the revolutionary movements elsewhere in Austria the new central government could not establish its authority throughout the realm. Just the opposite, provisional governments in Venice and Milan proclaimed the independence of these two provinces from Austrian rule and expressed the desire to become part of a united Italian state. The new government created in Budapest announced the separation of the Hungarian provinces from the rest of the monarchy; a Polish National Committee in Cracow proposed to do the same for the province of Galicia, as a precursor to the re-creation of an independent Poland.

This wave of revolutions from the Great Powers washed over many of the smaller countries of Europe as well. The rulers of the smaller German and Italian states did not dare a trial of strength with insurgents on the barricades, but generally appointed liberal governments after peaceful demonstrations and mass meetings. Rather the same was the story in Denmark, where mass meetings, led by liberal activists, culminating in a march to the royal castle on 21 March 1848, brought King Friedrich VII, just come to the throne two months previously, to concede to demands for a new, liberal, government ministry, and the granting of a constitution. A variation on this theme occurred in the Netherlands, where mass meetings in the capital, the Hague, and in Amsterdam, the kingdom's largest city, eventually produced demonstrations, and, on 24 March 1848, rioting in Amsterdam and clashes with the police. Bypassing both his conservative government ministers and the conservative majority in the Dutch parliament, the king appointed a commission to write a new constitution, headed by the jurist Johan Thorbecke, the leader of the liberal opposition. These measures calmed the public; the new constitution, which increased the powers of the parliament, and provided for

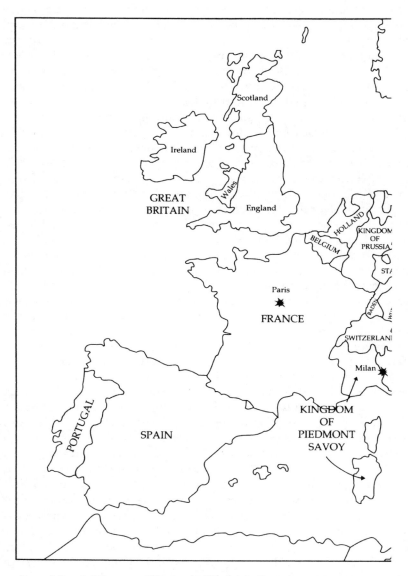

Map 3.1 Scenes of barricade fighting in January to March 1848.

direct election (albeit with a property franchise) to its lower house, was duly implemented.

The situation was somewhat touchier in Belgium, a constitutional monarchy not unlike the one just overthrown in France. Also like France, Belgium had a liberal and a radical political opposition, as well as a nascent labor movement, containing some socialist sympathizers. Belgian radicals had close ties to left-wing political activists in neighboring northern France and western Germany. Following the proclamation of the republic in Paris, a "Belgian Legion" was created there, drawing on Belgian workers employed in the French metropolis. Taking the train north to the border region, the legionaries gathered in an armed camp, and the legion, some two thousand strong, crossed into Belgium at the end of March 1848, joined there by leaders of the radical opposition in Belgium itself. The expected mass support from Belgian workers failed to materialize, and a small regular army contingent easily scattered the poorly armed legionnaires. Not waiting for more trouble, the Belgian government quickly proclaimed a series of reforms, including a lowering of the property franchise for elections to the Belgian parliament, leading to an increase in the size of the electorate by 70 percent – just the sort of reform de Tocqueville had suggested in vain for France a few months previously. Combining this measure with a decrease in taxes calmed the situation considerably.

The government of Sweden had to face a liberal opposition that was conducting a banquet campaign in favor of a reform to replace Sweden's Estates with a constitutional legislature. As in Paris, the banquets led to street demonstrations, but the Swedish army, unlike its French counterpart, took decisive action against the demonstrators, shooting some thirty of them. The king did appoint a new group of government ministers, but unlike the case in Belgium, the Swedish government did not follow up the military suppression of opposition with reform measures. Proposals for a new constitution were handled dilatorily by the government, and eventually rejected by the Swedish Estates, so that the Scandinavian country kept its feudal legislature until 1866, making it one of the last countries in Europe to still retain such a body. In Norway, then ruled by the king of Sweden, but with a separate governmental structure, including a constitution and a legislature elected by a property franchise, there were street demonstrations in the capital of Christiana (later to be renamed Oslo), which were suppressed by the military with no loss of life.

Things were still quieter in the Iberian Peninsula. Particularly in Spain, that had been through a series of revolutions and protracted civil wars in the 1820s and 1830s, that attracted European-wide attention, some response to the events of 1848 might have been expected. Spaniards, however, were quite worn out by the violent political conflict of the recent past. There was little enthusiasm in Spain for political activity of any kind, certainly not a revolutionary one, in 1848.

Finally, the Parisian uprising made its influence felt very far off in southeastern Europe, in the Danubian Principalities of Moldavia (today's Moldova) and Wallachia (part of today's Romania). Young men from the principalities, studying in Paris, some of them members of Romanian secret societies there, took part in the street fighting of February 1848. They resolved to carry the revolution to their homeland, and by April 1848 (it took a while to get back), had returned, to start banquets and mass meetings, in the respective capital cities of Iași and Bucharest, calling for constitutional and legal reforms. While the prince in Moldavia succeeded in suppressing the opposition, thanks to a private army of Albanian mercenaries, the agitation continued and intensified in Wallachia, until a new, revolutionary government was formed in June.

Three points can be made about this initial wave of revolutions. First, there is the relative moderation of their outcomes. Outside of Paris, the "revolution stopped at the foot of the throne," as contemporaries said. The republic was not proclaimed; monarchical government remained in place. Even the new government of Hungary, while announcing its separation from Austria was willing to recognize Ferdinand von Habsburg as its king. The provisional governments in Italy were republican in form. But the proclamation of a Venetian republic referred more to the pre-1789 old regime than to the post-1789 revolutionary era, for it seemed to be a restoration of the "Republic of Saint Mark," that had governed the island city and its maritime empire from the middle ages until its abolition by revolutionary French troops in 1797. Furthermore, the policy of the provisional governments of northern Italy, like that of the new ministries in central Europe, was a liberal one. These new governments granted basic civil liberties, including freedom of speech, the press, and assembly. They promised a constitution and the holding of parliamentary elections (often for a constituent assembly to write such a constitution) while refraining from more drastic measures.

A second point about this early phase of the 1848 revolution is the speed with which the previously existing governments collapsed. The barricade fights were all of relatively brief duration, the authorities usually giving in without attempting a serious trial of strength. Both contemporaries and later historians have sometimes asserted that the initial success of the 1848 revolutions was due to a failure of nerve on the part of the rulers; had they just cold-bloodedly committed the armed forces, the uprisings in the major capital cities could all have been handily suppressed.

Unlike most such historical "counterfactuals," in 1848 there actually was a counter-example to test this assertion, one soldier in the Great

Powers undergoing revolution, who did not lose his nerve and did try to suppress the uprising, Field Marshal Joseph Radetzky, commander of the Austrian troops in northern Italy. Radetzky had his soldiers fight it out with the Milanese insurgents for five straight days, until the pugnacious Field Marshal ordered the remaining troops under his command to evacuate the city, before they all deserted. His experiences suggest the weakness of the counter-argument, and the weakness of the state in 1848: the government could not rely on its troops to follow orders. The actions of the rulers of Denmark, the Netherlands, and the smaller German states demonstrated a distinct unwillingness to rely on their armed forces for a resolution of the conflict; even in Belgium, the government, after turning back a revolutionary threat by force of arms, hastened to implement reforms.

A third point to note was that the wave of revolutions did not reach the two peripheral Great Powers, the Russian Empire and Great Britain. Naturally, the news of revolution in France, the German states, Italy, and the Habsburg monarchy had an effect on the politics of the two countries. In the United Kingdom, the radical opposition, the Chartists, although in decline for almost a decade, were inspired by the victories of revolution in continental Europe to one final effort. Their great parade and demonstration in London, on 10 April 1848, to present a petition to parliament for universal manhood suffrage, was met by a massive show of force: police, the army and the "special constables," an 85,000–man militia, primarily composed of property owners. In the tsar's empire, there were no demonstrations or overt signs of political opposition. An underground secret society, the "Petrashevtsy," best known for one of its members, the then student and future novelist Fyodor Dostoevsky, was broken up by the police. Even if failing to bridge the English Channel and pass the closely guarded borders of the realm of the tsars, the revolutionary wave of February–April 1848 had spread across the European continent, from the Atlantic to Ukraine, from the shores of the Baltic to the shores of the Black Sea. We will now look at events in that revolutionary spring.

The "springtime of the peoples"

The republic proclaimed in France – an astonishing report for contemporaries, bringing back great and terrifying days, still on the fringe of living memory: the Jacobins and the reign of terror, the abolition of feudalism, Napoleon, the decades of warfare. Scarcely was this news absorbed, when it became clear that this time around the revolution would not be restricted to France, but was spreading throughout the continent. With remarkable speed, considering the poor quality of communications, news of the great events penetrated the most distant parts of

Europe. As early as 19 March 1848, there were proclamations of freedom and public celebrations in Uzhhorod and Mukachevo, the chief towns of the mountainous sub-Carpathian Ukraine, then in the northeastern corner of the Hungarian kingdom (part of today's Ukrainian Republic), about the most isolated part of Europe imaginable.

Peripheral as these towns were, the response of their inhabitants to the striking news of the revolution was entirely typical: a great outburst of jubilation, a massive celebration of the victory of freedom. Parades, speeches, church services, nocturnal illuminations – all the paraphernalia of festivity were pressed into service. A wave of fraternization swept the continent, uniting the most implausible elements. French priests blessed the planting of trees of liberty, previously the symbol of a godless radicalism. Protestants, Catholics, and Jews of Mainz all came to the Rhineland city's cathedral to celebrate jointly the great tidings of liberty. Romanians and Hungarians in Transylvania embraced each other. Czechs and Germans worked and spoke together on the "National Committee" in Prague. The Polish revolutionary Ludwik Mieroslawski, imprisoned by the Prussian police for his role in the abortive uprising of 1846, was released from jail in Berlin, to be greeted by a crowd issuing cheers for Poland. For a few brief weeks, Europe experienced the "springtime of the peoples," celebrating the end of a decades-long winter of oppression.

It was, of course, all an illusion. Social conflict, nationalist rivalry, interconfessional hostility, and differing, even contradictory, political agendas all waited, scarcely concealed beneath the surface of fraternity. Disillusioned contemporaries and subsequent historians have made the rapid emergence of these conflicts and the destruction of revolutionary euphoria, shortly followed by the destruction of the revolution itself, the main theme of the history of 1848. It is a main theme, and the nature and development of these conflicts and their disillusioning effects will be considered at some length in the rest of this chapter, but it is not the only one. Scholarship of the last several decades has revealed an equally significant feature of the revolution: the development of political organization and mass political participation on an unprecedented scale. In these developments one can still see, preserved and transformed, some of the aspirations and exaltations of the springtime of the peoples.

Much of the development of political organizations and the growth of political participation was a result of the emergence of sharp conflicts out of the euphoria of the springtime of 1848. Let us now turn to these conflicts, and consider them in three separate categories: (1) the development of popular mass movements; (2) the clash of nationalities and the beginnings of armed conflict; (3) the policy dilemmas of the new governments created by the revolution and the result of elections they called under a broad, often universal, manhood suffrage.

Points of conflict: (1) popular mass movements

The victory of revolution in the capital cities was a signal for the lower classes to resume the social conflicts they had engaged in over the previous decades, but to do so on a broader scale and with a greater anger and energy. These open and spontaneous clashes would begin in March 1848 and continue, almost uninterruptedly, through June of that year. Things calmed down somewhat then – helped along by doses of armed repression – but such conflicts would be resumed at irregular intervals until the summer of 1849. This constant background of popular disturbances, and the anxieties they provoked among many substantial citizens, would be a characteristic feature of the mid-century revolution.

Throughout the regions of serfdom and seigneurialism in central and eastern Europe, peasants refused en masse to perform their labor services and to pay their feudal dues. Not content with such boycotts, they physically assaulted the aristocracy, attacking and plundering their castles, seizing and destroying charters of feudal privilege, registers of feudal dues, and other written documents of their oppression. Peasant violence against feudal landlords was omnipresent: from Kikinda in the Banat (part of the province of Croatia-Slavonia), where the peasants seized the lands of their lord and divided it up among them, to Slotinicy in Bohemia, where peasants stormed the castle of Prince Auersperg, to Hechingen, in southwestern Germany, where thousands of peasants, armed with clubs, surrounded the prince and forced him to renounce all his seigneurial dues.

It is important to understand that the rural uprisings of the spring of 1848 were not limited to the regions of feudal and seigneurial agriculture, any more than pre-1848 peasant grievances were exclusively about feudal and seigneurial relations in the countryside. As we have seen, peasant resentment about use of the forest was the greatest source of social tension in rural society before the revolution; it was also the single most common and most prevalent source of violence in the countryside during the spring of 1848. Everywhere that there were forests, there were forest riots.

Peasants occupied forest land that had previously been held in common but had passed into the private ownership of large landlords, a common action throughout the mountainous areas of the Italian peninsula. Ownership was not the only issue involved. Even when the woodlands were owned by the state or by the villages themselves, they were administered by foresters, enforcing government regulations that prevented the countryfolk from using the forests as they wished. In the *arrondissement* of Embrun in the Department of the Isère, in the Alpine region of southeastern France, the peasants were furious with the Inspector of the Forests, whom they regarded as the "architect of their ruin." He could not leave his official residence to inspect the forests for fear of being murdered, which almost happened to his subordinates, who were regularly surrounded and severely beaten by outraged farmers. Beating foresters, or other government officials charged with enforcing forest regulations, burning down their homes and offices, chopping down stands of trees they were planting (coniferous pine or spruce trees, disliked by peasants, since, unlike the oaks they replaced, they provided no acorns to feed the swine) burning forest records and registers of forest offenses, disrupting court sessions devoted to forest crimes – these were common scenes in Europe during the spring of 1848.

Both occupation of the woods and assaults on foresters were precursors to the actual point of these peasant actions: making use of the forest without restriction. The revolutionary year saw repeated instances of collective chopping down of trees, gathering branches and underbrush, hunting, pasturing animals in the forest – in short, doing everything that the hard pressed peasants, still under the impact of the economic crisis of the mid-1840s, needed to survive. Almost forty years later, a witness testifying in a civil lawsuit concerning property in the village of Hardenberg, in the Bavarian Palatinate in the extreme southwestern corner of Germany, remembered how in 1848 the villagers were streaming out of the forest, pushing wheelbarrows filled with newly chopped wood.[1] His recollection is characteristic of how the mid-century revolution was experienced: more than any other way, it was the time when the peasants could do what they wanted with the forest.

If forest conflict was most typical in poorer, mountainous areas, where there was the most forest, there was plenty for peasants to be angry about in the flatter, more open and prosperous countryside. The division of the common lands was one substantial cause of dispute: peasants demanded that it be returned to common use, destroyed fences, hedges, and ditches marking its being placed in private possession, and threatened the beneficiaries of such division. Particularly in those areas where there existed sharp social divisions among the peasants themselves, poorer peasants and day laborers were likely to turn on the wealthier villagers. They might demand higher wages for farm work, an unusually sophisticated action; more typically, they would mob the affluent farmers and demand money

---

[1] Landesarchiv Speyer, J6/969, testimony of field watchman Friedrich Parr of Dürkheim, 2 May 1885.

or food from them. Creditors were everywhere victims of the wrath of their debtors, who extorted by force or threat of force the cancellation of their debts and the public burning of IOUs and promissory notes.

As both contemporaries and later historians asked, what did all this have to do with the revolution, or to put it differently, what was the connection between these social grievances and the political issues in the capital cities? The best answer is to note that the peasants themselves constantly justified their actions by reference to the political issues of the day: they marched into the forest behind the tricolor flags of the revolution; they shouted the political slogans prevalent in the capital cities as they assaulted foresters or demanded the return of the common lands. Consider this description of the great land occupation during the revolution in the mountains of Sila, in the province of Basilicata of the Kingdom of the Two Sicilies, one of the major centers of forest disputes in the decades before 1848. The states attorney went out to investigate in May 1848 and he reported:

[a]t a distance of eighteen miles, I was met by over 300 of the National Guard, who were preceded by the tricolor flag and followed by the poor and the young people. Along the road were stationed other leaders of the National Guard: the crowd grew, the number of wretchedly thin and haggard was in the thousands. Several hundred women with the tricolor flag met us not far from the village. They were dressed in tattered clothes, the very picture of poverty. All of them shouted "Long live the constitution; long live Italy," but they all demanded land to farm and bread.[2]

Government officials, journalists, politicians, and, more generally, members of the urban, educated classes frequently commented on this rustic attitude, condemning it as a "misunderstanding" of the true meaning of liberty, national unity, the republic, or constitutional government. And of course it was: seizing land in Sila had nothing to do with whether all the Italian monarchies would be united into one state; beating up foresters no direct connection with the creation of a government without a king. In another sense, the misunderstanding existed on both sides. If the peasants misunderstood the meaning of abstract political concepts, the educated, urban population had little interest in the significance of long-term social conflicts, particularly for the rural population, but more generally, for the lower classes. The change of regime in February–March 1848, though, had created a situation in which the lower classes would have a say – a significant one – in the process of government. For that reason, the

---

[2] Cited in Aurelio Lepre, *Storia del Mezzogiorno nel Risorgimento*, (Rome, 1969), 223.

politicization of their previously apolitical social conflicts would be a decisive factor in the further course of the 1848 revolution.

The barricade fighting and the change of regimes also inspired artisans, manufacturing workers, and urban laborers to express drastically and often violently the social conflicts in which they had been involved. A wave of strikes passed through Europe, following hard on the heels of the barricade fighting. Printers and typesetters were prominent in these actions, in Germany obtaining from newspaper publishers a nationwide agreement for a six-day working week. Construction trades, of all the crafts, the ones in which each master employed the largest number of journeymen, were another center of strike activity.

Once again, given the nature of pre-1848 society and social tensions, these more familiar forms of labor conflict were not the most important ones. More typical were actions by outworkers, surrounding and attacking the homes or offices of merchant-contractors who employed them. The rioters, perhaps waving tricolor flags and cheering liberty and equality, or national unity, demanded higher wages. They also posed other, equally significant, demands, going to the question of who controlled this form of production. Arbitrary fines, short-weighing or short-measuring, and truck payments (payments in goods instead of in cash) were to be abolished, workers were to be given the opportunity and financing to purchase their own implements of production, if they only rented them from the merchants, or even the chance to organize their own collective workshops, which would produce and market goods independently of the capitalists controlling the trade. The way such demands were raised suggests a strong element of revenge for years of ill-treatment: the thousands of weavers in the German silk center of Elberfeld who demolished the home and office of one merchant known for his practice of short-measuring cloth, or the crowd of textile workers in northern France who forced one manufacturer to walk barefoot from the villages of Malaunay to Maronne.

Another major issue in such disturbances was control over the labor market. "Outsiders" taking jobs from local people – whether Belgians in Paris or in northern France, peasants from neighboring villages selling simple craft goods in the marketplace of the city of Trier, or quarry workers from one village working in the next one – were assaulted and driven out. The "Belgian Legion," that assembled in France to invade Belgium and create a republic there, was composed in large part of Belgian workers who had been ejected from their jobs. Support for the legion on the part of the revolutionary provisional government in France was less for the purpose of revolutionizing Belgium than of ending the conflicts in the French labor market, by shipping the Belgian workers back home. Craftsmen in small workshops protested merchant contract-ors giving out jobs to outworkers toiling at home; tailors, in particular, became exercised at the thought of women taking their jobs away. Soldiers who improved their meager pay by working odd jobs when off duty were the targets of civilian laborers competing with them.

One version of this conflict over the labor market involved machine breaking. Railroads tracks and steamships were the most frequent targets, attacked by porters, carters, boat- and towmen, who feared for their livelihoods; metallurgical factories were assaulted by smiths and grinders who resented the competition. (Unlike the case with the first machine-breakers, the English Luddites of the early nineteenth century, textile mills were less likely to be the object of mob violence in Europe during 1848.) Some of these actions were particularly visible to educated con-temporaries, who followed closely the progress of steam power. They paid attention when whole villages of towmen opened fire on steamboats proceeding up the Rhine river, and brought riverine commerce to a halt for several months until the steamboat companies agreed to pay them compensation for their technological unemployment.

Historians have made a lot of this machine breaking, probably too much. Such actions were part of a broader pattern of attempts to regain control of the labor market and were far outnumbered by actions directed at other aspects of this market. All of these actions reflected both the immediate effects of the economic crisis of the mid-1840s – the high prices, followed by indebtedness, poor business conditions, and wide-spread unemployment – and even more, the broader conditions of the preceding two decades, characterized by falling real wages, a crowded labor market and a decline in artisans' control over the conditions of production. The increasing sense of grievance connected to all these developments came to the surface in outbursts of violent anger during the spring of 1848.

The same question about the politicization of such social conflicts posed for the peasants can also be raised in relation to the urban lower classes. At the very least, there was the same use of political slogans and symbolism to legitimate their grievances. City people, though, tended to go further, in two significant ways. First, they made energetic use of the newly guaranteed freedom of association. To ensure that their demands were met, to negotiate with (or exert pressure on) employers and mer-chant contractors, to bring their views before local government and the state authorities, craftsmen, workers, and laborers created organizations. Much of this organization was by individual craft, taking a wide variety of forms, ranging from regular if informal open meetings, to existing, revived, or newly organized craft guilds, to mutual benefit societies, or even, and most rarely, nascent trade unions. In addition, there also developed workers' associations, whose membership either was open to all "workers" (remember that in contemporary parlance, this included outworkers and small master craftsmen, not just wage laborers) regardless of trade, or consisted of a federation of different trade groups. Not surprisingly, the most elaborate example of these forms of association was found in Paris, where all the trades had their own organizations, which met regularly, negotiated with, and/or intimidated employers and merchant contractors. Thanks to the policies of the new republican regime, each trade elected delegates to an officially recognized, state-sponsored deliberative body, the "Luxembourg Commission," a veritable parliament of labor, that debated plans for broader social and economic reorganization.

This last example reveals the second main difference between the expression of social grievances on the part of the peasants and of workers or artisans. The latter were noticeably more aware of the political significance of their demands. More than anywhere else, this was the case in Paris, the political capital of Europe, whose poorer inhabitants were unusually attuned to politics, even before the outbreak of the revolution. In a broader way, this condition existed throughout larger cities in France, where socialist doctrines had found a substantial audience in the 1840s. The politicization of social conflicts in urban areas and manufacturing districts of Germany, Italy, the Habsburg monarchy or the Principalities of Moldavia and Wallachia was not quite so pronounced. Following the return of more politicized exiles, both workers and intellectuals, from abroad, the development of associations to press workers' and craftsmen's economic interests and social grievances, as well as the rapid growth of political life in urban areas, it would not be long – the summer of 1848 at the very latest – before the two were closely interrelated.

Some popular grievances had been common in city and country, felt by peasants, artisans, and laborers before 1848, and these were expressed violently on a wide scale in the spring of that year. Tax collection was one major complaint of the lower classes and the springtime of the peoples was also the springtime of spontaneous tax boycotts and the attempted murder of tax collectors. Barricade fighting in both Paris and Vienna included the assault on and destruction of the octroi barriers, the tax collection stations on the city walls where foodstuffs coming into the city were taxed, food prices increased, and ordinary people's standard of living visibly diminished. This experience in the capital cities was repeated many times in smaller walled towns, where the octroi was collected. Peasants were no more willing to continue paying property taxes than they were to go on paying their feudal or seigneurial dues. Customs agents were attacked, as in this quite typical instance, when several hundred men demolished the customs station in the border village of Mühlenbeck, in the north German Duchy of Braunschweig:

The mob began by smashing in the windows and doors; then the tiles were ripped off the roof and the destruction of the building continued, until . . . it was completely torn down and just the annex was left standing. The records and implements in the building were strewn about and tables and chairs thrown out into the street. The attempt to set the building on fire was thwarted, when the flames which had already encompassed the records and papers were stamped out by inhabitants of Brunsen who threw a door on the conflagration. At 3 a.m., the ruins of the customs building were set on fire, so that it has been completely destroyed.[3]

After such events, it is no surprise that smuggling showed a vast increase in the spring of 1848 and was carried out quite openly, while customs agents were far too intimidated to intervene against it.

Clashes between civilians and soldiers occurred sporadically at this time as well. The troops of General Radetzky, retreating from Milan to Austria's four northern Italian fortresses, the so-called "Quadrilateral," met jeering and sneers, brawled with civilians when quartered at night, faced sniper fire on their march, or, in a more friendly way, were greeted with the red, white, and green Italian tricolor, plied with food and drink, and induced to desert. Another region of military–civilian hostility was in the Rhineland, on the western edge of the Prussian monarchy. The government had sent troops there following the proclamation of the republic in Paris, fearing the new French revolutionary regime would invade Germany as its predecessor had done in 1792. However, the provisional government of the French republic had proclaimed its intent of carrying out a peaceful foreign policy, so the Prussian soldiers directed their fighting spirits at the Rhineland civilians, assaulting them, tearing down their tricolor flags, grabbing wives and girlfriends and carrying them off. Civilians retaliated, resulting in large-scale riots, with deaths on both sides, in a number of Rhenish cities.

There were also scattered outbreaks of violence related to religious differences. The most common kind were anti-Semitic riots, occurring on a large scale in eastern France, southwestern Germany, and in a number of Hungarian cities. Religious and economic motives were closely mixed in these. Peasant riots against their creditors tended to expand into attacks on all Jews in those regions where Jews were disproportionately

---

[3] Andreas Düwel, *Sozialrevolutionärer Protest und konservative Gesinnung. Die Landbevölkerung des Königreichs Hanover und des Herzogtums Braunschweig in der Revolution von 1848/49* (Frankfurt, 1996), 83.

over-represented in the ranks of rural moneylenders. The urban counterparts to these rural disturbances occurred in cities where an unusually
rigid guild system was in force, and master craftsmen felt increasingly
threatened by a growing immigration of Jews from the countryside to work
as unlicensed craftsmen or as peddlers and shopkeepers selling wares
produced outside of the guilds. The pre-1848 Hungarian authorities had
tolerated this population movement; with the revolutionary questioning of
their rule, guildsmen took advantage of the situation to go after those
whom they thought were threatening their interests.

There were other disturbances centered on religious issues as well.
Some of these involved clashes between different Christian confessions.
Scattered brawls and encounters between Protestants and Catholics took
place in religiously mixed areas of western Germany and in the city of
Nîmes in southern France. In the overwhelmingly Roman Catholic areas
of Mediterranean Europe, anti-clericalism was at first muted: the patriotic actions of Pius IX, and the support of much of the Catholic clergy for
the initial, anti-Austrian outbreaks, had temporarily softened potential
hostilities towards the church in Italy. Circumstances were similar in
France, where attacks on churches and the clergy, while occasionally
occurring in the spring of 1848 in the southeast of the country, were far
less common than they had been in the aftermath of the revolution of
1830. There was even less evidence of anti-clericalism in predominantly
Protestant parts of the continent, as we might see from Berlin, where the
victorious barricade fighters paraded past a badly frightened Prussian
king, singing hymns.

The center of popular hostility to organized religion in the spring of
1848 was in the Habsburg monarchy. In Vienna, the crowd stormed and
destroyed the convent of the Redemptorists, driving the *patres* out of the
city and forcing the archbishop to flee for good measure. Provincial
centers were not far behind, the crowd in Graz, capital of the province
of Styria, destroying the convent of the Jesuits and forcing them to flee.
The funeral of the Bishop of Graz in April 1848 became the scene of anti-
clerical demonstrations. The Catholic Church was especially closely
connected to the old order in Austria, so its overthrow seems to have
excited special hostilities that extended even to the lower levels of the
clergy. Particularly in the monarchy's eastern provinces, priests' voices
were raised in the spring of 1848 in favor of a more democratic reorganization of the church and for the abolition of clerical celibacy.

What all these riots, demonstrations, mass meetings, and newly
founded organizations showed was that the initial successes of the revolution in the capital cities had produced an enormous problem of the
re-establishment and even more of the re-definition of public order. The

new regimes would not just have to calm down angry citizens, suppress riots, revive the economy, and get public business and the administration of justice carried out in a regular fashion, they would have to do so within new, as yet unascertained parameters. Before 1848, part of public order in much of central and eastern Europe was the regular payment of seigneurial dues and the performance of feudal labor services. Would that still be the case? Similarly, strikes or even the organization of workers to preserve their collective interests against employers were disorderly acts before the revolutionary events of February–March 1848, but would they be afterwards? Would good citizens of the new regimes still pay the octroi or the property tax? Answers to these questions could not be sought in lengthy debate; they had to be devised and implemented immediately, by a very mixed group of individuals, ranging from the officials in the service of the new governments, carried over from the previous regimes, to the new men of the revolution, to miscellaneous, self-appointed groups of civilian volunteers.

Leaving aside, for the moment, the more complicated question of just what order was under the new regimes, and turning to the simpler issue of the creation of physically peaceful conditions, the new authorities faced a difficult task. Scarcely sufficient in calmer times, the few police were completely overwhelmed and intimidated, in no condition to do much of anything. The army could be used, and was, particularly in the countryside, to protect forests, resume tax collection, stop peasant violence against the lords. In Hungary, the new government even went so far as to declare the entire country in a state of siege in June 1848, primarily because of the ubiquity of peasant uprisings. But there were not enough soldiers to guarantee order everywhere. Additionally, using the army to control disorder could lead to more disorder as the riots between soldiers and civilians showed.

Since existing institutions were not up to the task of preserving public order, a new one was required. It already existed in liberal and democratic political theory, which held that the ultimate guarantee of the people's rights was an armed citizenry, organized into a militia, that is, a "national guard" or a "civic guard." First tried out in 1789, such an armed force existed continuously since then in France. The refusal of the National Guardsmen of Paris to fire on the demonstrating crowds both in July 1830 and in February 1848 had guaranteed the initial successes of the revolutions of both those years. In the spring of 1848, with the coming to power of liberal regimes, these armed corps sprung up throughout Europe, sometimes formed by the new authorities, sometimes appearing spontaneously and retrospectively legitimized. Governments were even willing to give the guards large numbers of weapons from military stores.

These guards were the ubiquitous armed presence needed to restore public order and, all things considered, they did a good job of it.

However, the activities of these guards raised the second and more difficult question about the restoration of order, namely what would this order be? Even before the militias took any action, the issue of eligibility for membership made the problems involved with the preservation of order painfully clear. As a rule, membership was restricted to property-owning solid citizens; the lower classes were excluded. In much of Italy, the organizers of the guards went further, and tried to prevent any peasants from joining the civilian militias and receiving arms. Paris presented the opposite picture: the insurgent workers who had created the republic on the barricades were in no mood to be turned away from bearing arms for it, and the new provisional government, following several angry demonstrations, was willing, for the moment, to do their bidding.

The upshot of these situations was that while the guards did restore order, the order they restored was usually an unsatisfactory one, for at least some social groups. The bourgeoisie of Paris was not pleased at an "order" of armed workers in the streets, allowing organized trade groups in each craft to negotiate with or intimidate employers and merchant contractors. Admittedly, in other urban areas – French industrial towns, such as Limoges or Rouen, would be good examples – the terms were reversed, and armed property owners intimidated the lower classes. The most common result was a situation that pleased no one, where the bourgeoisie remained afraid, and the urban lower classes angry and resentful. Much of the rural population, throughout the continent, was no less dissatisfied: the re-established order in the countryside included the resumption of tax collection, new limitations on use of the forest, in eastern Europe even a continuation in the payment of feudal dues or the performance of labor services while legislation abolishing them was thrashed out. As the spring of 1848 gave way to summer, the scope and intensity of popular disorders gradually decreased, but the ill will generated by them and by their suppression or pacification remained, creating strong possibilities for future political conflict.

Points of conflict: (2) national unity and national war

Since the demands for national self-determination and the creation of a unified nation-state were an intrinsic part of the program of the pre-1848 political opposition, the initial successes of the revolution were a signal for both popular demands and government policy to move in that direction. Once it was out in the open and pursued as a matter of public policy, all the problematic features of nationalism, previously hidden by the official repression of nationalist demands, became apparent. Nationalist efforts would come up against the existing European states, in spite of the revolutionization of their governments still not organized on national lines, against religious, regional, and dynastic loyalties, and, most of all, against each other.

The union of the many Italian and German states into one had been a basic nationalist demand, vigorously pursued following the outbreak of the revolution. For Italy, the immediate goal of the nationalist movement was the expulsion of foreign, that is Austrian, rule from the two northern provinces of Lombardy and Venetia. Following the insurgent victories on the barricades, this goal seemed nearly accomplished. Most of the two provinces were under the control of nationalist provincial governments; the remnants of the Habsburg troops entrenched themselves in the fortresses of the Quadrilateral and prepared for a siege.

These developments put substantial pressure on Carlo Alberto, King of Piedmont-Savoy, the one clearly anti-Habsburg Italian monarch. Like most of the rulers of the smaller and medium-sized states of Germany and Italy, Carlo Alberto had not waited for violent revolutionary action to encompass his realm, but had made a series of concessions to the liberal opposition, climaxing shortly after the proclamation of the republic in Paris, by the granting of a constitution for his kingdom, the calling of parliamentary elections, and the appointing of new, more liberal government ministers. The revolutions in the Habsburgs' northern Italian provinces less than two weeks later raised the ante: the arena of his actions could no longer be just the Piedmontese kingdom; it would have to be the entire Italian peninsula. The provisional governments of the two former provinces formally requested the intervention of the regular Piedmontese army to drive the Austrians out of their fortresses. Pressure was also applied from within Carlo Alberto's own realm by street demonstrations in favor of war in the port city of Genoa. Finally, suspicion spread that more radical elements, especially in Venice, were thinking of asking for armed assistance from the new republican regime in France. Carlo Alberto had no choice; on 23 March 1848, he declared war on Austria and sent his army marching towards Lombardy. "*Italia farà da sé*," Italy will do it alone, he proclaimed, asserting that the Italians would need no outside assistance in expelling foreign rulers and creating national unity. If this rejection of French military support catered to nationalist sentiment, it was also a step taken against the potentially radicalizing and pro-republican consequences of French intervention.

The war Carlo Alberto initiated would completely dominate the 1848 revolution in Italy. Even after the Austrians' victory in August 1848, Italian politics would remain focused on the situation in the north, and the possibility of renewing the campaign against the Austrians. Well before then, the Italian national war would have major political consequences within and far beyond the borders of the Italian peninsula.

Once Carlo Alberto had committed his army to the national war, liberals and radicals in the other Italian states demanded that their governments do the same. These demands had no strategic ramifications, since none of these forces were of any military significance, but for one Italian state, the Papal kingdom, the political consequences of any decision were enormous. Pius IX was an Italian prince, ruler of one of the peninsula's states, but he was Pope of all Catholics, of the Austrians, as well as of the Italians. The calls for war echoing in the streets of Rome put him in an impossible position. He finally agreed to send Papal troops north, ostensibly just to guard the frontiers against the Austrians, but not actually to enter into combat, only the general commanding the Papal forces promptly led his soldiers into battle, telling them that they were engaged in a holy crusade with the Pope's blessing. At the end of April, Pius ordered the Papal troops withdrawn, denouncing the war and offering his services as a mediator between the Italians and the Austrians. It was the beginning of his break with liberalism, nationalism, and the 1848 revolution, a move with broad European consequences. Devout Catholics all across the continent, who, as part of their religious and political views, supported the assertion or reassertion of Papal authority, would follow in his political footsteps, moving from welcoming the initial outbreak of the revolution, or at least showing a willingness to engage in cautious cooperation with it, to an increasingly open enmity.

In Germany, unlike Italy, the movement towards national unity in 1848 was less about national warfare, although there was also some of that, than about clashing nationalist claims to the same territory. One arena of competing nationalist claims was in Prussia's southeastern province of Posen (Polish: Poznań). This province, largely rural, economically little developed, with noble large landowners and many landless laborers was largely inhabited by Roman Catholic Polish-speakers, with a minority German and Protestant population, and a smaller Yiddish-speaking Jewish one, mainly in the towns. Revolutionary attacks on authority there had taken on a nationalist tone, as German officials were driven out and replaced by Polish-speaking nationalists, loosely coordinated by a Polish national committee in the provincial capital of Posen. Polish revolutionaries quickly converged on the province. Led by Ludwik Mieroslawski, recently released from jail in Berlin, they hoped to use the province as a center for a planned attack on Russia, with the intent of liberating the Polish territories under Russian rule.

The new liberal government in Prussia was, at first, in March 1848, prepared to go along with the Poles, and divide the province along ethnic lines, ceding the predominantly Polish-speaking regions to a Polish nation-state, perhaps even supporting the plans for war with Russia. However, in the course of April, clashes developed between German- and Polish-speaking inhabitants – or between Protestants and Catholics, for the differences were interpreted as much in religious as in national terms – with the Jews increasingly supporting the Germans. A German national committee was formed in Posen to compete with its Polish counterpart. German-speaking liberals and conservatives, both in Posen and in Berlin, increasingly came to support their "national" cause in this eastern province, and, by the end of April, Prussian troops were sent against Mieroslawski's insurgents. Armed largely with scythes beaten straight, they were no match for the regular army.

This conflict in Posen/Poznań, in conjunction with the suppression of the Polish national committee in Cracow, in the Austrian province of Galicia, marked the early end of the hopes of Polish nationalists for the 1848 revolution. Historians, particularly those of the mid-twentieth century, under the impact of the Second World War and the brutal Nazi occupation of Poland, have sometimes interpreted this rejection of Polish nationalist aspirations by most Germans (by May 1848, only a minority on the extreme left of the political spectrum supported the demand for the creation of a Polish nation-state on Prussian territory) as a fatal blow to the German revolution itself. When applied to the 1848 revolution, this judgment is an anachronistic one; events on the southeastern fringe of the Prussian monarchy (other provinces of the monarchy, with a large Polish-speaking population, such as Silesia and West Prussia, saw no Polish nationalist movement at all) were not decisive for the German revolution. The clash of nationalist movements in Posen/Poznań does show a problematic feature of the nationalist political program, the way that different nationalist groups might claim the same territory. There were other places in central and east-central Europe where this clash of nationalisms was more important for the German revolution.

One was the provinces of Schleswig and Holstein, at the northern end of central Europe. Largely inhabited by German speakers, with a sizeable Danish-speaking minority in Schleswig, the northernmost of the two provinces, bordering on the rest of the Danish kingdom, the provinces' pre-1848 situation did not conform to nationalists' ideas of how borders ought to be drawn. Both provinces were part of the Danish kingdom, and, like other parts of that kingdom, had their own separate estates and legal systems, although they were administered by the royal officials – some German- some Danish-speaking – in Copenhagen. Holstein was both a province of the Danish kingdom and also part of the German Confederation. Schleswig was not part of the German Confederation, but both provinces had always had a common ruler – although different ones – for centuries.

The outbreak of revolution in 1848 had made these circumstances untenable for both sides. The liberal government come to power in Copenhagen in March 1848 proclaimed the complete incorporation of Schleswig, but not Holstein, into the Danish kingdom, with the enthusiastic support of Danish nationalists, who wished to carry out the liberal, nationalist program of creating a united Danish nation-state. At the same time, German nationalists in both provinces rose against Danish rule and established a provisional revolutionary government. (One might say that the Germans, especially in Schleswig, were in a similar position to the Poles in Posen, while the Danes in Schleswig were more like the Germans in Posen, although German nationalists, inconsistently, but understandably, supported their own national cause in both regions.) Liberals and radicals throughout Germany rallied to the support of the insurgents. The new liberal government in Prussia, like its Italian counterpart in Piedmont-Savoy, sent troops to assist them.

A powerful symbol of the nationalist movement, Schleswig-Holstein, and events there were certainly more important for the outcome of the 1848 revolution in Germany than those in Prussia's predominantly Polish provinces, the armed clashes in these northern provinces were just not as central to a potentially united Germany as Lombardy-Venetia was to Italy. The war pitting the armies of the Italian states against the forces of the Habsburg Emperor, even when the latter were weakened and disorganized by revolution, was a serious and difficult struggle, very much an uphill battle. Danish armies, on the other hand, were no match for Prussian troops. Although the Schleswig-Holstein question would become, for a moment in September 1848, the center of the revolution in Germany, it did not play the same central political role that Lombardy-Venetia did for Italy.

Rather, the movement towards German national unity in 1848 began and continued for a long time in peaceful, parliamentary fashion, although the greatest difficulties of clashing nationalisms – difficulties that would have fatal effect on the 1848 revolution in Germany – emerged from its peaceful efforts. A group of parliamentary deputies from the different German states, and other political leaders, mostly drawn from the ranks of the pre-1848 liberal and radical opposition, met in Frankfurt am Main, the capital city of the German Confederation, at the end of March 1848. They issued an appeal for elections to a constituent national assembly that would write a constitution for a united German national state. Such a proposal had been anathema to the German princes and their conservative government ministers before 1848, but the new, liberal governments of the individual German states, come to power after the barricade fighting or threat of it in March of that year, were far more sympathetic, especially since many of the new government ministers were the friends and political associates of the parliamentarians meeting in Frankfurt. They willingly consented to the creation of such a parliament, and agreed to the beginning of May 1848 as the date for elections to it. They were duly held and the parliamentary body resulting from them, the Frankfurt National Assembly, took up its deliberations in the second half of May.

Just as the theory of national self-determination would have it, there was a parliament representing the will of the German people to constitute itself as a unified nation-state. Only – and here the problems of nationalism in practice began – where was the German nation? Who would vote for the deputies to this national assembly? To put it differently, the question dogging German nationalism in theory for some decades now required immediate resolution: what was to be done with the Habsburg monarchy and the Germans living in it?

The modestly liberal regime in Vienna following the fall of Metternich was willing to allow elections for a German National Assembly to be held on at least part of its territory, only which part? The lands of the Crown of St. Stephen, that is Hungary, were out of the question, and, as we will see below, the Hungarian authorities were not listening to Vienna at this time, anyway. The province of Galicia, with its Polish, Ukrainian, and Jewish population, was clearly not part of Germany. That left the Habsburg's old crown lands, the provinces that make up today's Austrian and Slovenian republics, and, particularly, the provinces of Bohemia and Moravia, today's Czech republic. As we noted in the previous chapter, German nationalists had felt it self-evident that Bohemia and Moravia were part of Germany; the fact that a large proportion of their inhabitants spoke a Slavic tongue no more told against their being German than the Breton spoken then in Brittany told against it being part of France.

As we also noted in the previous chapter, Czech nationalists in Bohemia and Moravia had a quite different idea of the significance of the Czech language. Like the German nationalists, they saw the revolution and the overthrow of Prince Metternich as allowing the fulfillment of nationalist aspirations, only different nationalist aspirations. The call for a German National Assembly brought these differences into the open. Leaders of the liberal opposition in Prague, invited to join the deliberations at the preparatory meeting in Frankfurt, promptly and publicly declined, identifying themselves as Czech, not German nationalists. One by one, German liberals and radicals resigned from the Prague National Committee, the revolutionary body in the Bohemian provincial capital set up in the wake of the Viennese barricade fighting. Czech nationalists paraded through the streets, singing their new nationalist song, with the refrain, "Forward against the German, forward against the murderer, against Frankfurt"; German nationalists in Prague and throughout Bohemia and Moravia responded in kind. Tensions in Prague between Germans and Czechs, expressed in public meetings, in clashes on the streets, and in attempts to gain control of the city's National Guard, mounted steadily in April and May 1848.

The Czech nationalists called for a boycott of the elections to the German National Assembly. They demanded, instead, the union of the provinces of Bohemia, Moravia, and neighboring Austrian Silesia, into a Czech political body, a Czech nation-state within the Austrian Empire. Not content with this step, they went further and created their own assembly, a sort of anti-German national meeting. This was the Slavic Congress, which met in Prague during the first two weeks of June 1848, bringing together delegates from the different Slavic nationalities of the Habsburg monarchy.

German and Hungarian nationalists immediately denounced the meeting as the result of a conspiracy of "Pan-Slavists," adherents of the unification of all the Slavic peoples under the tsar, the ruler of the Russians, the largest Slavic nationality. This accusation was largely a paranoid fantasy of the sort encouraged by extreme nationalism. There were just a handful of delegates from outside the Austrian Empire and the one real live Russian at the congress, the anarchist revolutionary Mikhail Bakunin, was hardly the tsar's agent. Indeed, Russian foreign policy throughout the events of 1848–49 was to oppose with diplomatic, financial, and, ultimately, military measures, any revolutionary movement whatsoever, regardless of whether Slavs, Germans, Magyars, Romanians or anyone else was behind it.

Pan-Slavism was far from the minds of the congress's organizers. They were Czech liberals, who, as good constitutional monarchists, were entirely loyal to the Habsburg Emperor, but desired to turn his empire into a constitutional one, with a dominant position in it for the Slavic national groups. Since individually, each of these national groups was relatively small, although when taken together they made up a majority of the Emperor's subjects, their different national movements would have to cooperate to reach common goals. The organizers saw their meeting as a counterweight to the meeting of German parliamentarians in Frankfurt, as a body that would prepare for an Austrian constituent assembly to write a constitution for the entire empire. To make the point clear to all participants, the congress met in a hall decorated with a large black and yellow Austrian imperial banner and with a replica of the Habsburg's insignia, the double eagle. The congress met with the endorsement and under the protection of the Habsburgs' provincial governor of Bohemia, Count Leo Thun, himself a German-speaking nobleman, but an enemy of German nationalism.

The Prague Slavic Congress was just one of many efforts occurring during the 1848 revolution to transform the Austrian empire. In that decentralized realm, encompassing so much of Europe, with many different nationalities and many foci of political action, yet retaining in the emperor and the armed forces common political institutions, the sequence of events during the revolution was complex and confusing. Ever since 1850, historians have struggled to find a way to explain the different, separate, and frequently mutually hostile, yet closely interconnected political movements, which made up the revolution in the Habsburgs' realm. In my opinion, a chronological narrative would generate more confusion than understanding, so I will discuss the events from March to June 1848 in terms of the different centers of revolutionary movements in Austria. There were, however, common features to events throughout the monarchy, so in the following discussion please keep the following points in mind.

(1)   Republicanism was not much to be seen in the Austrian Empire, at least in the early months of the revolution. The varied and opposing political movements were led by constitutional monarchists; they all wanted to see a political role for the imperial (for Hungarian nationalists the royal) family.

(2)   Once again, in the early months of the revolution, the different political movements were all nationalist; they all sought national self-determination and they all wanted to assert their legitimacy by obtaining some sort of assembly of the people, to constitute the nation.

(3)   Through all the chaos and confusion, the empire as an institution remained in existence. There was an emperor, complete with his court, a council of ministers, an administration, and, especially, an army. To be sure, the emperor was not right in the head; the court and the ministers were not necessarily in agreement on policy, or even in the same location at any one time; parts of the administration and especially the armed forces might be working at cross purposes to the point of incipient civil war; the whole apparatus of state was essentially bankrupt – yet there was always something there beyond the individual national movements.

(4)   Finally, the Habsburgs' realm was inhabited largely by peasants, most of whom had been serfs until the outbreak of the revolution. Relations between lord and serf, and the nature of rural property were decisive issues for the future of the monarchy; their influence can be found behind every single one of the three previous points.

Let us now consider the events of the spring of 1848 in terms of four foci of the revolution: Vienna, the capital city and seat of the imperial government; the movements of the Magyars in the Crown of St. Stephen; the Polish nationalist movement in the province of Galicia; the national movements of the Slavic peoples within the empire, particularly in its Hungarian provinces.

Vienna was in some ways a city resembling Paris, less in the political sophistication of its inhabitants than in the presence of a determined group of radicals, who were able to make use of the extent to which the post-revolutionary "order" was one that solid citizens regarded as very disorderly. The parallel to the disorderly city was a stubborn central administration, reluctant to give up its pre-1848 authoritarian ways. The interaction of an angry populace, an active group of leftists and a slow-moving bureaucracy made the spring of 1848 a time of constant confrontations.

The central authorities' first response to the insurrection of March 1848 was to create a new conservative government without the former conservative leader, Prince Metternich, who had fled to London. Unsatisfactory to the crowd, this solution had been followed by the naming of some liberal ministers, the granting of some civil liberties, and an imperial proclamation of the intent to engage in constitutional rule and to call elections to an Austrian constituent assembly to write this constitution. These elections were to be held under a stiff property franchise, and the capital city's radicals, among whom the students at the university were particularly prominent, mounted a mass demonstration in mid-May, leading to a reshuffling of the government portfolios and a promise to hold democratic elections. The disorder was too much for the court, though, which packed up Emperor Ferdinand and fled the city for the more peaceful surroundings of Innsbruck, capital of the conservative, loyalist, and lightly taxed province of the Tyrol. The constitutional monarch was now far from his government ministers, through whom he was supposed to rule. The ministers themselves were left confronting a disorderly capital city with an active radical political movement.

Largely drawn from the German liberal-nationalists, the ministers were sympathetic or at least not overtly hostile to the movement towards German national unity and supported the call for elections to the Frankfurt National Assembly. At the same time, they were unwilling to see the Habsburg monarchy be dissolved – hence their calling elections to an Austrian constituent assembly.

Preserving the monarchy meant, more than anything else, dealing with the interrelated issue of finances and the Italian provinces. As noted in the previous chapter, the silver generated in Lombardy and Venetia was crucial to the precarious state budget. The fiscal difficulties of the pre-1848 regime had only been increased by the revolution, which had been anything but soothing to the financial markets. The ministers were unsure what policy they should follow: concede both provinces to Piedmont-Savoy, in return for its agreement to pick up a big chunk of the Austrian public debt; work out a compromise solution – say ceding Lombardy but retaining Venetia – with the help of British mediation; fight it out to the finish. At one time or another, the government tried all of these alternatives; every single one of them, however, was very difficult given both the collapse of public finances and the revolutionary movements throughout the empire. Consequently, the central government was forced to compromise with these revolutionary movements, although, since there were so many of them, compromising with the revolution was itself no simple task.

One new power center arising out of the revolution was in Budapest. Following the peaceful victory of the revolutionary movement there in mid-March, the Hungarian Diet moved to this new national capital from its traditional meeting place in Pressburg and launched a vigorous work of political reform, carrying out the major points of the reform of the pre-1848 liberal program, including the introduction of civil liberties, the abolition of tithes paid to the Catholic clergy, and the abolition of serfdom – albeit with compensation to be paid to noble landlords. The Diet then set elections for a constituent Hungarian national assembly, with a franchise along liberal lines – abolishing special privileges for the nobility but introducing a property requirement for voting – and adjourned.

All these reforms paled before the truly decisive step of the post-revolutionary Diet: it created an Hungarian national government, inde-pendent of the central bureaucracy in Vienna, responsible only to the elected Hungarian legislature. This government acknowledged Ferdinand as its constitutional monarch – but only as king of Hungary, not emperor of Austria. The Hungarian government insisted that it receive and expend all taxes raised in Hungary, that it have the final say over the Hungarian regiments within the Habsburg army, particularly about their service outside the lands of the Crown of St. Stephen and, finally, that its authority extend over the entire area of the Crown of St. Stephen. This was also part of the liberal political program: turning Hungary into a unitary state along west European lines, which would mean ending the special status of the provinces of Transylvania and Croatia-Slavonia, and of the military border districts, previously outfitted with their own unique governmental institutions and administered separ-ately from Vienna, rather than from Budapest. These demands were a bitter pill for the new liberal government in Vienna to swallow, yet given its weakened condition and the war it was pursuing in northern Italy, where many of the Hungarian regiments were stationed, it had little choice.

Developments in the province of Galicia at first seemed to parallel those in Hungary. Polish nationalists, encouraged by the revolutionary wave of 1848, put aside for the moment the memory of the disaster of 1846, and created a national committee in Cracow, the province's largest city with the ultimate intent of seizing power in the province. However, in Lemberg [Polish: Lwów; Ukrainian: Lviv], the province's second largest city, there appeared a Supreme Ukrainian Council. It proclaimed that the province of Galicia, or at least its eastern half, was not the territory of the Polish, but of the Ukrainian nation. That nation, furthermore, regarded the Austrian emperor as its rightful overlord and saw its aspirations towards national self-determination – that meant, above all, opposing the dominant position of the Polish language and the Polish nobility in the region – best preserved under the guidance of the Habsburgs and their governmental administrators.

Polish political leaders fumed, demanding to know "[H]ow many nationalities have they left to invent?" The "they" were the Austrian government officials, particularly Galicia's provincial governor Count Stadion, whom Polish politicians accused of having founded this Ukrainian national council for the purpose of sabotaging the Polish revolution. Polish nationalists sarcastically described the Ukrainians as "Russian Austrians, alias Ruthenians, invented in the laboratory of Count Stadion." The Ukrainian nationalists were a Frankenstein's monster for Polish hopes, and the astute Count Stadion did indeed show the Ukrainians official favor, even subsidizing their national council with government funds, but he was far from inventing a nationalist movement, something Polish nationalists – as with every other kind of nationalist in mid-nineteenth-century Europe, when their own aspirations were opposed – were unwilling to admit.

The situation in Galicia, where a nationalist movement, largely dominated by a feudal nobility, still in the process of moving from *natio* to nation, was challenged by an opposing nationalism, with the support of the Habsburg officials, was repeated many times and in more drastic form in the Hungarian provinces of the monarchy. There, the decline of Habsburg central authority and the proclamation of a new, liberal Hungarian national regime, did not lead to the creation of a unitary Hungarian nation-state as the Magyar politicians expected. Rather, both the decline of absolutist rule and the attempted liberal replacement sparked the proclamation of as many different national states as there were national movements, resulting in a wild political free-for-all, into which violent antagonisms between lord and serf were mixed, and which was quickly exploited by both the council of ministers in Vienna and by the emperor's court. The upshot was a quick fading of the euphoria of freedom in March 1848, to be replaced by drastically escalating hostilities and an incipient, multi-front civil war.

The first step in this process was the calling of mass meetings, "national assemblies" of the different nationalist movements: the Croats in Zagreb on 25 March, the Slovaks in Liptovsky Sväty Mikulas on 10–11 May, the Serbs in Karlovci on 13 May and the Romanians in Blaj on 15–17 May. Attracting thousands of participants – there are said to have been 40,000 in Blaj, the largest of these meetings – the assemblies passed their own resolutions abolishing serfdom,[4] instituting various liberal reforms, and calling for independent nation-states, under the rule of the Habsburg emperor. The Croats went the furthest, their national meeting calling for and ultimately obtaining elections to a Croatian constituent national assembly in June 1848 and demanding the creation of a Croatian government, with the emperor as its constitutional monarch, but independent of both Budapest and Vienna – to have, as the Magyars were obtaining, control over both its own tax revenues and over the Croatian regiments in the imperial army. In the spring of 1848, the Habsburg monarchy seemed to be dissolving into three mutually hostile, separate national governments – a German in Vienna, a Magyar in Budapest, and a Croatian in Zagreb (leaving out its Italian provinces, which were doing their best to secede from the empire altogether) – with the emperor and his court not precisely attached to any of them. If other national groups were unable to obtain their own governments, it was not for lack of trying.

However, the situation was still more complex, and this additional complexity was what enabled the imperial regime to survive an apparently impossible situation. To see this, let us focus in on the Romanian national mass meeting in Blaj. Most participants, like most people who lived in the province of Transylvania, were serfs – and serfs who spoke different languages or dialects, although most spoke Romanian, as did most of the serfs of the province. For the serfs, the big news of the meeting, news that spread like wildfire throughout the province, was its abolition of

---

[4] Of course, the Hungarian Diet had already done this. It is remarkable how often serfdom was abolished in the Habsburg Empire during the 1848 revolution – by the Hungarian diet, by the assemblies of the non-Magyar Hungarian nationalities, by the Austrian Constituent Assembly in September 1848, by imperial proclamation in October of that year, as well as some additional miscellaneous instances, such as in the province of Galicia by Count Stadion in April 1848. This constant reiteration of the abolition of serfdom showed both the existence of competing governmental authorities and the universal recognition of the politically decisive nature of the issue for the future of the monarchy.

serfdom. Now the Hungarian Diet in Budapest had already done this six weeks previously, but the Diet and the Hungarian national government it had created intended to incorporate Transylvania into a unitary, Hungarian national state. The champions of Hungarian nationalism in Transylvania were, above all, the Magyar nobles, themselves serf-owners, and determined to resist the liberation of the serfs or, if it was absolutely unavoidable, to obtain the maximum possible compensation for it. Here we can see how the political ideas of western Europe produced different results when transposed to the very different social circumstances in the east of the continent: the liberal and nationalist regime in Budapest was attempting to gain control over part of its "national" territory, only its nationalist supporters there were enemies of liberal social and economic principles.

The organizers of the Blaj national assembly were liberal and even radical intellectuals, from that small group of people who thought of themselves as Romanian nationalists. They had rejoiced at the overthrow of Metternich and the end of oppressive Habsburg rule. After just a few months of revolution, however, they were faced with a government in Budapest that largely shared their political, social, and economic ideas, but also regarded them as enemies of the nation, and was determined to prohibit their political activity. They also had to confront the local supporters of that government, who saw them as dangerous troublemakers, stirring up the serfs to attack their lords. The situation left them with no choice but to seek a powerful ally, which could only be the imperial authorities.

The mass meeting in Blaj elected a delegation to bring the Romanians' case to the emperor. Curiously, though, the deputy chairman of this delegation was the Magyar aristocrat, Baron László Nopcsa, a man with a reputation as a particularly cruel and vicious exploiter of the serfs. But Nopcsa was also a politically conservative nobleman, a loyal servant of the Habsburgs, the cousin of the Chancellor, or imperial provincial governor, of Transylvania. Like an increasing number of conservative aristocrats, high-ranking army officers, leading state administrators, or senior clergymen, he came to an agreement with the Romanian nationalist movement, because it appealed to the authority of the emperor, and so opposed the claims to sovereignty of the revolutionary Hungarian government, thus providing a way to sabotage that government's proposals for political and social change.

So the stage was set in Transylvania, and in much of the rest of the Hungarian provinces, for a violent confrontation. The Hungarian authorities would move to arrest "traitors" – i.e., Romanian, Slovak, or Serb nationalists – and to restore order and protect property, that is to prevent the serfs from using their understanding of the proclamation of freedom and a constitutional regime as meaning they were free to assault their landlord, chop his wood, and, at the very least, cease paying him dues or performing their labor services for him. Especially in Transylvania, the government would meet fierce resistance from the serfs, organized by Romanian nationalist leaders. The ultimate outcome, a savage civil war, was already in sight by June 1848, and the war in Transylvania would be the most violent of all the events of the mid-century revolution, costing tens of thousands of lives. Yet for the leaders of the Romanians in the civil war, all outcomes would be a disaster. If they lost the war, they were lost; but if they won, they lost as well, since their victory would just bring back authoritarian Habsburg rule that they had opposed in the first place.

There is one more point about the situation that needs to be emphasized, the role of the imperial army. Here, we need to look to the province of Croatia-Slavonia and the neighboring military border district. One of the last acts of the conservative regime in Vienna had been the naming of a new Ban, or provincial governor of Croatia-Slavonia, and also commander of the border troops. In a political masterstroke, the conservative officials chose a colonel of the border regiments, Josip Jelačić.

There was nothing in his career showing particular military gifts. Since the border regiments had not fought the Turks for decades, most of their confrontations, and most of Jelačić's military experience, consisted of engaging cattle rustlers from neighboring Bosnia. Jelačić, however, socialized with and to a certain extent sympathized with the "Illyrians," the Croatian nationalist intellectuals. But unlike these intellectuals, he was a Habsburg officer, totally loyal to the empire. He could be counted upon to join together the border troops (many of them Serbs, ironically, in view of the future hostilities between Serbian and Croatian nationalists) and the civilians of Croatia-Slavonia, to lead them against the Hungarian government, and to ensure that Croatian nationalism was devoted exclusively to the imperial cause – all of which he did, quite successfully.

Jelačić refused to recognize the authority of the Hungarian government in Budapest. He demanded that his civilian subordinates, state officials in Croatia-Slavonia, break off all relations with it, and that his military subordinates, the Habsburg forces stationed there and on the military border, reject any orders coming from the new Hungarian Ministry of War. The constitutional monarchist Hungarian government, claiming sovereignty over the whole "national" territory, promptly removed Jelačić from his position, in the name of the lawful authority of the king of Hungary. Jelačić refused to budge, noting that he exercised his lawful authority in the name of the Emperor of Austria – emperor and king being the same person, the mentally retarded Ferdinand von Habsburg. Various messages reached Jelačić from the "constitutional" ministry in Vienna and from the imperial court, some supporting him, some opposing him, depending on whether the official in question thought that the empire's survival could best be obtained by placating Hungarian or Croatian nationalism.

There were now two civilian and military authorities in Hungary, both claiming to be legal and both issuing contradictory orders in the name of the monarch. Which legal authority were government officials and, especially, the officers and soldiers of the imperial (or royal) army to obey? The decentralized, feudal relations of governmental power characteristic of Habsburg rule, especially in the Hungarian provinces, did not fit a revolutionary situation, in which liberal, constitutionalist, and nationalist principles were being asserted. The incipient civil war in Hungary would find the imperial army on both sides at once, a circumstance that would only sharpen the conflict and make it more violent.

The application of nationalist principles to government policy in the spring of 1848 brought war to northern Italy and created the conditions for a civil war soon to break out in the Hungarian provinces of the Habsburg monarchy. Of all the nationalist movements, the one towards German national unification was the most peaceful – oddly enough, considering the future European wars German nationalism would help bring about. Even there, the question of whether the Germans of Austria should be included in a united German state sufficed to bring about a major political crisis. That Austrian empire was the very heart of nationalist contention in 1848–49, yet rather than a crescendo of nationalist demands tearing the realm to pieces, the different national movements fought each other, and cancelled each other out. The nationalities conflict in the empire was a strange affair, sometimes relatively peaceful, sometimes extremely violent, in which the contending parties were in fundamental agreement on basic political, social, and economic principles, yet fought each other bitterly and allowed the ultimate triumph of their common enemy, the authoritarian and conservative imperial government and its conservative supporters in the upper ranks of the nobility, army, state service, and Catholic Church.

Points of conflict: (3) governmental power and elections

If social conflict and nationalist rivalries helped bring the euphoric mood of the early spring of 1848 to a quick end, a third focus of contention also contributed to the growing tendency towards confrontation in revolutionary Europe. This focus was located within the new governments themselves that had emerged from the fighting on the barricades or the threat of such uprisings. Within these governments, we can locate three different sources of tension: the question of the retention of administrative and military personnel from the previous regimes; the nature of executive authority in the newly created or newly revised constitutional systems; and the outcome of elections to legislative bodies.

The new government ministers in the spring of 1848 had to decide whether it was necessary to replace senior government administrators and army officers. Answers varied with the new governments, but overall there was a noticeable preference for keeping existing officials in place. This tendency was weakest in France, where the revolution had brought the sharpest change of regime. The provisional government in Paris sent special agents, "commissars of the republic," to the provinces, to secure the new government's authority, thus bypassing the prefects, standard channel of government between the capital and the provinces. These commissars, engaged in the "republicanization" of France, saw a key means to achieve this end in the purging of the governmental bureaucracy. Virtually all the prefects were replaced, as were sub-prefects, and mayors of larger cities. To a lesser extent, prominent judicial officials, states attorneys, and presiding justices of the major courts were also expelled from office. Yet even here, the purge was far from general: some commissioners were far more restrained in their efforts; others were unable to overcome the resistance of the notables, the locally most influential men, who succeeded in retaining their favorites in administrative posts, or in replacing them with others equally to their favor.

Elsewhere on the continent, replacements were more modest: a few of the most reactionary, particularly compromised officials might resign or be transferred, often after public demonstrations were held against them, but to a great extent the administrative hierarchy remained intact. Generals and, more broadly, the army officer corps, changed even less. Even more significantly, the lower levels of government administration, the foresters, gendarmes, tax collectors, or customs agents, the officials with whom ordinary people, especially the peasants, came into contact, changed least of all. Particularly hated individuals who were driven out of office by popular disorders at the outbreak of the revolution would sometimes even be restored to office by the new governments. As one observer noted from provincial France, in the villages, "nothing has changed so that the country people believe that as in 1830 the government has only changed its name."

Keeping state officials in office did help preserve or re-create administrative and judicial continuity, and facilitate the process of creating a new political order, one characterized by the granting of basic civil liberties and the planned holding of elections. It did, however, raise the question of whether the officials and soldiers who had served the regimes just over-thrown would be willing to do the same for the new governments. At first, and helped by a certain amount of intimidation due to popular demon-strations, they were willing to do so. In the early days of the revolution, state officials and army officers hastened to display publicly and symbol-ically their loyalty to the new regimes, in France, declaring themselves republicans; in Italy, Germany, or Hungary, displaying the previously prohibited tricolor national flag.

However, the new central authorities themselves were not entirely homogeneous; in particular the executive powers were badly split. In February and March 1848, monarchs had renounced previous claims to absolutism and agreed to rule in constitutional fashion, appointing gov-ernment ministers whose presence in office would be confirmed by elected legislatures and arranging for the election of such legislatures where they did not exist. This change of royal policy was the result of political pressure, sometimes of revolutionary violence; it was far from being a voluntary decision, reached out of conviction. Monarchs con-tinued to surround themselves with informal advisors: courtiers, conser-vative aristocrats, and generals – a "camarilla," as contemporaries said, using a phrase invented in the Spanish revolution of 1820 – whose members were strongly opposed to the views of the liberal ministers, the official agents of the royal executive, according to constitutionalist doc-trine. This condition was most blatant in the Habsburg monarchy, where the monarch's own ruling ability was a fiction, and he and the camarilla that spoke in his name were for much of the revolution located in a different city than the constitutionally responsible Austrian government ministry. Such conservative camarillas opposed to the liberal ministers existed in Prussia, Bavaria, Piedmont-Savoy, the Two Sicilies, the Papal States, and in most of the newly constitutional monarchist regimes in the Europe of 1848. In the early months of the revolution, the camarillas, along with the monarchs they advised in extra-constitutional fashion, were relatively uninfluential; most actual power resided with the liberal government ministers. With the development of large-scale conflicts emerging from the revolution, the unofficial conservative advisors of the monarch would gain increasingly in influence, until, by the fall of 1848, they were ready to take back the government ministries and promote an open counter-revolution.

The French republic avoided this problem at first by not having a monarch. France developed a similar difficulty somewhat later on, when the constituent national assembly elected in April 1848 wrote a constitution containing an American-style, powerful, popularly elected president as chief of the executive branch of government. The presidential elections, held in December 1848, brought into the highest office of the republic a potential monarch, nephew of a one-time emperor, Louis-Napoleon Bonaparte. The republican president acted much like European monarchs, ignoring his cabinet, whose members were responsible to the legislature, and surrounding himself with his own coterie of advisors, who would help him turn his republican executive office into a monarchical one.

The legislative branch of government provided its own, equally pronounced set of conflicts. Many new, liberal regimes came to power in states possessing neither legislatures nor constitutions. One of their first actions was to schedule elections for a constituent assembly. Neglecting some of the smaller German and Italian states, between March and June 1848 elections were held in the Kingdom of the Two Sicilies, in the Papal States, in the Grand Duchy of Tuscany, in the insurgent provinces of Lombardy and Venetia, in France, throughout Germany, including portions of Austria, for a constituent national assembly, in the kingdom of Prussia for a Prussian constituent assembly, in the Hungarian provinces of the Habsburg monarchy (except Croatia-Slavonia) for a Hungarian national assembly, in Croatia-Slavonia for a Croatian national assembly, and in the other provinces of the monarchy for an Austrian constituent assembly.

Adding to the impact of this remarkable wave of elections was the generally broad franchise. France, as might be expected, led the way in democracy: elections to the constituent national assembly in April 1848 were direct and all adult males were entitled to vote. The elections to the German national assembly and to the Prussian constituent assembly were also held under universal manhood suffrage (or almost so), although they were usually indirect, the voters selecting electors, who in turn chose the actual parliamentary deputies. In theory, this was the case in the Austrian elections as well, but the instructions from Vienna to allow a democratic franchise reached most provinces after the elections themselves were held, so that a relatively modest property qualification was demanded. In Hungary, Croatia, and the Italian states, elections were direct, but a stiffer property qualification was imposed, disenfranchising between one-half and two-thirds of the adult men. The Hungarians added another restrictive provision, requiring voters to know the Magyar language, thus conveniently disenfranchising many of the other national groups. Croatians, for their part, refused to allow enemies of Croatian nationalism to vote. Even with these restrictions, the elections provided for an unprecedented political participation. Never had so many Europeans been able to vote, or had been called on to do so all at once. The vast majority of these new voters, especially those living in the countryside, were lacking in political experience. Pre-1848 governments, whether prohibiting public discussion of and participation in politics outright, strongly discouraging them, or limiting them to a small, affluent group, had done their best to create such a situation, and the low standards of living, the very partial spread of literacy, the limitations on communication and transportation, had done the rest. Most Europeans, when called upon to vote in the spring of 1848, had not been regular newspaper readers, had never joined a political club or association, had never attended a public demonstration or an organized discussion of politics. They had no clue as to what was going on. While the new regimes had granted the basic civil liberties that were a prerequisite to an expanded popular political participation, there was nowhere near enough time between the introduction of these freedoms and the actual holding of elections for any significant political campaigning to have occurred.

Under these circumstances, the advent of any widespread franchise was sure to produce some strange results. One possibility was sheer incomprehension, most common in rural areas of Austria. Peasants simply did not understand the indirect voting procedure and the whole idea of parliamentary rule. Villagers refused to select an elector, proposing instead to send one of their number to Vienna, to tell the emperor personally of their problems. Sometimes, an entire village would turn up *en masse* at the second stage of the indirect balloting, the meeting of the electors in a centrally located city. There, the more sophisticated townspeople would tell them that they did not understand elections and send them home, so the villagers ended up excluded from the process.

Particularly in the province of Galicia, but elsewhere in the monarchy as well, the elections were dominated by hostility between lords and serfs. Abstention was virtually universal in a number of Galician constituencies, peasants refusing to have anything to do with politics or a legislature, both domains of the hated nobility; noble, clerical, and urban voters, a small minority of those eligible for the franchise, determined the outcome of the elections. Peasants chosen as electors would come to the meetings of the electors, see noblemen present and walk out, announcing that they would not collaborate in their oppressors' plans to revive a Polish kingdom; they trusted their emperor. Sometimes rural and urban electors would engage in a riot rather than an election. After hearing that an estate steward had been chosen as an elector, two hundred peasants of Michalowice attacked their ostensible representative, and tore the ballots to pieces.

In much of central and western Europe, where feudalism had been abolished and the sharp contrasts between lord and serf did not exist, peasant ignorance of politics led countryfolk to follow the lead of the locally wealthiest and most influential men. A charming example of an early version of the practice of democracy comes from one village in the Prussian province of Westphalia, in western Germany. There, as was often the case, the elections were held in the church.

Early in the morning the congregation gathered in the church. The priest... held the services and following them gave a short speech. He explained that today was the day of the elections and since it was permitted to hold them in the church he requested his parishioners to behave as was appropriate in a sacred place. He called on them to keep in mind the importance of the election. In these great events, God's voice was to be heard; therefore he asked God to enlighten them and guide them in this important business. They would help decide on the entire future position of the Christian religion, of the holy church, of the entire nation, the government, and, finally, of the re-creation of the German Empire. They should only elect thoughtful men who would conscientiously vote for the most worthy candidates. Nothing seems to have been planned in advance. As the election began, everyone sat on the benches in the church; they held no discussions; they did not whisper to each other. Their names were read out, the ballots distributed. Each man wrote down a name on his ballot or had his neighbor write one for him. When the ballots were opened, read aloud, and counted, it turned out that the priest had been elected almost unanimously as an elector for the election of a deputy to Berlin [i.e., to the Prussian Constituent Assembly]; the elector to Frankfurt [the German National Assembly] was the former feudal lord of the village.[5]

Even in France, the most politicized country on the continent, many of the peasants could show a *naïveté* and incomprehension on the same scale as anything in Galicia. This attitude was particularly on display in the elections of December 1848 for a president of the French republic, which resulted in a landslide victory for Louis-Napoleon Bonaparte. Although the imperial pretender, hastening back to France from exile following the outbreak of the revolution, had been gradually gathering support, no one had expected such an enormous triumph. Observers had not counted on the peasantry, some of whom came to the polls thinking that they were voting for the great emperor Napoleon himself, not his nephew. Others asserted that Louis-Napoleon was so rich that he would pay all the taxes out of his private fortune, relieving them of any fiscal obligations.

The end result of this first, continent-wide trial run at democracy was a strange discrepancy between advocates of democracy and its beneficiaries. Elections held under a broad, sometimes universal male suffrage favored most those political forces that were the most skeptical about both elections and democracy. Everywhere, a majority of the candidates elected represented conservative or at best very moderately liberal viewpoints. Radicals,

---

[5] Cited in Wilhelm Schulte, *Volk und Staat. Westfalen im Vormärz und in der Revolution 1848/49* (Münster, 1954), 561.

that is, the supporters of democracy, people who had pressed for the broadest possible franchise, were the big losers in elections held under the franchise they advocated.

Indeed, the elections resulting from the revolution at times seemed to be a referendum aimed at repudiating the revolutionaries. Sandor Petöfi was a radical Hungarian poet, whose powerful song about Magyars refusing to live as slaves had been sung in great choruses of tens of thousands, during the Budapest demonstrations of March 1848 that had destroyed Habsburg absolutist rule in Hungary. When Petöfi went into the countryside to campaign for a seat in the Hungarian constituent assembly, the clergy and lesser nobility plied the peasants with food and drink and informed them that the republican intellectual was really a Russian spy. He was lucky to escape being lynched.

In the Prussian Rhine Province, both the liberal politicians who had led the opposition to absolutist rule in the United Diet of 1847, immediately preceding the revolution, and the radical activists, who had inspired large and impressive street demonstrations in many cities during March and April of 1848, met with little success in the elections to the Frankfurt National Assembly and the Prussian Constituent Assembly. Ordinary voters, especially in the countryside, but in most towns as well, rejected them and their political programs. Instead, they voted along religious lines, supporting candidates sponsored by the clergy of their Christian confession, opposing candidates of the other one. Whether chosen by the Protestant or the Catholic vote, the deputies so elected stood on the right wing of the political spectrum.

The most embarrassing failure of the left was in the very heart of the European revolutions, in Paris. The overthrow of Louis-Philippe and the proclamation of the republic had been the actions of the city's workers, highly politicized and imbued with socialist doctrines. These same armed workers had placed their stamp on the newly created republic, forcing the opening of the Parisian national guard to the lower classes, and, impelling the government to a spectacular if admittedly symbolic gesture, appointing as ministers without portfolio the socialist leader Louis Blanc and the working-class activist Albert Martin. Not stopping at political measures, the insurgent Parisians had won social and economic concessions as well: the "national workshops," a public works program for the unemployed, that at least sounded like the "social workshops" of Louis Blanc's socialist theories, and the legalization of the workers' committees of the different trades, allowing them to negotiate with employers and merchant contractors and granting them government funds to meet in the Luxembourg Commission, and discuss radical social and economic reforms.

The workers tried to cap this off with a victory in the elections to the constituent national assembly. Representatives of the trade committees met to name a slate of candidates for the Parisian region. However, this initiative was taken very late – on the very eve of the elections. The nature of the slate named revealed both the guild and artisanal roots of the early socialist movement and also that movement's distance from politics. The representatives of the trades committee tried to name candidates who would represent all the different trades. Corresponding to traditional guild practices, but completely inappropriate for universal manhood suffrage, this resulted in a slate of totally obscure figures, each one known only to the workmen in his particular craft, but left no time for a campaign to make their names known to the public. The candidates of the workers' committee were badly defeated at the elections, Parisian voters rejecting the unknown names proposed to them and choosing instead the mostly liberal-moderate, if republican, members of the provisional government.

What all these elections had shown was the power of the notables, the locally most influential and affluent men: former feudal lords, substantial property owners lacking titles of nobility, clergy, state officials, merchants, and the like. Among a mass electorate lacking political experience and political organization the decisions of the notables would determine the outcome of the voting, an outcome following the notables' own political sympathies, usually with the liberal center or the right. There were only two kinds of exceptions to this general picture. One occurred in various parts of the Habsburg monarchy, where angry serfs successfully pressed the election of their own candidates against those of their feudal lords. Such victories of the rural lower classes were not necessarily victories of the political left, since many peasants imagined that the emperor was on their side, and identified his enemies – radicals, nationalists, even liberals – with their enemy, the nobility. A second kind of exceptional outcome was more favorable to the left and occurred in those regions where many notables were themselves radicals – in much of southeastern France, for instance, or in southwestern Germany – and so could use the same social and economic influence usually wielded against the democrats in their favor.

The radical deputies chosen in these regions found themselves a distinct minority in the parliaments to which they were elected, where delegates of the center and the right had a dominant influence. This result set up the third of the group of conflicts emerging from the spring of 1848, as politically moderate to conservative assemblies met in capital cities, many of whose inhabitants had been politically radicalized. The potential for conflict in such a situation is obvious enough, but this potential was heightened by the example of the French Revolution. In 1792 and 1793, the Jacobins, the radical party of the revolution, had mobilized their supporters among the common people of Paris to purge conservative members of sitting parliaments or close them down altogether, and hold elections for new ones. Everyone politically active in 1848, on both the left and the right, was aware of the precedent and expected or feared its repetition.

The most famous example of such a confrontation in 1848 was in Paris itself, the so-called "June days," which led to a virtual civil war in the capital – a three-day-long armed conflict between insurgents and the government, with tens of thousands of armed participants on both sides and thousands of casualties. Yet the June Days were only one of many such dramatic conflicts, pitting radical leaders and their urban followers against a more conservative parliament, usually in conjunction with a government ministry responsible to it. There were at least eight such clashes, some admittedly abortive, in seven different capital cities, between May and November 1848. Historians have long focused on them, and written the story of the revolution primarily in terms of them. In more recent years, more scholarly attention has been paid to developments in the provinces, taking events in the capital city somewhat off the revolutionary center stage. If not quite the entire story of the revolution, these conflicts were nonetheless the most dramatic and the most likely to mark a major turning point in the revolutionary process.

The revolution in the balance

By the end of the spring of 1848, the European revolutions had reached a halfway point. Absolutist regimes had been overthrown; nationalist claims asserted; parliamentary governments either created or coming into existence. Fixtures of a society of orders, particularly feudal and seigneurial relations in agriculture, had been *de facto* dismantled and were in the process of being legally abolished. Civil liberties, including freedom of speech, press, association, and assembly, had been introduced; elections, under an unprecedentedly broad franchise had been held. All the preconditions of a vigorous political life and a widespread popular political participation were in existence.

For all these struggles and accomplishments, a good deal had been left undone or unclear. Basic political issues remained unresolved. Would national self-determination become the organizing principle of government in central and eastern Europe, and if so which nationalities? Would the newly created regimes be liberal ones, that is constitutional monarchies with a limited, property franchise, or democratic – that is republics with universal manhood suffrage? Equally unresolved were key questions of political power. Who would command the National Guard, what weapons would it have, and who would be entitled to bear them? Where would the ultimate base of power lie, with government ministers responsible to an elected parliament, or with a royal or presidential camarilla? With an elected legislature or the radicalized masses of a capital city?

The outcome of social conflicts remained similarly undetermined. What would the revolution mean for the peasants' right to gather wood in the forests, for craftsmen's right to organize themselves – and in what ways – and seek better conditions from employers and merchant contractors? Would taxes – and which ones – go up or down? Would the power of the police, customs officials, and tax collectors increase or decrease? Would soldiers continue to assault civilians and vice versa? Who would control village and municipal government and what powers would such institutions have over such disputed matters as the common lands or public works projects for the unemployed? And, perhaps most importantly, what relevance would these questions have for the resolution of the conflicts over political issues and political power?

We will turn now to the answers that events gave to these questions, approaching them in two different ways. Chapter Four will deal with them structurally and analytically, considering the development of new social and political institutions and practices emerging during the revolution, outlining different varieties of revolutionary experience. In Chapter Five, I will then adopt a narrative approach, looking at the major events and crises of the mid-century revolution, from the first in May 1848 until the very final confrontation in December of 1851.

4 Varieties of revolutionary experience

The new contours of public life

In the months following the barricade fighting of February–March 1848, a new space opened up for political activity in Europe. The\ liberal governments coming to power formally granted the classic civil liberties: freedom of speech, of the press, and of association and assembly. Even more significant as a guarantee of these freedoms in practice was the general weakening of state authority as a consequence of the revolutionary events, and the massive and widespread social conflict following them, which had the effect of making repressive actions, no matter what their legal basis or lack of it, substantially more difficult to carry out. In this chapter, we will explore some of these new possibilities for public life, go on to consider the different forms of association and organization that emerged and the people who took part in them, and conclude with a discussion of the long-term trends of political development over the course of the revolution.

The parliament as political focus

By the summer of 1848, Europe was crammed with parliaments. In the east and south of the continent, the very existence of such branches of government was a novelty. Everywhere, though, the parliaments of the year of revolution claimed significantly greater powers than their pre-1848 predecessors. In particular, many of the legislative bodies elected in 1848 were constituent assemblies, chosen for the purpose of laying down the basic rules of future political life. Most of these assemblies also strove to gain control of the executive, demanding that the government ministers be named by and from the parliamentary majority or at least responsible to it.

There were admittedly many variations on the theme of revolutionary legislatures. At the weakest end might have been the Croatian National Assembly, that met for six weeks and amiably adjourned, leaving government largely in the hands of the Ban Josip Jelačić appointed by the imperial authorities in Vienna. While new in the sense of having their members chosen by universal manhood suffrage, in elections with a very strong turnout, the Constituent National Assembly in France, and its successor, the Legislative Assembly elected in May 1849, could act within a well-established parliamentary tradition, since constitutionally guaranteed French legislative assemblies had met continuously since 1815, in spite of the changes in regime. The German National Assembly, known from the city where it met as the Frankfurt Parliament, was more of an institutional innovation. It created an all-German provisional government where none had ever existed before, and wrote a constitution for a permanent government of a German nation-state. When the time came to translate these documents and provisional institutions into permanent ones, and make good on its claims to power, the Assembly proved incapable, or perhaps found the task beyond its strength. The radical end of the spectrum of the legislatures of 1848 were those that acted in unconstrainably revolutionary fashion: the constituent assembly of the Roman Republic, emerging from the overthrow of Papal government towards the end of 1848, or, most strikingly, the Hungarian National Assembly, that broke with Habsburg authority and waged a year-long war against it.

Regardless of these differences, the legislatures of the mid-century revolution all acted as foci of political life. Deputies gradually came together into organized caucuses representing different political tendencies. The creation and realignment of these caucuses and their interaction shaped debate, guided the passage of legislation, and, via the increasingly common practice of parliamentary government, shaped state policy. In the French and German National Assemblies, as well as in the parliaments of the individual German and Italian states, these caucuses followed to a great extent the classic left–right spectrum created by the French Revolution of 1789.

As usual, things were different in the Habsburg Empire. There were tendencies towards the creation of caucuses arranged along a left–right continuum in the Hungarian National Assembly, but they were less pronounced, and the ever more important issue of the war between the Hungarian government and the Habsburg authorities would increasingly swallow other political differences. In the Austrian Constituent Assembly, political and national differences intersected in a complex fashion to determine the shape of the caucuses. All the Czech deputies, for instance, were gathered in one caucus, whose politics were constitutional monarchist, seeking to cooperate with the imperial authorities in reshaping the empire. The German deputies, on the other hand, were divided into three separate caucuses, one each on the left, center, and right; the Polish nationalist deputies into two, one on the left and the other in the center.

There was also a substantial group of deputies not belonging to any caucus, or, in fact having much to do with the work of this parliament, since they did not speak German, the language of the proceedings. These, mostly Polish- or Ukrainian-speaking peasants from the eastern provinces of the monarchy, could only know what was going on when they were informed by others. Notoriously, they usually voted as did the provincial governor of the province of Galicia, Count Stadion. On the issue of the abolition of feudalism and compensation for it to be paid to the former noble landlords – the major concern of these peasant deputies and a significant issue for the entire assembly – each caucus delegated an informal translator who would rush up to the peasants and explain the speeches, the proposed legislation, and the intricate parliamentary procedural maneuvering. Contemporaries noted with some amusement how these previously isolated and ignored representatives were suddenly surrounded by a host of their colleagues, each offering a different, politically edited version of the proceedings.

Parliamentary deputies, either as individuals or in caucuses, were also leading figures in extra-parliamentary politics. They were at the center of initiatives in France, Germany, and Italy to create nation-wide political parties – to be more precise, national federations of political clubs. When they could be spared from their legislative business, people's deputies were favored speakers at mass meetings and political rallies, typical forms of political life during the 1848 revolution.

The connection between the people and their representatives also worked in the other direction. Petitions flowed into the parliaments by the thousands during the revolution. In the spring of 1848, 339 groups of workers, typically craft associations, from Paris and the provinces petitioned the Constituent Assembly, either directly or via the Luxembourg Commission it had created, concerning the conditions of their trade, and making general demands for the "organization of labor." Peasants from Galicia petitioned the Austrian Constituent Assembly, calling on it to grant them ownership of the disputed common lands after the abolition of feudalism, and not to award these vital forest properties to the nobility. There were an estimated 25–30,000 petitions sent to the Frankfurt National Assembly, the precise number unknown since the register of petitions was incomplete.

The nature of petitions could range from the unsophisticated and unorganized, an individual asking for a personal favor or a village requesting intervention in a long-term local feud, to coordinated, large-scale political campaigns. Catholic clergy and lay activists circulated 1,142 petitions, with 273,000 signatures and sent them to the Frankfurt National Assembly, demanding that in the new German nation-state the church be empowered to manage its own affairs without government interference while continuing to administer public education. Free traders and protectionists in Germany engaged in a titanic battle of petitions to Frankfurt over economic policy; the latter were victorious, although probably because many of the craftsmen who signed were under the impression that "protectionism" would protect them from the competition of all manufacturers and merchant contractors, not just foreign ones. A similar petition struggle in the Austrian Empire was waged on national lines, the Ukrainian and Polish National Committees both collecting signatures for petitions to the Austrian Constituent Assembly over whether the eastern half of the province of Galicia (most of whose inhabitants spoke Ukrainian) should be separated from the western, predominantly Polish-speaking part. The Ukrainian committee collected over 100,000 signatures – an impressive total, although given the widespread illiteracy in the province, most must have been marks or crosses.

In and of itself, petitioning was an activity with little immediate consequence. Most petitions to the parliaments brought no results in 1848, and it is even far from clear that the parliamentarians paid much attention to them. Yet the long-term consequences of this experience were considerable. The mass movement of petitions in 1848 established parliament and its elected people's representatives as an alternative instance to the monarch and his officials, to which a citizen could turn to express grievances or demand a rectification of the existing situation. Even the ultimate failure of the revolutionary parliaments to establish their authority could not totally undo the implantation of this attitude; it would remain throughout the nineteenth century.

Newspapers

The end to censorship, a sudden surge of interest in public life: these were ideal conditions for the press and the mid-nineteenth-century revolution saw a veritable explosion of journalism in Europe. For instance, in three districts of the Prussian Rhine Province, for which we possess statistics, of the seventy newspapers published there in 1848, thirty-four, almost half of them, had been founded during the revolutionary year itself. Before the revolution, when official consent to start a newspaper was required, a good year would have seen the founding of one or two. The extent and variety of the press was greatest in the continent's political capital: there were at least 171 different newspapers – different counts, including more ephemeral periodicals, note more than twice as many – published in Paris during the spring of 1848. Total press-run of all the newspapers published in the capital city went from about 50,000 before the revolution to 400,000 by May 1848. On a broader scale, in the Austrian Empire there existed all of seventy-nine newspapers before the revolution, only nineteen of which had permission to discuss politics under the inspection of the censors. In 1848, the number of newspapers jumped to 388, of which 306 discussed political affairs – now without any censor telling them how. Similarly exact figures are lacking for the states of the Italian peninsula, but scattered evidence suggests that hundreds of newspapers were founded there during the mid-century revolution as well.

Most of the Austrian newspapers were German-language ones; in the monarchy's eastern provinces, where much of the population was illiterate, and where "national" literary languages had barely come into existence, the ranks of the press were much thinner. Croatian-language newspapers just went from five in 1847 to eight during the revolution; Slovak from six to eight; Slovene from one to six. These were all substantial percentage increases, although the absolute numbers of periodicals remained very small. The one Slavic nationality with a broad periodical press – not by coincidence, also the one with the highest literacy rates – was the Czechs. The thirteen Czech-language newspapers of 1847 grew to fifty-two during the year of revolution.

As newspapers became more common and were free to engage in political discussion, they gradually became differentiated. Each major political grouping developed its own periodical press, offering the reading public a wide choice of interpretations of the news. Like parliamentarians, editors became important political figures (without considering the many parliamentarians who were also editors). Just one example might suffice here, the newspaper editor Karl Marx, whose *Neue Rheinische Zeitung* [New Rhineland News] of Cologne, with its press-run of 6,000, was one of the larger left-wing newspapers in Germany and provided the chief way that Marx himself was involved in politics during the revolution.

The revolutionary period also saw a significant stylistic innovation in journalism: the first attempts at a popular press. With few exceptions, pre-1848 newspapers were written in a learned style, difficult to follow except for that small minority of the population possessing a secondary-school education. Of course, these were also the people most interested in politics. The events of the revolution politicized a much broader segment of the population, thus creating a journalistic problem, since the two groups of people – those interested in the news, and those able to understand literary writings – no longer coincided.

While most of the newspapers founded during the revolution continued to write for an educated audience, some journalists set out to produce a product for a generically popular group of readers, as indicated by the title of one such newspaper, the *New Cologne News for Townfolk, Countrypeople and Soldiers*. Edited by a woman (something most unusual at the time), the feminist Mathilde Franziska Anneke, the paper was characterized by a didactic but popular tone – much unlike the newspaper Marx edited, that was written in a complex intellectual style, very difficult for most people to understand – featuring for instance, the careful explanation of foreign words used in politics. Other journalists, however, did something even more innovative, bringing out newspapers aimed specifically at the peasantry, a social group hardly ever addressed before the revolution. In France, there was *La Feuille du Village* [The Village Sheet]; in Germany, *Die Dorfzeitung* [The Village News]; in Hungary, *Munkások Upága* [Workers' Newspaper] – this last, in spite of its name, directed primarily to a peasant audience and distributed to the rustics when they came to town on market days.

To this very brief discussion of the popular press, we should add a note on the politicization of other forms of popular reading matter. Calendars and almanacs had long circulated in Europe; besides a bible or a lives of the saints, they were the only reading matter that members of the lower classes would be likely to possess. Now one could purchase a *Democratic Pocket Calendar for 1849* or an *Almanac of the Friend of the People*. Fliers, broadsides, and lithographs – typically one-page sheets, containing some printed matter and rather more illustrations – offered likenesses of political leaders, songs, speeches or even political programs, views of barricade fighting, and satirical cartoons rather than the two-headed calves or axe-murderers that had previously been apolitical specialties.

In considering the effects of the press during the revolution, it is worth noting the context in which newspapers were read. Especially those directed towards a popular audience, but probably most periodicals, were not read privately and silently but publicly and out loud, in a tavern or coffeehouse, in a church, or at the meeting of a political club or other form of association. When we think of the experience of newspaper reading during the revolution, the primary image ought not to be the individual reader bent over his or her own copy, but a group of listeners gathered around a reader, who might interrupt an article to explain or comment on it, answer questions or respond to remarks.

Politics in the streets

During Mardi Gras of 1849, a curious event was observed in the little town of Sachsenburg in the Austrian province of Carinthia. The towns' democrats

[o]rganized a regular theatrical procession through the streets, singing various republican verses, and bearing stuffed figures representing the Field Marshals Count Radetzky and Prince Windischgrätz [both of whom had led troops in suppressing insurgent movements against Habsburg rule]. The procession ended at the marketplace where the two figures were led to the scaffold and condemned to death, the verdict being carried out by decapitation.[1]

At one level, this scene was just a prank, a masquerade, part of the tradition of pre-Lenten festivities in Catholic Europe. Carnival or Mardi Gras was a time of permitted license, when the mocking of authority was allowed, and could even be publicly celebrated with tumultuous parades and satirical verse, for on Ash Wednesday the fun was over and the world reverted to its normal, sober self. On another level, though, the depiction was more serious, the decapitation playing on the Jacobin practice of guillotining political enemies, the scene suggesting the wish to overturn permanently that authority which was only mocked at Mardi Gras.

During the mid-century revolution, there was a good deal of this sort of use of popular folklore for political ends. Carnival was one version, and the incident in Sachsenberg could be seconded by many similar ones in western Germany, southern France, Italy, and other areas of pre-Lenten revels. Another version of the politicization of popular culture was the use of the charivari for political ends. Known in England as "rough music," in Germany as "cat music," the charivari was a violent demonstration, typically carried out by young people, especially in the countryside, against those who had violated norms of sexual and marital behavior: the bride whose first child had arrived suspiciously soon after her marriage; the husband who beat his wife – or worse, let her beat him; the widower who married a much younger, single woman, depriving the eligible bachelors of a potential spouse. The charivari in response would take place at night, involving a crowd gathering to shout, scream, chant curses or sing obscene songs, splash manure on the house doors or even throw stones at the windows.

It was an easy step from denouncing moral failings to assaulting political enemies. The Catholic conservatives of the village of Rülzheim, in southwestern Germany, took that step on 26 December 1848, surrounding a meeting of radicals at the village inn, screaming, making various noises, throwing things, and eventually shouting at several departing leftists, "We'll beat you all to death!" Democrats brought a similar serenade to the prefect of the Department of the Lot in southern France, when they suspected him of concocting fraudulent election

[1] Wilhelm Wadl, "Die demokratische Bewegung in Kärnten im Jahre 1848," *Carinithia I* 174 (1984): 375–412.

returns, favoring right-wing candidates. Once again, these examples could be multiplied indefinitely.

Although at least partly organized, politicized charivaris and Mardi Gras festivities contained within them, as might be expected from the nature of the folkloric celebrations themselves, much that was anarchic and spontaneous. Other forms of politics in the streets, while frequently retaining elements of popular customs, were more carefully prepared and occurred in a more disciplined fashion. The most significant were the political mass demonstration and the public mass meeting.

Thinking of mass demonstrations brings to mind their twentieth-century form: the determined if restrained political show of force, characterized by organized marches of large numbers of demonstrators, perhaps concluding with a rally. Such demonstrations are usually planned to be peaceful, although acts of either demonstrators, or police, or both, can lead to them getting out of hand. The events of the fall of 1989 in eastern Europe provide a good recent example. In 1848, however, the political choreography of the twentieth century, establishing mass demonstrations as a unique form of political conflict, had not yet been established.

Mass demonstrations were often perceived as or actually were attempts at insurrection. The 30,000 demonstrators from all parts of the Grand Duchy of Tuscany, who gathered in the capital, Florence, on 22 January 1849, to demand that the legislature and grand ducal government enact universal manhood suffrage and support the efforts of the republican regime in Rome to unite all of Italy in revolutionary fashion, scarcely concealed their intent of overthrowing the grand ducal government. The authorities yielded to the demonstrators' demands; two-and-a-half weeks later, the grand duke fled, and a provisional revolutionary government took power.

The classic examples of such demonstrations were the two major mobilizations of Parisian workers, mounted by the Luxembourg Commission and some of the radical leaders on 16 April and 15 May 1848. The first of these demonstrations appeared to the provisional government as an attempt to overthrow it, or at least to purge its politically more moderate members. Therefore, the government had 100,000 armed National Guards, drawn from the ranks of property-owning Parisians, lining the route of the demonstration, chanting anti-socialist slogans and thoroughly intimidating the demonstrators – not all that different from how the British government had contained the radical Chartist demonstrators in London a week before. The second of these demonstrations really seems to have been an attempt to overthrow the government, the crowd invading the Constituent Assembly (which had been elected since the demonstration of the previous month), only to be dispersed by the National Guard.

If some mass demonstrations were not easily distinguishable from planned, or semi-planned uprisings, others, of a more peaceful nature, occurred in the context of public festivals. One example was the festival held in Cologne to celebrate the six hundredth anniversary of the beginning of the construction of the city's cathedral (construction had proceeded very slowly and the church was still not finished after 600 years), in mid-August 1848. Included in, indeed taking the center of the festivities, were large parades, speeches, and public gatherings, with thousands of participants and tens of thousands of spectators, in honor of Archduke Johann of Austria, who had recently been named imperial regent, that is head of state of the provisional German government, by the Frankfurt National Assembly. These were clearly political demonstrations, and contemporaries understood them as such, particularly as an attack on leftists, influential in Cologne, who, as republicans, were hostile to a monarch heading a potential united German state. The circumstances of the demonstrations – the anniversary of the cathedral, for instance, or their climax on 15 August, the Feast of the Assumption of the Blessed Virgin – mixed the political meaning in with popular and religious festivities.

The other variant on well-organized mass politics in 1848, the political mass meeting, might seem closer to similar events in the twentieth century. Planned and advertised in advance, the meeting would take place either out of doors, or in a large banquet or beer hall, so that as many spectators as possible could attend. There would be a cast of speakers, ranging from the prominent – parliamentarians, newspaper editors – through the local notables to the more obscure activists of socially modest backgrounds. Since mechanical sound amplification did not exist, people standing in the back could not hear what was being said. They did not necessarily lose the political import of the event, though, as such rallies were invariably accompanied by the display of non-verbal symbols: flags, banners, sashes, cockades (small pieces of colored cloth, placed in one's hat), pictures or busts of political heroes, perhaps posters and inscriptions as well. The impact of the meeting was sometimes heightened by a parade preceding, a banquet accompanying, or a dance following it.

We can point to precursors to such mass rallies, the banquet campaign in Paris for instance, that led up to the street fighting of February 1848. Yet there was one thing distinctly new about the meetings of the era of the revolution: they were not limited to cities and towns, but were held in the countryside as well. One series of such meetings has even passed into national mythology: the great agitation tour of the Hungarian revolutionary

Lajos Kossuth in the fall of 1848, when he went from village to village in the Hungarian plain, calling on the newly liberated serfs to fight against the invading Habsburg armies. Kossuth's actions in this martial context have been memorialized many times in painting and sculpture, becoming part of the Hungarian national tradition.

Kossuth's speeches were also examples of a new form of political mass mobilization, and as such unusual in eastern Europe during the mid-century revolution. Frequent and well-attended rural mass meetings were far more a feature of the central and western parts of the continent. Thousands attended such a rally in the countryside near the radical town of La Garde-Freinet, in the Department of the Var in southeastern France on 17 June 1849. The speakers went rather too far in attacking government policy (which by this time was becoming increasingly conservative). Their subsequent arrest nearly led to a major riot, as thousands of angry ex-spectators turned out in their defense. Another example of such a rally was the mass meeting sponsored by the democrats of Cologne on the Fühlingen Heath, north of the city, on 17 September 1848. As many as 8,000 people, from the city and the countryside appeared, and heard speakers, including Karl Marx's friend and close associate Friedrich Engels, call for revolutionary measures to create a republic in Germany. Those in the back who could not hear the speakers could still see the giant red flag raised on the platform.

Such mass meetings were particularly prevalent in rural areas of southeastern and central France, central and western Germany, and central Italy during the revolution. Some were very large, with thousands of participants, from both town and country, like the two examples given above. Far more, though, were smaller and less spectacular, just bringing together the inhabitants of a single village, to hear speakers come from a nearby town. Gathered together on the marketplace, in front of the church, or in the piazza, the peasant spectators were increasingly involved in a process of politicization that would help change the nature of political life.

Free to organize and associate

In the very center of the process of politicization was the creation of organizations and associations for political, social, economic, and religious purposes. Particularly in central and western Europe, much of the history of the revolution can be understood in terms of the formation of such groups, their affiliation and federation, their mutual interaction, and their role in the political mobilization of broad groups of the population. In a familiar pattern, the significance of such associations for the revolutionary process falls off as one moves east and south, yet as far off as the

Habsburg provinces of Bohemia and Galicia, in some parts of inner Hungary, or in some provinces of the Papal States and the Kingdom of the Two Sicilies, they were a factor to be taken seriously in political life. In this section, we will first take a look at political clubs, and then go on to consider other forms of organization, and some of the social groups that supported them.

Political clubs

The idea of a political club, a voluntary association whose members meet regularly to debate the questions of the day, and to organize petitions, election campaigns, public mass meetings or demonstrations – in short, to engage in organized political activity – dated from the French Revolution of 1789. That revolution had seen a proliferation of such organizations, including the most famous and influential of them, the radical Jacobin Club. As the armies of the revolutionary government spilled out across France's borders, they sponsored the creation of such clubs in neighboring countries as well. These groups had proven quite effective – indeed, too much so, the role of the Jacobins and other political clubs in stirring up the population and overthrowing the constituted authorities being so great that the revolutionary governments (even the extremely radical regime of Maximilien Robespierre) took steps to limit the associations' activities and eventually to prohibit them. By 1800, political clubs were illegal everywhere in continental Europe and either remained that way, or were only permitted to operate with police permission, until the introduction of freedom of association in 1848.

The spring of 1848 saw a rapid proliferation of political clubs, the movement beginning in the continent's political capital, Paris. One historian has counted about 200 clubs existing in Paris during the spring of 1848, with approximately 70,000 members, quite a substantial figure in a city of one million inhabitants. In that tumultuous spring, club meetings were turbulent and unorganized, at times chaotic. Gustave Flaubert, in his great novel *The Sentimental Education*, has left an acid portrait of these meetings: no regular agenda; much shouting and little listening; just about anybody taking part, including, to the author's barely repressed feelings of scandal, women; a lengthy speech by a left-wing Spanish exile in a language no one present understood.

If exaggerated for literary effect, Flaubert's portrait was not a total misrepresentation. Club meetings often were chaotic, and even when they were conducted in more orderly fashion it was difficult for them to result in effective political action, since club members had so many different points of view, ranging from moderate liberalism, through

Jacobin radicalism to pacifist and largely apolitical socialism, to revolutionary communism. There were efforts at turning these unwieldy bodies into an effective political instrument: a "Club of Clubs," made up of delegates from each of the groups, was formed, that hammered out a political platform and sent agents into the provinces to conduct a campaign for the elections to the French Constituent Assembly in April 1848. The mostly left-wing Parisian agents achieved little in the elections dominated by monarchist local notables; the Club of Clubs' recommendations were only partially followed in Paris itself, although its slate at least found more support than the totally unsuccessful ticket of the craftsmen's groups. Following the insurrectionary demonstrations of May 1848 in which some club leaders played a prominent role, and the uprising and street fighting of June 1848, many of the groups were dissolved by the government; others were placed under police surveillance.

The story of political association did not end in the capital city or with the spring of 1848. In October of that year, political activists on the left regrouped. Led by prominent parliamentarians, socialist and non-socialist radicals united to create a new political association, called Republican Solidarity. While its headquarters was in Paris, it concentrated its activities less on the capital city than on organizing support throughout the countryside. Either incorporating already existing left-wing groups or organizing them where none had previously existed, its leaders had created by January 1849 a network of some 350 affiliated clubs, with branches existing in three-fourths of all French departments. The increasingly conservative governmental authorities promptly dissolved the organization. Even then, political organizing did not stop but continued underground. In spite of mounting political persecution, activists formerly associated with Republican Solidarity organized over the following three years a network of 700 secret societies, mostly in towns and villages of central and southern France. There were perhaps 100,000 people affiliated with these groups, whose existence would be dramatically revealed in the last event of the mid-century revolution, the uprising against the *coup d'état* of Louis-Napoleon Bonaparte in December 1851.

Looking back at this chronicle of political clubs, we can trace a gradual process of politicization in France during the revolution. Once the new revolutionary regime proclaimed freedom of association, political organization began, at first centered among those who had been most exposed to politics before the revolution – above all Parisians, but also the inhabitants of other major urban centers. These first groups were still very disorganized and inchoate, containing within them many different, possibly contradictory political tendencies. As the revolution continued, political organization spread from the capital and the major cities into smaller towns and then the countryside. With the growth of political repression following major confrontations between radical movements in the capital and a more conservative legislature and government, the center of political organization shifted ever more from the metropolis to the provinces, and from large cities to small towns and villages.

Along with this shift in the locus of political organization went a change in the politics of political associations: from being discussion clubs, whose members had a wide range of views, making for much controversy, debate, and confusion, but little political action, they became organizations of the politically like minded, and hence more united in their actions, possessing the potential for creating nationwide federations, and for these reasons politically more effective. The most common and largest organizations in France were those of leftists, with conservatives running second and constitutionalist liberals, a poor third. In the Department of the Vaucluse, in the southeast of the country, the prefect counted sixty-two left-wing political associations in 1850, ten legitimist (i.e., conservative adherents of the Bourbon dynasty overthrown in 1830), and only one group of moderate republicans. He noted that there were an additional forty-two generically conservative groups, lacking any particular affiliation, most of which were really non-political clubs and associations.[2]

These same processes – the spreading of political association to the provinces and into small towns and the countryside, the creation of broader federations of political clubs, and the separating out of different political tendencies into different clubs and associations – occurred everywhere in revolutionary Europe during the mid-nineteenth century. The process varied in different countries, depending on their degree of urbanization, literacy or prior political experience; it, along with other aspects of the revolutionary events, could be overshadowed by the outbreak of war. Our knowledge of this process depends on the extent to which it has been studied by historians. While there are still gaps to be filled, overall, a number of recent studies have revealed the outlines of the process throughout the continent.

The German counterpart to Republican Solidarity was the "Central Association for the Preservation of the Accomplishments of March [1848]," founded in November 1848 by left-wing deputies to the Frankfurt National Assembly.[3] Some 950 clubs with half a million members were affiliated.

---

[2] Figures from John Merriman, *The Agony of the Republic: The Repression of the Left in Revolutionary France, 1848–1851* (New Haven and London, 1978), 61.

[3] Even Germans found the name overly Teutonic and referred to the group as the Central March Association.

Adding to this, the 260 clubs of a rival left-wing national federation that had held two national congresses in 1848 (one in June and one in October) as well as unaffiliated organizations, gives a total of about 1,400 democratic political clubs by the spring of 1849 with perhaps 700–750,000 members.

As in France, German radicals were the best and most organized of all political groups, but other political tendencies in central Europe, if not quite able to match the scope and scale of the democrats, were organized into broad federations as well. Some 250 constitutional monarchist political clubs became members of federations organized at two different national congresses, in July and September 1848. The theoretical difference that had long plagued German liberal nationalists – whether a united Germany should include the Germans of Austria, or, to put it differently, whether the kingdom of Prussia should have a dominant role in a united German state – proved equally divisive and irreconcilable in practice. These differences of opinion about the scope of a future German national state explain why there was little overlap in affiliation between the two congresses.

Even more active than the constitutional monarchists in Germany were the conservatives. At first regarding the outbreak of revolution as an unmitigated disaster, German conservatives gradually realized that all was not yet lost, that the revolution had not led to the feared introduction of a Jacobin regime, that the right retained strong bases of support in the armed forces, state officialdom, and the orthodox clergy. Consequently, conservatives began to re-emerge into public life in the summer of 1848, and to organize their political support. They remained cautious, accepting publicly some of the principles of the revolution, renouncing the open advocacy of absolutism or a society of orders. Indeed, German conservatives often adopted the liberal vocabulary, referring to themselves as constitutional monarchists, although putting much the greater emphasis on the "monarchist" than the "constitutional." As conservatives, they remained hostile to nationalism, stressing their loyalty to the individual ruling dynasties; conservative political clubs and their federations were thus not "national" groups, but organized in the individual German states.

In Prussia, the largest of these states, conservative groups, sporting such names as "Prussian Association," "Patriotic Association," or "League of Loyalty to King and Fatherland" (the fatherland to which members were to be loyal was Prussia, not Germany), numbered about 100 in the fall of 1848. By the spring of 1849, there were approximately 300 of them, with altogether some 60,000 members. Although only very loosely tied together in several federations lacking any real centralized

leadership, organized conservatives in just one of the German states outnumbered organized liberals throughout all of Germany.

There was yet another kind of political organization in central Europe
during the mid-century revolution, probably second in size only to the
democrats, the clubs of devout Catholics, the Pius Associations. The first
few such groups were formed shortly after the outbreak of revolution in
March–April 1848, but they seem to have developed on a large scale in
the fall of 1848 and winter of 1849. There were at least 500 politically
active local groups and many more either devoted primarily to religious
and charitable ends, or that had only an ephemeral existence. The Pius
Associations held two national congresses, the first in October 1848, the
second in May 1849.

While extraordinarily well organized, numerous, and widespread,
these Pius Associations were politically much less effective than the
other groups, primarily because their members could never decide on a
common political line. In the Catholic monarchies of central Europe, that
is to say in Bavaria and Austria, the Pius Associations were the conservatives, the equivalents of the Prussian Leagues of Loyalty to King and
Fatherland, representing those who stood for the pre-revolutionary status
quo, supporting at best minor modifications of it, and suspicious of liberal
or radical plans for a unified nation-state. Elsewhere in Germany, members of some individual clubs supported a specifically Roman Catholic
politics, separate and distinct from democrats, liberals, and conservatives
alike – thus foreshadowing developments of the years 1871–1933, when
such a specifically Roman Catholic political party, the Center, would
exist and play a major role in German politics. Still other Pius
Association members rejected the idea of an independent Catholic politics and supported constitutional monarchism. Just a tiny minority of
them sympathized with the democrats. The option chosen by the largest
number of groups was to renounce taking a political position altogether,
and to devote themselves to pious and charitable concerns.

These multiple political positions testify once again to the leading role
of parliamentary deputies in public life during the 1848 revolution. The
different political options of the Pius Associations reflected the different
viewpoints of devout Roman Catholic deputies who sat in the Frankfurt
National Assembly, the Prussian and Austrian Constituent Assemblies
and the parliaments of the smaller German states. While conferring on
specifically religious issues, especially those related to the public school
system and church–state relations, the deputies were not a homogeneous
voting bloc, but were found in various caucuses of the right and center.
Overall, though, it might be fair to say that the Pius Associations followed
a political course similar to the Pope after whom they were named: at the

outbreak of the revolution, adhering to the party of movement, with feelings ranging from outright enthusiasm to cautious sympathy; with the growth of conflicts and apparent tendencies towards radicalization, moving steadily towards the party of order, sometimes in the form of open support for conservative politics, sometimes in the form of a conscious decision to leave politics to the increasingly counter-revolutionary state authorities and limit participation in public life to pious causes.

One last kind of political club in the German states ought to be mentioned, namely groups founded by members of national minorities. Following the failure of their attempt to seize power and create a Polish nation-state in the Prussian province of Posen, Polish nationalists turned to political organization. They founded a *Liga Polska* that grew to 300 branches and 37,000 members by June 1849. Rather in the same way that the Pius Associations anticipated a future Catholic political party, this Polish League anticipated the future creation of a Polish nationalist political party that would exist in Germany from 1871 until the collapse of the German Empire and the re-creation of an independent Poland at the end of the First World War.

Somewhere between 1 and 1.5 million Germans joined a political club during the mid-century revolution. Since there were about 38 million Germans at the time (including the German-speaking inhabitants of the Austrian Empire), or 9–10 million adult males, this means that 10–15 percent of them had become involved in organized political life.[4] Such participation rates are noticeably higher than those of West Germany of the 1980s, when 3–4 percent of adults belonged to a political party. Compared with pre-1848 central Europe, when these sorts of political organizations and the participation in public life associated with them had been illegal, these statistics show how the 1848 revolution became the occasion for an enormous increase in political participation.

Historians have not studied the formation of political clubs in Italy during the 1848 revolution in comparable detail. Such clubs were few and far between in Lombardy and Venetia, no surprise since these provinces were the scene of warfare and then of Austrian reoccupation, subject to martial law. There do seem to have been a substantial number – just how many requires further investigation – in central Italy, in the Grand Duchy of Tuscany and the Papal States. As was the case in Germany and provincial France, while a few clubs were formed in the spring of 1848, most dated from the fall of that year and the winter of 1849.

---

[4] As will be seen below, women were also active in politics during the revolution, although in different ways from men. In Germany, it would seem that relatively few of them became members of political clubs.

Parallel to developments elsewhere in western and central Europe, Italian political clubs went through a process of political differentiation in the summer and fall of 1848, from which the democrats emerged as the largest and most active groups. By the end of the year, federations of democratic political clubs had been formed in Tuscany and the Papal States. At the beginning of 1849 their leadership was merged, with the support and encouragement of the veteran revolutionary Giuseppe Mazzini, forming a "Central Committee of Italian Political Clubs," with headquarters in Rome.

The main organized alternative to the Italian democrats was the constitutional monarchists, whose main strongholds were apparently in the Kingdom of Piedmont-Savoy. A central organization, the "Society for an Italian Confederation," was founded by the reforming priest Vincenzo Gioberti, whose 1843 book *On the Moral and Civic Primacy of the Italians*, advocating a Papal-led Italian confederation, had shaped constitutional monarchism in Italy. While Pius IX had proven a disappointment to the constitutional monarchists, Gioberti had not given up on the idea of an Italy united on liberal lines. There was some difficulty, though, in finding a replacement for his original idea of an Italy united under Papal leadership, which may help explain why his organization's national congress in October 1848 ended inconclusively.

Another open question about political organization in Italy during the 1848 revolution concerns the nature and extent of political clubs in the southern part of the peninsula. The Italian south had a long history of conspiratorial secret societies, dating from the "Carbonari" of the first two decades of the nineteenth century. Many of these groups seem to have been transformed into open and legal political clubs following the outbreak of revolution; one account notes thirty-eight of them in the province of Puglia, in the Kingdom of the Two Sicilies, alone. How typical this was, just what activities these and other southern political clubs engaged in, whether they underwent the same process of political differentiation and affiliation with a national confederation as did clubs further north – all these are matters in need of further study.

While there were political clubs formed in the Habsburg monarchy during the 1848 revolution, they were fewer and further between than in other parts of Europe. To be sure, there were democratic, constitutional-monarchist and Catholic-conservative political clubs formed in the imperial capital, all with membership in the thousands and loosely affiliated with their respective German political confederations. These Viennese clubs, however, had little contact with the Austrian provinces, where political organization set in late and only occurred in modest fashion. A typical example might be Klagenfurt, the capital of the province of Carinthia, where political clubs – democratic and constitutional-monarchist – were only founded in September–October 1848. Outside the provincial capital, the democrats extended their organizational reach to just a handful of market towns in the province over the following four to five months.

In all of Austria, outside of Hungary, the politically most lively and best organized region was the provinces of Bohemia and Moravia, where nationalist rivalries between Germans and Czechs interacted with differences between radicals and liberals, spurring on the formation of political associations. Fifteen German constitutional-monarchist political clubs from these two provinces held a regional conference in the summer of 1848 and affiliated with the corresponding federation in Germany. The Czech clubs, on the other hand, with the unusual name of the "Slavic Linden," were politically more left wing, sympathetic to democratic ideas, and in fact substantially to the left of the constitutional-monarchist Czech deputies to the Austrian Constituent Assembly. By the spring of 1849, there were fifty branches of the Slavic Linden in the two provinces, with, however, a quite modest total of some 2,000 members.

Most of the other Slavic nationalities of the monarchy could not even match that. There was a Croatian version of the Slavic Linden as well, but it had all of three branches, with a few dozen members between them. The Polish National Committee in Cracow did form some branch groups in the province of Galicia that might be seen as political clubs, but the extension of such clubs into the countryside, characteristic of political developments in much of central and western Europe, was impossible – and as Polish nationalists succeeded in doing in the Prussian province of Posen/Poznań – given the ex-serfs' deep hatred of the noble leaders of Polish politics. The Poles' nationalist opponents, the Ukrainians, had more success, forming about fifty branches of their national committee throughout eastern of Galicia, testifying to a greater degree of popular support, but also to the benevolent assistance of the Habsburg authorities. These circumstances in Galicia also suggest that in contrast to much of western and central Europe, where different political clubs represented varying points of view on the political spectrum – radical, liberal or conservative – in much of the Habsburg monarchy clubs represented members of different nationalist groups. Similar to the arrangements of the parliamentary caucuses in the Austrian Constituent Assembly, this state of affairs suggests that while the dynamics of politics in the west and center of the continent stemmed primarily from the clash of political opinions, in the Austrian Empire it came, above all, from the clash of nationalities.

The circumstances of political organization in Hungary started out somewhat differently from the rest of the Habsburg Empire. A strongly left-wing political club, the Budapest "Society for Equality" was founded by newspaper editors and deputies to the Hungarian National Assembly in July 1848. Its membership grew to over 1,000 by September. The founders of the group had envisaged a national federation of such clubs, and had begun to take steps in that direction, when this development, parallel to those further west, was interrupted by the outbreak of civil war, the invasion of Hungary by Habsburg troops in September 1848. Activists in the Society for Equality threw themselves into the war effort, supporting the new government of Lajos Kossuth that was determined to fight the emperor's soldiers, and joining Kossuth in agitating in the countryside to recruit peasant soldiers for the regime. As the war continued and grew in intensity, as the struggle of the Hungarian national government against the Habsburg armies, and the nationalist movements of the Romanians, Croats and Serbs allied with it, became ever more desperate, the armed conflict overshadowed all efforts at political organization. The Society for Equality and its potential affiliated political network ceased to exist, showing that the nationalities' conflict had superseded the clash of political opinions as the basis for political life in Hungary as well as the rest of the Austrian Empire.

The foregoing survey of the founding, spread, and federation of political clubs recounts one of the most important results of recent scholarship on the revolution of 1848, namely the portrayal of the revolution as a pioneering venture in mass political mobilization. Via club membership, literally millions of Europeans had their first opportunity to participate in politics. To cap off this section on the clubs, it might be worth giving some concrete form to the concept of "political participation" by considering what went on at a club meeting, and explaining just what the clubs actually did.

Clubs met at regular intervals, ranging form weekly to monthly. A major function of these sessions was transmitting information. More knowledgeable (this usually meant more bourgeois) club members would give speeches on the current political situation or other relevant issues. Even the better-educated members would be likely to have some difficulty with this sort of public speaking and they might resort to reading newspaper articles out loud. In the countryside, where the printed word was still unfamiliar, and literacy ranged from spotty to poor, this was the typical form of a club meeting: an innkeeper, schoolteacher, priest, pastor, or other at least modestly literate person would read newspaper articles to the peasants and explain them as best as he could.

Open debate and controversy, something usually associated with political clubs, and present to perhaps an extreme degree in the wild scenes in Paris during the spring of 1848, seem to have been less common in the expanded, provincial, and politically more homogeneous political world of the later phases of the revolution. Only a relatively limited number of members ever took the floor to speak, a set of circumstances actually set down in the statutes of the "circle of the people" (*Circolo del Popolo*), the democratic club of Florence. Only "affiliates," people selected by a ballot of the group's founders, were permitted to speak at meetings. While this statutory exclusion of popular participation was unusual, a reading of minutes or accounts of meetings elsewhere suggest that the same, often affluent or educated, leading members did most of the talking. The 1848 revolution may have introduced popular political participation on a broad scale, but political leadership remained largely an elite affair.

Another major function of the clubs was the organization of political activism. The mass demonstrations and political rallies discussed earlier in this section were typically organized by clubs. The "spreading" of political organization into the countryside was also a part of club activity. Rural political clubs were founded by members of urban groups, who would travel out to villages to give speeches to the peasants and drink with them, trying to gain their political allegiance.[5] In elections held during the 1848 revolution but after the initial attempts in the spring of that year, political clubs played a substantial role in nominating candidates, carrying out an election campaign, and getting voters to the polls. Finally, most of the attempts at insurrection, at pushing the revolution in a more radical direction, were organized and planned by the clubs. At the very least, club members attempted to lead and direct popular mass movements in an insurrectionary direction.

A final function performed by clubs was providing a mediating link between an upper level of political leadership – parliamentary deputies, or editors of large circulation newspapers, usually in the capital city – and rank-and-file political activists throughout the country. In contrast to the later nineteenth and twentieth centuries, this connection was not close and direct. Clubs and their federations were not the organized political parties of later decades. Communication and transport in 1848 were still far too primitive to allow for a large-scale political apparatus with a centralized leadership that could issue directives and start political campaigns across an entire national territory. The best that could be done at

---

[5] It is difficult to overestimate the extent to which popular politics in mid-nineteenth-century Europe involved the consumption of substantial amounts of alcohol. A large drinking capacity was probably the first qualification of any successful political agitator.

mid-century was to hold an occasional national congress bringing together activists from widely scattered regions on an ad hoc basis, and creating a skeletal leadership structure that would try, usually not too successfully, to coordinate their activities. The largest region across which any seriously coordinated political action could be expected was a province or French department.

What the clubs did do effectively was to spread broadly issues envisaged by a national leadership, popularize their political demands and the slogans, songs, and non-verbal political symbols expressing them. Clubs had a multiplier effect on political propaganda, providing a large audience for speakers, as well as for newspapers, almanacs, and other forms of written political statements. While the expansion of popular political participation in the wake of the 1848 revolution went well beyond the ranks of club members, the clubs themselves were the backbone of the new political life. There were, to be sure, other foci around which political participation could be organized – most commonly in the Austrian Empire, the war between the Hungarian government and Habsburg troops, the latter supported by Croatian and Romanian nationalists, the best example – yet, generally, without the presence of clubs, the first stirrings of political life induced by the outbreak of revolution in the spring of 1848 tended to disappear.

Association as a social and political theme

If political clubs were the most common version of association emerging from the 1848 revolution, and had unquestionably the largest membership, they were certainly not the only ones. Occupational and professional groups – among others, assemblies and associations of workers, artisans, peasants, teachers, and clergy – came into existence to press specific demands. Women, previously perceived, with few exceptions, as outside the political process altogether, formed their own groups and found ways to enter into public life. This process of formation of various kinds of associations, occurring both alongside of and in interaction with the founding of political clubs, left its stamp on the revolutionary experience of the mid-nineteenth century.

The 1848 revolution is often seen as the birthplace of the labor movement in continental Europe, a legitimate judgment, provided that one does not take the model of the labor movement of the late nineteenth and first half of the twentieth centuries, with its trade union federations and socialist or communist parties, and impose it on Europe c. 1850. There were recognizable trade unions formed in 1848 and subsequent years. Printers and typesetters were a particularly active trade everywhere, from

France to Italy to Hungary. The German printing workers even formed a national federation that gained a six-day week from the publishers and negotiated a tentative wage contract with them. (Ironically, Karl Marx himself got into a prolonged dispute with the labor force of the newspaper he edited, the *Neue Rheinische Zeitung*, about whether pay would conform to the national standard.) Cigar-makers were another active group, the Germans forming a national union federation that even outlasted – briefly – the revolution itself.

Yet such trade unions were not the typical form of workers' association during the revolution – and in view of the structure of the labor force, dominated by nominally independent small-producing outworkers, this was to be expected. Outworkers' aspirations ran more in the direction of obtaining independence from the merchant contractors who employed them and to whom they were indebted. The means to achieve this end would be the formation of cooperatives, for production, consumption, and marketing. Discussed before 1848 in socialist theory, and occasionally attempted in artisan practice, the revolution offered an opportunity to try out such associations on a large scale – not surprisingly, most of all in France. The Parisian trade associations formed in the spring of 1848 did not rest content with threatening or negotiating with merchant contractors, but sought to found producers' cooperatives, even obtaining some start up money from the Provisional Government of the republic. After the suppression of the uprising of June 1848 and the conservative turn in government policy, the Parisian workers' organization devoted themselves exclusively to the non-confrontational task of cooperation. Between 1848 and 1851, there were 300 cooperatives formed in Paris, counting workers from 120 different trades and involving some 50,000 members.

Many similar producers' associations were formed in provincial France, altogether at least as many as in the capital. In the country's second city, Lyon, the cooperative movement took a somewhat different tack, uniting workers from different crafts into three major consumers' cooperatives founded at the beginning of 1849. A federation of such cooperative groups, with headquarters in the textile city of Reims, in northeastern France, extended its influence over the manufacturing and industrial regions in the northern part of the country.

All of these cooperative groups included a mutual benefits fund as part of their operation, and to contemporaries this form of health and burial insurance was another example of the cooperative movement. Mutual benefit societies were not a novelty of 1848; they had been present beforehand, although requiring official approval for their operation. The revolution did see a substantial increase in the numbers of such societies, but the main change in them was ideological: the groups now appeared charged with the cooperative ideal.

Both producers' cooperatives and mutual benefit societies existed in central Europe, and new ones were founded in 1848, equally imbued with the idea of cooperation. The general thrust of the movement of association there, however, was in a somewhat different direction than in France, towards the formation of generalized workers' associations, whose members were drawn from the different crafts. Such groups appeared in the spring and summer of 1848 in larger urban centers – among many others, Cologne, Berlin, and Vienna – and increasingly in smaller provincial towns. A congress held in Berlin in August–September 1848 established a national confederation of these groups, the "Workers' Fraternization," that counted about 15,000 members in 170 different local associations by the spring of 1849.

Another peculiarity of labor organization in Germany was the existence of craftsmen's guilds in many parts of the country. Craftsmen forming associations – and everywhere in Europe, the large majority of organized "workers" were craftsmen – had to decide whether guilds should provide the basis for their organizations. In the first flush of popular activity and organizational effort in the spring of 1848, the centrality of the guild issue had been obscured. Various bodies, whether guilds, public meetings of craftsmen, or newly formed workers' associations, had issued a wide variety of often contradictory demands, that included the strengthening or re-establishment of guilds among many other measures. A national congress of craftsmen, meeting in Frankfurt – in the same city that housed the German National Assembly – during the summer of 1848, however, brought the issue of guilds to the fore.

The artisans expressed their skepticism about the free market economy, talked of the need for craftsmen to associate and called for a more progressive tax structure, restrictions on merchant contractors, and limitations on the use of machinery – measures that most central European craftsmen might agree to. The congress delegates went on to demand legal restrictions on journeymen setting up in business for themselves and insisted that only master craftsmen take part in their deliberations – unceremoniously showing the journeymen in attendance the door. The journeymen promptly held their own congress, that later affiliated with the Workers' Fraternization.

These two developments represented what would become from the 1848 revolution onwards a line of division in central Europe. While all artisans had some grievances in common and, during the 1848 revolution at least, expressed them in a common language, condemning capitalism and the unequal distribution of wealth and calling for measures of association against it, one group of craftsmen, master artisans, usually from areas such as Bavaria with a strong guild tradition, directed a good deal of their hostility towards the journeymen and demanded the restoration or strengthening of the guilds to discipline them. Another group of artisans, including most of the journeymen but many outworking masters as well, saw masters and journeymen cooperating against their main enemy the merchant-contractors. During 1848–49, adherents of both these positions could be found at different points throughout the political spectrum. As the revolution went on, the pro-guild, anti-journeymen masters tended to move towards the political right, becoming the forerunners of later nineteenth-century populist conservatives, while the second group of craftsmen increasingly supported the left, forming the basis for the future labor movement.

These organizations of artisans and workers were the most significant form of association outside the political clubs in Europe during the mid-century revolution. In summing up their accomplishments and limitations, we might note the following points. As a large-scale associational effort, the labor movement was restricted to France and Germany. In the less urbanized, less economically developed areas to the south and east of the continent, there were at most organizations of individual crafts, particularly printers and typesetters, but no labor movement. Even in the economically more advanced European regions, the size of the labor movement should not be exaggerated. Workers' organizations were overshadowed by more expressly political organizations: 50,000 members of Parisian cooperatives in 1848–51, as against 75–100,000 members of Parisian political clubs in the spring of 1848 alone; 15,000 members of the German Workers' Fraternization as against 500,000 members of the Central March Association. The late nineteenth- and twentieth-century state of affairs, where trade union membership far exceeded that of political parties, did not exist in the middle of the nineteenth century.

Everywhere on the continent the mid-century labor movement followed a common political trajectory. At the beginning of the revolution, it appeared to be an alternative to politics. Strikes, riots against employers, mass meetings of craftsmen, founding of unions, cooperatives, or workers' associations all occurred without much connection to the movements towards national unity or the elections to parliamentary assemblies. Even in Paris, the most politicized place in Europe, the workers' associations organized an election campaign to the Constituent Assembly without any connection to the campaign organized by the city's political clubs. As the revolution continued, and the process of politicization of the population went further, the nascent labor movement gradually became more closely tied to political organization.

In Florence, for instance, the typographers' mutual benefit society voted to store the society's flag in the meeting rooms of the city's democratic club; the flag, and the typographers carrying it, were then always present at the demonstrations sponsored by the society. The city's furriers, a craft with a long guild tradition, acted similarly, and early in 1849 took part as a body in the planting of a tree of liberty. Workers active in the formation of cooperatives in France were frequently also members of the national democratic federation, Republican Solidarity, or its underground secret society successor. In a similar way, members of local branches of the Workers' Fraternization in Germany would also be involved in their city's democratic club. Usually, the artisans and workers active in occupational associations would belong to left-wing political groups, although occasionally, as was the case with the guild-oriented German master craftsmen, their political connections would be on the right. Regardless of the specific political orientation, those occupational, guild, or trade union associations that had originally been an alternative to political action had become a constituent part of it.

There were sporadic efforts to take the movement of occupational association to the countryside, with relatively little success. Peasants were certainly as vigorous as workers and craftsmen at pressing their demands in riotous fashion during the spring of 1848, but were far less likely to form their own organizations and associations. The one major exception occurred on the margins, both of Europe and of the 1848 revolutions, in Norway. A rural schoolteacher, named Marcus Thrane, vaguely inspired by both socialist ideas and Protestant theology, began organizing a "Workers Union," that by 1850 had about 30,000 members, an impressive number in a country of less than one million inhabitants. Most of the members, like most of the Norwegian lower classes, were small farmers and cotters and the group's demands included provisions for distribution of land to landless peasants, and the formation of agricultural cooperatives. Thrane and several other leaders were arrested in 1851, and his movement suppressed. In rural areas, the main forms of association during the mid-century revolution were the political clubs. Unlike the European labor movement, whose precursors can at least be glimpsed in 1848, peasant leagues, farmers' special-interest groups, and agricultural cooperatives were, with this partial exception in Norway, all future developments.

More active occupationally were two more intellectual professions, teachers and clergymen. Both groups were involved in organizing efforts during the revolution, attempting to obtain redress for long-standing grievances and to improve their social influence and esteem. In central Europe, the initial wave of social conflict in the spring of 1848 affected elementary school teachers most of all white-collar occupations. If not resorting to force, as did the more plebeian elements in society, teachers repeatedly gathered in meetings, formed local and regional organizations, and sent petitions to the different parliamentary assemblies demanding improved salaries and working conditions, and, more than anything else, that the administration of the public school system be taken out of the hands of the clergy and given over to professional educators. A national congress was held, though, not by elementary school teachers but by the better paid and socially more esteemed German secondary school teachers, in the Thuringian city of Eisenach in September 1848.

French schoolteachers were similarly active, albeit in somewhat different fashion. Although complaints about low pay and poor working conditions were common enough in both countries, the main goal of their German counterparts, the professionalization of public education, had already been achieved in France. French schoolteachers were more aggressive, seeing the 1848 revolution as an opportunity to expand their social role. The very name of the "Central Republican Committee of Education," a Parisian body begun in the spring of 1848, and producing a national teachers' newspaper, identified the profession with the new form of government. As one teacher activist put it in a brochure entitled *The Gospel and the Republic, or the Social Mission of the Schoolteachers*, "It is up to you, teachers, to replace the priests who have abdicated."[6]

Those men of religion whom the teachers were planning to replace had their own plans for occupational reform and enhancement of their social position. Eastern Orthodox clergy in the Habsburg Empire demanded equality of status with Catholic priests and state support for their religion, a demand closely connected, as were the Orthodox priests themselves, with the Romanian and Serbian nationalist movements. The Orthodox bishop Andrieu Şaguna was the leading moderate nationalist among the Romanians of Transylvania, and Orthodox priests in the Principality of Wallachia would prove to be active supporters of the revolutionary government there, in its struggle to survive against foreign intervention and to coordinate Romanian nationalists throughout eastern Europe.

The Orthodox Archbishop Josip Rajačić was named Patriarch of the Orthodox Church among the Serbs of the Austrian Empire by the Serb nationalist mass meeting in Karlovci on 10–11 May 1848. Through 1848 and 1849, Rajačić would lead the Serbs of the Banat against the Hungarians, even at one point attempting to get the Tsar to intervene, when he felt that the Habsburg government was not doing enough to

---

[6] Quoted in Merriman, *The Agony of the Republic* 119.

protect the Serbs. He was strongly supported in his efforts by the ordinary Orthodox priests, who promptly became a target for Hungarian military actions against the Serb nationalists. Magyar troops systematically destroyed the Orthodox churches as bastions of their Serb nationalist enemies.

A similar close identification of clergy and the nationalist movement was apparent among the Uniates or Greek Catholics and the Ukrainians of the Austrian Empire. The Uniate bishop of Lemberg, Hryhory Jachymoryč, was the head of the Supreme Ukrainian Council in the province of Galicia, and the fifty local branches of the council in the province were formed with the assistance of the Uniate clergy. It is perhaps no surprise that clergy would take a prominent role in the revolutionary events in eastern Europe, since they were a literate and educated group among a population where illiteracy was widespread, and more secular forms of political organization, as well as individuals who could organize them, were relatively few in number. However, the 1848 revolution spurred on political activities, particularly by the Roman Catholic clergy, in western and central Europe as well. There were two major themes of clerical activism. One was the demand for the liberation from state control, or, as the Archbishop of Lyon, informed the priests of his archdiocese, following the proclamation of the republic in France: "You often used to long for that liberty which makes our brothers in the United States of America so happy. This liberty will now be yours."[7]

The other theme of clerical activism concerned relations of power within the Catholic Church itself. Following the outbreak of the revolution, there were widespread demands by parish clergy for diocesan or even national synods, that is, elected church councils, demands frankly directed against the power of the bishops and the Pope. On the margin of this movement, more radical calls were heard for the abolition of clerical celibacy, demands raised by meetings of priests in southwestern Germany and in the Austrian province of Bohemia, the separation of church and state, and even the creation of national churches independent of Rome. The closest such demands came to realization was in Hungary, where a leader in the church reform and anti-celibacy movement, the pastor of Hatvan, Michael Horváth, called a national synod for church reforms, with the sponsorship of the revolutionary Hungarian government. Before the synod could meet, the revolutionary government was overthrown by Habsburg and tsarist troops. Interestingly, the Croatian nationalists, the mortal enemies of the revolutionary

---

[7] Cited in Roger Price (ed.), *1848 in France* (Ithaca and London, 1975), 66–68.

Hungarian government, concurred with it in opposing clerical celibacy, whose abolition was one of the demands they made at their nationalist mass meeting of 25 March 1848.

In the end, the revolutionary movement brought little change to the Catholic Church. No national synods were ever summoned, although there were synods held in each of France's archdioceses, most of which were dominated by proponents of Papal authority. When, as was the case with the synod of the Archdiocese of Paris, decisions were reached that did not meet with Vatican approval, these decisions were simply ignored. There was a national conference of the German Catholic bishops in the fall of 1848 – the first of its kind, beginning a practice still continued today – and a further conference of all the Habsburg bishops in the winter of 1849, these meetings supported and reinforced Papal authority, rather than challenging it in the name of nationalism. More successful were organization and action of the Catholic clergy to rebuff efforts directed against its social position. When the revolutionary Hungarian government announced its intention of ending the specially privileged status of the Catholic Church and introducing the equality of all Christian confessions, bishops and lower clergy began a petition drive to the National Assembly, demanding that the state hand over to the church funds for education and religious functions it had previously controlled. In Germany, the Catholic clergy responded to schoolteachers' petitions in favor of the separation of church and school with the organization of counter petitions among the faithful in favor of religiously segregated and clerically controlled public education, in terms of signatures collected far outdoing the teachers' efforts. Far from being replaced by the schoolteachers, Catholic priests in France scored a major victory over them in 1850, when the Falloux Law restored to the church a partial role in the administration of public education.

In many ways, the two themes of Catholic clerical activism contradicted each other. Priests wanted to be free of government control, but demands of the lower clergy for more power within the church could only have been realized with government backing. In the end, the 1848 revolution and the ensuing counter-revolution would produce in most of Europe a lessening of state control over and a greater autonomy for the Catholic Church, but also a reinforcement of both the Church's position in society and of the ecclesiastical hierarchy and of the power of the Pope.

There were similar movements among Protestant clergy and religiously interested laymen, especially in central Europe, albeit on a smaller scale. A national congress of German Protestants, held in August 1848, was attended primarily by religious revivalists and political conservatives. Its major product, was the "Inner Mission," a joint effort of Germany's

Protestant churches at poor relief, social work, and the evangelization of the lower classes, whose falling away from religion the congress's attendees held responsible for the outbreak of revolution. These more conservative Protestant elements, were, like their Catholic counterparts, hostile to the schoolteachers' demands for professional autonomy and sponsored petitions against them. Religiously rationalist and politically more left-wing Protestants were also active, supporting the school-teachers, calling for provincial synods, and attempting to introduce more democratic elements into the administration of the different German Protestant churches, ultimately without much success.

If 1848 marked the still relatively feeble beginnings of the organized labor movement in continental Europe, it also marked the end of a close connection between political and religious revolutions. The French revolutionaries in the decade after 1789 had attempted first to reform and transform the Catholic Church in their country and then to create an altogether new religion in competition with it. In 1848 there were similar attempts to reshape existing religions, perhaps not quite so strongly as in the years after 1789, but the connection between political revolution and religious transformation was clear enough. Following the middle of the nineteenth century, political transformations and religious changes would go their separate ways, with religious upheavals, such as the First and Second Vatican Councils, decoupled from political revolutions. Religion would continue to play a very important role in European politics, and the clergy would, if anything, become politically more active, twentieth-century communist revolutionaries would propose the transcendental yet atheist project of creating a "new socialist man," but revolutions would generally not involve revolutionizing existing churches.

The 1848 revolution did create an environment in which everyone could organize and associate, act on behalf of their own interests, and, more generally, participate in public life. One of the most interesting aspects of the mid-nineteenth-century European revolutions was that everybody meant literally everybody – not just men, but women too. Before 1848, the idea that women could participate in public life seemed impossible, supported at most by a few socialists. With the outbreak of the revolution, the impossible idea became reality overnight.

As just one example of many, we might take the account of how the "married women and maidens" of the west German textile town of Elberfeld met in a "public meeting" on 31 March 1848. Explaining that their "hearts beat faster and stronger at the hope of a united Germany, yet bleed at the thought of the desperate condition of our workers," they called on their sisters just to wear the products of the nation's industry, so that their sex might assist in both the movement of national unification and help resolve the social crisis of the working class. The assembled women also called on men to follow their example in their purchase of clothing, but, additionally, to perform their manly duty and protect women and children from potential violence and anarchy.[8]

This meeting and the appeal it issued defines much of women's role in 1848. Women appeared in public, they met in a "public meeting" – previously, an action respectable women did not take, especially in a city like Elberfeld, many of whose inhabitants were extremely devout Protestants, suspicious of and hostile to anything that even remotely smacked of women's emancipation. They displayed their interest and participation in the great issues of the day, in this case the movement towards German national unity and the social conflicts emerging in manufacturing regions during the spring of 1848. Women thus asserted their right to a role in public life, but they did so largely in terms of their private role in the household and family. The women of Elberfeld would contribute to national unity by their fashions and shopping habits, by being charitable towards the poor, and, perhaps most importantly, by calling on men to take on their masculine role and publicly protect their homes and families.

As the process of politicization characteristic of the 1848 revolution continued, women's political participation, while remaining within these parameters, became more elaborate. Women expanded their support for the national cause: from the thousands of German women who collected money for a German navy (a popular nationalist cause in the revolution), to the women of Prague, who formed a "Club of Slavic Women" to promote girls' education in the national tongue. Women also formed clubs and associations to assist political refugees or imprisoned insurgents. One of the first of that kind, a women's group formed on behalf of those imprisoned after the Prague street fighting of June 1848, held two public meetings in August 1848, demanding that those arrested in the suppression of the uprising be released. The further nationalist initiatives of the Club of Slavic Women came from the impetus of these meetings. Such women's associations to assist victims of political persecution would become more common after the suppression of the uprisings of the spring of 1849.

Female participation in the mass meetings, festivals, and demonstrations (at least the more peaceful ones) characteristic of the revolution became ever more frequent. Women, for instance, made up half the participants in the mass banquet sponsored by the Cologne Democratic Society and the city's workers' association in March 1849 to celebrate the

---

[8] The appeal of the meeting is printed in the *Kölnische Zeitung* of 6 April 1848.

first anniversary of the outbreak of revolution in Germany. Women sewed flags for their town's civic or national guard and turned them over to the guardsmen in ceremonies at which female speakers reminded the armed men of their patriotic duties and their male counterparts responded by promising to defend their nation and its women and children. These ceremonies were among the few times that women spoke in public during the revolution. It was a hotly debated issue whether political clubs should admit women to their sessions at all. In the end, most, ranging from radicals to Catholic conservatives, agreed to do so, but only a handful allowed women to obtain membership or to speak at the meetings.

Women were occasionally found at the barricades, making up a small proportion of those killed, wounded or arrested in the street fighting in Prague and Paris in June 1848, or in Vienna in October of that year. There were a few women who became famous for their role in the armed fighting occurring during the revolution. Brandishing two pistols, Ana Ipătescu led the crowd in Bucharest on 1 July 1848 in defending the revolutionary government against a putsch organized by conservative soldiers. The romantic artist C.D. Rosenthal later memorialized her actions in a famous painting. A few women, armed and outfitted as soldiers, participated in the three radical republican uprisings in the southwest German Grand Duchy of Baden occurring in 1848–49: Emma Herwegh, wife of exiled German revolutionary Georg Herwegh, Amalie Struve, the wife of Gustav Struve, one of the leaders of the Badenese democrats, and Mathilde Franziska Anneke, wife of the communist revolutionary (and ex-artillery officer in the Prussian army) Fritz Anneke. Of course, all three of these women, whose participation was widely reported in the contemporary press making quite a stir, were married to male revolutionaries (Ana Ipătescu was as well), and played their political role in conjunction with their husbands. Their well-publicized actions were a more extreme variation of more common behavior of women in such insurrectionary situations, namely spurring on their men by shaming them for inaction and encouraging them to act. During the critical days of the German revolution in September 1848, some of the more left-wing women in the village of Zimmern in the kingdom of Württemberg, in southwestern Germany, went from door to door, getting other women in the village to sign a petition in favor of militant political action. A male democrat promptly announced at a mass meeting, "What a shame, if the men won't go, then the women will!" A less critical tone was struck by the women in radical villages of southeastern France, who told their men as they marched off to join the uprising of December 1851, "Bring back the good [cause] to us." The women went on to stand guard in the villages, in their men's absence.

Today's reader may get a little impatient at all these accounts of women supporting their men acting through or at most alongside of them, and wonder if women ever took part in the revolutionary activities on their own account, or if they ever raised demands for women's rights. The honest reply would have to be rarely. Even future feminists, such as the German women, Mathilde Franziska Anneke or Louise Otto-Peters, understood their political activity during the 1848 revolution – besides Anneke's military exploits, both of these women edited newspapers – in terms of a supportive, auxiliary role. Women did sometimes meet for debate on public matters in a few women's political clubs, found in such large cities as Berlin or Vienna. The Viennese women were particularly active, even petitioning the Austrian Constituent Assembly, calling on it to take more revolutionary measures. By contrast, the actions of their Berlin counterparts were not without their farcical elements, especially as the leader of the group, Lucie Lenz, was a police spy and the mistress of the chief of police. Women's associations were also present in smaller towns in provincial France and southwestern Germany. (The exact number or extent of these clubs has never been ascertained, and it is possible that there were more of them than are now known to have existed.) The one place where an independent female initiative existed was the center of the continent's avant-garde, the place where socialist ideas had had their greatest degree of influence (and remember that early feminism in Europe was closely connected with socialism), in Paris. "[T]he rights of women are constantly put forth in all the clubs," wrote one Parisian woman to her British friend, the veteran feminist Anna Wheeler in the spring of 1848, "could you not come over?"[9] This was a bit exaggerated, since many of the Parisian clubs had already developed what would become the standard practice of allowing women to attend meetings, but not to speak at them. Others, though, permitted women to voice their opinions; the "Fraternal Association of Democrats of Both Sexes" was, as its name suggests, a political club specifically designed to have both men and women as equal members. Even more to the point, and justifying the enthusiasm of Wheeler's correspondent, there existed political clubs exclusively for women – among others, the Club of the Emancipation of Women, and the Union of Women – and a women's newspaper, the *Voice of Women*, edited by the veteran socialist and feminist Eugénie Niboyet. Members of these clubs demanded that women have equal chances at public education, the right, while married, to control their own property, and that divorce be legalized. They insisted

---

[9] Quoted in Barbara Taylor, *Eve and the New Jerusalem: Socialism and Feminism in the Nineteenth Century* (New York, 1983), 61.

that the "right to work," a common demand in Parisian socialist circles not be limited to men, but include women who needed employment and, most shockingly, raised a demand found virtually nowhere else on the continent, that women have the right to vote.

The creation of trades' associations and their tentative unification into a labor movement was also a main feature of the Parisian spring of 1848, and women were active in this area as well. The original public works programs for the unemployed created by the provisional government was for male workers only. Unemployed women promptly protested and received their own, admittedly much smaller program. Women craftsmen of Paris employed in the needle trades were not shy about proposing their own solutions to the social problems of their crafts, ones differing from their male counterparts many of whom hoped to improve their position by excluding women from work.

As part of the general political crackdown following the suppression of the uprising of June 1848, the government prohibited women from attending the sessions of political clubs. The political activism of Parisian feminists continued nonetheless, and found a fair amount of support among male leftists, a state of affairs reflecting the strong influence of socialist theories on the radicals of the French capital. One leading feminist, Jeanne Déroin, even proposed to run as a democratic candidate for the elections to the Legislative Assembly in May 1849. Pierre-Joseph Proudhon, unlike most of the leading French socialists a pronounced misogynist, denounced the plan, and the demand for woman suffrage, that Déroin's candidacy was designed to articulate. He asserted that the organs women possessed to nourish the young made them unsuited for suffrage, to which Déroin promptly replied, by asking Proudhon to show her the male organ that qualified him to vote.[10] In the end, Parisian leftists decided not to support Déroin's candidacy, because the government had announced that it was unconstitutional, and any votes cast for her would not be counted.

Jeanne Déroin's initiative marks the highpoint of women's political activism during the mid-century revolution. Most female activity was, by today's standards, far less aggressive or self-assertive. If we look at women's activity and organization during the revolution by the standards of the 1840s, on the other hand, it appears far more impressive. Previously consigned to private life by all but the most avant-garde of thinkers, women conquered for themselves a definite, if admittedly limited, portion of the public sphere during the revolution. Future feminist initiatives

[10] This incident is described in Priscilla Robertson, *An Experience of Women: Pattern and Change in Nineteenth-Century Europe* (Philadelphia, 1982), 28.

to expand women's public role and to move towards an equality of rights between the sexes would be led by women who had gained pioneering political experiences in 1848.

These female efforts suggest something about the broader historical significance of the 1848 revolution. It was not limited to or exhausted by its most dramatic moments – by the barricade fighting, by the civil wars, by the general air of upheaval and somewhat naive enthusiasm character- istic of the spring of 1848 – all of which has led historians to talk of 1848 as the "romantic revolution." Of equal and probably greater importance was the less spectacular side of the revolution, the many opportunities it offered for political action and organization, that is, for participation in public life, to individuals and groups that had never had the opportunity to do so before. The revolution meant the chance to join a political club or occupational association, to read in the newspapers about the great issues of the day and to debate them (or at least to hear others read about or debate them), to attend a mass rally, to take part in a demonstration, to sign a petition, and to cast a vote. These were opportunities that outlasted the romantic moment in the spring of 1848 – indeed, for many Europeans, they only began to be possibilities in the second half of that year and in 1849. Without considering these less spectacular facets of the revolution, the more dramatic ones – the chain of uprisings and civil wars stretching from the late spring of 1848 through the summer of 1849 and then, in one final moment, the French uprising of December 1851 – are not entirely understandable. Even further than that, the pioneering experience of political participation in the mid-century revolution was one that helped shape the development of organized politics on the continent for much of the rest of the nineteenth century.

Tendencies of political development

In the previous sections of this chapter, we have seen something of the extent and the diversity of the forms of political action and organization that existed in Europe during the 1848 revolution. Now, let us look more systematically at these observations, posing three broad groups of ques- tions. First, who supported which political group? Within this rubric, it might also be useful to consider the contours of different forms of revolu- tionary action: how political leadership compared to the rank and file, how the membership in associations compared with involvement in street fightings or uprisings. Secondly, how did increasing political organization and differentiation change the course of the revolution? Here, we might wish to know if the same individuals or groups that were involved in social or political struggles in the spring of 1848 were still involved a year later, and how the nature of these struggles themselves had changed. Finally, we could ask how these general developments affected each of the different political groupings. Did their strength and influence increase or decrease as a result of growing tendency towards political organization and popular political participation? How did the actual political movements themselves, their doctrines and public profile, change as a result of changing circumstances?

Bases of political support

Between restrictions on suffrage and limitations on organization, political involvement before 1848 had been skewed distinctly in favor of the affluent and the educated. The great expansion of the political universe during the revolution did not sweep aside those who had previously been active in politics; just the opposite, it promoted them to positions of leadership. The legislators and journalists of 1848, the leading members of political clubs in large cities and in towns, the prominent orators, the organizers of rallies, demonstrations, and uprisings were the pre-1848 adherents of their respective political causes. This meant that leaders of the left during the revolution were likely to be from the educated middle class, with a smaller number of businessmen, landowners, rentiers, and, in eastern Europe, noblemen, most of whom had anti-clerical or free-thinking religious attitudes. Prominent constitutional monarchists were from similar social backgrounds, although civil servants, businessmen, and property owners were better represented in their leadership, while younger, less affluent professionals were less prominent. Leading conservatives included senior government and court officials, army officers, members of the nobility, religiously orthodox clergy, and other well-to-do but devout men.

What had changed was that these men had gone from being common soldiers to officers of a much expanded army. They now had a very substantial following, drawn from quite different social groups. This was particularly the case for the democrats, who could claim the largest number of organized supporters. In urban areas, artisans made up the largest group of leftists, whether calculated in absolute numbers, or as a percentage of a given social group, whether considering membership in a democratic political club or analyzing lists of those killed and wounded on the barricades. Craftsmen were noticeably more likely to be involved in left-wing politics than unskilled laborers and somewhat more likely than members of the industrial labor force.

These differences in political participation cannot be explained as a result of differing incomes, since artisans' incomes varied, some relatively well off, others, such as shoemakers and tailors – both notoriously left-wing crafts – earning only as much as day laborers did. A more plausible explanation lies in the long craft tradition of social organization, in the form of guilds or mutual benefit societies, an organizational tradition that carried over into politics. The way that unskilled workers who became involved on the left did so tends to support this explanation: they were seldom members of organized political associations, more commonly participants in demonstrations or insurrectionary uprisings.

Another important social group for organized left-wing politics were tavernkeepers – themselves often craftsmen, bakers or brewers. Meetings held in their establishments were good for business and as a group they threw themselves into left-wing politics, often standing out as activists and second-rank leaders of various sorts. They were active in this way in the country as well as in the city.

Innkeepers' activities bring up the other side of the democrats' popular support, too often lost in older accounts of the "urban revolution" of 1848. Organized left-wing politics did begin in the city and spread to the countryside somewhat later on during the revolution, only really starting in the summer of 1848, and gradually continuing throughout the following year – in France, the following three-and-a-half years. In the end, though, there were a very large number of peasants joining democratic clubs, attending left-wing political rallies, serving in the revolutionary army of the Hungarian government, supporting the revolutionary government of Wallachia against Turkish intervention, and participating in the uprisings of June 1848 in Calabria, May 1849 in southwestern Germany, or of December 1851 in central and southern France. Much of what made the democratic political tendency into a mass movement during the mid-century revolution was its success in attracting rural support.

Liberal political forces were less changed by the revolutionary experience. Liberalism remained a movement of the notables; the rank-and-file members of liberal political clubs were, socially speaking, quite similar to the leadership. Liberal clubs were dominated by businessmen and substantial property owners, professional men, and government officials. The latter were quite noticeable; in Germany, constitutional monarchist political associations were often known as "civil servants' clubs." As a popular political movement, liberalism never expanded to the extent that the democrats did. Still, liberalism of the mid-century revolution was not exclusively an elitist movement. Liberal political clubs included craftsmen as members and occasionally could be found in rural areas. Constitutional monarchist notables were able to exert their influence and win elections held under universal manhood suffrage.

Conservative and clerical notables were probably more successful than their constitutional monarchist counterparts in gaining popular support. Day laborers made up a substantial part of the membership of the Pius Association of the Rhineland city of Mainz; dockworkers of Marseilles, in southern France, were ardent Legitimists. Guild-oriented master craftsmen of Bavaria were firm conservatives, as were substantial numbers of outworking weavers in the textile centers of the Wupper Valley in western Germany.

Popular conservatism was still stronger in the countryside than in urban areas. Peasants of much of northern France voted solidly for candidates of the right during the elections of 1848 and 1849; their counterparts in the northeastern provinces of the kingdom of Prussia were equally likely to give their ballots to candidates of the right, and willingly signed up when Protestant pastors or noble landlords solicited their membership in Prussian Associations, Patriotic Associations, or other conservative political clubs. It was above all conservative, monarchist peasants who made up the armies of the emperor of Austria, the king of Prussia or of President Louis-Napoleon Bonaparte (theoretically head of state of the French republic, but rapidly on his way to becoming emperor) that ultimately crushed the revolutionary forces on the European continent.

This brief survey of the main political forces shows that they all had an educated and affluent leadership and at least some degree of popular following, or, to put it differently, the similarities in the social structure of their respective supporters seem to outweigh the differences. If we look more closely, however, we can make some useful distinctions. In considering economic factors, probably the best way to understand popular political loyalties is in terms of the attribution of prosperity to governmental action. Those members of the urban lower classes who saw the pre-1848 government as their supporter, as protecting them from the omnipresent threat of impoverishment, were more likely to be conservative. The Bavarian government sanctioned and protected the guilds that protected master craftsmen against potentially ruinous competition and unruly journeymen; the guildsmen sought to preserve the Bavarian regime unchanged during the German revolution. Much the same was the case with the Marseilles longshoremen. The authorities had tolerated for decades the city's dockers' guild, even though it had been, formally, illegal. The large lower class, mostly unskilled casual workers, of Naples was the beneficiary of the state's provisioning policies that kept bread prices low and the urban poor of the capital city content; they repaid their royal patrons with their support. Most of the urban lower classes lacked this tolerant attitude. They saw governments prohibiting their organizing efforts, favoring employers, interfering with their mutual benefit societies, raising taxes on basic foodstuffs – in short, making their already hard lives even more difficult. With such a point of view, they were far more likely to find their way into left-wing politics.

A similar combination of economic conditions and attitudes towards the state existed in the countryside. In western and central Europe, conservatism was dominant in the areas of affluent grain-growing, particularly on the north European plain. The relative prosperity of the peasant proprietors of those regions made them less disposed to look for drastic political change. These areas tended to have a social structure characterized by sharp contrasts between the dominant group, substantial, property-owning farmers, and the day laborers who worked for them – and who rioted against them at the outbreak of the revolution. This dimmed the farmers' enthusiasm for further confrontations and made them more likely to support the calls for the restoration of order issued by right-wing large or noble landowners. At the same time, these regions' rural lower classes did not become supporters of radical politics, but generally put their trust in the paternalist attentions of their monarchs and government officials to help them out of their plight and resolve their grievances.

If these grain-growing regions were likely to be the stronghold of peasant conservatism, the more hilly or mountainous areas, where grain-growing was less central to peasants' survival, since they relied more on use of the forest or the raising of market-oriented, non-subsistence crops, were more likely to see peasants on the left. These agricultural areas were generally less well off than the grain growing regions. The violent price swings of the years 1845–49 had been particularly difficult for peasants who cultivated grapes or olives, burdening them with debt contracted in years of high food prices, that then had to be paid off when prices plunged. Moreover, these regions tended to have a more egalitarian distribution of landed property, or at least a situation in which most farmers owned some land. The sharp contrasts between substantial farmers and landless laborers were not present; peasants could concentrate their anger on noble landowners or against the government authorities and their taxes and forest regulations, both circumstances favorable to left-wing politics. Long-term economic trends, differing social structures, and differing attitudes towards the state go a long way in explaining the political options chosen by the peasants of western and central Europe.

In eastern Europe, on the other hand, the decisive question in rural areas was serfdom and its abolition. Peasants would throw their support behind whatever group or institution successfully portrayed itself to them as responsible for the end of the hated feudal regime. In one area, the main beneficiaries of rural hostility to serfdom were the organized democrats. This was Silesia, divided between a larger portion in the kingdom of Prussia, and a smaller one in the Austrian Empire. Both parts of Silesia were leftist strongholds during the revolution, the most famous of the Silesian democrats being the law student and serf's son, Hans Kudlich, who introduced into the Austrian Constituent Assembly the legislation abolishing serfdom within the Habsburgs' realm. While Silesia was an ethnically mixed area, containing substantial numbers of German- and Polish-speaking peasants as well as a smaller number of Czech-speakers, national conflicts played a relatively minor role in the region's politics. German-speaking democrats from urban areas (townspeople throughout Silesia generally spoke German) succeeded in building support in the countryside through their strong advocacy of anti-feudal measures.

Affairs in the Principality of Wallachia were sort of similar to Silesia, although political life in the far southeastern end of Europe was far less sophisticated, precisely articulated or organized than in Silesia. There, urban democrats of Bucharest successfully mobilized the serfs of Wallachia in support of their revolutionary government with promises of an end to feudalism and to the oppression and land expropriations of the region's boyar nobility.

In much of the rest of eastern Europe, where political parties ranged from undeveloped to non-existent, peasants' options were more centered on nationalist movements. Two useful counterpoints can demonstrate how this worked in practice: Polish and Hungarian nationalist movements on the one hand, and Slovak and Romanian, on the other. Poland and Hungary were the two lands of the mass nobility, where nobles were 5–10 percent of the population, as compared to 0.5–1 percent elsewhere in Europe, where economic conditions of the nobility varied from great magnates to "noble" peasants, and where the nobility continued to play an unchallenged leading role in public life through the middle of the nineteenth century. In 1848, however, these two nobilities had drastically different degrees of success in gaining political support from their former serfs. Polish nobles in the Habsburg province of Galicia were lucky during the mid-century revolution not to be massacred by the peasants as they had been two years previously. They found no political support among the rural masses, whether Polish- or Ukrainian-speaking, who looked instead to the Habsburg emperor and his officials for the decrees liberating them from serfdom and for protection against the nobility. Freedom, to the peasants was freedom for the nobility; revolution meant the unlimited rule of the nobles. For that reason, the peasants saw themselves as conservative and counter-revolutionary, as monarchical loyalists. Peasants from twenty villages of Galicia petitioned the

Austrian parliament, "We fear Polish domination . . . we want to remain under the rule of our beloved monarch because then the lords will have no such freedom [to oppress the peasants]."[11]

In Hungary, while the peasants assaulted lords and their castles, refused to perform their feudal labor services or turn in their feudal dues, and stole wood from the forests, they also cheered the decrees abolishing feudalism of the Hungarian Diet, and its successor body, the Hungarian National Assembly – both institutions dominated by the nobility. Peasants – and not just Magyar-speaking ones, but Slovak- and Ukrainian-speakers as well – enlisted in the Hungarian national army, with its noble officers, to oppose the imperial forces; they followed the decrees of the revolutionary regime, carried out by the Hungarian county administrations, run by the nobility. While opposing noble domination, they were also willing to credit the nobility with ending it.

Considering the Romanian and Slovak national movements opens a different perspective, since they were led by just a few hundred intellectuals attempting to mobilize a group of serfs, largely lacking any sense of national identity, against a nobility speaking a different language. In Transylvania, the Romanian nationalists were able to accomplish this, leading tens of thousands of peasants in a long and bloody guerila war against the Hungarian government. Slovak nationalist efforts in the same direction had no result; their planned nationalist uprising a failure, its leaders forced into exile in Vienna. Slovak peasants saw Magyar nobles as taking measures to end serfdom and so the nationalist movement there failed to gain widespread support; Romanian peasants perceived the Magyar nobles of Transylvania as their oppressive enemies and cast their lot in with the nationalist intellectuals.

Another major factor influencing popular political options was religion. Members of minority religious groups, or of faiths different from that of the ruling dynasty were often political radicals, regardless of their social class. The "Greek" (that is, religiously Eastern Orthodox, ethnically Albanian) villages of the province of Calabria and the island of Sicily were known as centers of radical sympathizers and supporters of revolutionary insurgency. Protestants in southern France, even the substantial businessmen among them, became supporters of the socialist left in the years 1849–51, fearing that a restoration of royalist rule would mean an inquisitorial Catholic suppression of their faith. Protestant villagers of the Austrian province of Carinthia made no secret of their support for the Hungarian regime in its war against Habsburg rule, since the imperial

---

[11] Cited in Rosdolsky, *Bauernabgeordneten*, 212.

family was unquestionably Roman Catholic, while there was a strong Calvinist minority among the Magyars, particularly influential in the ranks of the leaders of the insurgent government.

By the same token, those who belonged to a majority religion, or to the same religion as the ruling dynasty, were more likely to incline to the right. Protestant pastors were always in prominent positions in the conservative political clubs of Prussia, and these clubs were clustered in the monarchy's predominantly Protestant eastern provinces, areas that had been ruled by the Hohenzollern dynasty for centuries. The same was true in Bavaria, only with all the confessional signs reversed: in this land ruled by the Catholic Wittelsbach dynasty, it was Catholic priests who led the conservative political clubs, and they were found in the heavily Catholic Alpine provinces, the core areas of Bavaria since the early middle ages. A similar point could be made about Hungary, where Roman Catholics played an unusually large role in the conservative, pro-Habsburg political forces, as Calvinists did in the revolutionary, anti-Habsburg ones.

It was not just differences between religions but differences within them that influenced political behavior. Free thought and anti-clericalism were usually associated with the left. While this connection could certainly be observed in urban areas, it was particularly crucial for left-wing politics in the countryside. Schoolteachers, a group in revolt against clerical authority, were frequently key connecting links between urban leftists and the peasants they hoped to organize. One French conservative newspaper denounced them in ferocious terms for moral and political failings calling teachers "perfidious missionaries who spend their time seducing girls, disturbing families, frequenting places of debauchery and perverting the children confined to their care."[12]

Even more to the dismay of conservatives, free-thinking clergymen were often leading rural leftists. Rationalist Protestant pastors in southwestern Germany, who had long been in trouble with their ecclesiastical superiors over their Unitarian views, showed a strong inclination in 1848 to interpret the Gospels to their peasant parishioners in terms of liberty, equality, fraternity, to plant trees of liberty and found democratic political clubs. They had their Catholic counterparts in Italian priests who had long chafed under Papal authority and orthodox doctrine, such as Father Barni, pastor of the Florentine suburb of Galluzzo. Barni founded a St. Lucia democratic club, and gathered the rustics around a tree of liberty, whereupon they proclaimed him an "apostle of Christ" and a

---

[12] Quoted in André Armengaud, *Les populations de l'Est Aquitaine au début de l'époque contemporaine* (Paris and the Hague, 1961), 380.

"true republican." After the suppression of the revolution, he would be indicted and convicted, not just for subversion, but for impiety as well.

Religious orthodoxy and strong devotion, on the other hand, usually went along with conservative politics. It is difficult to imagine someone in 1848 from the urban lower classes who was sympathetic to conservative politics and was not a regular churchgoer. Rural areas of strong piety – for instance, Brittany in western France, the Abruzzi in southern Italy or the Tyrol in Alpine Austria – were all strongholds of popular support for the right.

What would happen, though, when an individual was both devout and adherent of a minority religion, or one opposed to that of the ruling dynasty? Orthodox piety inclined him towards the right; religious opposition to the monarch to the left. Devout Roman Catholics in the Rhineland and Westphalia, the western provinces of the kingdom of Prussia, felt these cross pressures, as did pious Calvinists in Hungary. It was a true dilemma for the individuals concerned, and they could find no satisfactory solution to the problem, often zig-zagging across the political spectrum. The Eastern Orthodox in the Habsburg Monarchy were generally loyal to the Catholic Habsburg emperor, although the attempts of the Serbian Orthodox Patriarch Rajačić to gain military assistance from the Tsar, the leading Orthodox monarch, show that Orthodox loyalty to a Catholic emperor could sometimes – admittedly, in extreme conditions, as the Serbs of the Banat were engaged in a violent civil war with the Hungarian government – have its limits.

There was one religious minority worth a separate mention, the Jews. The revolution did, at least temporarily, improve their legal condition. As part of the reforms initiated by constituent assemblies, discriminatory legislation against Jews was abolished and their civic equality granted in Germany, Austria, Hungary, the Papal States, and the Kingdom of Piedmont-Savoy, although promptly revoked, after the failure of the revolution, everywhere but in the last named state. Jews also took on political leading roles for the first time as a result of the revolutionary events. Two of the ministers of the Provisional Government of the French Republic resulting from the insurrection of February 1848, Adolphe Crémieux in charge of the judiciary, and Michel Goudchaux in finances, were Jewish, the first Jewish government ministers in France. The leader of the revolutionary Venetian Republic, Daniele Manin, was of Jewish descent, although his family had converted to Christianity, and two members of his government were practicing Jews. The Hamburg attorney, Gabriel Riesser, the leading proponent of equal rights for Jews in central Europe, did not just represent his city in the Frankfurt National Assembly, but was chosen by the assembly's deputies as its vice president.

Many Jews prominent in public life during the 1848 revolution were associated with the radical left. Among the Jews who were democratic and republican activists were the doctors Adolf Fischhof and Joseph Goldmark, leading Viennese democrats, Johann Jacoby, an important left-wing deputy in the Prussian National Assembly, the German labor leader Stefan Born, or leading radical activists in western Germany, such as Ferdinand Lassalle in Düsseldorf, Ludwig Bamberger in Mainz, or Karl Marx (Marx had been baptized as a boy and raised as a Protestant) in Cologne. This may seem like no surprise, since Jews have generally been associated in the twentieth century with left-wing politics. It is less clear, though, if these prominent radicals were typical of Jews in mid-nineteenth-century Europe. Rather, Jews tended to divide, politically, along some of the same religious lines as did Christians. Urban, free-thinking Jews, often better assimilated into their cultural surroundings, as they were, for instance, in Vienna, Mainz or Budapest, were settled on the left of center, as we can see from the examples named above. Younger, less affluent individuals were sympathetic to the democrats or even the socialists, older better-off ones more inclined towards the constitutional monarchists. The Jews living in rural areas of both eastern and western Europe, as most did, were religiously Orthodox, and often spoke their own language, Yiddish, different from their Christian neighbors. They were far more likely to be politically conservative and supportive of monarchical authority, or, as was true of the Jews of the Austrian province of Galicia, the largest Jewish community in Europe outside the Tsarist Empire, took little part in the politics of the mid-century revolution.

Just as Jews have been associated with the left in the twentieth century, anti-Semitism has been associated with the right. Conservatives did make occasional use of hatred of Jews during the 1848 revolution, a course of action particularly common in the southern part of the German-speaking world. In Vienna, where Catholic and conservative journalists and political leaders frequently denounced Jews as responsible for the revolution, their agitation reached a highpoint on 20 July 1848, when a group of right-wing national guardsmen burst into the meeting of the democratic club screaming, "You republicans should all be hanged, you arrogant, dirty sow-Jews."[13] On a larger scale, deputies to the Frankfurt National Assembly with similar Catholic and conservative views strongly, although ultimately unsuccessfully, opposed the assembly's decision in favor of the emancipation of the Jews and making all religions equal under the law. Probably the most successful example of such anti-Semitic agitation

---

[13] Quoted in Wolfgang Häusler, *Von der Massenarmut zur Arbeiterbewegung: Demokratie und soziale Frage in der Wiener Revolution von 1848* (Vienna and Munich, 1979), 295.

came after the suppression of the revolutionary movement at the end of 1849 and the beginning of 1850. Catholic-conservative activists in Bavaria launched a massive and effective petition campaign to the king-dom's parliament, opposing the proposal of the Bavarian government to grant civic equality to the Jews. Such actions can certainly be seen as precursors of some particularly pernicious kinds of twentieth-century mass politics, but both the centrality of anti-Semitism to right-wing politics and the extent of its use remained relatively limited in the mid-nineteenth-century revolutions, when compared to conditions fifty or eighty years later.

All these observations suggest some of the ways in which the process of politicization was channeled during the revolution. If leadership of the different political tendencies was largely in the hands of usually affluent and educated pre-1848 activists, the popular following they recruited tended to break down along distinct lines that could be summarized in two main complexes: the interaction of economic conditions with state authority, and the relationship between religion and government. Those of the lower classes with strong social or economic grievances – whether declining real wages or the oppressions of serfdom – were likely to be sympathetic to the left, provided they saw the government authorities as responsible for their troubles. If they did not, or, worse, came to perceive the leaders of radical politics as responsible for their vexations, then they would enroll in the ranks of the party of order. Common people who had been doing better economically over the long term, or who saw the pre-1848 authorities as their allies, would join them in the conservative camp.

As for religion, we can say quite simply that the devout were usually to the right of center, free-thinkers, rationalists, and anti-clericals to the left. Contrasts between religious minorities and majorities, or the confession of the royal family, usually added to (although occasionally worked at cross purposes to) this basic antagonism. As with the social and economic factors, we can note here as well the importance of relations to the govern-mental authorities, in this case perceived simply and directly in terms of the monarch and his religion. Perhaps it is obvious, since revolutions are political events, yet it needs to be emphasized that political struggles in 1848, while sometimes between social classes or national groups, were also between supporters and opponents of the pre-revolutionary regimes.

The direction of political life over the course of the revolution

The political process during the mid-century revolution moved in the direction of expanded participation and of more cohesive, ideologically more explicit and more widespread organization. Taking a leading role in this process were the pre-1848 political activists, themselves educated and/or affluent, who sought to gain a mass following by trying to politicize the social conflicts typical of Europe before 1848 and expressed violently if often incoherently at the outbreak of the revolution. If we consider how this process affected political life as a whole, we can point towards two broad tendencies: the decline of the center, bringing with it an increasing political polarization, and a decentralization of the political initiative, away from the capital city, towards the provinces.

The major loser in this process was precisely those political moderates who seemed to have triumphed in the euphoria of the "springtime of the peoples." With their political vision of a society of substantial property owners, and so more wedded than either radicals or conservatives to a politics of the notables, of the affluent and educated, liberals proved over the long run least able to compete in the political game under the new, more democratic rules initiated in the uprisings of the spring of 1848. Liberals clung to a political scheme characterized by the informal influence of the notables at the local level and the actions of parliamentarians at the national. They were unwilling or unable to mobilize a large popular following, organize it into a widespread network of political clubs and call on it to engage in extra-parliamentary political action.

At first, this inability or unwillingness might not seem to have mattered much: the uprisings of the spring of 1848 had placed the liberals at the center of governmental power and the following elections, held under the influence of the notables, before political organization had a chance to take off, had provided them with a comfortable parliamentary position. This set of affairs was appropriate to liberal versions of the political process, characterized by a support for constitutional monarchism and a wish for peaceful legal reform, involving cooperation between a representative legislature and an executive. As the revolution continued, however, as national and social conflicts escalated, producing bloody confrontations, as warfare spread across northern Italy and the lands of the Crown of St. Stephen, the peaceful pre-conditions for legal reform vanished. Liberals might dominate the parliaments, but it was unclear just how widely these parliaments' authority would be accepted. Liberals might also be government ministers, but the senior bureaucrats and army officers needed to do the work of governing were not necessarily sympathetic to them, and the ultimate executive authorities – the monarchs, or, in France after December 1848, President Louis-Napoleon Bonaparte – who increasingly listened to a revived and strengthened conservative element, could easily dismiss them from office.

The same process that led to the weakening of the center produced a strengthening of the right and left, both democrats and conservatives proving more adept than liberals at organizing a mass following, both tendencies' more extreme and militant programs seeming more appropriate for a political environment characterized by growing social, political, and even military confrontation. By the first anniversary of the revolution, this process of increasing political polarization was well advanced. Those parliamentary bodies elected in the spring of 1848, largely dominated by liberal moderates – the German National Assembly, the Austrian Constituent Assembly, the French Constituent National Assembly – found themselves unable to control events, increasingly pushed off the center stage.

Another, less-known illustration of this process of political polarization is the results of elections held at later dates during the revolution. Usually overshadowed in historical accounts by the initial elections of the spring of 1848, these later ballotings took place under different circumstances: they were far more organized affairs, with slates of candidates put up and campaigns organized by political clubs and their national federations. Such elections brought two different results. Some, such as the balloting held at the end of 1848 or the beginning of 1849 for the parliaments of the Kingdom of Piedmont-Savoy, or for those of the kingdoms of Bavaria and Saxony (as well as, later on in 1849, for parliaments in some of the other, smaller German states) brought victories for the democrats. Other votes – the two prime examples being the elections to the parliament of the kingdom of Prussia in January 1849 and for the French legislative assembly in May of that year – resulted in a sharp split between left and right. Constitutional monarchists who had dominated the Prussian elections in May 1848 were greatly reduced in number eight months later; both conservatives and democrats scored major gains, dividing most of the seats between them. In France, the moderate republicans, the major grouping of the Constituent National Assembly, were almost non-existent a year later; the radical left, on the other hand, had more than doubled its seats, becoming the single largest caucus in the legislature. This expansion on the left was paralleled by a resurgence on the right: a substantial majority of the deputies elected were monarchists, but since they were divided between the supporters of three different dynasties – the Bourbons, the Orléans, and the Bonapartes – each of the individual monarchist parliamentary caucuses was smaller than that of the democrats.

If left and right had expanded during the revolution, while the center had shrunk, the arenas of political action had changed as well. In the spring of 1848, politics had been centered above all in the capital cities, and to a lesser extent in larger urban centers. While there had been plenty of activity and even substantial violence in the provinces, the small towns, and the countryside, relatively little of it was consciously directed at changing the form of government. The growing political tensions between moderate to conservative parliaments and a radicalized population of the capital cities leading to renewed fighting on the barricades once again focused politics on the capitals, between Paris and Prague in June 1848 and Vienna in October.

With this second round of street fighting, the leading role of the capital cities in the revolution came to an end. While this fighting was going on, the expansion of political clubs (or, in Hungary, of civil war) into the provinces had brought the issues of the revolution to large segments of the rural and small-town population, helping to politicize what had previously been apolitical social conflicts. In the next major round of revolutionary confrontations in the winter and spring of 1849, the capitals were quiet while the provinces were active. There was little happening in Paris, and nothing in Berlin, Vienna, Naples or Milan, while there were uprisings and revolutionary regimes created in central and southwestern Germany, and in the smaller states of central Italy, or while the revolutionary Hungarian government reorganized itself for its armed counter-offensive in the provincial town of Debrecen after Budapest had been captured by imperial troops. The last major struggle of the revolution, the French uprising against Louis-Napoleon's *coup d'état* in December 1851, took place entirely in the villages and small towns of central and southeastern France; neither Paris nor any of the major urban centers played a significant role.

This pattern of development suggests broad regional contrasts in provincial politics during the mid-century revolution. In the flatlands of northern France and Germany, and perhaps in the wealthy agricultural area of northern Italy as well (although here the presence of warfare makes a comparison of the course of events difficult), radical politics during the revolution was primarily a matter for artisans, outworkers and, to a lesser extent other members of the urban and manufacturing lower classes. The political sympathies of large landowners, both noble and commoners and of the urban bourgeoisie, whose ranks included a substantial number of merchants and manufacturers, ranged from constitutional monarchist to outright conservative. Democracy meant to these elites a threat to their property; the initial, if often qualified support they expressed for the revolution quickly vanished. In the countryside, sharp antagonisms between substantial property-owners and landless laborers dominated the scene. In so far as these rural social antagonisms were politicized at all, protagonists on both sides of them tended towards a conservative viewpoint, looking to constituted authority for support. To this outline of social forces, we need to note that these areas tended to be strongholds of religious orthodoxy.

In southern and central France, central and southwestern Germany and central Italy, on the other hand, most of these social preconditions were reversed. Not just artisans, but members of the urban middle class, merchants, property owners, and professionals, were likely to have sympathies for the left. Property in the countryside was distributed more equitably; social antagonisms did not pit one rural group against another, but most farmers against the government or the unfavorable market conditions for their crops. The religious factor was politically opposite here too, free thought prevalent among the urban middle class, and gradually spreading to the common people in both town and country.

While there are specific exceptions to which one can point, all in all, the northern regions were strongholds of the right, the southern ones of the left. Conservative political organizations were more common in the north; democratic ones were limited to the urban, lower-class minority. Initial revolutionary enthusiasm waned rapidly; news of the second round of violent confrontations in the capital cities encouraged the right and center, discouraged the left. By the fall of 1848, and certainly by the spring of 1849, the revolution was over; people gave up on politics or wished to return to a slightly modified pre-revolutionary status quo. The southern regions, on the other hand, were the centers of successful left-wing organizing efforts, bringing with them a network of political clubs and an increasingly politicized population. The news of the defeats of radicalism in the capital cities spurred on leftist politics, making these regions the centers of future revolutionary confrontations.

These shifts in the balance of political forces and the locus of political action also affected the different political movements, and it seems appropriate to close this chapter by seeing how they were changed by the experience of revolution. Liberalism, before 1848 in opposition throughout most of central and eastern Europe, and partly oppositional, partly governmental in the western part of the continent, became at the outset of the revolution everywhere the party of government. Almost at once, liberals moved from the party of movement to the party of order.

Liberal governments played a major role in the suppression of the second round of insurrection in the capital cities. They acted against the more peaceful manifestations of leftism as well, directing the police to spy on the sessions of democratic political clubs, prohibiting public meetings and demonstrations they sponsored, even (as was the case with the French Republican Solidarity) outlawing their national federations. This attack on the left was accompanied by a remarkable softness towards the right, liberal authorities refraining from disciplining military officers or high state officials who were quite open in their attacks on the revolution.

As recent studies of voting behavior in the revolutionary parliaments have shown, the liberal deputies, many of whom were leaders of the pre-1848 opposition, voted on crucial roll-calls with their former conservative enemies. Indeed, in many instances founders of liberal political clubs and local level activists were pre-1848 conservatives who came to see constitutional monarchism as the most appropriate way to continue conservative politics in the post-revolutionary environment.

If liberals moved towards the right, conservatives in the same period moved to the left. The 1848 revolution was a crucial period for European conservatives in coming to terms with social and political innovations of the French Revolution of 1789. During the revolution, conservative leaders gave up their previous, stubborn insistence on the preservation of feudal and seigneurial privileges, accepting a free market in rural land and labor – albeit with compensation for the former feudal lords. If not quite to so great an extent, prominent rightists also abandoned their former support for monarchical absolutism and a legislature elected by the estates, accepting a constitutional monarchy as the basis for their political activity. Conservatives threw themselves into the work of popular political organization with energy and initiative, achieving regionally impressive success.

A sign of the new orientation in right-wing politics was the congress called by large landowners of the eastern part of the kingdom of Prussia in June 1848, setting up an organization entitled, in good Teutonic fashion, "The Association for the Protection of Property and the Advancement of the Welfare of All Social Classes." Quickly dubbed by hostile contemporaries the "Junker parliament," from its domination by the landed interest, its name nonetheless suggests a desire to make conservatism the party of all property owners, businessmen, small farmers, and craftsmen, as well as noble landlords, and to define politics in terms of a confrontation between friends and enemies of property.

This viewpoint was not so dissimilar from the liberal vision of a society of property owners, and one of the major characteristics of the process of politicization during the revolution was the gradual alliance of the formerly hostile liberals and conservatives. Legitimists and Orléanists in France, decades long enemies, stood for parliamentary election on joint tickets as common members of the party of order. Conservative constitutional-monarchist political clubs and liberal constitutional-monarchist political clubs in Prussia cooperated in the parliamentary elections of January 1849. While differences between the two forces still existed, among others over the significance of nationalism for politics, or over attitudes towards religion, the joint front against the radical left increasingly outweighed them.

As the former liberal protagonists of the revolution dropped out of the party of movement to join their one-time conservative enemies in a revived and modified party of order, democrats found themselves by the end of 1848 the sole remaining adherents of the revolutionary state of affairs. Yet the experiences of the previous year – the initial outbreak of revolution and the widespread social conflict accompanying it, the disappointments of the first elections under universal manhood suffrage, the violent confrontations in the capital cities during the summer and fall of 1848, and the campaigns of provincial and rural organization, along with the founding of federations of political clubs – had changed the nature of the democratic movement. There were two new self-designations chosen by French democrats in the last months of 1848 that symbolize this new direction adopted by the political left, not just in France but more widely in Europe.

In November 1848, the parliamentary caucus of the left-wing deputies in the French Constituent National Assembly – the same group that founded the national political federation Republican Solidarity – renamed itself the "Mountain," after the caucus of leftist deputies in the Convention, the parliament of the First French Republic, in 1792–95. Following experiments with socialism, after demanding, as did some Parisian radicals, that the tricolor French flag be replaced with a red one, in short, after all the ultimately unsuccessful attempts to go beyond the Jacobin ideas of republican and democratic radicalism, the leftists of the continent's political capital fell back on the Jacobin tradition. Democrats throughout Europe followed them, and leftist politics during the later stages of the mid-century revolution was an orgy of symbolic references to the great events of 1793: wearing Phrygian caps, planting trees of liberty, issuing cheers for liberty, equality, fraternity, and toasts in honor of Marat and Robespierre.

Another phrase that also became current in France towards the end of 1848 shows that the Jacobin revival was not a literal return to the original Jacobinism of the 1790s, that toasts in honor of Robespierre did not imply a desire to repeat his political decisions. French leftists described themselves as supporters of the "democratic and social republic," or, as they quickly became known, as "democ-socs." Expressed in this phrase was the understanding that a successful left-wing political movement that could enjoy mass support – and in Europe of the middle of the nineteenth century that meant above all rural support – would have to articulate the long-term grievances of the population that had been so dramatically expressed in the social conflicts of the spring of 1848.

Along with the Phrygian caps and the trees of liberty, leftists also promised that a future democratic and republican regime would make wood from the forests easily available to the peasants, that it would offer low-interest loans to solve their credit problems. Democrats promised similar easy credit terms to urban artisans as well as government support for their experiments with cooperatives. Even more commonly, and more universally, leftists assured their potential supporters that a new regime would be one of lower and more equitable taxes, that government expenditures would be cut back and redeployed to the interests of the common people, that the intrusive and oppressive authority of customs agents, foresters, and police would be reduced to an appropriate and limited level. These messages were broadcast over all the institutions of political mass mobilization, from newspapers to pamphlets and fliers, from sessions of political clubs to mass meetings, banquets, and demonstrations.

This line of argument was a clear break with Robespierre's and the original Jacobins' notion of a "republic of virtue," in which popular government would promote a morally upright way of life. For the "democ-socs," republican and democratic regimes would instead guarantee prosperity to those unable to obtain it for themselves. The influence of the socialists was clear, in the idea of using the government to offset the unequal outcomes of the market, but the democrats wished to extend government action to include the many small property owners, particularly in the countryside, that majority of the population long neglected in socialist – and, more broadly, in almost all left-wing – thought. In this way, armed with popular support, the democrats hoped to resist the liberal-conservative alliance in the party of order and retain and expand the original, emancipatory principles of the revolutionary mass movements of the spring of 1848, by peaceful, parliamentary means if possible, by a violent, second revolutionary uprising if need be. These clashing aspirations of the realigned political forces stood behind much of the confused and continual conflict occurring in the mid-century revolution from the late spring of 1848 through its final confrontation at the end of 1851.

clashes btw former pol. allies

5   Polarization and confrontation

Patterns of confrontation, May–November 1848

The second half of 1848 was a period of the resurgence of the party of order and of the decline of the party of movement in Europe. In a series of dramatic confrontations the revolutionary forces were overwhelmed, sometimes by an alliance of conservatives and liberals, sometimes by a resurgence of elements of the pre-1848 regimes. Following these confrontations, governments were reshuffled and public policy took a strong turn to the right. If the revolutionary movement had suffered a severe setback by the end of 1848, counter-revolution had not yet completely triumphed. Constitutional monarchists retained some influence on government policy; basic civil liberties and the constitutional form of government, those major accomplishments of the spring of 1848, remained, precariously, in place. While increasingly harassed by the police, radical and democratic forces were still able to reorganize themselves and seek out new supporters, preparing a new round of political struggles in the first half of 1849.

First steps in southern Italy

The 1848 revolutions began in the Kingdom of the Two Sicilies; the reaction against them also took its first major step there. As always in Italy during the mid-century revolution, the war against the Austrians in the north set the background for political action. Radicals in the capital city of Naples and more militant members of the kingdom's parliament meeting there demanded that its armed forces be sent north to join the nationalist war, and that the constitution granted by the king at the outbreak of the revolution be modified to increase parliamentary control over foreign affairs. King Ferdinand responded by moving troops into Naples to intimidate the opposition. Barricades were built and on 13 May there was street fighting, quickly decided against the insurgents. The liberal government ministers resigned in protest, but Ferdinand simply replaced them with conservatives closer to his heart.

Foreshadowing future events, the most vigorous opposition to the royal putsch appeared not in the capital, but in the provinces. While there were demonstrations against the king and debate in the political clubs in a number of towns, opposition was most determined in Calabria, where democrats created a revolutionary government, enjoying substantial popular support and exerting its authority for about one month, until it was suppressed by royal troops sent against it. A modern detailed study of the Calabrian uprising is lacking, but historians have noted two basic reasons for the strength and popularity of the radicals there. One was circumstances in the countryside: a vigorous peasant movement, showing early signs of politicization (rustics shouting "death to the royalists!" as they seized disputed forests), interacting with a politically left-wing group of notables, themselves agricultural proprietors but less afraid of peasant movements than their counterparts elsewhere in southern Italy. The second was the presence in the province of a religious minority, a number of Greek Orthodox villages, whose inhabitants were strong supporters of the revolution and opponents of their Roman Catholic king's authority.

Ferdinand's actions, although a blow against the revolution, had not restored the pre-1848 situation. Social conflict in the countryside continued throughout the Italian south; oppositional newspapers and political clubs remained legal, if increasingly persecuted by the authorities, and Naples saw occasional anti-monarchist demonstrations, like the crowd that gathered on the evening of 29 January 1849 in the center of fishermen's quarter to chant democratic slogans. The kingdom's parliament still met after 13 May, although the events of that day had decided against its claim to a voice in conducting foreign policy. Most of all, the insurgents in Sicily whose January 1848 rising had begun the wave of revolutions, had gained control of virtually the entire island. Ferdinand's troops, rather than fighting the Italian national enemy in the north, would instead spend the rest of 1848 and much of 1849 restoring his authority in the rebellious off shore province. The Kingdom of the Two Sicilies was very much on the margin of European politics, yet the result of its struggles in May-June 1848 would be typical for more central regions. The forces of order were strengthened and the revolution was weakened but not yet destroyed. Future political struggles would, however, be centered in different regions from those in which they had previously occurred.

The June Days

Unlike Calabria, Paris was at the very center of political life in mid-century Europe; political confrontations there would have ramifications throughout the continent. Tensions had been rising in the capital city from April through June 1848 over two issues, one expressly political, one indirectly so, via tangled social and economic questions. Although inter-related, the two issues came to a head separately, reflecting the division between the labor movement and political radicalism during the early months of the 1848 revolution, decisively weakening the strength of the party of movement.

The political issue was centered on the conflict between the left-wing, republican activists, who had overthrown a king in February 1848, with the support from the politicized lower classes in Paris, and a center-right, monarchist constituent national assembly chosen in the democratic elections of April 1848 called by the new republican regime. The second issue concerned the socialist plans for the "organization of labor." No sooner had Louis-Philippe been overthrown, than the provisional government of the republic had created "national workshops," ostensibly modeled on the "social workshops" of the well-known socialist Louis Blanc. Soon employing 100,000 of the unemployed, these workshops had little to do with the state-supported consumer cooperatives of Blanc's socialist the-ory, but were much closer to the old regime "charity workshops," public works to keep the unemployed from starving. Expecting the socialist version, the politicized Parisian unemployed found instead meaningless activities – digging holes and filling them up again – for minimal pay. At the same time, employers were increasingly unhappy with these institu-tions. They saw them as encouraging the already considerable labor unrest, since workers could support themselves while on strike by taking jobs with the workshops.

To make matters worse, the workshops became mixed up with diffi-culties in fiscal policy. Coming to power in February 1848, the new republican authorities discovered a very substantial budget deficit, a result of low tax receipts during the previous, recessionary year. To balance the state budget – an action which even extreme leftists then regarded as necessary and appropriate – they introduced a temporary 45 percent surcharge on the property tax, the "forty-five centimes." Most painfully affected by this measure were small farmers, already burdened by payments on the debts they had contracted during the years of bad harvests and high food prices in 1845 and 1846. A wave of tax riots swept through southwestern France and monarchist politicians hastened to turn the peasants' anger against the Parisian workers, announcing that the increased taxes were going to pay for supposed socialist experiments in the capital.

The political issue came to a head in the mass demonstration of 15 May 1848, organized around a traditional demand of the republican left – freedom and independence for Poland and the starting of a great European war if necessary to achieve it. Socialist slogans were absent from the event. This separation between political radicalism and the labor movement could be seen organizationally as well. The demonstration was an affair of the political clubs; the trade associations and their representatives in the Luxembourg Commission played no role in it. Workers employed in the National Workshops remained at work, rather than take part.

The demonstration's organizers were intending, following Jacobin precedents of 1793, to intimidate or possibly to overthrow the constituent assembly. Their precise plans were unclear at the time and have remained so today, but in any event they were a failure, the demonstrators invading the assembly but turned back by the National Guard. The government retaliated swiftly, closing some clubs and arresting prominent figures in them, including the veteran revolutionary Louis-Auguste Blanqui, the recognized leader of the extreme left. Under prodding from the conservative parliamentarians, the authorities went further and used the demonstration as a pretext to strike a blow at the labor movement as well, abolishing the Luxembourg Commission and placing Louis Blanc under indictment.

By late May, all the forces of the left in the capital, both the radical democrats and the socialists (remember the two were by no means necessarily the same), had been defeated, their organizations weakened or dissolved, many of their leaders in jail or in hiding. The government resolved to follow up its victory by abolishing the National Workshops. Now up to this point the workshops had been, for all their left-wing implications, a force for the preservation of order. Under the energetic leadership of the young engineer Albert Thomas, the unemployed in the workshops had been kept at work and away from the anti-government demonstrations. Thomas had banned socialist or radical political agitation in the workshops during the elections of April 1848, while encouraging propaganda in favor of Louis-Napoleon Bonaparte.

Abolishing the workshops would complete the victory of the moderate republican government and the monarchist assembly over the leftists, but it would also destroy a key means for the preservation of public order in a city rife with social and political tensions. In view of the defeated and disorganized state of the left following the fiasco of 15 May, the government might have succeeded in peacefully eliminating the workshops had it not moved to do so in a clumsy and provocative way. Characteristic of the authorities' actions was their response to Albert Thomas's objection to their plans. When he sensibly pointed out the dangers to public order inherent in dissolving the workshops and leaving 100,000 unemployed in the streets, the government hustled him out of town secretly, under cover of darkness on the night of 26 May.

The following day, when the unemployed discovered how the popular director of their program had been disposed of, they mounted large demonstrations in his favor and against the government. Over the following weeks, petitions in support of the workshops were circulated, and mass meetings in support of them were held, encouraged by the remaining, as yet unarrested leaders of the trade associations and activists in the political clubs. From being a force for order in the capital, the national workshops had become the center of an increasingly determined opposition to the regime. The tensions reached a peak on 21–22 June, when the government announced that the workshops were to be dissolved and the unemployed would either be drafted into the army or sent to the provinces to drain swamps. Two days of mass meetings and demonstrations against this decision climaxed on the morning of the 23rd, when a group of demonstrators began building barricades. Within hours, they were to be found throughout the poorer neighborhoods of Paris. No one knew exactly how many people were manning them; estimates ranged between 15,000 and 50,000.

The republic born of the February 1848 insurrection now faced an insurrection against it. The street fighting in June was far more bitter and violent than in February, and resulted in many more casualties. Unlike Louis-Philippe, the republican government and the constituent assembly were determined to fight. They allowed the insurgents to set up their barricades. These were then systematically bombarded by artillery, blowing up the barricades and a fair portion of the houses surrounding them. Once a breach had been made, the infantry was sent in, for three days of hand-to-hand street fighting. In the end, some 1,500 combatants on both sides had been killed, as had been the Archbishop of Paris, struck by a stray bullet while trying to arrange a truce. The forces of order, embittered by the fighting and quite out of control, shot 3,000 captured insurgents on the spot; 12,000 more were arrested, 4,500 of whom were eventually deported to Algeria.

Here was front page news for the press across the continent, newly expanded and freed from the constraints of censorship, an event for everyone to know about and debate. One version of the events, widely spread in both conservative and liberal circles, saw it as a communistic rising of the lower classes, out to destroy authority, property, the family, and religion, seeking to loot and pillage, and to install anarchy and godlessness. The *Allgemeine Zeitung* of Augsburg, Germany's leading newspaper, with a moderately liberal editorial policy, under a headline, "Days of Terror in Paris," reported about the insurgents at the barricades that

[t]hey no longer seemed to be human beings but monsters, who took pleasure in the martyrdom of the solid citizens they challenged and who left no horror undone ... The people struck their blows with bestial anger, they became intoxicated before they went off to commit murder ... Such a revolutionary struggle has not previously existed; this one has been the frightful result of the most extreme moral decline of the masses.[1]

Substantial Parisian property owners certainly shared these views, cheering on the soldiers fighting the insurrection, and gloating at the firing squads for the defeated insurgents. 100,000 members of the National Guard from the provinces converged on Paris to help fight the insurrection, bourgeois hoping to preserve their property, peasants eager to settle with the unemployed eating up their extra 45 centimes in tax.

Oddly enough, there was one leftist in Europe who shared these views, if from a reversed perspective. Karl Marx, at the time of the uprising in the pages of the newspaper he edited, a few years later in his classic studies on *Class Struggles in France* and *The Eighteenth Brumaire of Louis Napoleon*, described the June Days as a colossal class struggle, pitting the working class of Paris against all other classes in French society – the capitalist bourgeoisie, the small property-owning petit bourgeoisie, and the peasants. While noting that the uprising was doomed, due to its lack of leadership and its inadequate support, Marx praised the heroism of the insurgents, suggested that their struggle revealed the futile character of the democratic aspirations of the spring of 1848 and foreshadowed the coming class struggles whose end would be the triumph of the workers and the creation of a communist regime. Marx's picture of a struggle between workers and property owners destroying the initial possibilities of the 1848 revolution and bringing to an end the aspirations associated with them, while initiating a new era of class confrontation, became for many years a standard part of the account of 1848 given by historians from many different countries and of different political loyalties.

However, its validity is open to question. To judge by the occupations of those 12,000 arrested for their part in the fighting, the largest group of insurgents were artisans – either journeymen, masters, or outworkers, the occupational records not distinguishing between them – and hence typical of the urban lower classes of mid-nineteenth century Europe. One might want to call this evidence of a working-class uprising, provided "working-class" is understood in the terms of the mid-nineteenth, and not the twentieth century. The enemies of the insurgents, though, were workers as well.

[1] *Augsburger Allgemeine Zeitung*, 5 July 1848, cited in Ulrike Ruttmann, *Wunschbild-Schreckbild-Trugbild. Rezeption und Instrumentalisierung Frankreichs in der Deutschen Revolution von 1848/49* (Stuttgart, 2001), 253.

The regular army troops were reluctant to storm the barricades, so most of the fighting against them was performed by the Mobile Guard, a special militia created by the new republican government in February for the unique circumstances of the capital city. Unlike the regular National Guard, its members were outfitted, fed, and quartered at government expense, as well as being offered a modest stipend. Service in such a militia would appeal to supporters of the republic in need of a job – unemployed Parisian workers for instance, the same sort of people who were employed in the National Workshops and were fighting on the other side of the barricades. Insurgents and members of the Mobile Guard were from precisely the same social groups. It is harder to understand the June Days as a workers' uprising against capitalism, if workers were doing the fighting against the insurgents.

The background to the June Days also does not coincide with Marx's concept of a class struggle, that is, of a situation in which economic and political antagonisms converge. In the spring of 1848, the Parisian labor movement, the trade associations, and the Luxembourg Commission, had gone their own way, separate from that of the radicals in the Parisian political clubs. The clubs and the associations had not cooperated, had in fact worked at cross purposes, in the elections to the Constituent National Assembly in April 1848 and at the demonstration of 15 May. The series of defeats that these movements suffered – from the poor showing of their candidates at the elections to the Constituent National Assembly, to the failed demonstrations of 16 April and 15 May, to the June Days themselves – reflected this lack of unity between political and economic mass movements. The desperate fighting on the barricades of 23–26 June 1848 expressed not the high point of a class struggle but the failure of one to materialize.

Most democrats of 1848 did not share Marx's view that the June Days pointed the way towards future political struggles. Some leftists shared the more conservative attitude that the insurgents were enemies of property and civilization, and supported the authorities of what was, after all, a republican government, in their attempt to repress the uprising. Most saw the events as a grave tragedy, pitting a labor movement and a republican government against each other, and placing radicals in the capital city at odds with potential allies in the provinces. Helpless at understanding how two groups who ought to have been friends and allies came into such violent conflict, democrats across Europe expressed suspicions of conspiracy and asserted that behind the uprising stood the machinations of tsarist or Bonapartist provocateurs.[2]

---

[2] While the long arm of the Tsar of all the Russias hardly reached as far as Paris, supporters of Louis-Napoleon Bonaparte were mixed up in the events and slogans in support of Bonaparte were frequently heard on the barricades.

Democrats realized that the labor movement would have to be more closely tied to the political left. In addition, to ensure that the radicalized lower classes of the capital city not be isolated from the rest of the country, leftists would need to consider the economic and social interests of other groups, particularly smallholding farmers. This was the insight behind the formation of Republican Solidarity in France and the parallel efforts at reorganization undertaken by leftists elsewhere in Europe in the closing months of 1848 and the beginning of 1849. The idea inherent within these efforts of a left-wing political movement as an alliance between classes would characterize the later phase of the 1848 revolution. Twentieth-century socialist movements, whether of the revolutionary, Bolshevik or the reformist, social-democratic variety, have also been successful precisely in so far as they have not relied exclusively on the workers but have organized supporters from other social classes.

Marx himself was too sharp a politician not to be aware of these differing interpretations of the June Days. It is generally not realized that for a while during the 1848 revolution, he toned down his own glorification of the Parisian insurgents and moved towards the more widely accepted viewpoint. In a speech before the democratic club of the city of Cologne, of which he was a leading member, on 4 August 1848, he told his fellow members that "the denial of mutual concessions and the perverted ideas of the relations between the classes has led in Paris to a bloody outcome." A revolutionary movement and government stemming from it, he went on, would have to have representatives from different social classes, since the rule of a single class was "nonsense."[3]

Whatever interpretations democrats made of the June Days, their outcome was certainly a defeat for the left in France. Following the insurrection, the government come to power in February 1848 was reshuffled. The more left-wing of the ministers were forced to resign; the most prominent among them, the former Interior Minister Alexandre Ledru-Rollin, would shortly become the leader of the reorganized parliamentary opposition. The new head of the government was the former Minister of War, General Eugène Cavaignac, who had led the armed forces that combated and suppressed the insurrection. No one could doubt Cavaignac's republicanism. It was a matter of family tradition, since his father had been a member of the Convention, the radical legislature of the first French Revolution in 1792–95, and Cavaignac himself had accepted setbacks in his military career because of his hostility to monarchical rule.

---

[3] Cited in Sperber, *Rhineland Radicals*, 302.

Cavaignac, however, had little sympathy for the ideas increasingly prominent in 1848 that a democratic and republican form of government would go hand in hand with the redistribution of income or the rectification of inequalities created by the market economy. He was a "pure republican," who envisaged a republic with a strong executive (like himself, for example) that could secure the protection of property demanded by liberal social and economic principles. In most of Europe, people with these social and economic viewpoints were constitutional monarchists, seeing a truly strong executive that could protect property only possible with a royal head of state. While certainly not what Cavaignac had in mind, his accession to power set the stage for the emergence of another strong executive figure, with military connections, who would claim to be the defender of property, and a monarch as well – Louis-Napoleon Bonaparte. The June Days pitted workers against workers and republicans against republicans: the outcome of their struggle was the beginning of the end of the republican regime in France and its replacement with a monarchy that would make defense of property against ostensible socialist threats a main point of its rule.

Counter-revolution in the Austrian Empire

By late spring 1848, the Habsburg Empire looked like a hopeless case: the monarchy's northern Italian possessions in revolt, invaded by a Piedmontese army and largely cleared of Austrian troops; three different "national" governments, in Vienna, Budapest, and Zagreb each claiming sovereign authority; Polish, Romanian, Slovenian, Serb, Czech, and Slovak national movements aspiring to a similar sovereign status; a mentally incompetent monarch and his court in flight from the capital to the provinces; a state treasury completely bare.

Yet by August, the outlook was entirely different. Most of northern Italy had been reconquered; the emperor and his court were back in Vienna and his government was discussing with a constituent assembly the future shape of the monarchy. While financial problems remained, the authority of the central government was widely recognized; only the Hungarians remained defiant, and steps were being taken to bring them back into line. This total reversal of the monarchy's prospects was the result of a series of developments, nowhere near so clear cut as the Parisian June Days, but equally significant as indications that the initial victories of the 1848 revolution would not be of long duration. As usual, events within the Habsburg's realm were complex and involved violent and peaceful political struggles occurring simultaneously but in widely separate places. To provide some conceptual order in this political chaos, it would be helpful to consider some of these struggles separately: first events in Prague, then those in northern Italy, and finally those in Hungary. The common thread running through all these struggles is the way that the Habsburg court and the army officer corps, the largely unreformed survivors of the pre-1848 absolutist regime, sought simultaneously to make use of and to suppress the new revolutionary forces, to restore their pre-revolutionary authority.

As we noted in the third chapter, the initial euphoria in the city of Prague, capital of the Austrian province of Bohemia, at the overthrow of absolutism had given way in the course of April and May 1848 to a growing hostility between German and Czech nationalist movements, complete with hostile incidents in the streets and confrontations between "German" and "Czech" divisions of the National Guard. German nationalists in Bohemia took part in the May 1848 elections to the German National Assembly; Czech nationalists boycotted them – a boycott highly successful in Prague, where pro-Czech demonstrators marched menacingly through the streets on the day of the elections, keeping the pro-German element at home. As a further stroke against the German National Assembly, Czech nationalists organized a Slavic Congress in Prague that met in early June 1848, to prepare the reorganization of the Austrian Empire along national lines, with the Slavic nationalities in a dominant position.

The main leaders of both the Czech and German nationalists were constitutional monarchists. They were firmly loyal to the Habsburg Emperor, and while they had very different ideas about the territories he should rule, or the organization of these territories along national lines, they agreed that he should rule in accordance with a constitution authorizing a legislature, elected by substantial property owners. A smaller, politically less influential group of radicals existed in each nationalist movement, typically students at the university and polytechnic institute, who espoused more democratic political viewpoints. Some of the democratic activists had not yet given up on the idea that German and Czech nationalists could cooperate, abandoned by the dominant, constitutional monarchist wing of their respective nationalist movements.

This was the setting at the end of May, when the commanding general of the Prague garrison, Prince Alfred Windischgrätz, returned from an extended vacation. A member of the high aristocracy, owner of large estates in Bohemia, German-speaking but opposed to both German and Czech national movements, deeply loyal to imperial authority and suspicious of constitutional arrangements limiting it, Windischgrätz was the very epitome of the feudal and absolutist regime that had been overthrown in March 1848. Indeed, after the outbreak of revolution, the civilian governmental authorities in Prague had suggested that the prince make his temporary vacation a permanent one. They were appalled at the thought that a post so sensitive for the preservation of public order should be filled by such an overt reactionary, and one whose brutality in suppressing the strike of Prague's cotton printers in 1844 had left a dismal memory among the city's lower classes. Windischgrätz's return to the garrison, they feared, would only lead to a confrontation between the soldiers and Prague's politicized inhabitants.

A confrontation, however, was precisely what the general and those at the imperial court who shared his opinions had in mind. On returning to his post, Windischgrätz took a series of provocative measures, including the redoubling of military patrols and the placing of artillery on the hills surrounding the city. Radical activists, predominantly Czech nationalist students, responded with mass meetings and public demonstrations, demanding the general's resignation, the withdrawal of the artillery and the handing over of rifles from the garrison to the National Guard, so that the citizen militia, and not the army could ensure public order. A large crowd of demonstrators marching through the city on the morning of 12 June clashed with soldiers, and within a few minutes barricades were being built throughout the city. Street fighting continued through the 17th, in spite of efforts by the Bohemian Provincial Governor and commissioners sent by the government ministry from Vienna to arrange a truce and a compromise. In the end, artillery bombardments forced the insurgents to surrender.

Not surprisingly, the radical leaders were arrested, but Windischgrätz went further, imposing martial law, purging the city's National Guard and subordinating it to the army, ordering the Prague National Committee dissolved, and sending home the delegates of the Slavic Congress, bringing that meeting to a premature end. A mixed civilian-military tribunal was created to prove that the uprising was the result of a revolutionary conspiracy; the court's investigation, taking place while the city was in a state of siege, was not hampered by any liberal safeguards designed to preserve the rule of law. The chief civilian official in Prague, the provincial governor, Count Leo Thun, who had persistently tried to mediate between Czech nationalism and Habsburg authority, even during the uprising itself, was unable to oppose General Windischgrätz, because he was dismissed from his office by the central government in Vienna.

These measures directed against the Czech nationalist movement might seem at first an odd thing for a general determined to uphold imperial authority to do, since the Czech nationalists were also strong supporters of the emperor, their Slavic Congress, the reader will recall, meeting in a room decorated with the black and yellow Austrian flag and the imperial eagle. The imperial authority they wanted, however, was one with a constitution and limited executive powers, not an absolutist regime based on the armed forces of the sort favored by Windischgrätz. While the Prague events were a triumph of absolutism over constitutionalism, there was more to them than that: they were a triumph of absolutism occurring to the applause of constitutionalists, due to the issue of nationalism. German nationalists in Prague, in Bohemia, in Vienna, in the neighboring kingdom of Saxony, in the Frankfurt National Assembly, indeed throughout the German-speaking world, praised General Windischgrätz's soldiers for their victory in the German cause against Slavic opposition. The struggles in Prague, as German nationalists saw them, were a major step forward in the creation of a German national state, guaranteeing that its authority would extend throughout the entire "national" territory.

This interpretation of the Prague events as a struggle between Teutons and Slavs was even more dubious than understanding the Parisian June Days as a struggle between workers and the bourgeoisie. Germans and Slavs were on both sides of the Prague barricades. The insurgents, drawn from the ranks of Prague's students and artisans, while predominantly Czech-speaking, included German-speakers as well, and many of Prague's German nationalist radicals were involved in the uprising. Like so many of the Habsburg army units, General Windischgrätz's troops were ethnically mixed, but mostly from Slavic nationalities.

Even more to the point, their commander was no German nationalist, and had not the slightest sympathies for the nationalists' program of creating a German nation-state as a constitutional monarchy, to say nothing of a democratic republic. With the exception of a small group of democrats in Vienna and isolated leftists elsewhere in central Europe, German nationalists failed to see that Habsburg troops, led by an absolutist general against Czech nationalists, could just as easily be unleashed on them. Their nationalist passions caused German nationalists to lose sight of the liberal political principles on which their nationalism was based. This attitude, common to all the contending national groups in the Habsburg Empire, would be one of the secrets of the empire's survival in spite of all the nationalist attacks against it.

As the events in Prague suggested, revolutionary movements in most of the Habsburg territories were directed at the transformation of imperial authority; those in northern Italy, on the other hand, were to separate the territory, absolutely crucial to the empire's finances, from Habsburg rule altogether. The victories of the forces of General Radetzky in northern Italy in the summer of 1848 were thus the most decisive military triumph of the embattled empire, responsible more than anything else for its survival in the year of revolution. That these victories emerged from the desperate situation of the spring of 1848 was the result of three factors: the hesitancies of the Italian revolutionaries and the Piedmontese government, the disparities in the military leadership of the opposing armies, and the diplomatic localization of the conflict.

Rather than attack Radetzky's defeated and retreating troops, the Piedmontese government used its armed forces in the spring of 1848 to assert its control over the two northern provinces. Plebiscites were held on whether Lombardy and Venetia should join the northern Italian kingdom, obtaining enormous majorities in favor of this step – a victory for the constitutional monarchists over the radicals who had led the uprisings in Milan and Venice and created the revolutionary provisional regimes in both provinces. Unable to mobilize popular support for their program of an Italian republic, the radicals had no good argument against King Carlo Alberto's armies.

More broadly, events in the liberated provinces went along the lines favored by the constitutional monarchists there and in the Piedmontese government. Suffrage was restricted to substantial property owners, as was membership in the National Guard. The rural lower classes in particular were denied any participation in the revolutionary movement, and their attempts to use the excitement at driving out the Austrians to gain access to forest and former common lands or to improve their position against the large landlords – the latter largely sympathetic to the moderate version of the revolutionary movement – were quickly suppressed. While the Italian revolutionaries were losing popular sympathy in the countryside, General Radetzky's remaining forces were mounting a vigorous campaign of terror there. On learning, in mid-April, that insurgent forces were stationed in the village of Montebello in Venetia, Radetzky sent a detachment of soldiers to drive out the insurgents, burn the village, and murder every man, woman, and child in it. Revolutionary enthusiasm in the countryside faded rapidly under these circumstances; with it went peasant support for the uprising, crucial to a victory over the Austrians, as the veteran revolutionary Giuseppe Mazzini had been asserting for decades.

Even without popular support and armed irregulars, the regular army of Piedmont-Savoy and its Italian allies ought to have sufficed to drive out the battered Austrian forces. But Carlo Alberto's generals were reluctant to close on the enemy. While they waited, the Pope, in April, withdrew his support and his armies; in May, following King Ferdinand's victory over the oppositional parliament in Naples, his contingents returned home to southern Italy. These delays not only weakened the Italians but gave Radetzky a chance to reorganize his troops and obtain reinforcements from the Tyrol, Austria's conservative Alpine province. When the two armies finally met in July, the Piedmontese generals displayed such a

breathtaking incompetence that Radetzky ordered his marksmen not to
fire on them, since their commands were so favorable for the Austrians.[4]
At the decisive battle of Custozza, on 23 July 1848, the Piedmontese were
routed, and Radetzky advanced victoriously southwards. Milan fell at the
beginning of August and by the middle of the month a cease-fire between
Piedmont and Austria had been arranged, leaving both northern provinces in Austrian hands, with the exception of the island city of Venice,
whose inhabitants, under the leadership of the republican lawyer Daniele
Manin, defiantly prepared for a siege.

The disastrous Piedmontese strategy seems more comprehensible
when one realizes that Carlo Alberto and his ministers were hoping not
to have to fight the Austrians at all. In spite of their boast that Italy would
do it alone, they expected that the support of England and France, and
the possibility of their armed intervention, would suffice to bring the
Austrian government to negotiate the cession of its Italian provinces.
The feeble regime in Vienna did make several moves in that direction
during the spring of 1848, but, in the end, the government and especially
the imperial court, decided to fight it out.[5]

British support for Italian national unity proved to be entirely verbal,
but the outcome of the war posed a serious dilemma for the regime of
General Cavaignac. Along with independence for Poland, Italian
national unity and an end to Austrian rule in the peninsula had long
been a foreign policy goal of French republicans. There were the memories of the great campaigns in northern Italy fought by the armies of the
First French Republic and Napoleon in the 1790s; more prosaically,
Austrian withdrawal would remove a Great Power presence from
France's southeastern border and perhaps open up the possibility of
regaining the French-speaking territory of Savoy, that France had ceded
in the Treaty of Vienna in 1815. At the end of July and again at the
beginning of September 1848, Cavaignac and his ministers debated
French intervention, coming within a hair's breadth of starting a campaign that could easily have led to a great European war.

Rather than going to war, the French government limited itself to
diplomatic protests. A number of reasons determined this position, but
the most important was probably the government's fear of the potentially
radicalizing effects of a major war. 'The precedent of the early 1790s,

---

[4] Peter Stearns, *1848: The Revolutionary Tide in Europe* (New York, 1974), 138.
[5] General Radetzky is traditionally said to have refused to obey orders to evacuate northern
Italy and thus saved the Habsburgs' cause by his disobedience, but he received so many
mutually contradictory orders from the government and the imperial court that he did not
so much disobey them as choose which ones to obey.

when the war between revolutionary France and the major European states had brought the Jacobins to power and led to the reign of terror, weighed heavily on statesmen in the mid-nineteenth-century revolution. It was precisely this precedent that led radical leftists to call for war (think of the demonstrations in Paris on 15 May 1848), and moderates, such as General Cavaignac and King Carlo Alberto, to shrink from it. No Great Power ever came under the rule of a radical regime in 1848, willing to wage such a revolutionary war. The Habsburgs' forces' many struggles against smaller insurgent armies were thus always localized, another factor allowing the Austrian Empire to survive.

Northern Italy was now in effect under a dictatorship of General Radetzky. He began his rule hoping to gain popular support. Tradition has it that peasants disgusted with the property-owning revolutionaries who had reigned in the two provinces since March 1848 called out on sight of the Austrian troops, "Hurrah for Radetzky; down with the lords!" The financial exigencies of the monarchy quickly changed the situation. Radetzky was ordered by the cash-starved government in Vienna to treat the provinces as conquered territory, have his troops live off the land, and extract their pay directly from the population. They did so with a vengeance, and although the general tried to direct their exactions at the large landowners, whom he held responsible for the movement against Habsburg rule, the organized and unorganized looting quickly cost the Austrians initial popular sympathies. Young men called to the colors took to the hills and forests *en masse*; a sullen silence settled over the region. Attempts by some of Mazzini's followers to begin new uprisings in the fall of 1848 were unsuccessful; northern Italy was subdued, held down by armed force, but deeply alienated from its Austrian rulers.

The defeat of Carlo Alberto's armies had been a major setback to revolutionary forces not just in Piedmont-Savoy but throughout Italy. There were demonstrations in favor of continuation of the war, most prominently in the Tuscan port city of Livorno, which briefly fell into the hands of revolutionary forces, but all were suppressed by the authorities. In Germany, on the other hand, the exploits of General Radetzky were regarded as great nationalist victories. Opinion was more divided than had been the case with General Windischgrätz's triumphs in Prague; German democrats, in particular, were sympathetic to Italian nationalism and were more likely to see in the events a victory of counter-revolution – a realistic appraisal. Constitutional monarchists, and a majority of the Frankfurt National Assembly, on the other hand, celebrated Radetzky's feats of arms, seemingly unaware that their nationalist enthusiasms were cheering on the destruction of their own nationalist aspirations.

Towards war with and in Hungary

In August 1848, the imperial court returned in triumph to Vienna. The emperor's authority had been re-established in northern Italy; Slavic nationalist movements had been neutralized or enlisted in the imperial cause. Much the same was true of the German nationalists; the Frankfurt National Assembly had even chosen a Habsburg prince to be Imperial Regent, head of state in a provisional German central government. All that remained from the concessions made in the spring of 1848 was the Hungarian national government in Budapest. Court and central government in Vienna now resolved to revoke these concessions and destroy the Hungarian government: the political scene in the Habsburgs' realm during the following year would be dominated by this effort.

Circumstances certainly seemed favorable to it, as the ministers and National Assembly in Budapest were having substantial difficulties in asserting control over their "national" territory. Conflicts in Transylvania and the Banat, combining clashes between Magyar nobles and restive serfs, and Hungarian against Romanian or Serbian nationalists, were continuously worsening, heading for civil war. Habsburg officials and army officers offered the anti-Hungarian irregulars both covert and open support, as well as promises of further aid from Vienna. From the point of view of power politics, however, the most significant conflict within the lands of the Crown of St. Stephen pitted the Hungarian against the Croatian national governments, since the Croatian authorities in Zagreb controlled regular armed forces, the troops of the border regiments.

Painfully aware of this, the Hungarian government ministers attempted to resolve the Croatian situation in the summer of 1848 through negotiations with the imperial court. They attempted to gain imperial support against Ban Jelačić and the Croatian government by offering to send Hungarian regiments to reinforce Habsburg forces in Italy, an offer that was accepted but made superfluous by Radetzky's victories. This was a constitutional monarchist strategy, tying the Hungarian government to the fortunes of the House of Habsburg. When the offer was discussed in the Hungarian National Assembly, the radical minority angrily denounced it, insisting that Hungarian troops should stay at home to guard Hungarian national self-determination, rather than being sent to fight Italians attempting to exercise the same right. The vote in the Assembly supported the government, and crowds, led by Budapest radicals, attempted to storm the parliament, but were narrowly turned back.

In a related yet independent negotiations, the Hungarians attempted to come to terms with Ban Jelačić himself.[6] These negotiations proved abortive, since the Ban rejected all Hungarian offers, even for Croatian independence, insisting as a pre-condition for negotiations that the finances and the armed forces of the entire Habsburg monarchy be placed under a unified central command. Such a pre-condition had little to do with Croatian national self-determination, but a lot to do with preserving Habsburg authority. It was certainly possible that the Hungarians were negotiating in bad faith, and had no intention of granting Croatian independence, but Jelačić's reply shows the extent to which the man Croatian nationalists recognized as their leader was more than anything else a loyal servant of the imperial crown.

Jelačić would become the center of the court's and the Vienna ministry's efforts to regain control of Hungary. At the end of August, they officially reinstated him as Ban and commander of the border troops; at the same time, they ordered the Hungarian government in Budapest to give up its plans for an independent Hungarian army. While no formal order was sent, word reached Jelačić from the court that it would look favorably on his taking military action against the Hungarian government. On 11 September, his forces crossed the Drava River, the border between Croatia and Inner Hungary.

This invasion brought on the great crisis of the Hungarian revolution of 1848. The Hungarian government was facing war on three fronts, against the Croats, in the Banat, and in Transylvania. Fighting against it on all of these fronts, were soldiers of the Habsburg monarch, the nominal Hungarian head of state. The survival of an independent Hungarian regime and the constitutional monarchist project of a Hungary headed by a Habsburg ruler could no longer be reconciled. Radicals in Budapest realized that their moment had come. Mass meetings sponsored by the Society for Equality – itself meeting and acting in defiance of a Hungarian government order for its dissolution – demanded a revolutionary response to the situation; large crowds surrounded the parliament building as the National Assembly debated about the crisis situation.

Unlike many other such tense situations during the mid-century revolution, the crisis of September 1848 in Budapest did not lead to a confrontation between radicals of the capital city and a moderate parliament. Instead, the parliament made concessions to the radicals: bypassing

---

[6] The reader should recall that the Hungarian government, claiming sovereignty over Croatia, had got Emperor Ferdinand (the official Hungarian head of state) to sign a decree deposing Jelačić from office, but the government ministers had no difficulty distinguishing between legal claims and the realities of power.

the Hungarian government, it appointed a National Defense Committee, headed by Lajos Kossuth, the veteran leader of militant Hungarian opposition to Habsburg absolutism. Kossuth was himself not officially connected to the Budapest radicals, but he acted decisively to meet their key demand, the raising of an army to fight the invading imperial forces. The final break between Vienna and Budapest followed a few days later, when the imperial government appointed Field Marshal Count Lamberg as special commissioner in Budapest and commander-in-chief of all the armies in Hungary – that is, of Jelačić's forces and of the Hungarians marshalling to oppose his advance. Arriving in the Hungarian capital on 28 September, Count Lamberg was attacked by an infuriated crowd, stirred up by radical activists, dragged from his carriage, beaten, and lynched. The court and the Vienna government responded by declaring the Hungarian parliament and government dissolved and by offically appointing Jelačić to replace Lamberg, steps that meant the official recognition of the war against the Hungarian regime long covertly if erratically sponsored by the court. The constitutional monarchist government ministry in Budapest resigned, its policy of conciliation with the emperor completely destroyed, and power passed into the hands of Kossuth and his National Defense Committee.

War between Austria and Hungary had begun. Against a scarcely organized army, it at first seemed that Jelačić's troops would quickly occupy Budapest. They conducted the campaign as they would a border skirmish against the Bosnians, looting massively as they went. Infuriated Hungarian peasants resorted to guerilla warfare, threatening the invaders' communications and supply lines. The meeting of Jelačić's troops with Hungarian regulars proved that cattle rustling was really the formers' forte. The Hungarians were victorious in several encounters in late September and early October 1848, forcing the Croatians to retreat along the Danube towards Vienna. The war continued and became more embittered on the other two fronts in Transylvania and the Banat, but the Hungarians had rebuffed Austrian efforts at a quick victory.

Counter-revolution and foreign intervention in the Danubian Principalities

Occurring in statelets far off on the southeastern fringes of Europe, the triumph of counter-revolution in the Principalities of Moldavia and Wallachia would have nowhere near the broader impact of the Parisian June Days or the victories of General Radetzky. Nonetheless, events in the Danubian Principalities are of interest for their internal dynamics in a region of servile agriculture, for their place in the Romanian nationalist movement during the mid-nineteenth-century revolution, and for the role played in them by foreign intervention, particularly by the forces of the tsar. The Russian invasion of Wallachia in September 1848 was an open manifestation of a threat that hung over the revolutionary movement throughout central and eastern Europe.

As the reader will recall from Chapter 3, the revolution in Moldavia was quickly suppressed by a private army of the prince in April 1848. Revolutionary leaders fled across the border to the town of Czernowitz, capital of the Austrian province of Bukovina (today the Romanian city of Cernăuti), where they formed a "Moldavian Revolutionary Committee," that attempted to coordinate the actions of Romanian nationalists in the principalities and in the Habsburg provinces of Transylvania and Bukovina. Among the committee's plans for action was the unification of the two principalities to form the nucleus of a Romanian nation-state.

Throughout April and May of 1848, there was a steady increase in political agitation in Wallachia, led by the students recently returned from Paris. Turning their attention from the capital city of Bucharest, where they already had considerable support, to the countryside, they sent some 3,000 agitators to urge the serfs to join the revolutionary movement. Indeed, the overthrow of the prince's rule began in the provinces, in the small Danube river town of Islaz, where a mass meeting on 21 June 1848, led by a captain of the civic guard and an Eastern Orthodox priest, proclaimed a revolutionary provisional government. The prince, rather like the rulers of smaller countries in central and western Europe, did not even try to oppose the insurrection, but fled the country. A provisional government was proclaimed in the capital, officially led by the Metropolitan, the senior Eastern Orthodox bishop, and with a membership composed of liberals and radicals.

As had been the case elsewhere in Europe several months previously, there quickly developed political tensions following the creation of a new government in Wallachia. Central to the clashes between conservatives, liberals, and radicals was the question of the abolition of serfdom. Conservatives, particularly the boyar nobility, were opposed to such an action, but if it were to occur, then they demanded that the lands cultivated by the serfs be turned over to the nobility as their property. Moderates and even radicals (many of whose leaders were themselves from families of boyar landowners) wanted an orderly abolition of serfdom, with compensation for the nobility, but for the peasants to retain some of their lands. Closely connected to this issue was the question of the franchise for elections to a planned constituent assembly, that would ultimately decide on the agricultural system, with the left insisting on a democratic franchise, and the conservatives demanding additional representation for large landowners. The peasants themselves added fuel to the political dispute by refusing, as had their counterparts in eastern and central Europe, to perform their servile duties or pay seigneurial dues.

In all these respects, developments in Wallachia seemed reasonably similar to those occurring to the north and the west in previous months. However, the Danubian Principalities had a special international status, and it was diplomacy and foreign intervention that would strongly influence domestic developments and finally sweep them aside. Officially, the two principalities were a part of the Ottoman Empire, and their rulers were nominally subordinate to the Sultan in Istanbul. However, as a result of Russian victories over the Turks two decades previously, the 1829 Treaty of Adrianople had made the tsar into the protector of the principalities. In addition, the diplomatic representatives of the European Great Powers, as was the case elsewhere in the Ottoman Empire, had legal jurisdiction over their nationals residing in the Principalities, and, informally, a considerable influence on their politics.

The Wallachian revolutionaries were careful to court the support of the Sultan, proclaiming that their plans for reform and renewal were not directed against Turkish sovereignty. However, the tsarist protective power was dead set against the revolutionary movement. The center of opposition to the revolutionaries was not so much the hapless prince as the Russian Consul General in Bucharest, who had pressed him to suppress the proclamation of a revolutionary government in Islaz. By contrast, the British Consul General had generally supported a cooperation of the monarch and the revolutionaries along the liberal lines of a constitutional monarchism. His position was endorsed by an emissary of the republican government in Paris. Following the flight of the prince and the proclamation of a revolutionary government, Russian troops moved into Moldavia and were stationed, threateningly, on the border with Wallachia. Rather than intervene directly, and antagonize the liberal western Powers, the tsar's government hoped to pressure the Sultan to send an army to end the revolutionary regime.

The threat of intervention thus determined the course of events in Wallachia during the summer of 1848. Emboldened by the prospect of Russian and possibly Turkish support, conservatives made several attempts to overthrow the government, each turned back by masses of the population of Bucharest, at one time led by the female revolutionary, Ana Ipătescu, as mentioned in the previous chapter. The revolutionary government attempted to raise an army against the possibility of intervention and intensified efforts to gain peasant support. In view of the emergency situation, elections had to be called off, and a commission attempting to create a legal end to serfdom was unable to conclude its work.

At the end of July, a Turkish army marched into Wallachia. The revolutionary government negotiated with the Ottoman representatives, agreeing to a reshuffling of cabinet portfolios, to increase the number of moderates in the government. At first, this seemed to satisfy the Sultan, but a change of opinion in Istanbul resulted in new orders for the Turkish forces to proceed against the revolutionary government. It met them, not with armed opposition, but with a massive display of passive resistance. Tens of thousands of peasants, led by their Orthodox priests, carrying both nationalist tricolor flags and religious paraphernalia, placed them-selves in the way of the Turkish forces marching on Bucharest. On 27 September, a Russian army crossed into Wallachia from Moldavia and brought the revolutionary regime there to an end.

The internal political dynamics during the brief reign of the revolu-tionary provisional government in Wallachia are reminiscent of those elsewhere on the continent in 1848, particularly in east-central Europe – the growing differences between radicals, liberals, and conservatives, the combination of religion and nationalism, the centrality of the peasantry and of the question of the abolition of feudalism and seigneurialism to the fate of the revolution. These dynamics, particularly the growing clash between radicalism and counter-revolution, were strongly affected by the threat of the military intervention of the tsar's armies. By contrast, the western Powers, France and England, more sympathetic to at least a liberal regime, were unable or unwilling to act in a similar fashion. This broader correlation of military forces would be repeated at other times in the year following the summer of 1848 and would play a role in the final victory of counter-revolution.

The crisis of September 1848 and the Frankfurt National Assembly

Through the summer of 1848, Germany had escaped the large-scale violent clashes that marked the mid-century revolution in France, Italy, or the Habsburg monarchy. Rather, the leaders of the constitutional monarchist majority in the Frankfurt National Assembly seemed to be succeeding in their program of national unification and peaceful reform. The major issue dividing them was the vexed question of whether the future united German state should include the Germans of the Habsburg Empire. Consequently, liberal parliamentarians, particularly the domi-nant figure among them, the Assembly's president, Hessian estate owner Heinrich von Gagern, decided to leave this most difficult issue for last, setting the assembly to work on first drawing up a constitution and declaration of basic rights for a future German state, before considering its boundaries. To lend additional authority to the assembly while it worked at this task, Gagern had it create a Provisional Central Power, an interim national government. True to constitutional monarchist doctrine, he had the assembly elect a prince as head of this nascent German state, the elderly Archduke Johann of Austria, a hero of the wars against Napoleon at the beginning of the nineteenth century.

This national government had no powers of its own, lacking an army or civil service, and tax revenues to support them. It was dependent for its authority on the cooperation of the governments of the individual German states. Assuming this cooperation was part of the strategy of the Assembly's leaders, and in view of the liberal governments that had come to office in the major German states since March 1848, the strategy seemed entirely plausible. The crisis of September, however, would cast doubt on the entire program, bringing up questions about the authority of the provisional national government and the assembly that created it, the policies of the governments of the individual German states, and the cooperation between the National Assembly and these governments. It would also demonstrate the emergence of a new diplomatic alignment, perceptible at the same time in Moldavia and Wallachia, less favorable to even moderate liberal policies.

The crisis emerged over the northern duchies of Schleswig and Holstein, whose largely German population had been in revolt against Danish rule since March 1848. The new, liberal government of Prussia sent regular troops to support them; the Frankfurt Assembly had endorsed this action, in effect declaring war on Denmark over Schleswig-Holstein, leading the smaller German states to send their own, largely symbolic, troop contingents. The movement in Schleswig-Holstein became a popular nationalist cause throughout Germany: mass meetings were held in support of the war, women gathered money and supplies for the fighting, volunteers were enlisted to go to the front.

As the war continued in the summer of 1848, and Danish forces were driven back, the Great Powers became involved, the British and the Russian governments concerned that Prussia or a united German state might control the passages connecting the Baltic and the North Sea. Under heavy diplomatic pressure, particularly from Russia, the Prussian government concluded an armistice with the Danes at the end of August, evacuating most of the disputed territory and dropping support for the provisional government set up by the German insurgents there. It was a move with wide and largely negative political ramifications.

Prussia's foreign ministry had taken the step without consulting the provisional German government or the Frankfurt National Assembly, thus challenging the Assembly's and government's claims to national sovereignty, in doing so throwing into doubt the whole movement for national unity. Furthermore, this action concerned a popular national cause, one that had won widespread support in the mass meetings characteristic of the year of revolution. It also involved yielding to the tsar, seen by liberals and radicals alike as the great enemy of political progress. Democrats in particular regarded the Prussian government's action as proof of the growing influence of the conservative camarilla on the king, evidence that he would rather have his troops fight with the Russians against the revolutionary movement than against the Russians for the nationalist cause.

Throughout Germany there were mass meetings and demonstrations against the Prussian government's decision and demands that the National Assembly continue the war – and expand it to a broader war against Russia if necessary. These were particularly common in the western regions of central Europe, including many in and around the city of Frankfurt itself, where the Assembly was meeting. The Assembly voted to condemn the Prussian government and to continue the war; for a moment it seemed as if the German National Assembly would take a similar course as the Hungarian one at the very same time, renouncing its alliance with monarchical authority in favor of waging a revolutionary war.

The German parliamentarians shied away from this, reversing their previous vote and endorsing the Prussian government's actions. Radical deputies to the National Assembly sponsored an enormous mass meeting in Frankfurt on 17 September 1848, vigorously denouncing this decision. The following day, an enraged crowd tried to storm the Assembly and purge its right-wing members, in an action similar to the one in Paris the previous May. Prussian troops sent to rebuff this assault immediately alienated the politicized lower-class inhabitants of Frankfurt who began building barricades and fighting with them. In street fighting similar to the Parisian June Days, if on a smaller scale, the insurgents were defeated by artillery fire followed by infantry assaults, although not before they captured and lynched two conservative deputies of the National Assembly.

The street fighting in Frankfurt was part of a broader wave of demonstrations and mass movements throughout western Germany, including an abortive insurrection in Cologne, the largest city in the Rhineland and a quickly suppressed republican uprising in the Grand Duchy of Baden. The result of the crisis was a defeat for the democrats, whose partly spontaneous, partly poorly planned insurgencies were easily defeated. Both the provisional central government and the individual German states made suppression of the democratic movement a major political priority, attempting to harass or prohibit clubs and their activities. The crisis was no victory for the German constitutional monarchists either, since it brought into question their program of creating national unity via cooperation with the individual German states. How could such a program succeed if the individual states, particularly the Great Powers among them, Austria and Prussia, were increasingly coming under the influence of conservative court figures hostile to the entire liberal program, including national unification, seeking instead close ties to the Tsar and his program of diplomatic and military opposition to the revolutionary movement? Crises occurring within these states in the two months following the street fighting in Frankfurt would increase the strength of conservative elements and make the liberals' dilemma more painful than ever.

The October crisis

Nothing better indicates the complex interconnection of events in the Habsburg monarchy during the mid-century revolution than the October crisis. Set off by the war in Hungary, that is by the attempts of the court and the government ministry in Vienna to reassert their authority over the lands of the Crown of St. Stephen, it provoked a major challenge to imperial authority in the capital city itself and, to a lesser extent, in the non-Hungarian provinces of the empire. The outcome of the crisis would go far towards determining the post-revolutionary shape of the empire and to settling the fate of the German and Slavic nationalist movements within and beyond its borders.

The crisis began on 6 October 1848, when the government ordered troops of the Vienna garrison to march towards Hungary in support of Jelačić's battered forces. As the troops were leaving the city, they were surrounded by a crowd of Viennese civilians, responding to the appeals of the city's well organized and active democrats. The Viennese radicals, having a low opinion of the strength of the Austrian Constituent Assembly, with its constitutional monarchist majority, and mostly Slavic deputies, doubting its ability to stand up to the court or the ministry, saw the Hungarian government as the one barrier between the court and the return of pre-1848 absolutist rule.

The soldiers mutinied and refused to march, supported in their disobedience by many detachments of the Vienna National Guard. A mob seized the Minister of War, Count Latour, on the street, and hanged him from a lamppost. The court packed up Emperor Ferdinand and once more fled Vienna, this time heading for Olmouc (German: Olmütz) in Moravia. There, they were joined by the conservative and centrist deputies to the Austrian Constituent Assembly, and almost all of the government ministers. The imperial capital came under the control of a Committee of Public Safety, whose members were mostly democratic activists and radical parliamentarians. The radicals' rule was likely to be of short duration, however, as orders went out from Olmouc to General Jelačić's retreating troops, already on the way back to Vienna, to make the city their new military objective. They were to be reinforced by the soldiers of the Prague garrison under the command of General Windischgrätz. This was far more force than the insurgent Viennese could muster, and the insurrection's leaders engaged in a desperate search for allies.

Hans Kudlich, the democratic deputy from Silesia to the Austrian Constituent Assembly, author of the proposal to abolish serfdom in the empire that the assembly had passed in September 1848, was sent out on a mission to raise the countryside in support of the radicals in the capital. There was support for insurgent Vienna in the provinces, only it was largely confined to the largest cities – Graz, Linz, Salzburg, Brno (in Moravia, German name Brünn), to a lesser extent Klagenfurt – where democratic clubs had been formed. Radicals forced government officials to declare a state of emergency, raised money for the Viennese, or sent armed contingents to join in the fight. Among the peasants, the Viennese democrats met with at best indifference, at worst outright hostility.

There was still considerable rural social discontent at the time, and in the mountainous areas of the small province of Bukovina, situated between Galicia and Hungary, a massive peasant movement against the nobility. Peasants did not connect this with the politics of the capital, though; some, prompted by the Catholic clergy and local officials, even denounced the democrats for opposing the emperor, the man they thought had abolished serfdom! Radicals returned the hostility, condemning peasant stupidity and ignorance, but Kudlich pointed out that the rural situation reflected the democrats' own failings:

In October [1848] we were punished for our sins of omission . . . the Viennese party of movement had only agitated in Vienna. It had built up the revolutionary explosive force to the most extreme levels but had neglected the hinterland, the provinces completely. There, the network, the organization, the clubs were lacking . . . [under these circumstances, Kudlich's attempts to gain support for the Viennese revolutionaries] disappeared in the great sea of indifference and phlegm.[7]

The last hope of the Viennese lay with the Hungarian army. Paradoxically, the nationalist logic of the revolutionary Hungarian government discouraged intervention: an independent Hungary, after all, ought to have nothing to do with Austrian affairs. Finally, under Kossuth's urging, the Hungarians did make an attempt at the very last

---

[7] Cited in Friedrich Prinz, *Hans Kudlich 1823–1917* (Munich, 1962), 128.

minute, after Vienna had been completely surrounded and besieged. They reached the suburb of Schwechat on 30 October, and were driven off.

The following day, Habsburg troops stormed the insurgent city. There was fierce fighting, second only to the Parisian June Days among major urban insurrections during 1848, but once again the combination of artillery bombardment followed by infantry assaults brought victory for the armed regulars and disaster for the insurgents on the barricades. Leaders of the uprising were taken out and shot. The victorious imperial troops looted their own capital as if it were an enemy city conquered in wartime, which perhaps it was.

The conquest of insurgent Vienna marked a defeat for the German nationalism of the radical leaders there, but was also a rebuff to the German nationalist movement beyond Austria's borders. The Frankfurt National Assembly had sent deputies as commissioners to mediate between the Austrian court and the Viennese revolutionaries, only to have the court treat its intervention in the crisis with open contempt. One of the commissioners sent to Vienna, the Saxon radical Robert Blum, a leading figure among the Assembly's leftists and a prominent democratic activist, was captured by imperial troops, brought before a court martial, and shot. After the Prussian government refused to recognize the National Assembly's authority in the crisis over the armistice in Schleswig-Holstein in September, six weeks later the other central European Great Power rejected in clearer and more brutal fashion the Assembly's claim to the exercise of sovereignty over German "national" territory.

In a reversal of the situation in June 1848, Czech nationalists cheered the exploits of General Windischgrätz's troops and saw the events in Vienna as a victory for Slavic forces over German nationalism. This was a misinterpretation of events even more blatant than that proffered by German nationalists after the street fighting in Prague. Once again, Germans were not pitted against Slavs. Windischgrätz's forces were ethnically mixed and the lower classes of Vienna, the bulk of those fighting on the side of the insurgents, included many Czech- or Slovenian-speaking migrants from rural areas, who had come to the capital city looking to work. As in June, the victory of the imperial forces was not a triumph for one nationalist movement but a victory over all of them and their plans for a constitutional Austrian empire.

Even before the street fighting was over, the constitutional monarchist government ministers were forced to resign; their replacements, above all the new Prime Minster, General Windischgrätz's brother-in-law, Prince Felix Schwarzenberg, scarcely hid their intent to revert to absolutist rule. The Austrian Constituent Assembly was not immediately dissolved but was reconvened at the end of November far from the turbulent imperial capital in the Bohemian provincial town of Kremsier (Czech: Kroměříž). The Czech constitutional monarchists, the leading element in the Assembly, quickly discovered how wrong their interpretation of the fighting in Vienna was. Court and ministers presented them with a *fait accompli* as the parliament reconvened, the abdication of the mentally retarded emperor Ferdinand and his replacement by his eighteen-year-old nephew Franz Joseph. Coming to the throne young, Franz Joseph would reign for an astonishing sixty-eight years, his death in 1916 heralding the end of the monarchy itself. For the beginning of his reign, though, the significant factor was that the court decided, behind closed doors, to make him head of state, without consulting the Constituent Assembly.

This change at the very top signified the new state of affairs. The parliamentarians continued to debate a new constitution for the empire, but their discussions had no bearing on state policy, that was devoted to removing the last obstacle to the reassertion of imperial authority. An army of 70,000 men under the command of General Windischgrätz was sent to reconquer Hungary for the Habsburgs. It made rapid progress, and by the end of December the Hungarian government had been forced to evacuate Budapest. The Austrian Empire seemed to have survived all the threats of 1848 and emerged stronger than ever.

The November crisis in Prussia

Encouraged by the victories of the Austrian court, Prussia's monarch, Friedrich Wilhelm IV, resolved in November 1848 to take a step that he had long contemplated and remove any countervailing forces to his authority. The main obstacle to his rule came not from the German National Assembly in Frankfurt, that had shown in the September crisis its inability to challenge Prussian policy, but from the Prussian Constituent Assembly, sitting in the monarchy's capital Berlin, and debating a constitution for the kingdom.

Republicans were a minority there, as they were in Frankfurt and Vienna, but the Berlin deputies pressed their constitutional monarchism more aggressively than other central European parliamentarians. Their proposals that army officers take an oath of loyalty to the constitution, not the monarch, that titles and privileges of nobility be abolished, and that the words "by the grace of God" be stricken from the royal title angered the monarch and were seen by his conservative advisors in the court camarilla as a direct attack on Friedrich Wilhelm's authority – as indeed they were.

Early in November, the king replaced his constitutional monarchist prime minister, General von Pfuel, who had been striving to reach an agreement with the Constituent Assembly, with Count Brandenburg, a Prussian version of Prince Schwarzenberg. The new prime minister promptly moved 50,000 troops into Berlin, ostensibly to "protect" the Assembly from the danger of a republican uprising, in reality to carry out a monarchist *coup d'état*. Intimidated and surprised, the civic guard of Berlin and the city's well-organized democrats provided no armed resistance. A majority of the Assembly voted to defy the king, calling on Prussians to boycott taxes as long as their representatives could not meet freely without military intimidation.

A wave of mass meetings and demonstrations in support of the Assembly swept through a number of regions in Prussia. Particularly in the monarchy's southeastern province of Silesia, and its western province along the Rhine river, this discontent took on more serious form, with attempts by demonstrators, usually led by radical activists, to seize government buildings and clashes between soldiers and armed insurgents or members of the civic guard. There were incidents and attempts at organized resistance elsewhere, but the capital remained quiet, and, in the end, the army was able to restore order throughout the country.

The government of Count Brandenburg then followed a somewhat different course from its counterpart in Austria. Rather than allowing the Constituent Assembly to continue debating, it sent the deputies home and issued its own constitution by decree. Prussia's conservatives thus made a bow in the direction of the 1848 revolution, conceding that both estates and royal absolutism were no longer acceptable forms of government. The constitution, however, eliminated all the offending proposals of the dissolved Constituent Assembly and put as few limitations on royal power as possible. Like Franz Joseph, the new Prussian constitution would have a long life, remaining in force until the end of the monarchy in 1918. While the authority of the court ultimately triumphed over the revolutionary forces in both central European Great Powers its victory in Prussia was accompanied by the establishment of a new constitution, in Austria by the accession of a new emperor to the throne.

The election of Louis-Napoleon Bonaparte as French president

The string of violent defeats suffered by the revolutionary forces in the second half of 1848 came to a peaceful conclusion in December of that year with the elections for the presidency of the French Republic. Since the suppression of the June uprising and the appointment of General Cavaignac to lead the government, it had been a foregone conclusion that the Constituent Assembly would create a strong executive power, and an equally foregone one that the general would put himself forward to fill the post. When both these eventualities came to pass, the election of General Cavaignac seemed a sure thing to virtually all political observers.

Neither liberal nor conservative monarchists put up their own candidate, and left-wing opposition to Cavaignac, if more apparent, was less effective. Following in the Jacobin political tradition, French leftists opposed the very idea of a strong executive power set against the legislature. The newly formed Republican Solidarity was still too busy trying to establish itself nationwide to take part in a campaign many of its members disapproved of, so that the three left-wing politicians who launched competing presidential candidacies could count on little organized support.

All calculations were upset by the candidacy of Louis-Napoleon Bonaparte. The imperial pretender received the tacit support of the other French monarchists, who saw him as a stalking horse for their dynastic wishes, making him the candidate of all those political forces, the right and much of the center, opposed to the republican form of government. He also received a substantial left-wing vote from politicized urban workers, who had bitter memories of Cavaignac's role in suppressing the June insurrection. Finally, Napoleon's nephew ran fantastically well in the countryside. Peasants of all political sympathies – and especially those with none at all – cast their vote for the man who would lower their taxes and bring back the wonderful days of his great uncle. Louis-Napoleon was swept into office with 75 percent of the votes cast.

While unique in his ability to garner support from voters across the political spectrum, as well as those outside it, once in office Louis-Napoleon followed an increasingly conservative political course. The government ministers he appointed were exclusively monarchists and, under their direction, the judicial and executive officials set out to suppress the political left, closing down political clubs, and banning Republican Solidarity in January 1849. These were not entirely different from the policies carried out by General Cavaignac, but the new strong man at the head of the regime lacked his predecessor's republican principles. Louis-Napoleon's election suggested that by the end of 1848 even France, the country revolutionaries throughout Europe looked to for guidance and leadership, was turning towards the restoration of monarchical authority, if perhaps in the form of a different dynasty than the one which had ruled before the revolutionary events began.

The second wave of revolution

Many histories of the 1848 revolutions conclude in December of that year, with the defeat of the revolutionary initiatives of the spring. The account of seemingly uninterrupted setbacks to the revolutionary forces given in the first section of this chapter certainly seems to fit this interpretation. But this explanation also has its weaknesses. If the revolutionary forces were defeated by the end of 1848, why were there six different revolutionary regimes in Europe five months later? Why did the spring of 1849 see a new round of uprisings, barricade fighting, and small-scale civil wars?

The events of the first half of 1849 are only understandable as a new initiative of the forces of revolution, arising from the development of political organization and agitation occurring over the previous year. As a consequence of them, new social groups could be enlisted by the party of movement and it could act in regions less affected by the defeats suffered in 1848. Since counter-revolutionary political forces had also had the opportunity to develop and organize over the course of 1848, the second wave of revolution involved clashes between two fairly well-organized political camps. The elements of spontaneity and surprise, so characteristic of the events of the spring of 1848, while not entirely absent a year later, did not play the same major role that they had at the outset of the revolution.

New political initiatives

Even before the dreary string of defeats of the revolutionary forces had come to an end, democrats throughout much of Europe were preparing new political initiatives, based on their previous and continuing organizational efforts. In France and Germany, these efforts were largely peaceful in nature, directed towards forthcoming elections. Republican Solidarity and its informal successor groups, created following its prohibition, looked towards the first elections to the legislature created by the Constituent Assembly. Held in May 1849, they produced a monarchist majority, but showed the existence of substantial left-wing minorities. As contemporaries said, a "red France" was revealed, in Paris and vicinity, and in the central and southeastern parts of the country, where the candidates of the "democ-socs," the reorganized left wing, scored strong and unexpected victories.

German democrats and the Central March Association took a somewhat different tack. Frustrated with the weakness and the right of center politics of the Frankfurt National Assembly, they turned away from it, concentrating their energies on elections to the parliaments of Prussia, Bavaria, Saxony, and a number of the smaller states. They achieved results at least as good as, and usually better than the ones obtained in elections to the Frankfurt Assembly the previous spring.

Events in Italy were more dramatic, organizational initiatives combined with mass demonstrations and overthrow of established governments. The movement was at its most radical in Rome, and it began in lurid fashion with the public stabbing on 15 November 1848 of the Pope's constitutional monarchist prime minister, Pellegrino Rossi. Although assassination by dagger might bring back memories of the days of the Borgias or Julius Caesar, what happened on the 16th was more significant and more in line with the politics of the mid-nineteenth century. Some 10,000 demonstrators, led by the city's democratic clubs, and including much of the civic guard, converged on the Quirinal Palace, the Pope's residence, demanding the appointment of a new, democratic council of ministers. Pius IX bowed to the threat of force, but fled the city a week later, to exile in the Kingdom of the Two Sicilies, pronouncing anathemas on the revolutionary government in his states. The Roman revolutionaries responded by holding elections in January 1849, under universal manhood suffrage, for a constituent assembly in the Papal States. The elected deputies voted the end of Papal rule and proclaimed a Roman Republic.

The ramifications of the Roman revolution, as its leaders intended, were not limited to the Papal States but reached throughout Italy. Following the defeat of Piedmontese forces in the war with Austria, Italian democrats had gradually been developing a new political strategy, based on combining a mass movement towards national unification with actions to liberate the northern provinces from foreign rule. Their idea was to see the election of a national constituent assembly, sort of an Italian version of the Frankfurt Parliament, that could create a central government able to resume the war with the Austrians and do a better job of it than the Piedmont and the other Italian states had done the previous spring.

The new regime in Rome provided a basis for these plans. The Roman Constituent Assembly became the precursor to the planned all-Italian one. Giuseppe Mazzini, veteran leader of the Italian revolutionaries, who had endorsed the new political strategy, came to Rome on the creation of the republic there. The formation of a central committee of Italian political clubs in revolutionary Rome was another aspect of this idea as well.

The central committee, readers will recall, owed a good deal to democrats in the Grand Duchy of Tuscany, who also supported this strategy. One of the more moderate democrats, Giovanni Montanelli, had been named by the Grand Duke to his ministry in October and had made the idea of an Italian constituent assembly part of official state policy. But both Montanelli and the Grand Duke hesitated to go along with the anti-Papal Roman revolutionaries, so the Tuscan democrats turned up the pressure. After the clubs organized mass demonstrations in the capital city of Florence in January, Montanelli resigned from office, more radical ministers came to power, and the Grand Duke fled, leaving a second central Italian state in the hands of an insurgent government.

While in the spring of 1848 the main struggles of the Italian revolution had been in the Kingdom of the Two Sicilies in the south and in the provinces of Lombardy and Venetia in the northeast, the democratic initiative six months later began in central Italy and moved on into the northwestern kingdom of Piedmont Savoy in early 1849. The democrats were victorious in parliamentary elections held there, and government policy began to consider cautious rapprochement with the revolutionary regimes in the center of the country and a renewal of the war with Austria – once again, the main point of Italian politics during the mid-century revolution.

By February 1849, democrats could claim varying degrees of influence in four different Italian states – Piedmont-Savoy, Tuscany, Rome, and the city-state of Venice, last survivor of the anti-Austrian insurgent governments of the spring of 1848. These four governments were far from a smooth cooperation. Conservatives and constitutional monarchists retained a substantial influence at the Piedmontese court and Carlo Alberto toyed with the idea of marching on the anti-monarchical and anti-Papal governments of central Italy before or while assaulting the Austrians. The Piedmontese and the Venetians, both on the front line against Habsburg troops, distrusted the central Italian regimes, fearing that they were all talk and no action when it came to the war. Those latter governments, politically more to the left, suspected the northerners of not being revolutionary enough, and being willing to subordinate Italian national unity to Piedmontese dynastic interests. Yet in one way or another, all these regimes supported steps towards national unity and resumption of the war with Austria, common elements of the politics of the party of movement in Italy during 1848–49.

The new democratic initiatives were least successful in the Habsburg Empire. Any attempts at a resurgence of the revolution there, or even at resistance to a return to absolutist rule, would involve uniting previously mutually hostile nationalist movements, a difficult task in view of the feeble state of political organization, the subordination of many elements in these movements to dynastic and counter-revolutionary interests, and bitter memories of the months of often violent confrontation just past. Under these circumstances, it is surprising that any efforts were undertaken at all, and their modest success compared with similar initiatives further west in Europe is understandable. As was the case elsewhere in Europe, it was the democrats who were responsible for these new initiatives, constitutional monarchists preferring to cling to both their nationalist hostilities and the increasingly dubious chance of cooperation with the imperial court.

One example of this new mood was the banquet organized by the students at the University of Graz on 13 March 1849 in honor of the first anniversary of the revolutionary barricade fighting in Vienna. German, Slavic, and Italian students celebrated a "festival of fraternity" in a large beer hall, and then, joined by inhabitants of the town, marched to the railroad station, to hear radical speeches denouncing the monarchy. On a more serious level, German and Czech democrats in the province of Bohemia began laying plans with radicals in the neighboring Kingdom of Saxony for a revolutionary uprising. Frankly amateurish in nature, this conspiracy is best known for the participation in it of two colorful and dubious figures, the Russian anarchist Mikhail Bakunin and the operatic composer Richard Wagner, yet their presence should not obscure the more interesting point that some German and Czech nationalists were willing to put aside their mutual hostilities to confront a common enemy.

Potentially the most consequential if ultimately the least successful attempt at reconciling conflicting nationalities came in embattled Hungary. With its armies retreating from the assaults of Habsburg forces in the valley of the Danube, late in 1848, the insurgent government faced military disaster on another front in mountainous Transylvania. Peasant guerillas, loosely led by Romanian nationalists, backed up by the Habsburg regulars (including many Romanian-speaking imperial border guards) of General Puchner, had largely driven the Hungarian national army from the province. Fighting had been particularly bitter, involving the burning of the castles of the Magyar nobility by the peasants, assaults and murders on noblemen, and retaliatory arson and murder of peasant villagers.

In desperation, the Hungarian government turned to a new military commander, the exiled Polish insurgent, József Bem. Raising fresh forces, including many Romanians from the neighboring Banat, Bem marched into Transylvania, and in a series of battles during the late fall of 1848 and winter 1849 subdued most of the peasant insurgents, drove the Habsburg regulars out of the province, and even defeated a small Russian expeditionary force sent to support the Austrian government. Bem belonged to the democratic wing of the Polish emigration; he sympathized with the Romanian peasants' opposition to the Magyar nobles. Trying to bring the cycle of arson and murder to an end, he amnestied defeated peasant insurgents, and, quite exceeding his orders as a military commander, toyed with the idea of recognizing Romanian nationalist demands and granting some form of autonomy to the Romanians in Transylvania in return for their support against the Habsburgs.

For some of the more left-wing of the Romanian nationalists, this was not an entirely unattractive proposition. Throughout much of 1848 they had pursued the goal of creating a greater Romania, linking the Hungarian provinces of Transylvania and the Banat, where the Romanian speakers were mostly peasants, with the Austrian province of Bukovina, where the peasants spoke Ukrainian and the nobility Romanian with the principalities of Moldavia and Wallachia, on the other side of the Carpathian mountains from Transylvania. The two Danubian principalities would provide the core structure of this projected Romanian nation-state. These plans, involving a linking of territory inside and outside the Austrian Empire, had gone badly astray. When Habsburg authority was threatened in the spring of 1848, imperial generals and officials were willing to make all sorts of promises to the Romanians; the new government of Prince Schwarzenberg, on the other hand, feeling more secure and increasingly determined to restore absolutist rule, ever more openly ruled out such concessions. The Russian and Turkish interventions of September 1848 had eliminated any possibility of including the Danubian Principalities in the Romanian nationalist project.

Negotiations between the Hungarian government and the Romanian democrat Avram Iancu, leader of the last group of unsubdued peasant guerillas, were carried on sporadically, between April and August 1849. The legacy of almost a year of bloody warfare proved too great an obstacle: each side deeply mistrusted the other and neither was willing to make decisive concessions. In August 1849, on the eve of the defeat of the Hungarians by Austrian and Russian troops, the National Assembly voted to grant Romanian demands for national autonomy and Iancu responded by vowing that his forces would remain neutral in the conflict. By that time, it was too late; both Hungarian and Romanian nationalist and democratic aspirations were destroyed.

The crisis of the spring of 1849

It was fortunate for the Habsburgs that the revolutionary movements in their realm were least able to reorganize themselves, because the cumulative effect of the second wave of revolution in the spring of 1849 was above all to threaten once again imperial authority, so painfully and bloodily restored the previous autumn. There were three components to this challenge, coming from Italy, Hungary, and the German states respectively. Each component combined military confrontations, diplomatic maneuvering, and revolutionary mass movements, although in different proportions. The Italian component was the most purely military. Pressed by the democratic movement within and outside the kingdom, the government ministers of Piedmont-Savoy and King Carlo Alberto increasingly felt that they had no choice but to resume the war with Austria. On 20 March 1849, they refused to renew the armistice of the previous summer and sent their forces marching towards the two northern provinces.

As the Habsburgs' war in Italy was beginning again, their war with the Hungarians was taking a drastic turn for the worse. In a brilliant campaign, fought during the winter in the mountains of Slovakia, Arthur Görgey, the Magyars' best general, had defeated the Austrian forces in northeastern Hungary. In the spring, he came down from the high country into the Danubian plain. Rendezvousing there with other elements of the Hungarian army, he attacked the main Austrian forces and in a series of battles early in April defeated them and drove them back towards Vienna. By mid-April 1849, the Austrian army and its Slavic and Romanian nationalist allies had been almost completely defeated on all three Hungarian fronts.

Future prospects for the Austrians in the war were not encouraging. The renewed military efforts were destroying what little remained of imperial finances. Attempts to raise fresh troops had led to conscription riots in the provinces of Carinthia and Bohemia, where young peasants and townsmen, encouraged by the democrats, had refused to join the colors and had assaulted the recruiters. Troops had to be diverted from the fighting to suppress these outbreaks.

The final challenge to Habsburg authority came from the nationalist movement in Germany. Having finished writing its constitution for a united German state by the beginning of 1849, the Frankfurt National Assembly finally had to face the awkward problem of what to do about the potential state's boundaries, in particular, whether or not to include the Germans of Austria. The government of Prince Schwarzenberg solved its problem by insisting on the unity of the Austrian Empire and demanding that the entire empire – including Hungary and the Slavic provinces – be united with the German states. As everyone realized, such a union could not be a nation-state, or any unified state at all. It could only be a revival of the pre-1848 German Confederation, instrument of Metternich's domination of central Europe, consistent with Schwarzenberg's plans to return to absolutist rule.

This decision created an opportunity for the pro-Prussian constitutional monarchists in the Assembly, who supported the creation of a German nation state without Austria, the "little Germans," as their enemies dubbed them. Up until this point, the little Germans had always been a decided minority: deputies from Catholic regions and southern Germany, suspicious of both Prussia and Protestants, had opposed them, as had almost all of the democrats. The clearest test of sentiment on this point had come in June 1848 when the Assembly had debated which prince was to be chosen as head of state of the provisional national government. Archduke Johann of Austria had been elected by a huge majority, while one deputy's proposal to name Friedrich Wilhelm IV of Prussia to the post had been greeted by widespread and derisive laughter.

For their minority status, the pro-Prussian constitutional monarchists were a well-organized and politically effective caucus. They moved swiftly to capitalize on Schwarzenberg's obstinacy by making a deal with the Assembly's democrats, agreeing to their demands for universal manhood suffrage for elections to a future German parliament, and a strengthening of this parliament *vis-à-vis* the executive. In return for this, most democrats agreed to support the little Germans' proposal to make the King of Prussia the head of this new nation-state, that is, to elect him Emperor of the Germans. The Assembly did this at the end of March 1849.

Such a step was in line with the constitutional monarchists' program of creating a German nation-state in cooperation with the individual German monarchs and their governments. It was also, for the Austrians, a diplomatically threatening move. If the Assembly's offer was accepted by Friedrich Wilhelm IV, it would mean that the military power of Prussia, the Habsburgs' century-old rival for hegemony in central Europe, would be placed in the service of the German nationalist movement. The Austrians would then be facing nationalists combined with regular armed forces on three different fronts.

The outcome of the spring crisis

The latent or overt conflicts existing in March 1849 between the Habsburg Empire and the three nationalist movements were resolved by May of that year, with the victory neither of the empire nor of the nationalist movements, but with the transformation of the situation into a conflict between a group of revolutionary regimes and the party of order dominating each of the Great Powers of continental Europe. We can begin to see how this outcome emerged by considering the situation in Italy. The Piedmontese return to war was very brief. On 23 March 1849, three days after the resumption of hostilities, General Radetzky's soldiers met Carlo Alberto's troops, little improved from the previous summer, at Novara and decisively defeated them. The hapless Carlo Alberto abdicated the throne in favor of his son, and Piedmont-Savoy was forced to sue for peace. This left the revolutionary regimes in Venice, Florence, and Rome as the only Italian governments opposed to Austrian domination of the peninsula.

Dealing with the Hungarians was a more complicated matter. To secure the Habsburg position against them and against the German nationalists, Prince Schwarzenberg began, at the beginning of March 1849, by dissolving the Austrian Constituent Assembly. He took a leaf from the page of his Prussian counterpart Count Brandenburg by decreeing a constitution for the Austrian empire. This constitution was even more of a one-sided matter than the Prussian one, since it left virtually all power in the hands of the emperor. More importantly, it insisted on the unity of the entire monarchy, and a strongly centralized executive power, thus rebuking claims of any of the nationalist movements, whether Hungarian, Slavic, Romanian, or German. Temporarily "suspended" after it was decreed, the constitution was abolished in 1851, so that it never went into effect. It is best understood as a symbol of the determination of the court and senior government officials to control the empire, refusing to grant any serious powers to an elected legislature, as proposed by constitutional monarchists in 1848, while also rejecting the idea of a return to pre-1848 circumstances, when feudal assemblies, such as the Hungarian Diet, could mount a challenge to centralized rule.

This move was a final blow to any remaining hopes of Hungarian constitutional monarchists that some sort of arrangement could be reached between them and the Habsburgs. In mid-April 1849, the Hungarian National Assembly declared the House of Habsburg dethroned and proclaimed its national independence. The leader of the National Defense Committee, the nationalist hero Lajos Kossuth, was named interim president, for the duration of the war. The final step in turning the Hungarian situation into a conflict between revolution and counter-revolution was the decision of the Habsburg court, a few days later, to ask for full-scale Russian intervention. In a remarkable break from normal diplomatic practice, the Austrians offered no financial or territorial concessions, and the tsar asked for none. His armies would be employed in Hungary solely for the purpose of defeating revolutionary initiatives in Europe.

It seemed most unlikely that the German situation, one carefully crafted by the pro-Prussian constitutional monarchists to provide for cooperation between the Frankfurt Assembly and the Prussian monarchy, would lead to a revolutionary confrontation. Indeed, twenty-eight of the smaller German states agreed to accept the constitution written by the Assembly, and it seemed quite possible that Friedrich Wilhelm IV would as well. To be sure, the Assembly's constitution made an unpleasant number of concessions to the democrats, but these could have been negotiated away. Had Friedrich Wilhelm become emperor of a German state with a constitution similar to the one his ministers had decreed for his Prussian kingdom in December, it would have meant a substantial increase in the power of the Hohenzollern dynasty by means of a favorable compromise with the most moderate elements in the party of movement.

Prussia's king refused to give a definite answer to the Assembly's offer for almost a month, before finally condemning it at the end of April and announcing his counter-revolutionary intention of dissolving the Assembly. Austrian pressure on him to decline the offer had been substantial, but with the Habsburg court wondering if it would have to evacuate Vienna before the advancing Hungarians, accepting Frankfurt's offer would have meant little risk. In the end, it was the king's own extreme conservative political convictions, strengthened by the councils of his unofficial advisors, the equally conservative court camarilla, as well as the advice of the tsar's diplomats, that brought the decision.

The news of Friedrich Wilhelm's refusal to accept the constitution sparked a mass movement in its favor. Throughout central Europe, but particularly in the southeastern, central, and western parts of Germany, there were mass meetings and demonstrations in support of the constitution. Members of the public as well as armed civic guards and army reservists gathered and took an oath of loyalty to the constitution, pledging to fight, weapon in hand, in its defense. Curiously, at these gatherings held in support of a monarchical constitution, observers noticed the presence of many red flags, the symbol of radical republicanism. Even more curiously, speakers at the meetings denounced Friedrich Wilhelm, their erstwhile emperor, as a tyrant and blood-soaked murderer.

What was happening at the end of April and early May 1849 was that the architects of the constitution, the pro-Prussian constitutional monarchists, were giving up on their efforts towards national unity, since the Prussian king's refusal even to negotiate with the National Assembly ruined their plans for cooperation between the assembly and the German monarchs. Steadily increasing numbers of moderate deputies left the National Assembly and returned home. The movement in favor of the constitution had been taken over by the democrats and would be conducted in extra-parliamentary fashion. The demonstrations and mass meetings for the constitution occurred primarily in leftist strongholds; the whole campaign was loosely coordinated by the democrats' national political federation, the Central March Association. As the left wing of German politics came to dominate the movement for national unity, it took on increasingly radical, republican overtones.

By the second week of May, demonstrations had given way to armed conflict, complete with the seizure of arsenals, the building of barricades and fighting in the streets. Most struggles occurred in the provinces and the countryside; capital cities, scenes of previous centers of street fighting,

Berlin, Frankfurt, Munich, Vienna, remained quiet. One highpoint of this activity was in Saxony. Always a stronghold of the left during the revolution, the democrats, some of whom were already planning an uprising with Czech radicals, brought twenty thousand people into the streets of the capital city of Dresden, forced the royal family to flee, and created a revolutionary regime. It was short lived, suppressed in a few days by Prussian troops, after street fighting in Dresden, in the familiar pattern of artillery bombardments followed by infantry assaults.

The revolutionaries achieved their greatest success in the extreme southwestern corner of Germany, in the Palatinate, the Bavarian province on the west bank of the Rhine, and, on the other side of the river, in the Grand Duchy of Baden. As with Saxony, both areas had been centers of radicalism during the revolution, and, also as in Saxony, the radicals seized power in both of them, creating revolutionary regimes. Crucial to the success of these uprisings was the behavior of the armed forces in these medium-sized German states. Rather than trying to suppress the insurgents, many of the Bavarian soldiers stationed in the Palatinate, and the entire army of the Grand Duchy of Baden, went over to them. It would require Prussian soldiers to suppress the revolutionary movement in southwestern Germany, and while these soldiers were busy from mid-May through mid-June 1849 putting down uprisings elsewhere and being concentrated for a march on the southwest, the two insurgent regimes had a chance to consolidate their rule.

The rule of the insurgent governments and their ultimate defeat

The three Italian, two German, and the Hungarian insurgent governments of the spring of 1849 were the closest leftists would ever come to seizing power in the mid-nineteenth-century revolution. Very much as had been the case almost a year earlier in the Principality of Wallachia, all these regimes, from their very beginnings, faced the threat of invasion by the forces of counter-revolutionary Great Powers. Programs of social reform and political democratization had to be put aside; preparation for or actually waging war overshadowed everything else. This meant securing the authority and enforcing the rule of revolutionary governments for two main purposes: conscripting an army and raising funds to pay for it.

This task was least difficult in Hungary and in Venice, which had been at war with Habsburg forces for up to a year; at most, all that changed was the name of the government in whose name it was being carried out. The other regimes had to create their own governmental apparatus especially as the state officials, left over from the regimes that had just been overthrown were, at best, reluctant to carry out the revolutionary authorities' orders. To enforce their rule, the revolutionary regimes turned to sympathetic political activists, members of local democratic clubs. The extent and activity of these clubs, formed in the political organization and agitation of the previous year, marked the limits of the authority of the insurgent regimes.

The governments would need every bit of that authority, since they were forced to take unpopular and openly dictatorial measures: the conscription of young men into their hastily organized armed forces, the financing of these armed forces by imposing special taxes or forced loans, or by printing paper money, and the requisitioning (i.e., the seizure with only the most nebulous promises of compensation) of food, clothing, shelter, transport vehicles, and animals for their armies. All these measures sparked resistance. Young men, particularly in the countryside, fled into the forests and hills rather than join the armies; shopkeepers and businessmen refused to accept the paper money, or would only use it at far below its face value; the affluent inhabitants tried every trick of delay to avoid paying the forced loans.

These conditions were exploited by the democrats' conservative enemies, supporters of the overthrown governments. In the southern provinces of the Papal States, the most devout and loyal parts of Pius IX's realm, the Catholic clergy denied the sacraments to anyone participating in the elections to the constituent assembly called by the Roman revolutionaries. Following the proclamation of the republic and its ever more rigorous preparations for war with Austria, this discontent became more widespread and violent. One of many examples would be the villagers of Ginatreto, who refused to report for conscription, instead gathering at the parish church, ringing its bells, tearing down the republican flag planted there and raising the Papal insignia in its place. Similar incidents were common in all the revolutionary regimes.

There was some talk of attempting to conciliate the disaffected, the democrats of Bologna, for instance, suggesting to the government in Rome that it gain support of the peasants by repealing the tax on grain and making up for the loss of revenue by dismissing all the forest watchmen, "evil men . . . of no usefulness or true service."[8] The state of emergency and imminent danger of war, common to all the revolutionary governments, militated against most attempts at conciliation. Instead,

---

[8] Cited in Domenico Demarco, *Una rivoluzione sociale. La repubblica romana del 1849* (Naples, 1944), 129. In all of the areas governed by insurgent governments, peasants – whether radical, conservative, or apolitical – once again took advantage of the situation, as they had so often during the mid-century revolution, to raid the forests on a massive scale.

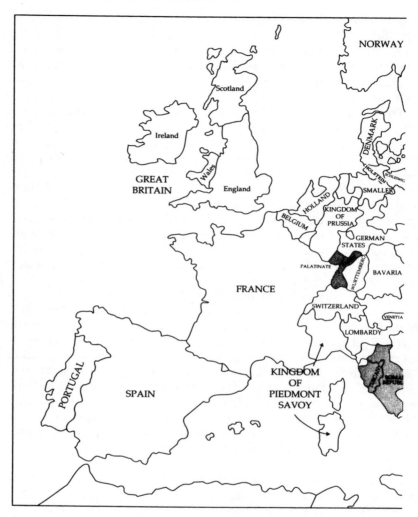

Map 5.1 Revolutionary regimes in the spring of 1849

SWEDEN

RUSSIAN
EMPIRE

KINGDOM
OF
PRUSSIA

SAXONY

Bohemia
Moravia

Galicia

AUSTRIAN EMPIRE

Hungarian
Provinces

MOLDAVIA

Transylvania

CROATIA

BOSNIA

SERBIA

WALLACHIA

OTTOMAN

EMPIRE

KINGDOM
OF TWO
SICILIES

GREECE

the civic guards, radical volunteers, or the newly raised armed forces were used to intimidate or suppress opposition. Armed confrontations followed. In several provinces of the Papal States, these reached the point of virtual civil war, as armed bands of pro-republican radicals and pro-Papal conservatives sought to slaughter each other.

The revolutionary government in the Grand Duchy of Tuscany, many of whose leaders were politically more moderate, was not prepared to take such drastic steps. Following the news of the Piedmontese defeat at Novara and the victorious advance of the Austrians, demonstrations in rural areas against the revolutionary government and in favor of the Grand Duke and the Pope became ever more common. The government made no attempt to repress them, eventually allowing itself to be ousted by the civic guard of Florence, whose leaders negotiated for a return of their monarch. In all of Tuscany, only the inhabitants of the port city of Livorno, a stronghold of radical forces throughout the revolution, were willing to carry on resistance. It required an assault by Austrian soldiers to bring the revolution there to an end.

The other revolutionary governments were able to suppress the opposition, raise an army, and prepare for war. As the conflict approached, the hopelessness of their situation became ever more apparent. Even in the best of circumstances, these were small powers facing much larger ones. The Hungarian and Badenese regulars loyal to the revolution could hardly be expected to stand up to the armies of one or more of the Great Powers; the improvised, ragged, and wretchedly outfitted armies hastily raised by the other governments had even less of a chance. If the insurgent regimes, and with them the mid-century revolutionary movement were to be saved, there would have to be intervention by a militarily powerful force, turning the localized conflicts into a great European war.

There could only be one source of this intervention, the army of the French Republic, so, in May–June 1849, all eyes were once again on Paris, the insurgent governments all sending delegations asking for military assistance. However, President Louis-Napoleon Bonaparte, his conservative government ministers, and the monarchist majority in the newly elected French legislature were far from having any sympathies for their fellow republicans elsewhere in Europe. Just the opposite, the president was under heavy pressure from French conservatives to intervene in Italy, not in support of the Roman Republic, but to destroy it and restore the rule of the Pope.

This was a painful demand for Louis-Napoleon, who was personally sympathetic to Italian nationalism and who, as a young man, had participated in the 1830 uprising against the Pope's rule. In mid-April 1849, he had sent a French expeditionary force to the territory of the Roman

Republic, with a noticeably ambiguous mission: it was unclear if it was to defend the republican regime there against a forthcoming Austrian intervention, or to overthrow it and restore the Pope. The first six weeks of the force's presence were equally ambiguous. An assault it made on the city of Rome was turned back by the revolutionary armed forces, under the command of Giuseppe Garibaldi, the latter beginning a long and glorious career as a military insurgent, that would make him one of the most celebrated figures in Europe. The expeditionary force then turned to diplomacy, only negotiations between its representative and the Roman Republic on restoring Papal authority brought no results.

At the beginning of June, under steadily increasing conservative pressure, Louis-Napoleon issued his troops unequivocal orders to destroy the republican government in Rome and re-establish Papal authority. This created a crisis in French politics, bringing to a head the issue of French intervention in the ongoing wars between the insurgent regimes and the other Great Powers. Ledru-Rollin, leader of the leftist caucus in the legislature, denounced the president's action as unconstitutional – for the constitution included a clause stating that the republic would never use its armed forces "against the liberty of any people" – and demanded Louis-Napoleon's impeachment. Voted down by the monarchist majority, Ledru-Rollin and the other radical parliamentarians called for a mass demonstration in Paris against the government's foreign policy.

Held on 13 June 1849, the demonstration proved a fiasco, the 6–8,000 marchers vastly outnumbered by the troops sent against them. Most of the leaders were arrested; to evade arrest, others, including Ledru-Rollin himself, had to flee the country. The protest found little echo in provincial France with the exception of Lyon, where it was strongly supported by the city's silkweavers, who went from demonstration to insurrection and built barricades in their neighborhoods. The army was sent against them, and after embittered street fighting, including the liberal use of artillery, their movement was suppressed.

The outcome of events in France sealed the fate of the revolutionary governments elsewhere in Europe. Prussian soldiers marched into southwestern Germany, and in a six-week-long campaign from mid-June through late July, defeated the armies of the revolutionary governments there.[9] French troops, after a month-long siege, captured Rome, restoring Papal authority. The island city of Venice and the revolutionary government of

---

[9] Increasingly isolated from events, the remaining members of the Frankfurt National Assembly had fled to Stuttgart, capital of the Kingdom of Württemberg, hoping for support from the government there. Instead, on the news of the Prussian victories, the kingdom's government dissolved the assembly and dispersed the deputies.

Hungary held out longest, but the besieged and blockaded Venetians were forced to surrender at the end of August, and the last Hungarian forces still fighting against the soldiers of the Austrian and Russian Emperors, ceased their resistance a month later. The second major wave of revolution had ended with a decisive victory of the counter-revolutionary armies.

In the underground, 1849–51

The victorious powers sealed their victory over the revolutionary regimes with a subsequent repression. Several hundred captured insurgents were shot on the spot or executed after trials before military tribunals. Thousands more were brought before civilian courts, or forced to flee to Great Britain or the United States, finding no, or, at best, temporary refuge from persecution on the European continent. If we neglect some acts of sadistic brutality – for instance, whipping Hungarian women in the public square – that seem to have been favored by certain Austrian officers, the repression was relatively limited, and by the standards of the mass murders committed by twentieth-century dictatorships, quite mild.

Contemporaries, naturally, did not see it that way; for them, the repression was vigorous and brutal. Yet it also did not entirely quiet the situation and bring the revolution to a complete close. Although intimidated and persecuted, the democratic movement continued, in some ways and places, its existence over the next two years. In Norway, admittedly a very peripheral area for the 1848 revolution, political radicalism even built steadily across 1849–50, only reaching its peak in 1851. Clashes between liberals and conservatives also continued in 1850–51, as adherents of these ideas attempted to install different versions of a post-revolutionary regime. The prospect of a war between the Great Powers and a new outbreak of revolution – two developments closely connected by contemporaries – loomed large on several occasions. It would only be at the end of 1851 that the mid-century revolutions would reach their conclusion.

One arena of continued radical activity was exile. Political refugees from France, Germany, and Italy rushed into Switzerland, enjoying the toleration (or at least not the immediate hostility) of Europe's one substantial republic, living on the borders, holding meetings, and trying to stay in contact with comrades in their native countries. Some refugees went across the Atlantic Ocean to the United States (a few, such as Garibaldi, headed for Latin America), the most hospitable of destinations for émigrés, and also one offering lucrative opportunities to raise funds for new revolutionary projects. Taking up residence on the other side of the

Atlantic, though, meant renouncing any influence on events in Europe, at a time when the outbreak of a major war or of a new wave of revolution seemed to be still a possibility.

The great center of emigration was London. The British government was committed to a policy of granting political asylum and was willing to let the refugees do as they pleased. As a Great Power in its own right, it was less susceptible to pressure from counter-revolutionary regimes to curtail the activities of exiles, or even to extradite them, than were than smaller lands of refuge, such as Switzerland, Belgium, or the Netherlands. *Emigrés* in London founded a number of political groups, the most important of which was the work of Giuseppe Mazzini, the "European Democratic Committee for the Solidarity of Parties, without Distinction of Nationality," known for short as the European Democratic Central Committee. Mazzini gathered an impressive group of prominent radical revolutionaries, including the former president of insurgent Hungary, Lajos Kossuth, the leader of the French "democ-socs," Alexandre Ledru-Rollin, Ion Bratianu, who had been the Bucharest chief of police under the revolutionary government of Wallachia, as well as a substantial number of radical deputies to the German National Assembly. Issuing appeals and preparing for an expected or hoped for imminent new round of revolution, the activities of the committee were followed nervously by the agents and spies of the continental Great Powers.

Another venue of left-wing political activism in late 1849 and 1850–51 was continental Europe itself. The areas that had been scenes of revolutionary regimes and civil wars and lay under martial law were impossible for leftists, of course, and political repression in the Austrian Empire and most of the Italian states was particularly rigorous. But in much of France and Germany, there were still opportunities for legal political action: publishing newspapers, holding public meetings, taking part in by-elections to the French legislative assembly, or to the parliaments of the medium-sized German states, such as Saxony or Württemberg, where the democrats attempted to retain many of the legislative and constitutional accomplishments of the revolutionary period. As time went on, and reactionary elements gathered strength, these legal options became steadily more limited.

Increasingly, leftists were forced underground, into conspiratorial secret circles, back away from the public realm in which they had been so effective during 1848–49. Although present everywhere, these secret groups were by far most prevalent in France. The second revolutionary wave of the spring of 1849 had crested rather feebly there, without the widespread insurgencies characteristic in the German and Italian states or in Hungary. Although many of the national parliamentary leaders of the

French left, such as Ledru-Rollin had been forced into exile, some democratic parliamentarians remained in office, and, more importantly, activists in the provinces, not compromised by participation in the
demonstrations of 13 June 1849, continued to organize energetically,
creating an ever larger network of secret societies, especially in villages
and small towns of central and southeastern France. This revolutionary
underground was a mass movement, not the isolated conspiracy of a
handful of activists found elsewhere in Europe at the beginning of the
1850s. Repression could check the activities of the French secret societies,
but, as the police and state's attorneys were painfully aware, not supress it.
Nervous conservatives and government officials in 1850–51 kept getting
glimpses of organized hostility to their rule in revolutionary songs or
slogans wafting out of taverns, in cries on the street, in the nocturnal raising
of red flags, and in the writing of subversive inscriptions on walls.

While leftists were acting in semi-legal, half-conspiratorial fashion, the
center and the right were still engaged in an open politics. The main
question they had to resolve was whether government policy would be
overtly reactionary, returning to its pre-1848 ways, or if it would incorporate some constitutional monarchist elements from the revolution
itself. This was an issue particularly salient in the states of Germany and
Italy, where it was usually equivalent to the question of the degree of
Austrian influence, since the Habsburgs threw their diplomatic and military weight behind a policy of reaction. Constitutional monarchists
retained the most influence on government policy in the two traditionally
anti-Habsburg powers, Prussia and Piedmont-Savoy.

In 1850, it seemed for a brief moment as if the combination of moderately liberal policies in Prussia and a continuation of the revolutionary
movement in one of the smaller German states might lead to a clash
between the two central European Great Powers and a major war.
Prussian diplomats sought in 1849 and 1850 to create a small-German
nation-state, under Prussian leadership, roughly in the boundaries proposed by the constitution written by the Frankfurt National Assembly,
but lacking the democratic features of the Assembly's Constitution, such
as elections with universal manhood suffrage. This proposal, known as
the "Erfurt Union," was, in effect, an endorsement of and an attempt to
implement the ideas of the pro-Prussian constitutional monarchists of
1848 and 1849. As such, it involved an effort to expand Prussian power in
central Europe *vis-à-vis* Austria, and so met up with the strong resistance
of Prince Schwarzenberg's government, that looked to a return to the pre-
1848 German Confederation.

At the same time, the ruler and government ministers of the Principality
of Hessen-Kassel (notorious for decades, before and after 1848–49, for

their extremely reactionary attitudes), a smaller state in the western part of Germany, were refusing to obey or recognize the principality's constitution, a product of the 1848 revolution. Not only was the vast majority of the principality's legislature opposed to this course of action, but so were the civil servants, and even the army officers, a situation suggesting the imminent outbreak of revolution. The Austrian government announced its support of the Prince, the Prussian government its support for the constitution. By November 1850, Prussian and Austrian troops were facing each other in Hessen-Kassel and war seemed ready to break out. Under heavy pressure from the Tsar, and from his conservative advisors, Prussia's Friedrich Wilhelm IV abandoned the policy of his government ministers and backed down at the last minute, in a diplomatic concession later dubbed by nationalist German historians, "the humiliation of Olmütz." Prussia dropped the cause of the Hessian constitution and agreed to the restoration of the German Confederation, and with it recognition of Austrian primacy in central Europe.

This potential clash between Austria and Prussia notwithstanding, hopes, fears, and expectations of a new outburst of revolution were centered on France. To take just one example of many, in December 1849 the miller Tommaso Gentili of the village of San Vito, near Rome, had told people at his oil mill, that in the near future the "red cap" would once again be raised in Rome and the "Romans would shout long live the French Republic and the French would shout long live the Roman Republic."[10] Since it was soldiers of the conservative, increasingly monarchist government of the French Republic who had suppressed the revolutionary government of the Roman Republic and restored the rule of the Pope, Gentili's comments might seem naïve. Yet he was correct in expecting that any serious opposition to the reaction and counter-revolution increasingly dominant in Europe would come from France. The major and final confrontation of the mid-century revolution did occur there in 1851. It showed, in a greatly magnified way, the mixture of all the elements of the post-1849 European political scene – repression of the left, underground democratic organizing, struggles within the center and the right over the future course of government policy.

Following the demonstration of 13 June 1849, and the arrest or flight or many of the leaders of the left, nothing was left to check monarchist forces. The state authorities proceeded to repress any and all manifestations of democratic and republican ideas as vigorously as they could. Political clubs and newspapers were obvious targets, but by 1850,

---

[10] Cited in Franco Rizzi, *La coccarda et le campane: Communità rurali e Repubblica romana nel Lazio (1848–1849)* (Milan, 1988), 213.

the French Republic had reached the point where someone publicly shouting "long live the republic," was liable to be arrested and charged with sedition and the expression of subversive ideas.

None of this was in any way different from repression elsewhere in Europe, but the differences between liberals and conservatives over the post-revolutionary order took on a unique cast in France. In particular, a counter-revolutionary return to monarchical government involved a competition between different dynasties. Mostly liberal, constitutional-monarchist adherents of the Orléans family, come to the throne in the revolution of 1830 and overthrown in 1848, clashed with conservative Legitimists, supporters of the Bourbons, the dynasty overthrown by the Jacobins in 1792, restored in 1814/15 and overthrown once again in 1830. As was the case elsewhere in Europe, liberals and conservatives in France had increasingly cooperated against the democrats in 1848 and 1849, and continued to do so afterwards. A high point of their coopera-tion was the law of 31 May 1850 that eliminated universal manhood suffrage, cutting the poorest 30 percent of the voters from the electoral rolls. In the end, though, Legitimists and Orléanists were unable to agree on a common monarch for a restoration, as the Legitimist pretender, the Count de Chambord, refused to accept basic liberal principles, such as the constitutional monarchy.

Another unique factor of French politics was a third option, namely the restoration of the Bonaparte dynasty. The Bonapartist pretender, Louis-Napoleon Bonaparte was already president and in 1850–51, he maneuv-ered skillfully to present himself to the French bourgeoisie as the man of order, who would suppress the dangers to property emerging from the underground democrats and socialists, while simultaneously portraying himself to the common people as the friend of democracy, the enemy of monarchist parliamentarians' efforts to limit the franchise. While thus trying with some success to appeal to conservatives, liberals, and radicals simultaneously, he was also using his constitutional power as commander-in-chief of the armed forces to move generals favorable to his ambitions to key commands, while sending hostile ones off to the Algerian desert.

By the second half of 1851, the tension in French politics had mounted noticeably. Presidential elections were scheduled for the following spring. The democrats placed their hopes in them, while for Louis-Napoleon, they were a political deadline, since the constitution prohibited the re-election of the president. For a while, it seemed possible that conservative and liberal legislators might agree to amend the constitution to allow Louis-Napoleon another term in office, while they tried to work out their political differences. Some of the liberal supporters of the Orléans dynasty, looking forward to a presidential candidacy by an Orléans prince (former king Louis-Philippe having died in exile in London in 1850) thwarted these efforts.

The solution for the president was a *coup d'état*, to make himself first president for life, and, following that, emperor. Launched on 2 December 1851, the coup met scattered resistance in Paris, but the few barricades erected there were quickly taken by the army. There was massive opposition, not at the urban sites of previous insurrections but in rural areas and small towns where the radical secret societies called out their members to fight. Opposition to Louis-Napoleon's coup followed closely on membership in the secret societies, and the insurgents, about 100,000 in all, marched into battle waving red flags and chanting slogans of the "democ-soc" left. It was, in many ways, a belated version of the second wave of revolution that had encompassed much of the rest of Europe in the spring of 1849, and it shared the same fate. The poorly armed insurgents, while able to take on and overpower the gendarmes, and seize local government offices, were no match for the regular army, which crushed the uprising in a few days.

The uprising enabled Louis-Napoleon to legitimize his coup retrospectively, proclaiming himself the man of order, who had destroyed the red menace, in this way gaining the support – sometimes enthusiastic, sometimes reluctant – of both conservative Legitimists and liberal Orléanists. With this final defeat of the left in the country that was the center of the party of movement and the repository of post-1849 hopes for a revolutionary revival, the European revolutions of the mid-nineteenth century came to an end. The reaction era of the 1850s began, and the hopes raised in the spring of 1848 seemed buried once and for all.

6 The mid-century revolutions in European history

The anatomy of a revolution

The origins of the 1848 revolutions are best understood in terms of the coming together of longer- and shorter-term socioeconomic and political causes. A basic precondition for the revolution was the gradual decline in popular standards of living over the previous twenty to twenty-five years. To a great extent, this state of affairs reflected the decline of an agrarian-artisan economy, and its replacement by a more efficient one, characterized by a more productive agriculture, an improved market network, and a growing industrial sector. In central and eastern Europe, these structural changes were accompanied by a gradual movement from a society of orders to a civil society of property owners, involving changes in those property relations, particularly serfdom and the guild system, that hindered the development of a market economy and society. While historians might understand these developments as part of a favorable transition, leading to increased economic growth and higher standards of living, contemporaries had no way of knowing that their troubles were transitional, that after mid-century things would gradually improve. All that could be perceived was the decline, creating a permanent and widespread discontent.

The harvest failures of 1845–46, followed by the recession of 1847, topped off and intensified these long-term changes. Starvation was avoided in continental Europe, although for the poorer, mountainous areas it was a near thing, and for those of modest means, already suffering from the gradual declines in their real income, the years of high food prices meant taking on a heavy burden of debt. The unemployment and falling price levels, caused by the recession and the rich harvests of 1847–50 made that debt difficult to pay off. The upshot was a chronic state of dissatisfaction, an essential background to the initial disorders and uprisings of the spring of 1848, but remaining throughout the revolutionary events and helping to explain some of the impetus behind the further surges of revolutionary activity.

258

There are two long-term political causes of the mid-century revolutions, both containing several factors and both working in interaction with socio-economic developments. One was the increasing demands that all European states placed on their inhabitants – raising taxes, recruiting and garrisoning soldiers, or closely regulating use of the forest. In and of themselves, these were hardly measures likely to increase a government's popularity, but two additional circumstances exacerbated their effects. Declining standards of living meant that the authorities were trying to pump resources out of a population that had ever less available. Also, as a result of the great territorial shakeup begun with the French Revolution and finally concluded at the Congress of Vienna in 1815, many monarchs ruled over new subjects, unfamiliar with their rulers, lacking ties of dynastic and religious loyalty. Such subjects would resent their new overlords in any event; all the more if these new rulers made additional demands on them.

Ironically, the more demands that states placed on their subjects, the fewer means they had to enforce them. Coercive and administrative personnel, such as police or tax collectors, were few and far between. Indeed in Europe of the 1830s and 40s, the more absolutist the government, the fewer means it had of enforcing its will, short of bringing in the army. This multiple gap that opened up between increasing demands of the state, its declining popular legitimacy, and its insufficient means of coercion was an essential precursor to the outbreak of revolution.

The second long-term political cause of the revolution was the gradual development of oppositional politics, or, as contemporaries might have said, the growing strength of the party of movement, in most European countries. Borrowing their ideas and frequently the symbols expressing them primarily from the French Revolution of 1789, members of the party of movement took aim at absolutist and feudal or seigneurial institutions; they advocated the granting of basic civil rights, an end to privilege and the realization of equality before the law, the creation of representative institutions, and generally felt that all these measures required the framework of a nation. A constitution, popular sovereignty, pro-nationalist government policies – these were key demands of oppositional politics.

The party of movement itself was split to a greater or lesser extent into a moderate, constitutional monarchist, and a radical, republican, and democratic wing. Differences between the two groups were sharper and more distinct as one moved from east to west, reflecting the greater legal possibilities for political debate in the post-1830 constitutional regimes in the western part of the continent. Before 1848, most members of the party of movement were from affluent and/or educated backgrounds, as were most of the politically interested population of any viewpoint.

They were at best loosely organized and possessed relatively few ties to the lower classes, especially in the countryside.

Generally, both political organization and popular political participation increased as one moved from east to west in Europe and from the country to the city. Certainly, it was in France that popular political participation of the urban lower classes was greatest before the revolution. For related reasons, it was in France that socialist doctrines developed on the fringes of the party of movement and found a popular audience.

The combination of a growing, politicized opposition with an increasing if not expressly and self-consciously political popular discontent, hardly augured well for most regimes. The weakness of the established order became manifest in the years after 1845. While the party of movement became increasingly aggressive in France, ever since 1789 the center of hope for political change, the main pillar of the existing system, the Austrian Empire, crippled by a desperate financial situation, seemed ever less able to respond to political challenges. The victory of the radicals in the Swiss Civil War of 1847 brought home to all politically interested contemporaries that the continent stood on the brink of a revolutionary outbreak. Everyone was prepared for the revolution, so that once it began it spread to almost the entire continent. Even in some of the smaller states, where no revolutionary outbreak occurred, or an actual outbreak proved abortive, such as Denmark, Norway, Belgium, and the Netherlands, there were mass political movements and major governmental reforms.

More significant than events in the smaller states was the lack of revolutionary activity in the two Great Powers on the rim of Europe, Russia, and Great Britain. These nations provide the other side of the coin, lacking the preconditions that brought revolution to much of the continent. Further advanced in the development of industry, agriculture, and market relations than continental countries, the difficult transition to a more productive economy and increasing popular standards of living had been accomplished in England and Scotland by the mid-1840s. The organized radical opposition to the government, the Chartists, whose movement had been powerful, widespread, and extremely threatening to the government and ruling groups eight to ten years before the outbreak of revolution on the continent, was already in decline by 1848. British radicals were excited by the proclamation of the republic in Paris, as were adherents of the party of movement everywhere in Europe, and Chartism did briefly revive in 1848, but neither the mass demonstrations mounted by the Chartists in London, nor their attempts at revolutionary conspiracy in the industrial cities of northern England could match earlier efforts and provided no major threat to the established order.

This optimistic prognosis cannot be applied to one part of the mid-century United Kingdom, namely Ireland, where standards of living continued their decline throughout the 1840s, culminating in the horrors of the potato famine. Unlike continental Europe, there was widespread starvation in Ireland; perhaps one million people died from hunger and disease. The extreme nature of the famine helps explain why there was no revolution in Ireland, although there was certainly plenty of impetus towards it, and Irish immigrants seem to have been major supporters of Chartist plans for insurrection in England during 1848. Another factor needs to be emphasized, however, the enormous police presence. There were some 13,000 police stationed in Ireland at mid-century, one for every 500 inhabitants: fourteen times as many per capita as in Prussia, the absolutist "police state," four times as many as in France, the most heavily policed country in continental Europe. Police forces were substantial in parts of England, particularly the capital city, as well. The greater ability of the liberal state in Great Britain, with its parliament and elaborate legal system, to enforce its will, when compared with the surprisingly feeble forces of repression in the absolutist monarchies on the continent, also helps explain why the United Kingdom rode out the revolutionary wave with little rocking of the boat.

The tsar's empire, for all its extreme absolutism, was also a regime lacking the effective administrative apparatus of the liberal states of western Europe. The presence of a particularly rigorous form of serfdom certainly provided reason enough for popular discontent. However, in Russia, the transition from an old-regime society of orders to a nineteenth-century civil society of property owners, already well underway before mid-century in the Austrian Empire, and even in the Danubian Principalities of Moldavia and Wallachia, was, at best, in its earliest stages. Political, cultural, social, and economic organizations were lacking; the party of movement in the tsar's realm was limited to a few circles of revolutionary conspirators – easily penetrated by the police – and a handful of potential liberal reformers, hoping in vain that the autocratic regime would cooperate with them. The outbreak of the 1848 revolutions raised hopes among both Russian reformers and revolutionaries, but it also increased the fears and hostility of the absolutist government, leading it to step up its repression of political dissent.

Considering that there was no serious revolutionary challenge to existing authority in Britain and Russia during 1848–49, it is reasonable to wonder if this might have been a major reason for the ultimate failure of revolutionary movements in other European countries. In one sense, this question has no answer, since we cannot rerun the history of 1848–49 including this time the tricolor flag flying from the Winter Palace in

St. Petersburg or from the Parliament in Westminster and seeing what would have happened. In a more modest way, however, we can approach this question by looking at the policies of the two non-revolutionary Great Powers towards the 1848–49 revolutions and seeing the effects of these policies on the revolutionary movement.

British policy in 1848 was basically favorable to the moderate, constitutional-monarchist wing of the revolutionary movement. British diplomats favored an Italy united under Piedmontese rule, and a united Germany under a Prussian king. Both steps would have weakened the Austrian monarchy and British foreign policy then, as throughout most of the nineteenth century, showed that regime little favor. On the other hand, London was no friend of the more radical side of the revolution; the government openly disapproved of the labor movement and socialist schemes so prominent in Paris before the June Days brought an end to them and installed a government more to British liking. The great European war that was an integral part of the radical political program met with particular disapproval and British diplomats moved to oppose it on the two occasions in August–September 1848 when it seemed that it might break out, between the Germans and Russians over Schleswig-Holstein and the French and the Austrians over northern Italy. In the end, though, Britain's policy was above all, detached, offering to help mediate disputed questions, rather than see them resolved by warfare. For this reason it is hard to see British influence as decisive on revolutionary events in one way or the other.

Russian policy was not detached in 1848–49. Quite the opposite, the tsar's government was hostile to any kind of revolution, whether moderate or radical, fearing, in particular, the possibility of another Polish uprising, and so took energetic measures against it. From the spring of 1848 onwards, the Russian army was mobilized, poised at the frontiers to intervene against revolutionary movements. On two separate occasions, it was sent into action: in September 1848, against Romanian nationalists in the Principality of Wallachia, and in June 1849 against the revolutionary government of Hungary. These actual interventions were only the tip of the iceberg. Particularly in central Europe, the possibility of a Russian intervention was a constant presence during the revolution. Russia threatened war against Prussia and other German states over Schleswig-Holstein; the tsar's diplomats promised Friedrich Wilhelm IV armed intervention should radicals seize power in Berlin, a promise that the beleaguered monarch was only too happy to accept.

This was a formidable record, and one can only agree with mid-nineteenth-century radicals who saw the Russian government as the "gendarme of Europe," a force aimed against the revolutionary movement. Yet even here, there is good reason to wonder just how decisive the actions of the tsar really were. His forces never had to fight the great European war that radicals advocated because the radicals never succeeded in gaining control of the government and hence the armed forces of one of the other Great Powers. Although this involves entering the realm of speculation, there is no reason to think that if such a war had broken out, Russian intervention would have been particularly effective. On all occasions when Russian forces fought in the nineteenth and early twentieth centuries – against the British and French in the Crimea in 1854–56, against the Turks in 1878, against the Japanese in 1904–5, and against the Germans in 1914 – they performed quite poorly. If the threat of Russian intervention seemed so powerful in 1848, it was because the radicals did not have control of the government of a Great Power to oppose it. In the end, a consideration of both British and Russian policy leads to the conclusion that the primary reasons for the failure of the 1848 revolutions must be found within the revolutionary movements themselves.

The same causes that led to the outbreak of the revolution were responsible for the ultimate defeat of the revolutionary forces. Once the initial victories of the revolution had been scored, and the pre-1848 restrictions on the free expression of political ideas abolished, it did not take long for serious divisions within the party of movement to appear. Powerful differences, indeed steadily increasing hostilities, emerged between constitutional monarchists and republican radicals, between German and Czech or Hungarian and Romanian nationalists.

As the party of movement was breaking up and engaging in internecine conflict, the party of order was re-emerging as a major political force. Ironically, it was the overthrow of the authoritarian pre-1848 regimes and the creation of a freer and more open public life that revealed the extent of those regimes' supporters and allowed them to organize themselves effectively. The Prussian conservative leader, Ernst-Ludwig von Gerlach, looking back on the revolutionary events in 1853, noted that conservatives had "seized the artillery of the revolution and turned it against the revolution itself, via public speeches, the free press and political organization."[1] Although Gerlach explicitly limited his observations to Prussia, they could easily be applied more broadly.

The supporters of the party of order were the mirror image of those of the party of movement, rallied largely from the same causes, just with opposite effects. Political conservatives in 1848 included people who had

---

[1] Cited in Bernhard Ruetz, *Der preussiche Konservatismus im Kampf gegen Einheit und Freiheit* (Berlin, 2001), 68.

done well over the previous quarter century – farmers who had taken advantage of rising grain prices, or businessmen who had profited from government contracts. Prominent in their ranks were those possessing dynastic or religious loyalties to their monarchs, including many middle-level and senior officials in the armed forces and state service, who retained their posts in spite of the revolution. In the end, the party of order would prove to be more unified, than its opponents, better at mobilizing the powers of repression and coercion, more coordinated at an international level. As a result of the weakness and mutual hostilities of their supporters and the growing strength and unity of their enemies, the new regimes created in the spring of 1848 proved short lived.

The revolution of 1848 and the canonical European revolutions

The conclusions to the previous section raise the issue of comparison, of placing the revolutions of 1848 in the succession of "canonical" or "classic" revolutions of modern European history – those of 1789 and 1917, of course, to which should be added, although still in the relatively recent past, those of 1989 as well. As was the case with "1848," where the year is shorthand for a multi-year process of revolution, political conflict, civil war, and finally repression, counter-revolution, and reaction, we should note that the comparison is really between 1848–51 and 1789–99, 1917–23, and 1989–91.

Spread of the revolutions

One area of comparison is the spread of the revolutions. At least as far as Europe is concerned, 1848 was the most widespread of the classic revolutions. The revolutionary events of the years after 1789 were primarily a French affair. Admittedly, there were independent echoes of the storming of the Bastille or the proclamation of the republic in many European countries, but autonomous revolutionary movements were found in just a few countries. Outside of France, they existed in Great Britain, particularly in Ireland, although in England and Scotland as well, and in the Polish Commonwealth, in the midst of its final division among the Great Powers of Eastern Europe. The great impact of the French Revolution of 1789 occurred in continental Europe through military action, and the revolutionary movement spread to Switzerland the Low Countries, the German and Italian states, and the Habsburg monarchy, primarily via the victorious French armies. Although possessing modest indigenous roots in those countries, it remained largely a foreign imposition, and was generally understood as such.

This is very much in contrast to the events of 1848, where revolution spread from one country to the next by force of example, not by force of arms. As a result, in most of continental Europe political participation was far more widespread in the revolutions of the middle of the nineteenth century than in the last decade of the eighteenth. The extent and readership of political newspapers, the membership in political clubs, the electoral turnout, the creation of professional and occupational associations – all these were vastly greater in Europe outside of France in 1848–51 than in 1789–99.

One has to wonder about France itself. In 1793–94, the government organized thousands of Jacobin clubs in France, but these were state-sponsored and state-created groups. By contrast, the political clubs of 1848 were independent creations of civil society. The many and active Parisian political clubs of the spring of 1848, the 350 local branches of Republican Solidarity in 1849, or the 700 secret societies of 1850–51 need not fear comparison with the number of Jacobin clubs before their founding became official government policy. Turnout at most elections during the French Revolution of 1789 was in the range of 20–30 percent of eligible voters; the 84 percent turnout at the elections to the Constituent National Assembly in April 1848 was much higher and set a record for French politics that stood until 1928.

The twentieth-century revolutions of 1917–23 and 1989–91 involved political participation and political organization on a very large scale, dwarfing earlier efforts. Both twentieth-century revolutionary waves, though, were limited in the areas they affected. The first one involved primarily the defeated powers of the First World War, the Russian, German, and Austro-Hungarian Empires; revolutionary movements in the victorious or neutral powers were much more feeble; social and political conflicts were less dramatic and far less violent and ruthless. Admittedly, there were exceptions, such as the revolution and civil war in Ireland, leading to the creation of an independent Irish Free State and the partition of the island. The revolutions of 1989–91 were concentrated exclusively in the communist states of the eastern bloc; the inhabitants of the democratic and capitalist states of the western part of the continent were spectators, watching the revolutions on TV, but showing no interest in emulating them in their own countries.

By contrast, the 1848 revolutions spread throughout Europe in states with very different forms of government. If the primary thrust of the revolutions was against absolutist regimes, and smaller constitutional monarchies, such as the Low Countries, the Scandinavian lands, and the states of the Iberian Peninsula, were less affected, the crucial event for the outbreak of revolution was the overthrow of the French July Monarchy, the very model of a constitutional-monarchist regime. If we count the Swiss Civil War of 1847 as part of the revolutionary events of the mid-nineteenth century, then they reached the one major republic existing in Europe.

Seen from a European perspective, the 1848 revolutions were the most widespread; in a global view, they appear as the most Eurocentric, the ones that made the least impression on the rest of the world. The French Revolution of 1789 had a truly global impact. A few examples would include the invasion of Egypt by Napoleon's troops, that changed the nature of relations between the European and Islamic worlds, the revolution in Haiti, in which former slaves created their own republic, or the controversies and struggles in the first years of the United States, where nascent political parties were, in part, aligned between friends and enemies of the French Revolution. The Russian Revolution of 1917 can count its offshoots in China, Vietnam, or Cuba; the communist movement emerging from that revolution had an enormous effect on the world for much of the twentieth century. Ramifications of the 1989 revolutions reached as far as Johannesburg and the results of the collapse of the Soviet Union, following on the revolutions against communism in east-central Europe, leaving the United States as the most powerful country in the world, continue to reverberate on a global scale.

No such global changes can be attributed to the 1848 revolutions. The provisional government of the French Republic did abolish slavery in France's West Indian colonies of Guadeloupe and Martinique. Public opinion in the United States was strongly supportive of the revolutionary movement, and US foreign policy openly endorsed it, but US influence on Europe counted for little in the middle of the nineteenth century. Unlike the influence of the French Revolution of 1789 on the political struggle between Federalists and Democratic-Republicans during the 1790s, the 1848 revolution was not a partisan or hotly debated issue in American politics. It is true that a number of the political refugees from the 1848 revolutions became second-rank actors in American political affairs, particularly in the struggle against slavery, leading up to the Civil War, but these rather modest consequences of the 1848 revolutions outside of Europe seem much less significant when compared with the much broader ones emanating from the events of 1789, 1917, or 1989.

Probably the primary reason for these relatively slight global effects of the 1848 revolutions was that they occurred at a low point in European political involvement with the rest of the world, after the end of the early modern colonial empires in the age of the French Revolution and before the onset of the late-nineteenth-century "new imperialism." Much of the global impetus of previous and successive waves of revolution in Europe was transmitted via colonial empires, movements against these colonial empires, and relations between European countries and their former colonial possessions. In 1848, there was only one significant colonial empire in existence, the British, and Great Britain was little affected by the revolutions of that year.

Comparative successes and failures of the 1848 revolutions

Historians' comparisons between the 1848 revolutions and other major uprisings of modern European history have usually been implicit in nature, contained in questions of relative success or failure. They center around the questions of why the initial victories of the 1848 revolution were so short lived, why the revolutionaries were so unsuccessful in creating a new regime, and why the authorities chased from office in the spring of 1848 returned to power within a year or two.

To pose these questions is, implicitly, to raise a comparison, to ask why the 1848 revolutions had a different outcome from those of 1789 or 1917, when the overthrown authorities did not return to office and long-lasting new regimes were created. Although we are still not that far away from 1989, it does seem clear that the communist regimes of eastern Europe overthrown then, and in 1990 and 1991, will not be revived as the pre-1848 governments were. The usual answer to the questions offered by historians is that the 1848 revolutions were not successful because the 1848 revolutionaries were not revolutionary enough. They lacked the energy and drive, the willingness to take drastic and ruthless measures, demonstrated by their Jacobin predecessors and Bolshevik successors. Sometimes this is attributed to personal failures of the revolutionary leaders, who appear as blowhards and big mouths, able to talk a good revolution but frightened by the daring and bloodshed required for effective action.

A more sophisticated version of this argument, ultimately going back to Karl Marx, although widely adopted by non-Marxists as well, attributes the failings of the 1848 revolutionaries to specific social and economic developments. In 1789 and the early 1790s, so the argument goes, revolutionaries from the middle class could uninhibitedly mobilize popular support for an assault on the absolutist regime and on feudal and seigneurial institutions, the common people not following any conscious political goals of their own. In 1848, the development of an organized working class and socialist movement made this impossible: the middle-class revolutionaries were too scared of what the masses might do to engage in this sort of popular mobilization. Instead, their revolutionary activities were half-hearted, characterized by a search for compromise with the pre-1848 authorities. But the labor movement, this argument continues, was still too weak to seize power on its own accord; that would have to wait for the twentieth century. 1848, in this sense, was the revolution that fell between two stools – the bourgeois of 1789 and the proletarian of 1917.

A closer look at the revolutions, however, suggests that differences in the situations of 1789 and 1848 are nowhere near so great as the different outcomes they are supposed to explain. The most important point to note is that in both revolutions there were moderate, compromise seeking, and radical, intransigent revolutionaries; both 1789 and 1848 had their con-stitutional monarchists and democratic republicans. While it may be true that at the outset of the revolution, the constitutional monarchists of the French Revolution of 1789 – men such as Lafayette, Mirabeau, Barnave, or the members of the moderate political club, the Feuillants – showed more verve and energy than their counterparts sixty years later, they were still no Jacobin intransigents. By 1790–91, they were quite willing to compromise with the pre-revolutionary authorities by creating a strong constitutional monarchy, with the king as chief executive, commander-in-chief of the armed forces, possessing a veto over decisions of the legislature. They planned to grant the nobility compensation for their abolished seigneurial privileges, and had no hesitations about introducing property requirements for voting or about using the National Guard to protect property and suppress popular disorders. Nor were they reluctant to take measures against emerging radicals and republicans. In short, they were guilty of all the compromises and half measures that historians have regarded as the reason for the failure of the 1848 revolutions.

Conversely, in 1848–49, there was no lack of daring and resolve – whether demonstrated in the initial barricade fighting, in the later and more brutal battles in Paris or Vienna, or in the revolutionary regimes emerging in the first half of 1849. Kossuth and Garibaldi need not take a back seat to Robespierre and Marat. The usual explanation thus turns into yet another question: why were the more determined revolutionaries able to seize power in the early 1790s, while their counterparts in 1848 could only do so in peripheral areas of Europe?

The growth of industrialization and the rise of the working class pro-vide the least of the answers to this question. In mid-nineteenth-century southern and eastern Europe, there was no industrialization or factory labor force. Even in the economically more developed central and west-ern portions of the continent, where the beginnings of both these could be observed the political activists of 1848 and the activists in the early labor movement as well, were largely craftsmen – masters, journeymen, and outworkers – very much the same people who made up the sans culottes of Paris during the reign of terror. The role of the labor movement itself in the radical politics of 1848 has been exaggerated in retrospect; class struggle and class consciousness as they would be understood in the late nineteenth and twentieth centuries were far from being the keys to the political left.

If we ask why 1848 was not 1789, the answer must be that 1848 was not 1789 precisely because it was sixty years later; politically conscious Europeans had had six decades to mull over the French Revolution, consider its consequences, recoil from it, attempt to imitate it, or try to improve on it. In 1789, there was just one Great Power encompassed by the revolution, just one country where revolutionary nationalism came to the fore. The war begun in 1792 between revolutionary France and counter-revolutionary European powers radicalized the revolution and brought the most extreme elements to power. By 1848, the politics of nationalism, developed in conscious or unconscious imitation of the original of sixty years previously, had spread across Europe. Particularly in the Austrian Empire, but more generally throughout Europe in 1848, these revolutionary nationalisms clashed with each other, weakening the revolution rather than radicalizing it, a situation cleverly exploited by the Habsburgs' servants to bring the revolutionary movement to an end.

More generally, all political elements in 1848 had learned the lessons of 1789. Conservatives were acutely aware of the danger of being too passive, of allowing revolutionaries to dominate events, above all of losing control of the armed forces. No monarch was willing to repeat the fate of Louis XVI. All of them were unwilling to depend exclusively on the constitutional monarchist ministers forced on them by the initial revolutionary events and gathered about them a reliable camarilla of conservative advisors skeptical of any concessions, who insisted, successfully, that the monarch rally and organize supporters in the provinces and the capital city, and, in related fashion, ensure the loyalty of his troops and use them for counter-revolutionary action at the appropriate moment. Louis XVI received similar advice, only it took him two years to accede to it; his attempt in 1791 to flee a capital city dominated by the radicals for the safety of loyalist troops in the provinces was a dismal fiasco. Emperor Ferdinand of Austria – more precisely, the courtiers who determined the mentally retarded monarch's actions for him – fled from the Viennese radicals not once, but twice, the first time just two months after the beginning of the revolution. After both flights, safe in the provinces, the royal court, in part making use of differences between competing nationalist movements, was able to command loyal troops to destroy revolutionary movements within the empire. Much the same was the case with Ferdinand's Prussian counterpart, Friedrich Wilhelm IV, who preferred to reside during the turbulent phase of the 1848 revolution in the garrison city of Potsdam, surrounded by loyal troops and a conservative camarilla, rather than in the royal capital of Berlin, where the constitutional government ministers did their work.

Similar memories plagued the moderates of 1848, the constitutional monarchists, and the French pure republicans. They noted all too well how militant measures taken by their predecessors after 1789 had paved the way for the Jacobins to come to power. Consequently, they were reluctant to repeat them, going slower on purging the officer corps or the civil service of adherents of the overthrown regimes, seeking compromises with monarchical (or, in France, Louis-Napoleon's potentially monarchical) authority. Above all, they refused the temptation of starting a great European war of the same sort that had brought the French radicals to power in 1792, although the war in northern Italy offered General Cavaignac that opportunity in the summer of 1848 and the September crisis of 1848 provided German constitutional monarchists with a similar chance. But by refusing to take these drastic steps, the constitutional monarchists undermined their own position, and they were gradually forced to cede power back to representatives of the pre-revolutionary regimes. It was only in the smaller states of Europe, in Hungary under Kossuth, and, to a lesser extent, in Piedmont-Savoy, that the moderates were willing to launch a nationalist war in alliance with the radicals, and these small powers lacked the population, and economic and military strength to upset all of Europe with a revolutionary war – although, for a while, the Hungarians came close.

Finally, the mid-nineteenth-century radicals had learned the lessons of the French Revolution of 1789 too well for their own good. The success of the Jacobins in mobilizing the masses of the capital city to overthrow or intimidate moderate governments and parliaments convinced 1848 leftists that they could do the same. Only in 1848, the moderates and conservatives also remembered what had happened fifty-five years earlier, and rather than repeating the Jacobins' revolutionary triumphs, radicals ended up with bloody disasters in the streets of Paris, Frankfurt, and Vienna. The development of a socialist movement in France, and to a much lesser extent in Germany, was a new element in 1848, one very much not present in 1789–95, but the chief political role of the socialists was to be a bogeyman, an additional element compelling conservatives and moderates to work together against the radicals.

Socialists had learned another lesson from the French Revolution, one different from other 1848 radicals, but no less damaging to the left. At least initially, many of the socialists of 1848 rejected political action as useless for working people, placing their hopes in the creation of trade associations and cooperatives. The lack of coordination between the Parisian labor movement and the political clubs stemming from this attitude greatly weakened leftists in the capital city during the spring of 1848 and prepared for the disaster of the June Days.

These considerations suggest a more basic point about social science theories of revolution. Many of these, whether deriving from some variant of Marxism or from anti-Marxist modernization theories, understand revolutions as occurring in a given set of social circumstances, independent of time and place. Such general theories of revolution have always had a hard time explaining the outcome of 1848, and this difficulty reveals their ahistorical character, their unwillingness to consider the role of memory and experience in human events. What made 1848 different from 1789 was above all that in 1848 people remembered what had happened in 1789 and acted on those memories, thus creating a different outcome.

By far the more interesting story of the left in 1848 is the way that leftists gradually learned to use the slogans and symbols of the radical phase of the original French Revolution while giving them a different social and political content, striving to organize popular support, in the provinces and among the peasants, trying to bring together social grievances with political solutions. Such efforts involved some fundamental rethinking for both the socialists and the Jacobins among the mid-nineteenth-century leftists, bringing them together, at least temporarily, in a common enterprise. These efforts were behind the second wave of revolution in the spring of 1849. Like the nationalist wars of Hungary and Piedmont-Savoy, this second revolution could not gain control of the government of any Great Power, so was ultimately suppressed by superior military force.

In the end, the mid-century revolutions were defeated by soldiers loyal to the monarchical authority of the tsar, the Austrian emperor, the king of Prussia, the king of the Two Sicilies, and the soon to be emperor Louis-Napoleon Bonaparte. Ties of religious and dynastic loyalty, of civilian and military authority, and of reliance on the state for prosperity had proven stronger than the divided and mutually quarreling forces of nationalism, social and economic discontent, and of aspiration towards the realization of popular sovereignty and civic freedom. This outcome also explains the great difference between 1848 and the successor wave of revolutions, beginning in Russia in 1917 and reverberating around Europe for the next six years.

In these twentieth-century revolutions, the lines of military and bureaucratic authority, as well as the ties of dynastic and religious loyalty, had been shattered by the First World War, allowing revolutionary forces to gain the upper hand, in spite of determined and organized resistance from conservative and moderate forces. Even then, among the states undermined by total war, it was only in the future Soviet Union that the revolutionaries were able to triumph unambiguously, while scoring only moderate successes in Germany and Austria, and being badly defeated by vehement counter-revolution in Hungary and Italy. Still, these events of 1917–23 suggest one way that 1848 formed a turning point for revolution in European history.

Following 1789, revolution had led to war. It was one of the lessons people had learned from the French Revolution, and expectations of, fears about, and hopes for a great European war were a constant undertone to the events of 1848–49. The outcome of the revolution suggested a new connection: an army remaining loyal to its commanders could defeat any revolutionary movement. Revolutions could succeed – or even break out – only when the repressive force of the army had been shattered by military defeat. Henceforth, it was not revolution that would lead to war, but defeat in war that would lead to revolution: in France in 1870, in many European countries following the First, and in some ways following the Second World War, or in Portugal in 1974.

We can pose here, although certainly not answer, the question of whether the eastern European revolutions of 1989 were a continuation of or a break with this post-1850 state of affairs. It could be argued that these revolutions emerged from what was, in effect, a defeat in the Superpower warfare of the late twentieth century, an economic collapse of the eastern bloc brought on by the attempts of the Soviet Union and its subordinate states to match the massive arms buildup of the United States and its NATO allies. Conversely, it could also be argued that the arms spending was not the primary reason for the collapse of the Soviet bloc economies, and that the causes of the loss of the authority and legitimacy of the communist governments lay elsewhere: in the very claims of the communist states to control all elements of the economy and society, and the rise of independent efforts to counteract this claim, in the all too open contrast between an affluent western Europe and North America, and an eastern bloc conspicuously lacking in consumer goods, or a host of other social and economic developments, some characteristic of the late twentieth century generally, others typical of the communist countries themselves.

What can be said here is that the quick succession of reform movements and revolutions in the summer and fall of 1989, moving from Hungary and Poland to East Germany, and from there to Czechoslovakia, Romania, and Bulgaria, caused political scientists, sociologists, and even journalists to dust off their history books and read up on the revolutions of 1848.

The way that the outbreak of revolution in one country encouraged it in the next seemed strikingly similar to what had happened 140 years previously. Yet it is interesting to note that in an age of total electronic communication the revolutionary wave took some six months to cross most of eastern Europe, while at the middle of the nineteenth century, on a continent with a very sketchy rail net, and a partially constructed telegraph system, the upheavals of the spring of 1848 occurred in about one-third the time they would require in 1989.

Aspirations and accomplishments of the 1848 revolutions

If the new regimes created in 1848 had vanished by 1851, the same cannot be said of many of the changes brought about during the revolution. Some of these changes were permanent, unaffected even by the return to power of counter-revolutionary forces. Others were latent, suppressed in 1849, and only gradually re-emerging over the following twenty years.

By far the most significant and never altered consequence of the revolution was the abolition of serfdom and other seigneurial institutions. These changes, won by rural uprising and decision of the revolutionary parliaments, were nowhere reversed, even by the most reactionary of the post-revolutionary governments. The peasants of central and eastern Europe did have to pay their former lords some compensation, but here as well, even the reactionary statesmen of the 1850s endeavored, via various state-sponsored cheap loan schemes, to alleviate this burden. Where serfdom persisted in Europe after the mid-century revolution, it was in those countries that had not experienced the revolutionary events, the most significant example being the Tsarist Empire.

A second main consequence of the revolution was the introduction of constitutional government in pre-1848 absolutist monarchies. Unlike the abolition of serfdom, this accomplishment did not always survive the end of the revolution. While the kingdoms of Prussia and Piedmont-Savoy retained their constitutional form of government, even in the reactionary 1850s, the Two Sicilies, the Papal States, and, most importantly, the Austrian Empire repealed all such accomplishments of the revolution and reverted to absolutist rule.

In the Austrian case, the central government was even more absolutist than it had been before the revolution, since the pre-1848 feudal legislatures, the Diets, were not revived, leaving no institutions to check the power of the emperor and his civilian and military officials in Vienna. This state of affairs was not of long duration. The military setbacks of the 1860s forced the Austrian government to return to constitutional rule. By the end of that decade, some form of constitutional regime existed in virtually every European country, the one exception being once again, the Tsarist Empire.

The 1848 revolutions also had an agenda-setting function, raising issues and posing demands that were not fulfilled at the time, but would determine the direction of future developments. Nowhere was this more apparent than in the realm of nationalism. Demands for national self-determination first appeared on a European-wide scale in 1848, and the revolution saw the first attempts at Italian and German national unification, as well as the first nationalist threats against the multi-national Austrian Empire. These questions would come to the fore again in the 1860s, although sometimes in ways not envisaged in 1848.

German national unity would be achieved, some two decades after the Frankfurt parliamentarians attempted it, through the actions of Prussia's prime minister, Otto von Bismarck. In a celebrated phrase, Bismarck compared himself to the constitutional monarchists of 1848, noting that they had tried to have their way with speeches and parliamentary resolutions, but he would carry out his policy with force and violence, by means of "blood and iron." It is just as useful, though, to compare his policies with those of his predecessor Count Brandenburg. Bismarck took up again the latter's policy, first tried out in the aftermath of the 1848 revolution, of co-opting the German nationalist movement by creating a Prussian-dominated, "little German" national state. While Brandenburg and the Prussian statesmen of 1849–50 wished to use purely diplomatic means and backed down at the threat of force, Bismarck showed no such hesitations. To obtain his goals, he led Prussia into three separate wars, with Denmark in 1864, with Austria in 1866, and with France in 1870, each time showing great diplomatic skill in keeping the conflicts isolated and avoiding the great European war that the constitutional monarchists in 1848 were afraid to provoke.

The end result, the German Empire of 1870–71, looked a lot like the united German state proposed in the constitution written by the Frankfurt National Assembly in 1849: a "little Germany," excluding the Germans of the Austrian Empire, a constitutional regime with a democratically elected parliament and the king of Prussia, taking the title of emperor, as chief executive. There was a crucial difference, though. The constitutional monarchists of 1848 had envisaged a cooperation between the nationalist movement and the major German monarchs, but with the nationalists, and the Frankfurt parliamentarians representing them, as the senior partners. Bismarck, following more successfully in Count Brandenburg's footsteps, had reversed the terms of cooperation, giving the Prussian monarchy the leading role, a result embodied in the empire's constitution that, in comparison to the version proposed in

1849, greatly strengthened the monarchical chief executive and weakened substantially the power of parliament.

This comparison, however, hides the way another important issue of 1848–49 was resolved in 1870–71. During the mid-century revolution, pro-Prussian constitutional monarchists represented a minority among German nationalists. They were noticeably outnumbered by the democrats, with their pronounced leanings towards republicanism, and their strong hostility towards the Prussian monarchy, and by Catholics and south Germans, suspicious of Prussia, and pro-Austrian, all of whom were cool or downright hostile towards a monarchical little German national state of the kind that Bismarck brought into existence. If the founding of the German Empire in 1870/71 subordinated the little German constitutional monarchists to the Prussian monarchy, it also brought a victory for their version of nationalism, a victory they were unable to achieve on their own during the 1848 revolution.

Italian national unification in the 1860s, with the creation of a constitutional-monarchist national state around the Kingdom of Piedmont-Savoy, followed a similar path, with a similar relation to the 1848 revolution as did German national unification at the same time. The opening move, in 1859, was the same as ten years previously, a military assault of the Piedmontese kingdom on the Austrian provinces in northern Italy. However, King Vittorio Emmanuele and his prime minister Emilio di Cavour, a constitutional monarchist veteran of politics in 1848, renounced the idea of Italy going it alone, that Vittorio Emmanuele's unfortunate father, Carlo Alberto, had tried during the revolution. In their war, they accepted the help of France, the assistance of Louis-Napoleon's authoritarian empire seeming (and being) far less dangerous to them than potential aid from the new republican regime had been for Vittorio Emmanuele in 1848. With the assistance of a Great Power, the Piedmontese were victorious in 1859, forcing the Austrians to cede the province of Lombardy.

Here, the Italian and German story diverges somewhat, for the subsequent – and decisive – events showed a more revolutionary character. Uprisings in the small duchies of central Italy, overthrew the governments there and brought them into the Piedmontese kingdom. The greatest obstacle to national unity, though, lay in the south in the arch-conservative governments of the Papal States and the Kingdom of the Two Sicilies. At this point, Giuseppe Garibaldi, the military hero of the Roman Republic of 1849, launched his celebrated expedition to the island of Sicily. The idea of an incursion by an armed band of revolutionaries, to spark an uprising and bring on a revolution, had been a mainstay of Italian radicalism since the 1830s; when tried, such excursions had always ended in disaster.

This one did not. Garibaldi and his one thousand red-shirts, found themselves in the midst of a massive peasant uprising in Sicily and southern Italy. As was the case in 1848, some of the southern peasants rose up against the large landowners, asserting radical and revolutionary slogans, while others chanted conservative and monarchist ones, but this made little difference. The uprisings themselves destroyed governmental authority, facilitated the march of Garibaldi's irregulars, and allowed Piedmontese forces to annex most of the two southern kingdoms. By 1861, just small parts of the peninsula remained outside the nation-state, and they would be incorporated over the following decade.

Yet if more radical forces had played a role besides the constitutional monarchists, and insurrections had complemented military campaigns in the creation of Italian national unity, the final result in 1871 was a constitutional Kingdom of Italy with a powerful executive from the Piedmontese royal family, and a legislature elected by a very stiff property franchise, excluding over 90 percent of adult males. As in Germany, the creation of Italian national unity was the culmination of hopes first raised in 1848, the successful completion of initiatives first proposed then. What was fulfilled in the 1860s, though, were the constitutional-monarchist versions of the aspirations of 1848, while the democratic ones were frustrated.

The national unifications of the 1860s also had a profound effect on the Austrian Empire. One major reason that the multi-national empire had survived the first wave of nationalist movements in 1848, was that no Great Power supported militarily any of the nationalist challenges to imperial authority. In 1859, Italian nationalism had acquired French military support; in 1866, little German nationalism had the assistance of Prussian soldiers. Habsburg forces, hampered in their actions by the still unresolved financial difficulties of the monarchy, were no match for these. The loss of the empire's possessions in northern Italy and of its influence in Germany once again raised the specter of its dissolution into smaller nation-states.

The survival of the empire was due to the Compromise of 1867, that turned the Austrian Empire into the Austro-Hungarian Empire, dividing the monarchy into Austrian and Hungarian realms, each with its own constitution, council of ministers, and legislature. Common to both realms were the armed forces and foreign policy, and the monarchical chief executive remained the same person, although Franz Joseph reigned in Austria as emperor and in Hungary as king, bearer of the Crown of St. Stephen. It was a solution akin to what Hungarian constitutional monarchists had envisaged in 1848, but had been unable to achieve, since neither indigenous radicals nor the imperial court were willing to let them have it.

Looking more broadly at the Compromise of 1867, we might say that it corresponded to the wishes of both the Hungarian and the German constitutional monarchists of 1848, each dominating the respective halves of the empire. Polish constitutional monarchists, who soon acquired an influential position within the province of Galicia (in the Austrian half of the empire) also had reason to be content with this arrangement. For the other nationalities, Romanians, Croats, Czechs, Serbs, Slovenes, Slovaks, and Ukrainians – ironically, precisely those nationalist movements that had been so loyal to imperial authority in 1848 – the Compromise offered little or nothing. Much of the future history of the empire would be the efforts of these nationalist groups to obtain self-determination, creating a national conflict that would ultimately lead to the empire's destruction and its replacement by nation-states whose boundaries and competing national claims had still not been fully resolved, even at the end of the twentieth century, as was above all apparent in the civil wars in the former Yugoslavia.

To sum up this section, we might say that the 1860s saw the victory of the constitutional monarchism of the revolution of 1848 and the constitutional monarchist version of the nationalism of the mid-century revolution. To a great extent, though, this victory for nationalism and constitutional monarchism, was not a result of the actions of constitutional monarchists or nationalists themselves, but of the armed forces of the Great Powers. These succeeded where the revolutionary movements and the parliaments of 1848 had failed. As a result of this, the aspirations towards political democracy, that strongly accompanied the nationalism of 1848, were more muted in the nationalist victories of the 1860s.

The 1848 revolutions as political mass movement

Another way to see the place of the mid-nineteenth-century revolutions in European history is to turn away from their outcome and concentrate on the revolutionary experience. As repeatedly asserted throughout this book, such an approach would involve considering the 1848 revolutions as political mass movements. We might ask what was unique about these movements, how they affected future structures of political life, how they related to past revolutionary movements, and how these movements were remembered and commemorated.

More than anything else, the mid-century revolutions were an enormous outpouring of popular political participation, organized and disorganized, violent and peaceful, encompassing, admittedly to a different extent, all social classes, members of all religious confessions, and inhabitants of most countries on the European continent. In this respect, the 1848 revolution stands alone in its century. Political participation on the European continent reached a level never approached since 1800 – and that would not be seen again for a good fifty years. Taking the continent as a whole, the franchise would not be as democratic, clubs and organizations as widespread, demonstrations as common or as vigorous, until the beginning of the twentieth century. The 1848 revolutions were a giant leap forward over all the improvements in communication and transportation of the following decades, improvements commonly understood as facilitating political participation and organization.

It would seem reasonable to assert that such a unique, remarkable event would have a powerful resonance and would decisively shape future developments. Another, equally plausible assertion, would point to the exceptional, almost freakish character of the 1848 revolutions, and for that reason see their significance for the future as limited. Historians have adopted both interpretations and there is evidence to support both of them.

The argument for the long-term effect of the 1848 revolution is most cogent and convincing when applied to France. Both historians and political scientists have long noted that the elections to the Legislative Assembly of May 1849 strongly foretold future political divisions: areas making up the "red France" of 1849 would continue to support the left well into the twentieth century, their inhabitants moving from the "democ-socs" of the mid-century revolution, to the Radicals and Socialists of the later nineteenth and early twentieth centuries and the Communists of the middle decades of the twentieth. Those regions supporting the party of order in the May 1849 elections would retain their monarchist loyalties through much of the nineteenth century, gradually moving on to the moderate and conservative republican groupings of twentieth-century French politics. Such long-term lines of political loyalty point towards the powerfully shaping effect of the 1848 revolution, particularly its later phase, subsequent to the Parisian June Days, characterized by political realignment and the bringing of organized political life to the small towns and villages of provincial France. As Maurice Agulhon, the dean of French historians of the 1848 revolution has trenchantly put it, the mid-century events were the "apprenticeship of the republic," when much of the political world of modern France came into existence.

A plausible argument could be made for a similar shaping effect of the 1848 revolution on political culture in Italy. Nationwide elections of the sort held in France during the mid-century revolution never came to pass on the Italian peninsula, so comparably definitive conclusions cannot be drawn. Still, it is interesting to note that the strongholds of radical political clubs and the centers of the second wave of revolutionary events– Tuscany, as well as the Bolognese and other northern provinces of the Papal States – would reappear in the late nineteenth century as centers of the socialist movement, and, after 1945, as the heart of the "red belt," the center of electoral and organizational strength of the Italian Communist Party. These observations underline, once again, the significance of the later phase of the 1848 revolution.

Nationwide elections comparable to those in France were held in Germany during the 1848 revolution, namely the May 1848 voting for deputies to the Frankfurt National Assembly. The results of these elections, the evidence from the formation of political clubs and from further elections held in various states during the rest of the revolution, suggest a quite different relationship of the mid-century events to future political life, namely a sharp discontinuity. The political map of late nineteenth- and twentieth-century Germany was quite different from that of 1848. A few elements of continuity did exist. The kingdom of Saxony had been a strongly radical area in 1848 and its inhabitants would continue to favor the left through the early decades of the twentieth century. Overall, though, the main strongholds of the left during the mid-century revolution were in central and southwestern Germany; by 1900, these strongholds were mostly in the north, areas that in 1848 had been at best politically moderate and often quite conservative.

It is difficult to draw a similar comparison for the Habsburg monarchy, given the rudimentary character of political life there and the complications introduced into the left–right political spectrum by the different national groups. To the extent that it is possible, it would seem that more of a German than a French or Italian pattern prevailed there. One aspect of political life in the multi-national empire was set by the 1848 revolution, the nationalities conflict. The different national groups that emerged during the revolution, as well as the demands for self-determination they raised, and the intolerance they showed for other nationalities, would remain the same throughout the further history of the monarchy and would bedevil its successor states after 1918, down to the present day.

A number of different reasons could be offered for these differing pictures, but probably the most important would relate to the relationship between left-wing politics and the labor movement. In the early phases of the 1848 revolution, organized labor and the political left were frequently disconnected; in the later phases of increasing polarization and organization the labor movement was incorporated into the left, but just as one part of it – and far from the most important part. This picture was broadly true throughout Europe, but in the decades after 1850, the relationship between the labor movement and the political left began to diverge.

In central Europe, leftist politics came increasingly to be identified with the organized urban working class; other social groups and organized interests fell away from the left, changing the social and regional profile of politics from what they had been in the middle of the nineteenth century. In the Mediterranean countries, on the other hand, while organized labor became steadily more important for the left, other social groups, particularly small farmers and small property owners, continued to play a role in radical politics, thus preserving the arrangements first created at the end of 1848 and in 1849.

Looking fifty or sixty years into the future from 1848, one sees an ambivalent relationship; looking back sixty years, the relationship is noticeably more straightforward. The revolutions of the mid-nineteenth century were clear successors to the French Revolution of 1789: social and economic preconditions to both revolutions were distinctly similar; the main political groupings of 1848 all ultimately stemmed from analogous groups first created between 1789 and 1793. We might take this comparison a step further and suggest that the 1848 revolutions brought the experiences of 1789 to a much wider group of Europeans.

These reflections all suggest what is possibly the single best way to understand the revolutions of the mid-nineteenth century. They were a greatly expanded, partially revised, and, with "success" narrowly defined as long-term change of regime, ultimately unsuccessful version of the French Revolution of 1789. Their outbreak and ultimate suppression both closed the cycle of revolution begun in 1789 and opened the way towards a different version of politics on the European continent.

Remembering and commemorating 1848

In this post-1848 world, much of the impact of the revolution lay in its commemoration. For at least one hundred years after 1848, the most energetic voices raised in memory of the revolution came from the labor movement. By the 1870s, for instance, German socialists would, on 18 March, the anniversary of the barricade fighting in 1848 Berlin, march to the Friedrichshain cemetery where the insurgents who died on the barricades were buried. On the twenty-fifth anniversary in 1873, over 20,000 demonstrators are said to have participated and the demonstrations continued even in the years when the German socialist party had been outlawed. Socialists in France, Italy, and in many parts of the Austro-Hungarian Empire were also aggressive in cultivating the memory of the revolutionary struggles of 1848. It is, at least in part, this embrace of the heritage of the mid-nineteenth century revolution by late nineteenth- and twentieth-century socialists and communists that has contributed to historians' tendencies to see the 1848 revolution primarily in terms of the labor movement.

By contrast, supporters of other political tendencies were more ambivalent in their relationship to the 1848 revolution. In an 1898 debate in the German parliament on the occasion of the fiftieth anniversary of 1848, conservatives and liberal nationalists denounced the revolutionaries of that year as "rabble" and praised Otto von Bismarck as Germany's nationalist hero. Italian nationalist liberals of the 1890s had a more positive attitude toward 1848, although their praise went to Piedmont's Carlo Alberto, and they had little good to say about Mazzini, Garibaldi, or the mass movements of the 1848 Italian revolution. Probably, nationalists in parts of the Austro-Hungarian Empire had the most favorable take on the 1848 revolution especially in Hungary, where the 1848 revolutionary leader Lajos Kossuth had received an enormous hero's funeral in 1894, after a life spent in exile. When Hungary became an independent country after the collapse of the Austro-Hungarian Empire at the end of the First World War, 15 March, the anniversary of the proclamation of an independent Hungarian government in 1848, was made into a national holiday – although only in 1928, the eightieth anniversary of the revolution, but also ten years after the creation of an independent Hungary. The generally conservative governments of interwar Hungary, while certainly supportive of nationalism, were rather ambivalent about many aspects of the heritage of 1848.

There were non-socialists, generally on the left side of the political spectrum, who had a more positive attitude toward the 1848 revolution, members of the French Radical Party, for instance, who sponsored the first serious historical scholarship on 1848 at the beginning of the twentieth century. The Weimar Republic, the attempt at a democratic government in Germany between the end of the First World War and the Nazi seizure of power in 1933, officially adopted a strongly pro-1848 stance. The black-red-gold tricolor of the revolution became the national flag, and the government celebrated the eightieth anniversary of the revolution in 1928 with considerable pomp, praising in particular the democratically elected deputies of the Frankfurt National Assembly, who had tried to create a united German nation-state in a constitutional, legal, and largely peaceful way. It is perhaps no surprise that a democratic and republican government emerging from the disaster of a lost total war, waged by an authoritarian empire, would take this stance. However, this attempt to make the 1848 revolution into a founding event of a democratic German republic only encouraged the republic's enemies to reject its memory.

The 1848 revolution has enjoyed two more phases of broader commemoration, at its centenary in 1948, and its sesquicentenary in 1998.

The first of these, falling in the aftermath of the Second World War, had perhaps two major characteristics. One was the widespread acceptance and endorsement of the 1848 revolutions. There were various commemorations throughout Europe, on both sides of the rapidly forming border between the western nations and the eastern bloc, with communists and anti-communists each claiming to be the true heirs to the events of the mid-nineteenth century. The nationalist element of the revolution was strongly emphasized in a Germany on the brink of division, and in eastern European countries whose communist leaders increasingly emphasized their nationalist credentials to hide their close cooperation with and increasing subordination to the Soviet Union. The one major exception to this general barrage of praise came from the Italian Christian Democrats, the political party endorsed by the Catholic Church, which condemned the revolutionaries who had driven Pope Pius IX out of Rome.

There was one somewhat newer feature of the 1948 commemorations, the praise of 1848 as a "European" event, interpreting it as the ancestor to the European unity movement emerging from the results of the Second World War. This connection of 1848 with a united Europe was very typical of the sesquicentenary commemorations, which thoroughly rejected any nationalist themes and emphasized the ways that the mid-nineteenth-century revolutions had crossed national boundaries, and how its leaders had been inspired by pan-European ideals. This version of events does require a rather selective view of nationalism at the middle of the nineteenth century. Ironically, these commemorations which rejected nationalism were by far the most common and frequent in Germany and Hungary, two of the nations for whom the 1848 revolutions were very important for nationalist political aspirations.

Rather as in 1948, fifty years later everybody was in favor of 1848. The strongly socialist tone so common in previous commemorations was very muted in 1998, a consequence of the end of communist rule in Europe and the general decline of the labor movement in most advanced industrial societies. Perhaps somewhat oddly, the events of 1989 did not get that much mention in 1998, although 15 March is once again a national holiday in post-communist Hungary. The celebration of the popular character of the revolution of 1848 as political mass movement, previously reserved for the workers, took on wider contours in 1998. The role of women was emphasized in many commemorations, both popular and scholarly, as was, more generally, the idea of the revolution as involving a surge of political participation across wide stretches of the population. Particularly in affluent, southwestern Germany, this sort of commemoration of the revolutionary experience took on a form that was both high tech and popular, with multi-media exhibitions, computer databases, electronic interactive displays, public festivals, outdoor theater, and even a comic book. At the end of the twentieth century, the 1848 revolutions were no longer controversial. They had been endorsed in a broad political consensus, remembered as an unpolitical spectacle, or were simply ignored, as was the case in Italy and Poland, where indifference and lack of commemoration were the characteristic responses to the revolution's one hundred fiftieth anniversary.

As should be clear from this brief sketch of commemorations of the 1848 revolutions, it is possible to remember them in very different ways, to emphasize different aspects of them, and to draw very different political conclusions from them. Of course, this observation is true of any major historical event. Especially now, at the beginning of the twenty-first century, when the questions posed by the 1848 revolutions have, in Europe at least, largely been resolved, the choice of themes to be used in understanding and portraying these revolutions seems largely subjective and a matter of individual preference.

If the reader will permit me to choose one aspect of the complex and tangled events of 1848–51 as exemplifying both their unique character and their relations to preceding and following forms of public life, it would be the democrats' campaign of agitation, realignment, and organization, starting in the summer and fall of 1848. Begun after the initial impetus of the revolution had faded, and counter-revolution had scored its first successes, this campaign both looked forwards towards new forms of organized public life that would be ever more central to future politics and was conducted with a rhetoric and symbolism closely connected to the Jacobinism of 1793. Unlike the original Jacobins, though, who saw their democratic and republican ideas as leading to a reign of virtue, a hard and sometimes inhumane regime of upright public morality, the mid-nineteenth-century radicals developed a political vision linking democracy and republicanism to the self-determination of and material improvement in the lives of embattled small producers, who faced an unfavorable market and a hostile state. To borrow a phrase from the politics of the twentieth century, we might call this radicalism of 1848 Jacobinism with a human face. Like the twentieth-century political movement from which I borrow this phrase, the "socialism with a human face," proclaimed in the Prague spring of 1968, it was a failed ideal, one that perhaps was just a political phantom with no real chance of success. Nonetheless, it was a distinct and interesting aspiration inspiring some of the mid-nineteenth-century revolutionaries, one still worth contemplating today.

Bibliography

CHAPTER ONE

Some useful works on agriculture and rural society in Europe during the first half of the nineteenth century include Roger Price, *The Modernization of Rural France* (New York, 1983); Ted Margadant, *French Peasants in Revolt: The Insurrection of 1851* (Princeton, 1979); Wilhelm Abel, *Agricultural Fluctuations in Europe from the Thirteenth to the Twentieth Centuries*, trans. Olive Ordish (New York, 1980); B. H. Slicher van Bath, *The Agrarian History of Western Europe A.D. 500–1850*, trans. Olive Ordish (New York, 1963); Hanna Schissler, "The Junkers: Notes on the Social and Historical Significance of the Agrarian Elite in Prussia," in Robert Moeller (ed.), *Peasants and Lords in Modern Germany* (Boston and London, 1986), 24–51, or Marta Petrusewicz, *Latifundium: Moral Economy and Material Life in a European Periphery*, trans. Judith C. Green (Ann Arbor, 1996). For the student with foreign language abilities, a few suggestions would be Carlo Pazzagli, *L'agricultura toscana nella prima metà dell'800* (Florence, 1973); Maurice Aymard, "Rendements et productivité agricole dans l'Italie moderne," *Annales Économies Sociétés Civilisations* 28 (1973): 492–97; František Lom, "Die Arbeitsproduktivität in der Geschichte der tschechoslowakischen Landwirtschaft," *Zeitschrift für Agrargeschichte und Agrarsoziologie* 19 (1971): 1–25. A fine study of the institution of serfdom and its end can be found in Jerome Blum, *The End of the Old Order in Rural Europe* (Princeton, 1978). The author's older work, *Noble Landowners and Agriculture in Austria, 1815–1848* (Baltimore, 1948) is also quite helpful.

On crafts, outworking, and the urban lower classes, the studies of William H. Sewell Jr. are particularly helpful. *Work and Revolution in France: The Language of Labor from the Old Regime to 1848* (Cambridge, 1980) is an excellent general introduction; *Structure and Mobility: The Men and Women of Marseilles 1820–1878* (Cambridge and New York, 1985); "Social Change and the Rise of Working Class Politics in Nineteenth-Century Marseilles," *Past and Present* 65 (November 1974): 75–109 are more detailed studies. Other works that might be recommended are Michael J. Neufeld, *The Skilled Metalworkers of Nuremberg* (New Brunswick and London, 1989); Peter Kriedte, Hans Medick, and Jürgen Schlumbohm, *Industrialization before Industrialization: Rural Industry in the Genesis of Capitalism*, trans. Beate Schempp (Cambridge, 1981). James H. Jackson Jr., *Migration and Urbanization in the Ruhr Valley 1821–1914* (Atlantic Highlands, NJ, 1997) contains a useful chapter on pre-1850 economy and society. Joan Scott, "A Statistical

Representation of Work: *La Statistique de l'industrie à Paris, 1847–1848*," in Joan Scott, *Gender and the Politics of History* (New York, 1988), 113–38, is an important piece on the place of women in the crafts. A few significant foreign-language works would include, for Germany, Friedrich Lenger, *Zwischen Kleinbürgertum und Proletariat* (Göttingen, 1986) and for Italy, Alain Dewerpe, *L'industrie au champs: essai sur la proto-industrialisation en Italie du nord (1800–1880)* (Rome, 1985) or Gian Mario Bravo, *Torino Operaia: Mondo del lavoro e idei socialie nell'età di Carlo Alberto* (Turin, 1968).

Nineteenth-century economic histories tend to focus on industrialization, which, for the European continent, really means the years after 1850. A few general works that pay particular attention to the first half of the century are Maurice Lévy-Leboyer, *The French Economy in the Nineteenth Century*, trans. Jesse Bryant and Virginie Pérotin (Cambridge and New York, 1990); the possibly over-optimistic David Good, *The Economic Rise of the Habsburg Empire 1750–1914* (Berkeley, Los Angeles, and London, 1984); Knut Borchardt, "Germany 1700–1914," in Carlo Cipolla (ed.), *The Fontana Economic History of Europe: The Emergence of Industrial Societies*, 2 vols. (Glasgow, 1973) 1: 76–157. Most of the works mentioned above contain general discussions of economic developments and social structure in the first half of the nineteenth century. Other possibilities include Catharina Lis, *Social Change and the Labouring Poor: Antwerp, 1779–1860* (New Haven and London, 1986). Marta Petrusewicz's book, *Latifundium*, noted above, dealing with a large estate in southern Italy, is very helpful for understanding social structure and economic development in the Mediterranean world. Three French-language books that deal with broader topics in an interesting way are Pierre Ayçoberry, *Cologne entre Napoléon et Bismarck* (Paris 1981), a convincing description of the social structure of a German city, André-Jean Tudesq, *Les grands notables en France (1800–1849)*, 2 vols. (Paris, 1964), a massive and classic study of the social elite of an entire country, and Jean-Louis Halpérin, *Avocats et notaires en Europe* (Paris, 1996), a helpful account of the legal professions.

Good studies of the state in action during the first half of the nineteenth century are John A. Davis, *Conflict and Control: Law and Order in Nineteenth-Century Italy* (Atlantic Highlands, 1988); Steven C. Hughes, *Crime, Disorder and the Risorgimento: The Politics of Policing in Bologna* (Cambridge and New York, 1994); Alf Lüdtke, *Police and State in Prussia, 1815–1850*, trans. Peter Burgess (Cambridge, 1989); Mary Lee Townsend, *Forbidden Laughter: Popular Humor and the Limits of Repression in Nineteenth Century Prussia* (Ann Arbor, 1992); and David Pinkney, *The Police State of Louis Napoleon III*, whose first chapter deals with conditions before 1848. Gunter E. Rothenberg, *The Military Border in Croatia, 1740–1881* (Chicago and London, 1966), is an introduction to some of the peculiar governmental institutions of the Austrian Empire. A general overview is Robert Goldstein, *Political Repression in Nineteenth Century Europe* (London, 1983).

On the place of religion in the society and politics of mid-nineteenth-century Europe, Edward Berenson, *Populist Religion and Left-Wing Politics in France, 1830–1852* (Princeton, 1984); Jonathan Sperber, *Popular Catholicism in Nineteenth Century Germany* (Princeton, 1984), Robert Bigler, *The Politics of German Protestantism: The Rise of the Protestant Church Elite in Prussia, 1815–1848* (Berkeley and Los Angeles, 1972), or the relevant sections of the massive work of Nicholas Hope, *German and Scandinavian Protestantism 1700–1918* (New York and Oxford, 1995), might be consulted. On literacy and education, see Carlo Cipolla, *Literacy and Development in the West* (Baltimore, 1969); Anthony La Vopa, *Prussian Schoolteachers: Profession and Office 1763–1848* (Chapel Hill, 1980); Leonore O'Boyle, "The Problem of an Excess of Educated Men in Western Europe 1800–1850," *Journal of Modern History* 42 (1970): 472–95.

Virtually all the works cited above contain some discussion of forms of social conflict. A few additional works, centering specifically on conflict, that might be mentioned in addition are two broad general studies, Charles Tilly, Richard Tilly, and Louise Tilly, *The Rebellious Century 1830–1930* (Cambridge, MA, 1975); Charles Tilly and Edward Shorter, *Strikes in France, 1830 to 1968* (Cambridge and New York, 1974) and several shorter, detailed investigations. Josef Mooser, "Property and Wood Theft: Agrarian Capitalism and Social Conflict in Rural Society, 1800–50. A Westphalian Case Study," in Moeller, ed.,*Peasants and Lords in Modern Germany*, 52–80; and James M. Brophy, "Violence Between Civilians and State Authorities in the Prussian Rhineland, 1830–1846," *German History* 22 (2004): 1–35, show the conflicts created by the actions of the Prussian state. Ladislau Gyémánt, "L'intégration de la paysannerie dans le mouvement national roumain de transilvanie durant la période 1790–1848," *Revue Roumaine d'Histoire* 20 (1981): 245–68; Luigi Parente, "Stato e contadini nel mezzogiorno d'Italia tra il 1830 e il 1845," *Cahiers internationaux d'histoire economique et sociale* 13 (1981): 252–311, both deal with social conflict in economically less developed rural areas.

CHAPTER TWO

Michael Broers, *Europe after Napoleon* (Manchester and New York, 1996) is a brief and stimulating introduction to the major political tendencies of pre-1848 Europe. Several useful and more specialized studies of the theory and practice of politics in Europe during the decades before the revolution of 1848 would include André Jardin and André-Jean Tudesq, *Restoration and Reaction 1815–1848*, trans. Elborg Forster (Cambridge, 1983); Irene Collins, *The Government and the Newspaper Press in France 1814–1881* (London, 1959); Ronald Aminzade, *Class, Politics, and Early Industrial Capitalism: A Study of Toulouse, France* (Albany, 1981); John Gillis, *The Prussian Bureaucracy in Crisis 1840–1860* (Stanford, 1971); Dagmar Herzog, *Intimacy and Exclusion: Religious Politics in Pre-Revolutionary Baden* (Princeton, 1996) and George Barany, *Stephen Szechenyi and the Awakening of Hungarian Nationalism, 1791–1841* (Princeton, 1968). The works of Ayçoberry, Berenson, and Tudesq, cited in the bibliography to the previous chapter, are excellent on pre-1848 political life. Most studies of the 1848 revolution (see the next section of the bibliography) also include discussions of the pre-1848 scene. For the student with a good reading knowledge of Italian, *L'Italia tra rvioluzione e riforme 1831–1846* (Rome 1994), the published proceedings of a 1992 scholarly congress on the history of the *Risorgimento*, contains a number of very interesting essays on political, social, cultural, and religious developments in Italy during the years leading up to the revolution of 1848.

As to specific political movements, Robert J. Berdahl, *The Politics of the Prussian Nobility: The Development of a Conservative Ideology, 1770–1848* (Princeton, 1988), offers a discussion of German conservatism. Two biographies of prominent conservatives that are particularly helpful for understanding conservatism are Frank J. Coppa, *Cardinal Giacomo Antonelli and Papal Politics in European Affairs* (Albany, 1990), and, especially, David E. Barclay, *Frederick William IV and the Prussian Monarchy 1840–1861* (Oxford and New York, 1995). Alan J. Reinermann, "The Failure of Popular Counter-Revolution in Risorgimento Italy: The Case of the Centurions, 1831–1847," *The Historical Journal* 34 (1991): 21–41 shows conservatism as a political movement; Hermann Beck, *The Origins of the Authoritarian Welfare State in Prussia: Conservatives, Bureaucracy and the Social Question, 1815–1870* (Ann Arbor, 1995), shows it as bureaucratic practice. For the student with a good reading knowledge of German, Hans-Christof Kraus, *Ernst Ludwig von Gerlach. Politisches Denken und Handeln eines preussischen Altkonservativen*, 2 vols. (Göttingen, 1994), is an illuminating biography of an important conservative political figure. Origins of liberal ideas are discussed in Pierre Manent, *An Intellectual History of Liberalism*, trans. Rebecca Balinski (Princeton, 1996) and Guy Howard Dodge, *Benjamin Constant's Philosophy of Liberalism: A Study in Politics and Religion* (Chapel Hill, 1980). Both James J. Sheehan, *German Liberalism in the Nineteenth Century* (Chicago, 1978) and Dieter Langewiesche *Liberalism in Germany*, trans. Christiane Banerji (Princeton, 2000) have good discussions of pre-1848 conditions. Andrew Janos, *The Politics of Backwardness in Hungary 1825–1945* (Princeton, 1982), includes a discussion of the relationship between mid-nineteenth-century liberalism and economic development. Iván Zoltán Dénes, "The Value Systems of Liberals and Conservatives in Hungary 1830–1848," *Historical Journal* 36 (1993): 825–50, is a very helpful comparison. Bruce Haddock, "Political Union without Social Revolution: Vincenzo Gioberti's *Primato*," *Historical Journal* 41 (1998): 705–23, is a brief introduction to some of the ideas of Italian liberals.

Radicalism and early socialism have been extensively studied. For Italy, see Clara Lovett, *The Democratic Movement in Italy 1830–1876* (Cambridge, MA, 1982) and Roland Sarti, *Mazzini: A Life for the Religion of Politics* (Westport, CT, 1997). The student who can read Italian should consult Franco Della Peruta, *Mazzini e i revolutionari italiani. Il "partito d'azione" 1830–1845* (Milan, 1974), a book that details very vividly the social and political context of a leading democrat in Italy and Europe. Beyond that, it is probably the single best work on political life in Italy during the 1830s and 40s. On radicalism and early socialism in France, see the works of Sewell and Berenson, cited above. In addition, the student can consult Alan Spitzer, *The Revolutionary Theories of Louis-Auguste Blanqui* (New York, 1957); Robert J. Bezucha, *The Lyon Uprising of 1834* (Cambridge, MA, 1974); Christopher H. Johnson, *Utopian Communism in France: Cabet and the Icarians, 1839–1851* (Ithaca and London, 1974) or Jacques Rancière, *The Nights of Labor: The Workers' Dream in Nineteenth-Century France*, trans. John Drury (Philadelphia, 1989), this last only if prepared for a heavy dose of post-modernism. The student with German-language abilities should try Cornelia Foerster, *Der Preß- und Vaterlandsverein von 1832/33* (Trier, 1982), a fine study of early German radicalism. Biographies of Karl Marx and Friedrich

Engels are legion; one that places them in their contemporary political context – admittedly in a critical way – is Oscar J. Hammen, *The Red '48ers: Karl Marx and Friedrich Engels* (New York, 1969).

It is hard to think of a more heavily and less satisfactorily investigated topic than nationalism and nationalist movements. Perhaps the single best work on the topic is Miroslav Hroch, *Social Preconditions of National Revival in Europe*, trans. Ben Fowkes (Cambridge, 1985). Historians have often turned to social scientists for explanations of nationalism, and have generally received little of use from them. Two rare exceptions to this desultory record come from anthropologists: Maryan McDonald, *"We Are Not French!" Language, Culture and Identity in Brittany* (Cambridge and New York, 1989), a study of the 1980s that offers thought-provoking material for considering the 1840s, and Katherine Verdery, *Transylvanian Villagers: Three Centuries of Political, Economic and Ethnic Change* (Berkeley, Los Angeles, and London, 1983). Studies of nationalism and the nationalities conflict in the Habsburg Empire all too often just reproduce, in partisan fashion, nineteenth-century nationalist hostilities. Some English-language works not entirely caught up in this tendency are Arthur Haas, "Metternich and the Slavs," *Austrian History Yearbook* 4/5 (1968–69): 120–49; Gunther E. Rothenberg, "The Habsburg Army and the Nationality Problem in the Nineteenth Century," *Austrian History Yearbook* 3 (1967 pt. 1): 70–87; Radu R. Florescu, "The Uniate Church: Catalyst of Rumanian National Consciousness," *Slavonic and East European Review* 45 (1967): 329–42; Laszlo Deme, "Writers and Essayists and the Rise of Magyar Nationalism in the 1820s and 1830s," *Slavic Review* 43 (1984): 624–40; Keith Hitchins, "The Sacred Cult of Nationality: Rumanian Intellectuals and the Church in Transylvania 1834–1869," in Stanley Winters and Joseph Held (eds.), *Intellectual and Social developments in the Habsburg Empire from Maria Theresa to World War I* (New York and London, 1975), 131–60; Francis Loewenheim, "German Liberalism and the Czech Renascence," in Peter Brock and H. Gordon Skilling (eds.), *The Czech Renascence of the Nineteenth Century* (Toronto and Buffalo, 1972), 146–75; Derek Sayer, "The Language of Nationality and the Nationality of Language: Prague 1780–1920," *Past and Present* 153 (1996): 164–210; Jan Kozik, *The Ukrainian National Movement in Galicia: 1815–1849*, trans. Andrew Gorski and Lawrence Orton (Edmonton, 1986). An unusually useful work on the development of nationalism in eastern Europe, written in a west European language, is Wolfgang Kessler, *Politik, Kultur und Gesellschaft in Kroatien und Slawonien in der ersten Hälfte des 19. Jahrhunderts* (Munich, 1981).

The works mentioned above on political practice and individual political movements in central and western Europe all contain discussions of nationalism. In addition to them, the student might consult: George L. Mosse, *The Nationalization of the Masses* (New York and Scarborough, 1975); Richard Hinton Thomas, *Liberalism, Nationalism and the German Intellectuals 1822–1847* (Cambridge, 1951); Hagen Schulze, *The Course of German Nationalism: From Frederick the Great to Bismarck 1763–1867*, trans. Sarah Hanbury-Tension (Cambridge and New York, 1991); and the excellent recent study, Brian E. Vick, *Defining Germany: The 1848 Frankfurt Parliamentarians and National Identity* (Cambridge, MA, 2002). Barbara Ann Day-Hickmann, *Napoleonic Art: Nationalism and the Spirit of Rebellion in France, 1815–1848* (Newark, DE, 1999) and Bernard Ménager, *Les Napoléons du peuple* (Paris, 1988) consider Napoleon and French nationalism.

CHAPTERS THREE, FOUR, AND FIVE

In commemoration of the one hundred fiftieth anniversary of the 1848 revolutions there were a very substantial number of scholarly conferences, colloquia, exhibitions, and lecture series, many of which have since been published as books. The topics, scope, and quality of these varied enormously. Several, however, stand out because of the attempt to offer a continent-wide perspective. The most massive of these collections of essays, and the most extensive and detailed work on the mid-nineteenth-century revolutions, is Dieter Dowe, Heinz-Gerhard Haupt, Dieter Langewiesche, and Jonathan Sperber (eds.), *Europe in 1848: Revolution and Reform*, trans. David Higgins (New York and Oxford, 2001). The book's nine hundred pages include essays on the events of 1848 almost everywhere in Europe. In addition, the work contains thematic essays on topics such as the peasantry, the labor movement, and the women's movement in the 1848 revolutions, on the language of revolution, revolutionary parliaments, and many more. It also has an extensive multi-lingual bibliography. R. J. W. Evans and Hartmut Pogge von Strandmann (eds.), *The Revolutions in Europe 1848–1849: From Reform to Reaction* (Oxford, 2000), has brief introductions to the 1848 revolutions in the larger European countries. Essays in this volume on responses to the 1848 revolutions in the Russian Empire and the United States cover topics not considered in the larger book. There were a substantial number of German-language collections of essays that appeared in conjunction with the revolution's one hundred fiftieth anniversary. Two that deserve mention are Christian Jansen and Thomas Mergel (eds.), *Die Revolutionen von 1848/49. Erfahrung – Verarbeitung – Deutung* (Göttingen, 1998), containing the work of younger scholars with a strong focus on the new cultural history, and Helgard Fröhlich, Margarete Grandner, and Michael Weinzierl (eds.), *1848 im europäischen Kontext* (Vienna, 1999), that has some interesting essays on events in east-central Europe. In contrast to collections of essays, the sesquicentenary of 1848 did not see the publication of any new English-language general history of the 1848 revolutions. There remain three older, English-language surveys. The oldest, Priscilla Robertson, *Revolutions of 1848: A Social History* (Princeton, 1952) is colorfully written in the explanatory tradition of the "romantic revolution" and still makes marvelous reading, but is now rather dated. Peter Stearns, *1848: The Revolutionary Tide in Europe* (New York, 1974) offers an interpretation of the 1848 revolutions in terms of sociological modernization theory. The most recent work, Roger Price, *The Revolutions of 1848* (London, 1989) is a brief sketch, designed primarily for college teachers. The bibliographies of Robertson and Stearns are particularly useful for their listing of memoirs and other primary sources.

The student interested in the 1848 revolution in France is especially fortunate, since there exists an extensive English-language literature. Maurice Agulhon, *The Republican Experiment, 1848–1852*, trans. Janet Lloyd (Cambridge, 1983) is a marvelous work of synthesis; Roger Price, *The French Second Republic: A Social*

History (Ithaca and London, 1972), is also a good introduction, concentrating more on Paris. A large number of significant monographs are also available. Maurice Agulhon, *The Republic in the Village: The People of the Var from the French Revolution to the Second Republic*, trans. Janet Lloyd (Cambridge, 1982) is a classic, as enlightening on pre-revolutionary social, economic, political, and cultural developments as it is on the revolution itself. John Merriman, *The Agony of the Republic: The Repression of the Left in Revolutionary France 1848–1851* (New Haven and London, 1978) is excellent on events in the provinces and the later years of the revolution. Mary Lynn Steward McDougall, *The Artisan Republic: Revolution, Reaction and Resistance in Lyon 1848–1851* (Kingston and Montreal, 1984) is a fine study of France's second city. Two major works on Paris during the revolution are Peter H. Amman, *Revolution and Mass Democracy: The Paris Club Movement in 1848* (Princeton, 1975) and Mark Traugott, *Armies of the Poor: Determinants of Working-Class Participation in the Parisian Insurrection of June 1848* (Princeton, 1985). On a very different aspect of Parisian life, see T. J. Clark, *The Absolute Bourgeois: Artists and Politics in France, 1848–1851* (Princeton, 1982).

Roger Price (ed.), *1848 in France* (Ithaca and London, 1975) is a good collection of primary sources. Among the many contemporaries who commented on events, Karl Marx's two great polemics, *Class Struggles in France* and *The Eighteenth Brumaire of Louis-Napoleon* (both in numerous editions) have left their mark on the historiography of 1848 and are still very much worth reading, even if many assertions in them may now seem not entirely supportable. There are strikingly few literary treatments of 1848, but the novelist Gustave Flaubert has left two very nasty portraits, one of the revolution in Paris, in *The Sentimental Education*, and one of events in the provinces, in *Bouvard and Pécuchet* (also available in different English-language versions).

In addition to all these, the works of Aminzade, Berenson, Collins, Johnson, Ménager, Sewell, and Tudesq, cited in the bibliography to Chapters One and Two, contain important accounts of aspects of the revolution. Two major studies of French peasant politics in 1848 and the 1851 uprising against Louis-Napoleon's *coup d'état* are Ted Margadant's *French Peasants in Revolt*, (mentioned in the bibliography to Chapter One), and Peter McPhee, *The Politics of Rural Life: Political Mobilization in the French Countryside 1846–1852* (Oxford, 1992). Ideally, one should read the two books in tandem, since their contrasting explanations of peasant politics, and, in particular, the role of non-rural outsiders in political leadership, make for interesting comparisons. The ambitious student with a good reading knowledge of French, who would like to explore the topic further, might try tackling a *grande thèse*, one of the massive monographs produced by French academics. Four good choices are Pierre Vigier, *La seconde république dans la région alpine*, 2 vols. (Paris, 1963), the work that began the current wave of reinterpretation of the mid-century revolutions; Alain Corbin, *Archaisme et modernité en Limousin au XIXe siècle 1845–1880*, 2 vols. (Paris, 1975); Rémi Gossez, *Les ouvriers de Paris* (Paris, 1967); or Pierre Lévêque, *Une société en crise: la Bourgogne au milieu du XIXe siècle* (Paris, 1983). The one hundred fiftieth anniversary commemorations did not result in any major re-interpretations of the 1848 revolution in France, but they did produce an excellent bibliography, that the advanced student might wish to consult. Volume 14 (1997, no. 1) of *Revue d'histoire du xixe siècle* contains several very helpful review articles on the historiography of the 1848 revolution in France and a very extensive bibliography of works on the topic written between 1948 and 1997.

Wolfram Siemann, *The German Revolution of 1848–49*, trans. Christiane Banerji (New York, 1998) is by far the best general English-language history of the 1848 revolutions in Germany. The previous standard work, Theodore Hamerow, *Restoration, Revolution, Reaction: Economics and Politics in Germany, 1815–1871* (Princeton, 1957), is now outdated. Some more recent and more specialized English-language works include the detailed, regional study of Jonathan Sperber, *Rhineland Radicals: The Democratic Movement and the Revolution of 1848–1849* (Princeton, 1991). Frank Eyck, *The Frankfurt Parliament 1848–1849* (London, Melbourne, Toronto, New York, 1968) is a good account of the unfortunate German National Assembly, written from a subtly conservative viewpoint. The work of Brian Vick, *Defining Germany*, noted in the bibliography to Chapter Two, supersedes Eyck's work for one very important aspect of the history of the National Assembly, its attitude toward the national question.

P. H. Noyes, *Organization and Revolution: Working-Class Associations in the German Revolution of 1848–1849* (Princeton, 1966), provides an at times tendentious discussion of the early German labor movement; Hammen's biography of Marx and Engels, cited in the bibliography to Chapter Two, has a good deal to say about communists and the labor movement in the German revolution. The essays in Werner E. Mosse, Arnold Paucker, and Reinhard Rürup (eds.), *Revolution and Evolution: 1848 in German-Jewish History* (Tübingen, 1981) consider the revolution's impact on a religious minority. James Harris, *The People Speak! Anti-Semitism and Emancipation in Nineteenth Century Bavaria* (Ann Arbor, 1994), discusses an organized anti-Semitic campaign emerging from the defeat of the revolution. Two articles, William J. Orr Jr., "East Prussia and the Revolution of 1848," *Central European History* 13 (1980): 303–31, and Ralph Canevali, "The 'French False Alarm': Revolutionary Panic in Baden, 1848," *Central European History* 18 (1985): 119–42, offer an introduction to the revolutionary events in two very different German regions. A number of the chapters in the collection of essays edited by Dowe et al. (cited at the beginning of this section) are very helpful on the 1848 revolution in Germany: in particular, Dieter Langewiesche's short summary of 1848 in Germany (120–43), Michael Wettengel's unusually good account of political clubs in the German revolution (529–57), Heinz-Gerhard Haupt and Friedrich Lenger's essay on the labor movement (619–37), and Willibald Steinmetz's on political discourse (830–68). Finally, Friedrich Engels, *Revolution and Counter-Revolution in Germany* (numerous editions) is, like Marx's books on France, a polemic by a contemporary deeply involved in events, still worth considering today.

The commemorative wave of 1998 washed most heavily across the German landscape and the student with German-language skills has a lot to choose from. One collection of essays deserving mention is Christoph Dipper and Ulrich Speck (eds.), *1848 Revolution in Deutschland* (Frankfurt and Leipzig, 1998) that provides brief summaries of the state of scholarship, with useful bibliographies. Important recent scholarly monographs include Michael Wettengel, *Die Revolution von 1848/ 49 im Rhein-Main-Raum* (Wiesbaden, 1989); Wolfgang Schwentker, *Konservative*

Vereine und Revolution in Preussen 1848/49 (Düsseldorf, 1989); and Manfred Gailus, *Strasse und Brot: Sozialer Protest in den deutschen Staaten unter besonderer Berücksichtigung Preussens 1847–1849* (Göttingen, 1990). Two products of 1998 are the massive work of Rüdiger Hachtmann, *Berlin 1848. Eine Politik- und Gesellschaftsgeschichte der Revolution* (Bonn, 1997); and Sabrina Müller, *Soldaten in der deutschen Revolution von 1848/49* (Paderborn, 1999), a very interesting study on an important topic – the military in the 1848 revolution – that has been rather neglected. Rüdiger Hachtmann, "150 Jahre Revolution von 1848: Festschriften und Forschungserträge," *Archiv für Sozialgeschichte* 39 (1999): 447–93 and 40 (2000): 337–401, is an excellent and very detailed guide to the latest German-language literature on 1848.

There is no modern general history of the Italian 1848 revolutions in English – or in Italian, for that matter. A somewhat idiosyncratic introduction to the events of 1848 on the Italian peninsula can be found in the essay of Simonetta Soldani, in Dowe et al. (eds.) *Europe in 1848*, 59–90. The chapters in that same volume by Christoph Dipper on rural revolutionary movements (416–40) and Charlotte Tacke on revolutionary festivals (799–829) also have useful material on aspects of the 1848 revolution in Italy. Paul Ginsborg, *Daniele Manin and the Venetian Revolution of 1848–49* (Cambridge, 1979), is an excellent monograph with very helpful discussions of pre-revolutionary politics and society and of events outside of its special regional focus. Maud Tyler, "A Dissenting Voice in the Risorgimento: Angelo Brofferio in Mid-Nineteenth Century Piedmont," *Historical Journal* 33 (1990): 403–15 is a useful short discussion of Italian constitutional monarchism. Outside of these, English-language offerings are slim. Clara Lovett's history of the democratic movement in Italy contains good chapters on the mid-century revolution. Alan Sked, *The Survival of the Habsburg Empire: Radetzky, the Imperial Army and the Class War 1848* (London and New York, 1979) has much that is informative on events in the two northern provinces; the student might compare his interpretation with that of Ginsborg. Otherwise the student must have recourse to textbooks. The most recent of these is John Davis (ed.), *Italy in the Nineteenth Century 1760–1900* (Oxford, 2000), which also contains the most up-to-date bibliography.

The best introduction to the Italian-language literature can be found in Simonetta Soldani, "Contadini, Operai e 'Popolo' nella rivoluzione del 1848–49 in Italia," *Studi Storici* 14 (1973): 557–613, which contains bibliographical references to many older studies. Two of the more significant of these older works are Domenico Demarco, *Una rivoluzione sociale: La repubblica romana del 1849 (16 Novembre 1848–3 Luglio 1849)* (Naples, 1944) and Carla Ronchi, *I democratici fiorentini nella revoluzione del '48–'49* (Florence, 1963). Two of the few Italian-language monographs on 1848 published since Soldani's essay are Franco Rizzi, *La coccarda e le campané: Communità rurale et Repubblica romana nel Lazio (1848–1849)* (Milan, 1988), an excellent study of popular culture and popular politics in a rural area just outside of Rome, and Enrica Di Ciommo, *La nazione possibile. Mezzogiorno e questione nazionale nel 1848* (Milan 1993), a thought-provoking intellectual history of democratic and liberal political movements in the Kingdom of the Two Sicilies.

There is no English-language history of the 1848 revolution in the Habsburg monarchy. Actually, good general works on this topic in any language (at least in any that I can read) are hard to find. The best one can do is individual chapters in books on larger topics. The essay of Jiři Kořalka on 1848 in the Habsburg monarchy in Dowe et al. (eds.), *Europe in 1848* (145–69) is the most recent summary and is particularly useful for constitutional developments and forms of political organization. The account of the 1848 revolution in Alan Sked, *The Decline and Fall of the Habsburg Empire 1815–1918* (London and New York, 1989) offers another perspective, one more centered on war and diplomacy. The best textbook account is in Robin Okey, *The Habsburg Monarchy: From Enlightenment to Eclipse* (New York, 2001), which stresses the tenacity of imperial institutions and the importance of the nationalist movements of the smaller Slavic nations. Rudolf Jaworski and Robert Luft (eds.), *1848/49 Revolutionen in Ostmitteleuropa* (Munich, 1996) is a useful collection of essays, primarily on the Czech lands of the Habsburg monarchy, but also containing pieces on the rest of the monarchy and on the eastern regions of the German states. The individual essays discuss many different subjects, but a number of them focus on nations, nationalism, and the nationalities conflict. By far the best discussion of popular politics and particularly peasant movements, so important to understanding events in the empire, is the work of Roman Rosdolsky, *Die Bauernabgeordneten im konstituierenden österreichischen Reichstag 1848–1849* (Vienna, 1976). More recently, Brigitte Biwald, *Von Gottes Gnaden oder von Volkes Gnaden? Die Revolution von 1848 in der Habsburgermonarchie: Der Bauer als Ziel politischer Agitation* (Frankfurt, 1996) supplements, but by no means replaces Rosdolsky's work. Stanley Z. Pech, "The Nationalist Movements of the Austrian Slavs in 1848: A Comparative Sociological Profile," *Histoire Sociale—Social History* 9 (1976): 336–56, is a helpful discussion of the development of political organization during the mid-century revolution.

Most studies tend to deal with specific regions and/or nationalities of the empire. Oddly, the areas that make up contemporary Austria are among the least investigated. In English, there is the older work of John Rath, *The Viennese Revolution of 1848* (Austin, 1957). The student with a good command of German can try Wolfgang Häusler, *Von der Massenarmut zur Arbeiterbewegung: Demokratie und soziale Frage in der Weiner Revolution von 1848* (Vienna and Munich, 1979) or Gerhard Pfeisinger, *Die Revolution von 1848 in Graz* (Vienna, 1986). For the Czech lands of the monarchy, Stanley Pech, *The Czech Revolution of 1848* (Chapel Hill, 1969) is a standard work, that can be usefully supplemented by Lawrence Orton, *The Prague Slav Congress of 1848* (Boulder, 1978) – also helpful as a broader-scale, English-language account of political movements in Eastern Europe – and the Marxist-Leninist version offered by Josef V. Polišenský, *Aristocrats and the Crowd in the Revolutionary Year 1848*, trans. Frederick Snider (Albany, 1980). Istvan Deak's *The Lawful Revolution: Louis Kossuth and the Hungarians, 1848–1849* (New York, 1979) is a wonderful biography of one of the towering figures of the revolution and offers much of substantial interest on politics in the entire realm of the crown of St. Stephen – not just among its Magyar inhabitants – before and during the revolution. A particular virtue of Deak's work is his discussions of the interrelationship of events in Hungary and in other parts of the empire. Laszlo Deme, *The Radical Left in the Hungarian Revolution of 1848* (Boulder, 1976) and Domokos G. Kosáry, *The Press during the Hungarian*

Revolution of 1848–1849 (Boulder, 1986) are also worth looking at. Catherine Horel, *Juifs de Hongrie 1825–1849: Problèmes d'assimilation et d'émancipation* (Strasbourg, 1995), has an excellent section on the Jews of Hungary and the 1848 revolution; her discussion of the Hungarian Jewish community in the pre-revolutionary decades is also quite useful. The chapter by Wolfgang Höpken in Dowe et al., *Europe in 1848*, on the agrarian question in the Habsburg monarchy (443–71) offers a summary of the research published in eastern European languages on serfdom, peasant movements, and popular nationalism in the eastern half of the Austrian Empire during 1848. The essay also demonstrates how much more needs to be done in this area.

On the revolution in Transylvania and the Romanian nationalist movement, the student can consult the works of Katherine Verdery and Keith Hitchins mentioned in the bibliography to Chapter Two. Another book of Hitchins', *Orthodoxy and Nationality: Andrieu Şaguna and the Rumanians of Transylvania, 1846–1873* (Cambridge, MA and London, 1977) is also helpful. Cornelia Bodea, *The Rumanians' Struggle for Unification 1834–1849*, trans. Liliana Toedoreanu (Bucharest, 1970) is official, government-sponsored history, but not without useful information. A very informative discussion of what the historical literature on the revolution and civil war in Transylvania has not yet done is Radu R. Florescu, "Debunking a Myth: The Magyar-Rumanian National Struggle of 1848–49," *Austrian History Yearbook* 12–13 (1976–77): 82–89. The work of Jan Kozik on the Ukrainian national movement, cited in the bibliography to Chapter Two, contains a detailed account of the 1848 revolution in Galicia. John-Paul Himka, *Galician Villagers and the Ukrainian National Movement in the Nineteenth Century* (London, 1988), has additional, excellent material on peasants during the revolution and on struggles between serfs and noble landlords. Paul R. Magocsi, *The Shaping of a National Identity: Sub-Carpathian Rus' 1848–1948* (Cambridge, MA, 1978) has a brief discussion of the events of 1848 in one of the most isolated corners of the empire, and, indeed, of all of Europe.

There is, so far as I am aware, no complete English-language account of the 1848 revolution among the Croatian and Serbian nationalities in the Habsburgs' realm. Besides Deak's book on Kossuth, and the essays of Jiří Kořalka and Wolfgang Höpken noted above, the student might have a look at Ivo Banac, "The Confessional 'Rule' and the Dubrovnik Exception: The Origins of the 'Serb-Catholic' Circle in Nineteenth Century Dalmatia," *Slavic Review* 42 (1983): 448–74; and Wayne S. Vucinich, "The Serbs in Austria-Hungary," *Austrian History Yearbook* 3 pt. 2 (1967): 3–47. The books on the Austrian army of Gunter Rothenberg (noted in the bibliography to Chapter One) and of Alan Sked (noted in conjunction with Italy during 1848) both have useful material on Croatians and the military border guards during the revolution. Gunter Rothenberg, "Jelačić, the Croatian Military Border and the Intervention against Hungary in 1848," *Austrian History Yearbook* 1 (1965): 44–68 is an excellent brief account.

On the 1848 revolutionaries in exile, Rosemary Ashton, *Little Germany: Exile and Asylum in Victorian England* (Oxford, 1986) is both charming and illuminating. Christian Jansen, *Einheit, Macht und Freiheit. Die Paulskirchenlinke und die deutsche Politik in der nachrevolutionären Epoche 1849–1867* (Düsseldorf, 2000) is much slower going, but contains very important material on exile politics, both in the years 1850–51, when it seemed like the 1848 revolution might not yet be over, and then afterwards, when it was clear that it was.

On the Swiss Civil War of 1847, the precursor to the 1848 revolutions, Joachim Remark, *A Very Civil War: The Swiss Sonderbund War of 1847* (Boulder, 1993), is an elegantly illustrated, but rather superficial political and military history of the war. The essay by Thomas Christian Müller, "Switzerland 1847/49: A Provisional, Successful End of a 'Democratic Revolution'?" in Dowe et al. (eds.), *Europe in 1848*, 210–37, goes much deeper. The essays in that volume by Hans-Henning Hahn on 1848 in the Polish lands (170–85) and, especially, by Lothar Maier on the mid-nineteenth-century revolutions in the Danubian Principalities of Moldavia and Wallachia (186–209) are important accounts of little-known events in Europe's eastern regions. Developments in countries that did not experience a revolutionary outbreak are best followed by the essays in the same volume by Horst Lademacher on Belgium and the Netherlands (259–86), Steen Bo Frandsen on Denmark (289–311), Anne-Lise Seip on Norway (313–24), and Göran Nilsson on Sweden (325–37).

To conclude this section, let me mention several topical questions that cross national boundaries. On the economic crisis of 1845–48, the student might consider the works of Wilhelm Abel and Roger Price noted in the bibliography to Chapter One, as well as M. Bergman, "The Potato Blight in the Netherlands and its Social Consequences," *International Review of Social History* 12 (1967): 390–431. On diplomatic relations during the revolution, see Lawrence Jennings, *France and Europe in 1848* (Oxford, 1974); Werner E. Mosse, *The European Powers and the German Question 1848–1871*, 2nd edn. (Cambridge, 1969); Ian W. Roberts, *Nicholas I and the Russian Intervention in Hungary* (Basingstoke and London, 1991), and Alan Sked's book on the Habsburg army.

A overview of the role of religion and religious confession in the 1848 revolutions can be found in the essay of Jonathan Sperber, in Dowe et al. (eds.), *Europe in 1848*, 708–28. Two monographs that provide valuable insights are Austin Gough, *Paris and Rome: The Gallican Church and the Ultramontane Campaign 1848–1853* (Oxford, 1986) and Stefan J. Diedrich, *Christentum und Revolution: Die christlichen Kirchen in Württemberg 1848–1852* (Paderborn, 1996).

For the role of women in the revolution, the place to start is the essay of Gabriella Hauch, "Women's Spaces in the Men's Revolution of 1848," in Dowe et al. (eds.), *Europe in 1848*, 639–82. It presents an excellent survey of the literature, provides a wealth of examples, and advances an interesting thesis. Two more specialized studies are Joan Scott, "Work Identities for Men and Women: The Politics of Work and Family in the Parisian Garment Trades in 1848," in her *Gender and the Politics of History* (cited in the bibliography to the first chapter), 93–112; and Stanley Zucker, *Kathinka Zitz-Halein and Female Civic Activism in Mid-Nineteenth-Century Germany* (Carbondale, IL, 1991). The works of Pech on 1848 in the Czech lands and of Sperber, on the mid-century revolution in the Rhineland, both have discussions of women's political activities. The student who can read German should look at Carola Lipp (ed.), *Schimpfende Weiber und patriotische Jungfrauen: Frauen im Vormärz und in der Revolution 1848/49* (Moos and Baden-Baden, 1986), which remains the single best work on women during the mid-century revolution. Several more general works have useful discussions of

1848: Priscilla Robertson, *An Experience of Women: Pattern and Change in Nineteenth-Century Europe* (Philadelphia, 1982); Claire Goldberg Moses, *French Feminism in the Nineteenth Century* (Albany, 1984) and Ute Frevert, *Women in German History: From Bourgeois Emancipation to Sexual Liberation*, trans. Stuart McKinnon-Evans (New York and Oxford, 1989).

CHAPTER SIX

There are three good discussions of 1848 in the United Kingdom. John Saville, *1848: The British State and the Chartist Movement* (Cambridge, 1987), is the most comprehensive. The essay by John Belchem, "The Waterloo of Peace and Order: The United Kingdom and the Revolutions of 1848," in Dowe et al., (eds.), *Europe in 1848*, (242–57) emphasizes the Irish dimension of events. Miles Taylor, "The 1848 Revolutions and the British Empire," *Past and Present* 166 (2000): 146–80, offers an interesting and stimulating, if not always entirely convincing, global perspective. A comprehensive account of the social changes that had diminished popular support for radicalism in England by 1848 can be found in Theodore Koditschek, *Class Formation and Urban-Industrial Society: Bradford 1750–1850* (Cambridge and New York, 1990); for a broader discussion of political and socio-economic differences between the United Kingdom and the countries of continental Europe in this period, see Jonathan Sperber, "Reforms, Movements for Reform and Possibilities of Reform: Comparing Britain and Continental Europe," in Arthur Burnes and Johanna Innes (eds.), *Rethinking the Age of Reform: Britain 1780–1850* (Cambridge, 2003), 312–30. J.H. Seddon, *The Petrashevtsy: A Study of the Russian Revolutionaries of 1848* (Manchester, 1985) and Priscilla Reynolds Roosevelt, *Apostle of Russian Liberalism: Timofei Granovsky* (Newtonville, 1986) both explain the extreme weakness of the party of movement in Russia and its frustrations during the year of revolution in much of the rest of Europe.

General discussions of the place of the 1848 revolutions in European history usually coincide with the anniversaries of the revolution. A classic discussion during the centenary was François Fejtö (ed.), *Opening of an Era, 1848* (London, 1949). Some more recent re-evaluations can be found in the introductory essays to the two collections edited by Dowe et al. and by Evans and Strandmann, described at the beginning of this section. A number of more specialized works containing broader considerations on mid-century revolutions would include Sewell, *Work and Revolution in France*, Agulhon, *The Republican Experiment*, Sperber, *Rhineland Radicals*, Pech, *The Czech Revolution*, Lovett, *The Democratic Movement in Italy*, all cited in the previous sections of the bibliography. Three books that discuss later forms of nationalism and the movements towards national unity of the 1860s in light of the events of 1848 are Raymond Grew, *A Sterner Plan for Italian Unity: The Italian National Society and the Risorgimento* (Princeton, 1963); Theodore Hamerow, *The Social Foundations of German Unification*, 2 vols. (Princeton, 1969–72); and Pieter Judson, *Exclusive Revolutionaries: Liberal Politics, Social Experience and National Identity in the Austrian Empire, 1848–1914* (Ann Arbor, 1996).

Some general theories of revolution can be found in Crane Brinton, *The Anatomy of Revolution*, 2nd edn. (New York, 1965); Ted Gurr, *Why Men Rebel*

(Princeton, 1970); Barrington Moore, *Social Origins of Dictatorship and Democracy* (Boston, 1966); Theda Skocpol, *States and Social Revolutions: A Comparative Analysis of France, Russia and China* (Cambridge and New York, 1979); and Charles Tilly, *European Revolutions, 1492–1992* (Cambridge, MA, 1993). All have difficulty with the 1848 revolutions, or simply ignore them. Three studies of the predecessor wave of revolution that suggest comparisons with 1848 are R.R. Palmer, *The Age of Democratic Revolutions*, 2 vols. (Princeton, 1959–64), often criticized, but full of thought-provoking suggestions, and two general histories summing up the latest views on the French Revolution of 1789: D. M. G. Sutherland, *France, 1798–1815: Revolution and Counterrevolution* (New York, 1986) and William Doyle, *The Oxford History of the French Revolution* (Oxford, 1989). Jonathan Sperber, *Revolutionary Europe 1780–1850* (London, 2000), argues that the 1848 revolutions closed a cycle of European history beginning in 1789. The student with German can turn to Irmtraud Götz von Olenhusen (ed.), *1848/49 in Europa und der Mythos der Französischen Revolution* (Göttingen, 1998), for a discussion of the impact of the events of 1789 on those of 1848. Two recent works trace lines of continuity and discontinuity between the Parisian 1848 revolution and the Paris Commune: Roger V. Gould, *Insurgent Identities: Class, Community, and Protest in Paris from 1848 to the Commune* (Chicago, 1995); and Martin Johnson, *The Paradise of Association: Political Culture and Popular Organizations in the Paris Commune of 1871* (Ann Arbor, 1996). Two books on the successor wave of revolution, 1917–23, also providing useful hints for comparison, are Sheila Fitzpatrick, *The Russian Revolution 1917–1932* (Oxford and New York, 1984) and James Cronin (ed.), *Work, Community and Power: The Experience of Labor in Europe and America 1900–1925* (Philadelphia, 1983). There has been a lot written on the revolutions of 1989, but much of it does not go very far beyond the surface of the events or seriously consider the 1989 revolutions in the context of other classic revolutions of modern European history. Two interesting accounts by historians as journalists are Timothy Garton Ash, *The Magic Lantern: The Revolution of '89 Witnessed in Warsaw, Budapest, Berlin, and Prague* (New York, 1990); and Robert Darnton, *Berlin Journal 1989–1990* (New York, 1991). Charles S. Maier, *Dissolution: The Crisis of Communism and the End of East Germany* (Princeton, 1997), is a thoughtful reflection on the historical significance of the 1989 revolution that includes some consideration of 1848.

On commemorations of 1848, see in particular two collections of essays: Axel Körner (ed.), *1848: A European Revolution? International Ideas and National Memories of 1848* (Houndsmills, Basingstoke and New York, 2000) and Charlotte Tacke (ed.), *1848 Memory and Oblivion in Europe* (Frankfurt, 2000). The essay by Robert Gildea, "1848 in European Collective Memory," which is printed in both the Dowe et al. (eds.) and Evans and Pogge von Strandmann (eds.) collections of essays is an interesting attempt at an interpretative synthesis. Beatrix Bouvier, "On the Tradition of 1848 in Socialism," in Dowe et al. (eds.) *Europe in 1848*, 891–915, discusses 1848 and the labor movement. The extensive review essay by Rüdiger Hachtmann on recent German-language publications on 1848, noted above, includes a helpful discussion of the 1848 commemorations in central Europe.

Many of the web sites constructed in conjunction with the revolutionary sesquicentenary are no longer in existence, a testimony to the extremely transitory nature of the Internet. One site that might be worth pursuing (although there is no guarantee of its continued existence) is an English-language site on 1848 in Germany, http://www.serve.com/shea/germusa/1848.htm

Short biographies

FRANCE

LOUIS BLANC (1811–82)

Parisian socialist journalist and inventor of the extraordinarily popular slogan, "the organization of labor." In February 1848, he was named Minister without Portfolio in the Provisional Government and chairman of the Luxembourg Commission that was to investigate the conditions of the working class and propose remedies. Blanc was forced to flee to England after the June Days and remained in exile until the proclamation of the Third Republic in 1870. He sat as a left-wing deputy in the National Assembly until his death.

LOUIS-NAPOLEON BONAPARTE (1808–73)

Son of the great Napoleon's brother Louis, Louis-Napoleon attempted, unsuccessfully, in 1836 and 1840 to seize power in France. Standing as the right-wing candidate in the presidential elections of December 1848, he attracted a broad range of voters from across the entire political spectrum. In office, he proved extraordinarily skilled at conspiracy and intrigue, finally mounting a successful coup in December 1851, crushing a left-wing rising against it. His rule as Emperor Napoleon III was marked by a constant search for popularity through glorious military victories in the Napoleonic tradition. Defeat in the Franco-Prussian War of 1870/71 led to the proclamation of the republic and end of his reign. He died in exile in London.

EUGÈNE CAVAIGNAC (1802–1857)

From an old Jacobin family, Cavaignac was an officer in the engineering corp of the French army transferred to Algeria in 1832 because of his republican sympathies. A "pure republican," opposing radical social and economic reforms, Cavaignac was named Minister of War in May 1848 and, after commanding the troops that suppressed the Parisian June uprising, was chosen prime minister. Widely expected to be elected president of the republic in December 1848, he was badly defeated by Louis-Napoleon Bonaparte. Cavaignac was one of the few "pure republicans" to be elected to the legislative assembly in May 1849. Briefly arrested after Louis-Napoleon's *coup d'état*, he remained largely in retirement until his death.

JEANNE DÉROIN (1805–94)

A self-educated Parisian seamstress, Déroin became involved in the early socialist movement. The leading female figure in the French Revolution of 1848, Déroin was active on the left, founding the Club for the Emancipation of Women, and the Fraternal Association of Democrats of Both Sexes. She advocated women's rights, including female suffrage, and attempted to stand for the legislative assembly in the elections of May 1849. Indicted by the ever more conservative government in 1850, she was acquitted by the jury but forced to flee the country following Louis-Napoleon's *coup d'état* in 1851. Déroin lived in England the rest of her life, where she remained an active feminist.

ALEXANDRE LEDRU-ROLLIN (1807–74)

A lawyer and recognized leader of the republican opposition during the July Monarchy, Ledru-Rollin was named Interior Minister of the provisional government in February 1848. Caught between the insurgents and the forces of order in May and June 1848, he was forced to resign his portfolio and became head of the reorganized "democ-soc" left-wing parliamentary opposition, in which capacity he ran an unsuccessful candidacy for president in December 1848. After the failed demonstration of June 1849, he was forced to flee the country. He lived in exile until 1870, returned to France in poor health, and died soon afterwards.

GERMANY

MATHILDE FRANZISKA ANNEKE (1817–84)

A freelance journalist in the 1830s and 40s, she moved in radical and eventually communist circles. She was one of the most prominent women active in the 1848 revolution in Germany, editing a newspaper in Cologne designed to explain complicated politics in simple language for a popular audience. Following the failure of the revolution, she fled to the United States and spent most of the rest of her life there. She continued to work as a journalist and remained active in radical politics, supporting the anti-slavery and the women's rights movements.

ROBERT BLUM (1807–48)

From a modest background, Blum became a leader of the radical wing of the political opposition in the kingdom of Saxony during the 1840s. His political pamphlets and almanacs, as well as his activity in the rationalist sect, the German-Catholics, made him known throughout central Europe. During the 1848 revolution, Blum was one of the leaders of the left in the Frankfurt National Assembly, and a popular speaker at extra-parliamentary mass meetings. Sent by the assembly to Vienna in October 1848, he joined the insurgents in their fight against imperial troops. Following the latter's victory, Blum was captured and shot, his death making him a widely mourned martyr of the democratic movement in Germany.

FRIEDRICH WILHELM IV, KING OF PRUSSIA (1795–1861)

Coming to the throne in 1840, he disappointed the hopes many liberals placed in him, by denouncing the doctrines of constitutional monarchism and refusing to consider a constitution or parliament for Prussia. Forced to appoint liberal ministers after the outbreak of revolution in March 1848, he conspired against them with the camarilla, his circle of unofficial conservative advisors. In April 1849, he refused the Frankfurt National Assembly's offer to become emperor of a united Germany, once again disappointing liberals. His brother and successor, Prince Wilhelm, was more willing to work with liberal nationalists and would be crowned emperor of a united Germany in 1871.

HEINRICH VON GAGERN (1799–1880)

A substantial landowner and leader of the liberal opposition in the Grand Duchy of Hessen-Darmstadt, Gagern was one of the most prominent of the pro-Prussian constitutional monarchists in central Europe. During the 1848 revolution, Gagern was first president of the Frankfurt National Assembly and later prime minister of the provisional central government it had created, largely on his initiative. His efforts at national unification were foiled by the king of Prussia's refusal to accept the assembly's offer of the imperial crown. Unlike many of his former political associates, Gagern opposed Otto von Bismarck's efforts to create a "little German" national state in the 1860s, preferring a more pro-Austrian position.

KARL MARX (1818–83)

The founder of modern communism began his political career in the 1840s, as editor of a liberal oppositional newspaper in Prussia, *The Rhineland News*, and, following its prohibition, as member of an émigré secret society, the Communist League. During the 1848 revolution, Marx edited *The New Rhineland News* and attempted both to further an independent labor movement and to promote an insurgent Jacobin radicalism. In the spring of 1849 he was forced to flee to exile in England. Marx's politics became steadily more focused on the labor movement over the following decades, but, unlike most German exiles, he rejected any reconciliation with Bismarck's German national state, remaining a revolutionary émigré until his death.

ITALY

CARLO ALBERTO, KING OF PIEDMONT-SAVOY (1798–1849)

Coming to the throne in 1831, he at first followed a conservative and clerical domestic policy, if opposing Austria in foreign affairs. Gradually opening himself to liberal and nationalist influences, he granted a constitution in the spring of 1848 and twice led Piedmontese and other Italian troops in a nationalist war against Austria. He was defeated both times, and following the second defeat at Novara in March 1849, he abdicated in favor of his son, Vittorio Emmanuele, who would become the first ruler of a united Italian kingdom.

GIUSEPPE GARIBALDI (1807–82)

Son of a merchant marine captain, he joined the secret society Young Italy and after a failed insurrection in 1833 was forced to flee into exile. Returning to Italy in 1848, he became famous for his heroic leadership of the military forces of the Roman Republic against French troops. In the 1850s, Garibaldi decided that national unification had to have priority over republicanism. His celebrated expedition to Sicily in 1860 overthrew the southern Italian kingdom and paved the way for a united Italy, under the rule of the King of Piedmont-Savoy. Garibaldi remained active in Italian politics until his death, belonging to the radical opposition in the united Italian kingdom.

VINCENZO GIOBERTI (1801–52)

A priest, he was forced to flee to France in 1831 following his involvement in a revolutionary conspiracy in the Kingdom of Piedmont-Savoy. His proposal in 1843 that the Pope become leader of Italian nationalism was widely acclaimed by constitutional monarchists and popular throughout the peninsula, although his parallel calls for reform in the Catholic Church were less well appreciated. Gioberti was Prime Minister of Piedmont-Savoy in the winter of 1848–49, and followed a policy of cautious cooperation with the democrats in their moves towards national unification and renewed war with Austria. Following the Piedmontese defeat at Novara, he was forced to resign. He lived in exile in Paris until his death.

GIUSEPPE MAZZINI (1805–72)

Involved in revolutionary politics at a young age, he founded the radical secret society Young Italy in 1831. It counted tens of thousands of members throughout the Italian peninsula, although all the uprisings it attempted were failures. During the 1848 revolution, Mazzini believed that national unity, the creation of a unitary Italian republic and the war with Austria would all have to be prosecuted simultaneously. He saw the revolutionary regimes in Tuscany and the Papal States as moving in this direction and became one of the leaders of the Roman Republic. Following its suppression, he was forced into exile. Returning to Italy in the 1860s, he remained a convinced republican, unreconciled with the Kingdom of Italy.

POPE PIUS IX (1792–1878)

As Bishop of Imola (1832–46), he developed a liberal reputation so that Italian nationalists and liberals placed great hopes in him on his election to the Papacy in 1846. They were disappointed by his opposition in 1847 to liberal reforms in the

Papal States, and then by his refusal in 1848 to join the nationalist war against Austria. Following the revolution in Rome in November 1848, he was forced to flee and only returned after the military suppression of the Roman Republic. The experiences of revolution made him into an extreme conservative, both theologically and politically. He opposed Italian national unification and refused to recognize the annexation of the Papal States by the Kingdom of Italy.

AUSTRIA

JOSIP JELAČIĆ (1801–59)

From a family of noble army officers, he was in the 1840s commander of a regiment of Croatian border guards and also known as a friend of Croatian nationalist intellectuals. Named Ban of Croatia and commander of the border troops in March 1848, he successfully tied Croatian nationalism to the imperial cause and firmly opposed all efforts of the Hungarian government to exercise its authority. In September 1848 Jelačić led an invasion of Hungary by imperial forces and in October took part in the suppression of the Viennese uprising. He held high military office until his death and has remained a great hero of Croatian nationalism.

LAJOS KOSSUTH (1802–94)

From a family of the lesser Magyar nobility, Kossuth was a lawyer and journalist, and a leader of pre-1848 Hungarian opposition to Habsburg absolutism. A great parliamentary and popular orator, Kossuth became the dominant figure in Hungarian politics in the more radical phase of the 1848 revolution, leading the country into war with the imperial forces and to its proclamation of independence. Following the defeat of the Hungarian army by Austrian and Russian troops, he was forced into exile, where he remained for the rest of his life, unreconciled to Habsburg authority. His revolutionary deeds and nationalist intransigence have made him the great Hungarian national hero.

HANS KUDLICH (1823–1917)

Son of a Silesian serf, Kudlich was a law student in Vienna at the outbreak of the revolution and quickly became involved in democratic politics there. He was elected to the Austrian Constituent Assembly where he offered the celebrated motion for the abolition of serfdom. Of all Austrian radicals, the most aware of the importance of the peasantry, Kudlich attempted in October 1848 to organize rural support for the Viennese insurgents. In March 1849, he was forced to flee into exile, ultimately to the United States. An attempted comeback in Austrian politics during the 1870s failed, and Kudlich spent the rest of his long life in the USA.

FRANTIŠEK PALACKÝ (1798–1876)

With his *History of the Czech Nation* (begun in 1836), Palacký became the main spokesman for Czech nationalism. In 1848, he hoped to combine Czech and other Slavic nationalisms with a constitutional Austrian monarchy, following these goals in opposing the German National Assembly, helping to organize the Prague Slav Congress, and leading the Czech caucus in the Austrian Constituent Assembly. His aspirations were frustrated by the influence of neo-absolutism in the Habsburg court. Deeply disappointed that the Compromise of 1867 brought no concessions to Czech nationalism, Palacký became increasingly disillusioned with the Habsburg monarchy that he had so loyally supported and sought to reform in 1848.

COUNT JOSEPH RADETZKY (1766–1858)

An Austrian army officer, who fought with distinction in the French Revolutionary and Napoleonic Wars, Radetzky was named commander of Austrian troops in northern Italy in 1831. During the 1848 revolution, he fought bitterly and unrelentingly to save the Italian provinces for the Habsburg monarchy. His two great victories at Custozza in July 1848 and at Novara in March 1849 did so, and probably saved the monarchy itself as well. As civilian and military governor of northern Italy from 1849 until his retirement in 1857, he engaged in a policy of revenge and repression that ultimately completed the alienation of the population from Austrian rule.

Index

Aachen, 67
Abruzzi, 198
agriculture, 5–12, 23, 24, 25, 40–41, 43, 54,
    61, 70, 78, 109–11, 125–26, 181, 194,
    203–04, 258, 260
Alsace, 20, 51, 69, 300
Amsterdam, 10, 117
Anneke, Fritz, 23
Anneke, Mathilde Franziska, 162, 187, 188
anti-clericalism, 38, 51, 69–70, 71, 81–82,
    87, 97, 105, 131, 185, 191, 197, 204
anti-Semitism, 52, 130–31, 199–200
aristocracy,
    political loyalties and activities of, 70,
        70–71, 74, 76, 77, 78, 88, 143, 145,
        145, 149, 151, 152, 153, 191, 193,
        195, 196, 205, 217, 218, 222, 226–27
    privileges of, 11–12, 21, 22, 23, 28, 31,
        32, 34, 42–43, 52, 58, 68, 70, 73,
        103, 124, 142, 145, 159, 195, 205,
        226, 234, 269, 273
    social and economic condition of, 10, 12,
        20, 21, 21–22, 101, 159, 195
armed forces, 9–20, 29–30, 78, 96, 134,
    135, 137
    and civilians, 48, 130
    conscription into, 29, 47–48, 212, 247
    and counter-revolution, 1, 2, 120, 121,
        121–22, 146–47, 163, 208, 212,
        214, 215, 217, 217–21, 223, 224,
        225, 227–28, 243, 246, 250–51,
        251–52, 257, 269, 271, 299, 303, 304
    and public order, 30, 214
    revolutionary, 1, 87, 106, 196, 203, 225,
        232, 240, 246, 247, 250, 275–76, 302
artisans
    organizations of, 13, 17–18, 26, 69, 77,
        86, 86, 128–29, 153–54, 178,
        179–80, 189, 258
    political activities and loyalties of, 88,
        160, 179–80, 203, 204, 207, 213,
        251, 268–69

social and economic condition of, 13,
    13–19, 22, 24, 24–25, 43, 44–46,
    178, 179, 187, 189, 258
Auersperg (Prince) 124
Augsburg, 212
Augustinis, Matteo de, 95
Austrian Empire, 3, 264, 265, 273, 274,
    275, 280, 304
    economic and social conditions in, 5, 8,
        11, 13, 16, 18, 21, 21–22, 25, 32, 42,
        43, 106, 107–08
    and German national unity, 95–96,
        138–40, 228, 242–43, 254–55, 274
    as a Great Power, 29, 96, 106–07, 116,
        242, 254–55, 262, 276
    pre-1848 government, administration
        and politics of, 8, 9, 29, 31–32, 47,
        48, 58–59, 60, 63, 64, 65, 72, 73, 89,
        98–105, 260
    revolution of 1848 in, 9, 10, 11, 12, 13,
        14–15, 16–17, 18, 19, 20, 39,
        117, 121, 122, 123, 124, 129, 130,
        131, 138–47, 149, 150, 151, 153,
        154, 157–58, 158–59, 160, 161,
        162–63, 165–66, 166–67, 171,
        173–75, 182–83, 183–84, 186, 187,
        188, 193, 195–96, 196–97, 198,
        199, 216–25, 231–34, 235, 242,
        243–44, 246, 251–52, 253, 269,
        279, 280, 300–01, 303–04

Baader, Franz von, 77
Baden, 11, 14, 19, 56, 62, 73, 230, 246, 250
Bakunin, Mikhail, 139, 240
Bamberger, Ludwig, 199
Banat, 13, 124, 182, 223, 225, 241
Barnave, Antoine, 268
Barni (Catholic priest) 197
Bărnuţiu, Simon, 99
Basilicata, 5, 41, 109, 126
Bavaria, 16, 52, 56, 171, 180, 193, 197,
    200, 202, 237, 246

306   Index

Belgium, 10, 11, 12, 13, 25, 33, 56, 57, 63, 87, 120, 122, 253, 260, 265
Bem, József, 17, 18, 240
Berlin, 10, 13, 14, 16, 18, 52, 117, 123, 179, 188, 203, 234, 245, 280
Berryer, Pierre-Antoine, 79
Biellese, 49
Bismarck, Otto von, 76, 274–75, 281, 301
Blaj, 144, 145
Blanc, Louis, 83, 85, 101, 153, 210, 299
Blanqui, Louis-Auguste, 63, 85, 211
Blum, Robert, 16, 138, 233, 300–01
Bohemia, 5, 11, 13, 124, 138, 139, 217, 219, 240, 242
Bologna (city and province), 10, 16, 64, 71, 279
Bonaparte, Louis-Napoleon, 16, 17, 18, 19, 20, 93, 150, 168, 193, 201, 211, 214, 216, 235, 236, 250, 251, 256, 257, 270, 271, 275, 299
Bonaparte, Napoleon, 92, 93, 266, 299
Born, Stephan, 199
bourgeoisie,
    political activities and loyalties of, 67–68, 70, 71, 72, 78, 87, 91, 100–01, 114, 122, 133, 145, 164, 175, 191, 203, 204, 213, 256, 267–68
    social and economic condition of, 20, 21, 22, 25–26, 34, 45, 46, 48, 86, 111, 127, 130, 198, 210, 232, 247
Brandenburg, Friedrich Wilhelm Count von, 13, 14, 16, 121, 226, 227, 235, 274
Bratianu, Ion, 253
Bratislava, 10, 15, 17, 21
Braunschweig, 18, 130
Bremen, 31, 56
Breyell, 49, 61
Brittany, 34, 45, 198
Brno (Brünn), 46, 232
Brophy, James 48
Brunsen, 127, 130
Brussels, 86, 87, 210
Bucharest, 16, 121, 226, 227, 228, 235, 274
Budapest, 10, 15, 21, 31, 49, 56, 61, 71, 117, 130, 142, 153, 175, 199, 216, 223, 224, 225
Bukovina, 38, 226, 232, 241
Bulgaria, 272

Cabet, Etienne, 83
Calabria, 12, 13, 41, 98, 196, 209
Carinthia, 162, 174, 196, 242
Carlo-Alberto, King of Piedmont-Savoy, 9, 17, 97, 134, 135, 220, 221, 222, 239, 242, 243, 275, 281, 301–02

Cavaignac, Eugène, 12, 13, 215–16, 221, 222, 270, 299–300
Cavour, Emilio di, 275
Central March Association, 169, 180, 237, 245
Cernăuti, see Czernowitz
Chambord, Count Henri de, 256
China, 266
Civic Guard, see National Guard
clergy,
    political activities and loyalties of, 74, 76, 79, 97, 105, 114, 123, 131, 145, 152, 153, 154, 159–60, 171, 182–85, 191, 193, 197, 198, 212, 232, 238, 247, 302–03
    social position of, 22, 27, 33, 35, 39, 50, 51, 97, 182
Club of the Emancipation of Women, 188
Club of Slavic Women, 186
Cologne, 19, 48, 60, 64, 162, 165, 179, 186, 199, 230
communism, 177, 266, 278
    doctrines of, 80, 83–86, 188, 189, 213
    in the 1848 revolution, 129, 153, 159, 168, 181, 210, 211, 212, 267, 269
    origins of, 42, 83
    and radicalism, 83–84, 85–86, 167–68, 206, 210–11, 214
    supporters of, 86, 88, 215, 260
conservatism,
    after 1850, 244, 252, 254–55, 275, 276
    before 1848, 73–79, 95, 104, 106–07, 115, 251
    doctrines of, 74–76, 84, 91–92, 199, 205
    in the 1848 revolution, 79–80, 145, 149, 152, 153, 158, 163, 169, 170–71, 184–85, 187, 199–200, 201, 202, 203, 204, 205–06, 217, 219, 230, 231, 233, 235, 236, 239, 242, 245, 247, 250, 263–64, 269–70
    and religion, 75–77, 135, 153, 171, 184, 197, 203
    supporters of, 78, 180, 193, 198, 199–200, 247, 250, 263–64, 271
Constant, Benjamin, 65, 66
Copenhagen, 30, 136
Cracow, 11, 78, 117, 136, 143, 174
Crémieux, Adolphe, 198
Croatia, 10, 11, 13, 15, 31, 32, 77, 99–100, 103, 142, 146, 150, 223, 224, 303
Cuba, 266
Custozza, battle of, 13, 221, 304
Czartoryski, Adam, 102
Czechoslovakia, 272
Czernowitz, 11, 226

Debrecen, 17, 203
Denmark, 10, 30–31, 117, 122, 136–37, 229, 274
Déroin, Jeanne, 189, 300
Dostoyevsky, Fyodor, 122
Dresden, 18, 246
Dubrovnik, 100
Düsseldorf (city and district), 5, 17, 19, 199

economic development.
    political opinions about, 68–69, 72, 77, 82, 85, 206–07
    trends in, 8–9, 12–19, 23–26, 40, 46, 53–54, 109–12, 128, 194, 210, 258, 264, 283
education and educators, 33–34, 69, 82, 87–88, 91, 99, 100–01, 160, 175, 181–82, 197
Egypt, 266
Eisenach, 182
Elberfeld, 16, 127, 185–86
Elections, 278, 279
    before 1848, 8, 56, 57, 61, 64, 72, 112, 113
    during the 1848 revolution, 11, 12, 13, 15, 16, 17, 18, 120, 137, 138, 139, 141, 142, 144, 149, 150–55, 168, 176, 189, 193, 202, 211, 214, 217, 220, 235–36, 278, 279, 299, 303
Embrun, arrondissement of, 125
Engels, Friedrich, 2, 80, 85–86, 166
Essen, 50
European Democratic Central Committee, 19–20, 253

feminism, 75, 84, 85, 188–90, 300
Ferdinand I, Emperor of Austria, 16, 107, 117, 141, 147, 224, 231, 234, 270
Ferdinand I, King of the Two Sicilies, 208, 209, 220
Fischhof, Joseph, 199
Flaubert, Gustave, 167
Florence, 15, 16, 17, 113, 164, 181, 239, 250
Fourier, Charles, 83
France, 252, 272, 274, 280, 281
    colonial empire of, 266
    economic and social conditions in, 5, 8, 9, 10, 11, 13, 20, 23–24, 25, 33, 34, 44, 46, 51
    as a Great Power, 12, 29–30, 105–06, 221, 228, 250, 251, 275
    pre-1848 administration, government and politics of, 9, 29, 30, 49, 56, 57, 60–61, 66, 70, 72, 76, 78–79, 83–84, 85, 86, 87, 92–93, 105–06, 112–13, 167, 260

revolution of 1848 in, 1, 3, 9–10, 11–12, 12–13, 15–16, 17, 19, 71, 116, 127–28, 129, 130, 131, 148, 149–50, 152, 153–54, 155, 158, 159, 160–61, 162, 164–65, 166, 167–69, 177, 178, 179, 180, 181, 182, 184, 187, 188–89, 193, 197, 198, 201, 202, 203, 204, 205, 206, 221, 235–36, 237, 250–51, 253–54, 255–57, 266, 270, 278, 299–300
    revolution of 1830 in, 70, 71, 87, 93, 105–06
Frankfurt am Main, 10, 13, 14, 56, 137, 230, 246, 270
Franz I, Emperor of Austria, 107
Franz Joseph I, Emperor of Austria, 16, 234, 276
Fraternal Association of Democrats of Both Sexes, 188
French Revolution of 1789, 260, 272
    effects of, 10, 17–18, 20, 38, 39, 54–55, 74, 92, 107, 205, 259, 264, 266
    as a political model, 55, 58, 66, 80, 103–04, 106, 112, 115, 121, 130, 132, 152, 155, 167, 206, 211, 221, 236, 259, 269–71, 280
Friedrich VII, King of Denmark, 117
Friedrich Wilhelm IV, King of Prussia, 8, 10, 16, 17, 75, 76, 114, 115, 234, 243, 244, 245, 255, 262, 301
Friedrich Wilhelm III, King of Prussia, 77

Gagern, Heinrich von, 61, 228, 301
Gaj, Ljudevit, 99, 100, 104
Galicia, 5, 8, 11, 12, 34, 35, 43, 63, 102, 117, 138, 143, 151, 159, 160, 167, 174, 183, 195, 199, 277
Galluzzo, 197
Garibaldi, Giuseppe, 1, 18, 251, 252, 268, 281, 302
Genoa, 134
Gentili, Tommaso, 255
Gerlach, Ernst-Ludwig von, 75, 76, 77, 263
Gerlach, Leopold von, 76
German Confederation, 20, 94, 95, 96, 107, 136, 242, 252, 254, 255, 280
Germany, 264, 265, 272, 281, 282
    East, 272
    economic and social conditions in, 8, 10, 11, 12, 16, 18, 19, 21, 23, 25, 33, 34, 41–42, 44, 45, 50, 52
    movement toward national unity of, 10, 13, 17, 18, 20, 91, 93–96, 97–98, 135–38, 147, 158, 165, 170, 217, 219, 223, 228–29, 229–30, 231, 274–75, 301

Germany, (cont.)
  pre-1848 administration, government
    and politics of, 30, 56, 57, 61–62, 63,
    64, 68–69, 70, 71, 73, 74, 77, 78, 82,
    83, 84, 86, 113
  revolution of 1848 in, 1–2, 10, 11, 12, 13,
    14, 15, 16, 17, 18–19, 117, 122, 124,
    125, 127, 128, 135–36, 137–38,
    149, 150, 152, 154, 158, 159–60,
    161, 163, 165, 169–72, 178, 179–80,
    181–82, 183, 184–85, 185–86, 187,
    188, 192, 193, 195, 197, 198, 219,
    228–31, 233, 234, 235, 237,
    244–46, 251, 253, 270, 300–01
Giantreto, 247
Gioberti, Vincenzo, 16, 97, 173, 302
Goldmark, Joseph, 199
Görgey, Arthur, 242
Goudchaux, Michel, 198
Graz, 131, 232, 240
Great Britain, 10, 12, 14, 24, 29, 57, 66, 68,
    69, 122, 221, 227, 228, 229, 260–61,
    262, 263, 267
Gregory XVI, Pope, 97
Grün, Karl, 84
Guizot, François, 67, 68, 69

Hague, The, 10, 117
Haiti, 266
Hamburg, 52, 56, 198
Hansemann, David, 67
Hardenberg, 125
Hatvan, 183
Havliček, Karel, 90
Hechingen, 124
Hecker, Friedrich, 82, 89
Heidelberg, 62
Heine, Heinrich, 45
Heppenheim, 89
Hermannstadt, 32
Herwegh, Emma, 187
Herwegh, Georg, 187
Hessen-Kassel, 20, 254, 255
Horváth, Michael, 183
Hungary, 281, 282
  economic and social conditions in,
    21–22, 35, 38, 61
  nationalities conflict in, 103–04, 104–05,
    143–47, 195, 196, 223–24, 240–41,
    303
  pre-1848 administration, government
    and politics of, 9, 28, 31–32, 52, 61,
    69, 73, 89, 112, 131, 303
  revolution of 1848 in, 10, 11, 12, 13,
    14–15, 16, 17, 18, 19, 77, 117, 123,

    130, 131, 132, 138, 142–43, 143–47,
    149, 150, 157–58, 165–66, 177, 178,
    182–83, 184, 192, 196, 197, 198, 201,
    203, 223–25, 230, 231, 232–33, 234,
    240, 241, 242, 244, 246, 251–52, 262,
    263, 270, 271, 281, 282, 303

Iancu, Avram, 241
Iași, 11, 121
industry, 5, 12–13, 17, 20, 26, 40, 46, 68, 69,
    77, 78, 79, 111, 133, 178, 258, 260, 268
Innsbruck, 12, 141
insurrection, 9, 10, 11, 12, 13, 14, 15, 16,
    18, 19, 20, 30, 43, 63, 98, 116–17, 121,
    122, 129, 133, 135, 137, 141, 155,
    164, 165, 203, 208, 209, 211, 212–14,
    218, 222, 230, 238, 240, 245, 246,
    257, 268, 275, 276
Ipatescu, Ana, 187, 227
Ireland, 8, 110, 261, 265
Islaz, 13, 226, 227
Italy, 252, 264, 272, 280, 282, 283
  economic and social conditions in, 8, 9,
    10, 11, 16, 20, 21, 23, 33, 109
  movement toward national unity of, 87,
    91, 93–94, 95, 96–98, 134–35, 208,
    275–76, 302
  pre-1848 administration, government
    and politics of, 31, 57, 63, 64, 68, 70,
    71–72, 80, 81–82, 87–88, 113–14
  revolution of 1848 in, 1, 3, 9, 11, 12, 13,
    14, 15, 16, 17, 18, 19, 116, 126, 129,
    130, 131, 134–35, 159, 163, 164,
    166, 172–73, 178, 181, 196, 202,
    203, 204, 208–09, 219–21, 222,
    238–39, 241–42, 243, 247–50,
    250–51, 251–52, 278, 302

Jachymoryč, Hryhory, 183
Jacobinism, see radicalism
Jelačić, Josip, 10, 13, 14, 15, 16, 146, 158,
    224, 225, 231, 232, 303
Johann, Archduke of Austria, 229, 243, 303
Johannesburg, 266
Joseph II, Emperor of Austria, 11, 54

Karlovci, 144, 182
Kikinda, 124
Klagenfurt, 174, 232
Koblenz, 64
Kolowrat, Count Anton 104, 107
Košice, 103
Kossuth, Lajos, 1, 15, 18, 19, 61, 165, 166,
    175, 225, 232, 244, 253, 268, 270,
    281, 303

Krefeld, 16, 52
Kremsier (Kroměříž), 234
Kudlich, Hans, 195, 232, 303
Kuranda, Ignaz, 104

La Garde-Freinet, 166
Lafayette, Marquis de, 268
Lamartine, Alphonse de, 1
Lamberg, Field Marshal Franz von, 15, 225
Lampertloch, 51
Lassalle, Ferdinand, 199
Latour, Count Theodor von, 231
Lauenburg, 30
Ledru-Rollin, Alexandre, 14, 112, 215,
    251, 253, 254, 300
Lemberg, 12, 16, 99, 143, 183
Lenz, Lucie, 188
liberalism,
    after 1850, 254, 256, 275, 276, 277
    before 1848, 8, 9, 61, 62, 65, 66, 67, 68,
        69, 70, 71, 72–73, 87, 93, 94–97,
        102, 104, 105, 112, 113, 114, 115,
        259, 301, 302
    doctrines of, 65–70, 73, 75, 78, 81, 81,
        82, 91, 94–95, 96, 97, 103, 132
    during the 1848 revolution, 10, 11, 12,
        13, 117, 120, 135, 137, 138, 139,
        141, 142, 143, 145, 149, 150, 152,
        153, 167, 170, 192, 201, 204–05,
        212, 216, 217, 230, 234, 239, 240,
        242, 243, 244, 245, 261, 270, 301,
        303–04
    supporters of, 70, 87, 173, 174, 192
Liga Polska, 172
Limoges, 133
Linz, 232
Liptovsky Sväty Mikulas, 144
List, Friedrich, 69
Livorno, 14, 18, 222, 250
Lombardy, 9, 12, 13, 14, 48, 96, 107, 134,
    141, 142, 150, 172, 220, 239, 275
London, 10, 12, 20, 63, 86, 122, 141, 164,
    253, 260, 299
Lot, Department of, 163
Louis XVI, King of France, 58, 269
Louis-Philippe, King of the French, 9, 71,
    93, 106, 116, 153, 210, 212
Lübeck, 56
Lviv, see Lemberg
Lvov, see Lemberg
Lyon, 13, 19, 44, 45, 63, 178, 183, 251

Mainz, 19, 123, 193, 199
Malaunay, 127
Manin, Daniele, 1, 198, 221

Marat, Jean-Paul, 268
Maronne, 127
Marseilles, 19, 20, 63, 79, 87, 193
Martin, Albert, 153
Marx, Heinrich, 42
Marx, Karl, 2, 42, 45, 60, 80, 161, 162, 166,
    178, 199, 213, 214, 215, 267, 301
Mazzetti, Giuseppe, 34
Mazzini, Giuseppe, 17, 19, 63, 87, 97,
    98, 173, 220, 222, 238, 253, 281,
    302
Medick, Hans, 53
Metternich, Prince Klemens von, 10, 64,
    74, 77, 78, 100, 104, 106, 107, 116,
    141, 145, 242
Michalowice, 151
Michelet, Jules, 85
Mieroslawski, Ludwik, 123, 135
Milan, 9, 48, 113, 117, 122, 203, 220
Minghetti, Marco, 71
Mirabeau, Count Honoré de, 268
Modena, 114
Moldavia, 11, 12, 13, 14, 15, 63, 121, 241,
    261
Mönchengladbach, 52
Montanelli, Giovanni, 239
Montauban, 52
Montebello, 220
Montevarchi, 81
Moravia, 15, 138, 139, 174
Mühlenbeck, 130
Mukachevo, 123
Müller, Adam, 74, 75
Munich, 117, 246

Naples, 12, 25, 70, 84, 95, 116, 193, 203,
    208, 209
National Guard, 11, 113, 132–33, 156, 164,
    165, 187, 211, 213, 214, 217, 218,
    220, 235, 238, 245
nationalism, 89–92
    Croatian, 99–100, 103, 104–05, 144,
        146, 174, 216, 224, 277, 303
    Czech, 99, 100, 104, 138–39, 158,
        174, 216, 217–19, 233, 277,
        303–04
    Danish, 137
    definitions of, 90
    and education, 90–91
    French, 91, 92–93, 104, 236, 299
    German, 1–2, 91, 93–95, 95–96, 97–98,
        104, 135, 136–39, 141, 158, 170,
        174, 185, 186, 219, 242–43, 244–45,
        247, 251, 254, 255, 262, 274–75,
        276, 281, 282, 301

nationalism, (cont.)
  Hungarian, 1, 31, 101–02, 103–04, 117,
    142, 145, 175, 183, 196, 223,
    224–25, 232, 241, 244, 251, 263,
    270, 271, 276, 281, 282, 303
  Italian, 1, 91, 93–94, 95, 96–98, 117,
    126, 134–35, 173, 208, 220,
    238–39, 241, 241–42, 262, 270,
    275–76, 281, 302, 303
  Polish, 101–03, 117, 135–36, 143, 160,
    172, 174, 195–96, 216, 277
  political implications of, 90–92, 94–98,
    103–05, 134–35, 137–39, 146, 147,
    155, 282
  Romanian, 99, 101, 103, 144–46, 182,
    195, 196, 216, 226, 228, 240–41,
    262, 277
  Serb, 99, 103, 144, 146, 182–83, 198,
    216, 223, 277
  Slovak, 99, 103, 144, 195, 196, 277
  Slovenian, 99
  social context of, 91, 94, 126, 144–45,
    195–96, 220
  Ukrainian, 99, 100, 143, 174, 183
Netherlands, 10, 11, 15, 30, 33, 38, 49,
    56, 117–20, 122, 253, 260, 264,
    265, 277
Niboyet, Eugénie, 188
Nîmes, 52, 131
Nopcsa, László, 45–46
Norway, 11, 19, 20, 56, 120, 181, 252
Novara, battle of, 17, 243, 302
Nuremberg, 44

Offenburg, 89
Olmouc (Olmütz), 15, 20, 231, 232, 255
Oslo, 120
Ottoman Empire, 14, 15, 30, 32, 192, 227,
    228, 241, 263
Otto-Peters, Louise, 188
outworking, 13–17, 18–19, 25, 45–49, 54,
    127, 129, 178, 193, 213, 269
Owen, Robert, 83

Palacký, František, 100, 219, 303–04
Palatinate, 19, 41, 125, 246
Palermo, 9, 116
Papal States, 8, 9, 10, 11, 16, 17, 19, 63,
    113, 114, 149, 150, 167, 172, 198,
    238, 247–50, 251, 255, 273, 275, 302
Paris, 30, 59, 61, 184
  economic and social conditions in, 9, 13,
    18, 44, 46
  and European politics, 63, 86, 87, 105,
    108, 129, 209–10, 212–13, 214–15

labor movement in, 9–10, 11–12, 13,
    129, 153–54, 159, 164–65, 168,
    178, 180, 189, 214, 262
  revolution of 1848 in, 1, 9–10, 11–12,
    12–13, 19, 20, 62, 116, 129, 133,
    153–54, 160, 164–65, 178, 180,
    187, 188–89, 203, 209–14, 237,
    251, 265, 268, 270
parliaments,
  constitutional, 8, 57, 72, 89, 274, 275,
    276
  during the 1848 revolution, 1, 2, 11, 12,
    13, 14, 15, 16, 17, 18, 19, 20, 61,
    137, 138, 139, 141, 149, 150, 153,
    154, 164, 168, 169, 171, 174, 176,
    179, 195, 196, 201, 202, 208, 209,
    211, 212, 214, 215, 216, 217, 223,
    228–29, 230, 231, 232, 233, 234–35,
    237, 238, 242–43, 244, 245, 250,
    251, 256–57, 274, 299, 300, 301
  feudal, 9, 31, 32, 58–59, 61, 103, 112,
    114–15
peasants,
  cultural, economic and social condition
    of, 5, 9–12, 25, 32, 33, 34, 40–43,
    51, 52, 109–10, 111, 124–26, 140,
    156, 232, 258, 259, 273
  political activities and loyalties of, 3, 5,
    9–12, 25, 32, 33, 34, 40–43, 51, 52,
    61–62, 77, 90–91, 101, 102–03,
    109–10, 111, 124–26, 140, 144–45,
    146, 148, 151–52, 153, 156, 159,
    165–66, 168, 174, 176, 181, 192,
    193, 194–96, 197–98, 205, 206–07,
    209, 210, 213, 220, 222, 227, 228,
    232, 232, 236, 240, 241, 247, 258,
    259, 263–64, 271, 273, 280
Petőfi, Sandor, 153
Pfuel, Ernst von, 234
Piedmont-Savoy, 13, 14, 281
  economic and social conditions in, 9
  and Italian national unity, 9, 16, 17,
    96–97, 113, 134, 142, 220–21,
    239, 242, 243, 254, 262, 275–76,
    281, 302
  politics and government of, 9, 16, 17,
    113, 134, 273, 301–02, 302
  revolution of 1848 in, 17, 134, 149, 198,
    202, 239, 270, 271, 302
Pius Associations, 15, 171–72
Pius IX, Pope, 8, 9, 11, 16, 19, 97, 113, 115,
    131, 135, 173, 220, 238, 282, 302–03
Po Valley, 11
Poland, 31, 272, 283
police, 28, 110, 122, 148, 156, 259, 261

political organizations,
  activities of, 4, 12, 13, 14, 15, 16, 18,
      19–20, 175–77, 180–81, 186–87,
      201, 205, 207, 211, 224, 232, 235,
      236, 237, 238–39, 245, 247–50,
      257, 260, 261, 268
  before 1848, 62–65, 69–70, 86, 88–89,
      94, 98, 100, 259–60, 301, 302
  extent of, 151, 166, 180, 196, 232, 254,
      265, 278
  formation of, 159, 167–72, 172, 188–89,
      197, 204, 205, 206, 238, 253–54, 279
  membership of, 172, 176, 187, 188,
      191–93, 204
  see also secret societies
Portugal, 35, 272
Posen, 11, 12, 135–36, 137, 172, 174
Poznań, see Posen
Prague, 11, 13, 99, 123, 138, 139, 140, 186,
      187, 203, 217, 218, 219, 222, 232
press
  before 1848, 59–60, 62, 151, 300, 301
  during the 1848 revolution, 100, 160–62,
      178, 212–13, 253, 300, 301
Pressburg, see Bratislava
Proudhon, Pierre-Joseph, 83, 85, 189
Provence, 51
Prussia, 273
  economic and social conditions in, 8, 12,
      16, 17, 41–42
  and German national unity, 2, 10, 11, 14,
      17, 18, 20, 62, 95, 96, 137, 229–30,
      242–43, 244–45, 254, 255, 274–75,
      301
  as a Great Power, 29, 96, 231, 244–45,
      276
  pre-1848 administration, government
      and politics of, 12, 28, 28–29, 41–42,
      48, 49, 53, 57, 58, 62, 64, 71, 75–76,
      76, 77, 78, 84, 114–15, 153, 261
  revolution of 1848 in, 10, 11, 12, 16, 17,
      117, 150, 152, 153, 160, 193, 195,
      197, 198, 199, 205, 231, 234–35,
      237, 263, 301
Puchner, General Anton von, 15, 240
Puglia, 173

Radetzky, Joseph, 9, 14, 122, 130, 163, 219,
      220, 220, 221, 222, 243, 304
radicalism,
  after 1850, 275–76, 278, 279, 281
  before 1848, 8, 56, 63, 64, 80–83, 86–89,
      97–98, 112, 115, 300, 302
  doctrines of, 80–83, 85–86, 97–98,
      206–07, 213, 214, 215, 270, 283

  in the 1848 revolution, 1, 9, 11, 12, 13,
      14, 15, 16, 17, 18, 19–20, 116, 134,
      137, 141, 145, 152, 153, 158,
      162–63, 164, 165, 166, 168, 169–70,
      173, 174, 175, 180, 181, 182, 183,
      186, 187, 188–89, 201, 202, 202, 203,
      204, 210–11, 214, 215, 218, 219, 220,
      224, 225, 226, 228, 230, 231–32,
      232, 234, 235, 236, 237, 238, 239,
      240, 241, 242, 245–46, 246–50,
      251, 252–54, 255–56, 257, 267,
      268, 270, 283, 300, 301, 302, 303
  supporters of, 87–88, 141, 169–70, 181,
      191–92, 193–94, 194–95, 196–97,
      197–98, 199, 203, 204, 213, 215,
      217, 268–69
Rajačić, Josip, 182
Raumer, Friedrich von, 95
Reims, 178
religion, 34–38
  conflicts over, 38, 50–53, 77, 115,
      130–31, 136, 159–60, 183–85,
      196–97, 199–200, 250
  and politics, 38, 69–70, 70–71, 72, 74,
      75–77, 77–78, 79, 80, 81–82, 96, 97,
      114, 135, 152, 165, 171–72,
      196–200, 271, 300, 302–03
  social role of, 34–35, 247–50
  and the state, 27, 31, 52, 72, 203, 204,
      209, 242
  see also, clergy
Republican Solidarity, 16, 17, 168, 206,
      215, 236, 264, 265
revolutions of 1848,
  economic and social preconditions of, 47,
      55, 109, 258
  interpretations of, 1–3, 123, 213, 215,
      267–71
  legacy and commemoration of, 160, 177,
      184, 185, 189–90, 215, 277–83
  and other revolutions, 154–55, 185, 205,
      221–22, 264–73, 280, 282
  outcome of, 123, 147, 155–56, 207, 219,
      228, 261–64, 271
  political preconditions of, 23, 30, 39, 50,
      53, 55, 59, 61, 62, 64–65, 73, 78, 89,
      92, 93, 98, 105–08, 112–16, 240,
      259–60
Rhineland, 13, 50, 69, 109, 130, 153, 160,
      193, 198, 235
Ricciardi, Guiseppe, 84
Riesser, Gabriel, 198
riots, 9, 30, 39, 45, 49, 50, 110, 124,
      125–26, 127, 128, 129–30, 130, 131,
      151, 180, 210, 225, 231, 247

Robespierre, Maximilian, 268
Rodi, 49
Romagna, 21
Roman Republic, 16, 17, 18, 19, 31, 93,
    121, 173, 238, 250, 255, 272, 275,
    302
Romania, 18, 19, 31, 121, 272
Rome, 16, 173, 238, 251, 255, 275, 302
Rosenthal, C.D., 187
Rossi, Pellegrino, 238
Rouen, 133
Rülzheim, 163
Russia, 12, 13, 14, 15, 19, 29, 63, 122, 139,
    226, 227, 228, 229, 230, 240, 244,
    252, 260, 261, 262–63, 274

Sachsenburg, 162
Şaguna, Andrieu, 182
St. Etienne, 13, 16
Saint-Simon, Henri de, 83
San Vito, 255
Salzburg, 232
Saxony, 13, 17, 18, 73, 202, 219, 237, 240,
    246, 300
Schleswig-Holstein, 10, 14, 30, 136–37,
    229, 262
Schwarzenberg, Prince Felix, 16, 233, 241,
    242
Scialoja, Antonio, 70
secret societies, 20, 63, 86, 87, 89, 94,
    98, 102, 122, 168, 173, 253, 254,
    257, 302
Serbia, 63
serfdom and seigneurialism, 26, 28, 77,
    132, 140, 145
  abolition of, 11–12, 102, 103, 104, 142,
    144–45, 159, 194–96, 232
  extent of, 11, 21
  opposition to, 42–43, 68, 77, 102–03,
    105, 124, 144, 145, 151, 154, 194,
    223, 232, 240, 259
Sibiu, see Hermannstadt
Sicily, 8, 9, 11, 14, 15, 18, 116, 149, 196,
    276, 302
Silesia, 16, 136, 195, 235
Slavic Linden, 174
Slotinicy, 124
Slovakia, 43, 242
socialism, see communism
Society for Equality, 175
Smith, John Prince, 68
Spain, 10, 30, 35, 120–21, 266
Stadion, Count Franz, 11, 143, 144
state officials, 20, 22, 28, 30, 34, 65, 100–01

  during the 1848 revolution, 140, 146–47,
    154, 156, 204, 218, 246–47, 257
  hostility toward, 9, 41, 49, 125, 163–64,
    207, 231
  political activities and opinions of, 57, 70,
    72, 78, 95–96, 143, 145, 149, 191,
    192, 224, 244, 264
Struve, Amalie, 187
Struve, Gustav, 187
Stuttgart, 19, 247, 251
Styria, 131
Sweden, 58, 96, 120
Switzerland, 8, 10, 56, 87, 115–16, 252,
    253, 260, 264, 266, 275

taxes, 16, 25, 27, 28, 30, 31, 48–49, 49–50,
    82, 129–30, 132, 141, 144, 156, 207,
    210, 247
Thalfang, 42
Thomas, Albert, 211
Thorbecke, Johan, 10, 117
Thrane, Marcus, 19, 181
Thun, Count Leo, 140, 218
Tocqueville, Alexis de, 112, 120
Toulouse, 61, 63
Transylvania, 11, 14, 15, 16, 17, 18, 35, 52,
    99, 101, 103, 142, 144–46, 182, 196,
    223, 225, 240, 240, 241
Trier, 42, 127
Turin, 19
Turkey, see Ottoman Empire
Tuscany, 9, 13, 14, 17, 18, 63, 81, 113, 150,
    164, 172, 173, 222, 238, 239, 250,
    279, 302
Two Sicilies, Kingdom of, 238, 273
  economic and social conditions in, 5, 8,
    25, 41, 49, 276
  and Italian national unity, 12, 96, 209
  pre-1848 administration, government
    and politics of, 8, 28, 41, 49, 70
  revolution of 1848 in, 9, 11, 12, 13, 14,
    15, 17, 18, 116, 126, 149, 150, 167,
    173, 208–09
Tyl, Josef, 99
Tyrol, 31, 141, 198, 220

Union of Women, 188
United States, 266
Uzhhorod, 123

Var, Department of, 166
Vaucluse, Department of, 65, 169
Venetia, 9, 12, 13, 14, 96, 134, 141, 142,
    150, 172, 220, 239

Venice, 9, 14, 18, 113, 117, 121, 134, 198, 220, 239, 246, 251, 252

Vienna, 13, 18, 106, 216, 269
  economic and social conditions in, 13, 16, 179, 233
  revolution of 1848 in, 10, 12, 14, 15, 16, 117, 129, 131, 141, 173, 187, 188, 199, 199, 203, 231–32, 233, 246, 268, 300, 303

Vietnam, 266

Villeneuve-Bargemont, Count, 77

Vittorio Emmanuele, King of Italy, 275, 275, 302

Wagner, Richard, 240

Wallachia, 11, 12, 13–14, 15, 63, 121, 182, 192, 195, 225, 226–28, 241, 261, 262

warfare, 20, 29, 107, 136, 263, 299
  during the 1848 revolution, 9, 11, 12, 13, 14, 15, 16, 17, 18, 19, 134–35, 136, 137, 166, 175, 190, 208, 219–22, 223, 224, 225, 229–30, 231, 232–33, 234, 240, 241–42, 243, 244, 262, 263, 270, 302, 303, 304
  and national unity, 95, 96–97, 107, 133–35, 137, 147, 229–30, 239, 274, 275–76, 302, 302, 303
  and revolution, 71, 81, 98, 105–06, 107, 115–16, 135–36, 203, 221–22, 230, 260, 264, 266, 269, 270, 271–72

Weitling, Wilhelm, 83

West Prussia, 136

Westphalia, 13, 16, 41, 77, 152, 198

Wheeler, Anna, 188

Windischgrätz, Prince Alfred, 13, 16, 17, 163, 217, 218, 219, 222, 232, 233, 234

Woerth, Canton of, 51

women, 48, 56, 130
  political activities of, 4, 76, 84–85, 172, 185–90, 229, 300
  in political thought, 75, 84–85, 189
  social and economic position of, 18–19, 19–20, 189
  see also, feminism

Workers' Fraternization, 179, 180, 181

Workers Union, 19, 20, 181

working class,
  organization of, 19, 128–29, 177–79, 192, 193, 267, 270–71
  political activities and loyalties of, 86, 129, 133, 153–54, 164, 179–80, 180–81, 191–92, 193, 193–94, 203, 211–12, 213–14, 236, 251, 260, 268–69, 279–80
  social and economic conditions of, 13, 13–17, 19, 22–23, 25, 46–47, 54, 86, 111, 127–28, 129, 133, 153–54, 164, 179–80, 180–81, 191–92, 193, 193–94, 203, 210, 211–12, 213–14, 218, 236, 251, 260, 268–69

Wupper Valley, 16, 71, 78, 193

Württemberg, 19, 187, 247, 251

Zagreb, 10, 100, 144, 216

Zimmern, 187

Zürich, 87

NEW APPROACHES TO EUROPEAN HISTORY

4 ROBERT JÜTTE *Poverty and Deviance in Early Modern Europe*
5 JAMES B. COLLINS *The State in Early Modern France*
6 CHARLES G. NAUERT, JR *Humanism and the Culture of Renaissance Europe*
7 DORINDA OUTRAM *The Enlightenment*
8 MACK P. HOLT *The French Wars of Religion, 1562–1629*
9 JONATHAN DEWALD *The European Nobility, 1400–1800*
10 ROBERT S. DUPLESSIS *Transitions to Capitalism in Early Modern Europe*
11 EDWARD MUIR *Ritual in Early Modern Europe*
12 R. PO-CHIA HSIA *The World of Catholic Renewal 1540–1770*
14 W. R. WARD *Christianity under the Ancien Régime, 1648–1789*
15 SIMON DIXON *The Modernisation of Russia 1676–1825*
16 MARY LINDEMANN *Medicine and Society in Early Modern Europe*
17 DONALD QUATAERT *The Ottoman Empire, 1700–1922*
18 REX A. WADE *The Russian Revolution, 1917*
19 JAMES R. FARR *Artisans in Europe, 1300–1914*
20 MERRY E. WIESNER *Women and Gender in Early Modern Europe*
   Second edition
21 CHARLES W. INGRAO *The Habsburg Monarchy 1618–1815*
   Second edition
22 JULIUS R. RUFF *Violence in Early Modern Europe*
23 JAMES VAN HORN MELTON *The Rise of the Public in Enlightenment Europe*
24 DANIEL GOFFMAN *The Ottoman Empire and Early Modern Europe*
25 NIGEL ASTON *Christianity and Revolutionary Europe, c. 1750–1830*
26 LEONARD V. SMITH, STEPHANE AUDOIN-ROUZEAU, AND ANNETTE
   BECKER *France and the Great War*
27 ROGER CHICKERING *Imperial Germany and the Great War, 1914–1918*
   Second edition
28 ULINKA RUBLACK *Reformation Europe*
29 JONATHAN SPERBER *The European Revolutions, 1848–1851*
   Second edition